Neil Craig.

THE QUEEN'S SCOTLAND

THE HEARTLAND

CLACKMANNANSHIRE PERTHSHIRE AND STIRLINGSHIRE

By

NIGEL TRANTER

HODDER AND STOUGHTON
LONDON SYDNEY AUCKLAND TORONTO

TOWNS AND VILLAGES

A key to the towns, villages and natural features of Clackmannanshire, Perthshire, and Stirlingshire shown on the map and mentioned in the text.

Aberfeldy	I5	Brig o' Turk	E10	Forest of Atholl	GH2
Aberfoyle	D11	Buchanan	D13	Forest of Mamlorn	C7
Abernethy	M9	Buchlyvie	E12	Forgandenny	K9
Abernyte	N7	Birnam	K6	Fernan	G6
Aberuthven	J9	Burrelton	M7	Forteviot	K9
Airth	I13	Butterstone	K5	Fortingall	G5
Alloa	I12			Fowlis Wester	I8
Almondbank	K8	Callander	F10		
Alva	I11	Cambus	I12	Garden	E12
Alyth	M5	Campsie	F14	Gargunnoch	G12
Amulree	I7	Campsie Fells	G13	Gartmore	D11
Ardler	N6	Caputh	K6	Gartness	D13
Ardoch	H10	Cargill	L7	Gask	J9
Ardvorlich	F8	Carron Valley	G13	Gilmerton	I8
Arnprior	F12	Carse of Gowrie	M8	Glen Artney	G9
Auchenbowie	H13	Cast. Campbell	J11	Glencarse	M8
Auchterarder	J9	Castlecary	H14	Glen Devon	J10
		Clackmannan	I12	Glen Dochart	D8
Baldernock	E14	Clunie	L6	Glendoick	M8
Balfron	E12	Collace	M7	Gleneagles	I10
Ballinluig	J5	Comrie	H8	Glen Falloch	B9
Balmaha	C12	Coupar (Angus)	M6	Glenfarg	L10
Balquhidder	E9	Craigend	E14	Glen Garry	G2
Bankfoot	K7	Crianlarich	C8	Glen Gyle	C9
Bannockburn	H12	Crieff	I8	Glen Lednock	G8
Bardowie	E14			Glen Lyon	F5
Ben Lawers	F6	Dalguise	J5	Glen Ogle	E8
Ben Ledi	E10	Denny	H13	Glen Shee	L2
Ben Lomond	C11	Devon Valley	J11	Glen Tilt	I3
Ben More	C8	Dollar	J11	Grandtully	I5
Ben Venue	D10	Doune	G11	Grangemouth	I13
Ben Vorlich	F9	Dowally	J5	Greenloaning	H10
Ben-y-gloe	J2	Dron	L9	Guildtown	L7
Ben-y-Vrackie	I4	Drymen	D12		
Blackford	I10	Dull	H5	Inchture	N8
Blacklunas	L4	Dunblane	H11	Inchyra	M8
Black Wood of		Dunipace	H13		
Rannoch	E4	Dunkeld	K6	Kenmore	H6
Blair Atholl	I3	Dunning	K9	Kilbagie	I12
Blair Drummond	G11	Dunsinane	M7	Kilbryde	G11
Blairgowrie	M6	Dupplin	K9	Killearn	E13
Blanefield	E14			Killiecrankie	I3
Bonnybridge	H13	Errol	M8	Killin	E7
Boquhan	F12			Kilmadock	G11
Braco	H10	Falkirk	I14	Kilspindie	M8
Br. of Allan	H11	Fallin	H12	Kilsyth	G14
Br. of Balgie	E5	Fingask	M8	Kilsyth Hills	G13
Br. of Cally	L5	Fintry	F13	Kinbuck	H10
Br. of Earn	L9	Fintry Hills	F13	Kincardine	G11
Br. of Lochay	E7	Firth of Tay	N8	Kinclaven	L6
Brightons	I14	Flanders Moss	F11	Kinfauns	L8

v

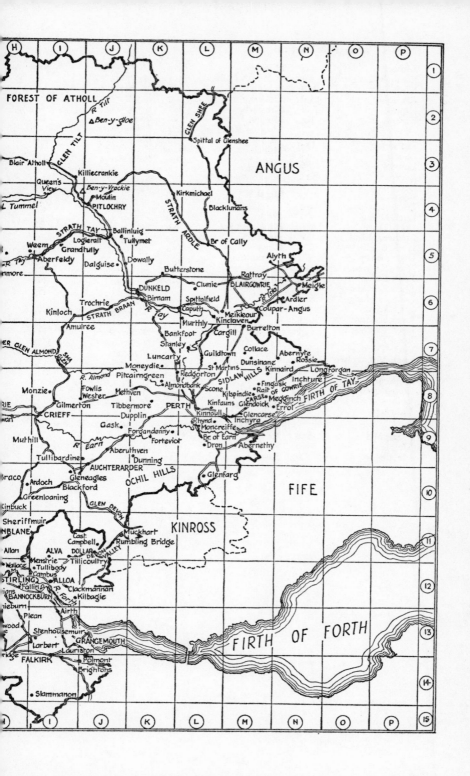

LIST OF ILLUSTRATIONS

ACKNOWLEDGMENTS

A. D. S. Macpherson: plates 1, 3, 4, 6, 8, 11, 17, 21, 22, 25, 31, 32, 35, 37, 38, 39, 43, 44, 46, 47, 48, 49, 50
Planair Aerial Photography: plates 2, 7, 16, 41
The National Trust for Scotland: plate 5
W. A. Sharp: plates 9, 13, 23, 42
John Partridge: plates 10, 28, 29, 30, 40
John Mackay: plates 12, 14, 18, 20, 34, 36
Ministry of Public Building and Works, Edinburgh: plates 15, 19, 24, 26, 27, 33 (Crown Copyright Reserved)

INTRODUCTION

In this renewal and extension of THE QUEEN'S SCOTLAND series, I have followed a somewhat different course from Theo Lang, who skilfully edited the first four volumes, which dealt with Scotland south of the Forth and Clyde, plus Fife and Kinross-shire. Partly out of personal preference, partly from a desire to ensure that every aspect of interest of every locality in the areas concerned is included, I have written every word myself, with no introduction or editing of the work of others. This has involved an enormous amount of research and of travel, for every place described has been visited afresh—or for the first time—for this work; so that the result is as first-hand and up-to-date as it is possible to be. It is, of course, a personal picture therefore, one man's view of the scene; with no doubt one man's idiosyncrasies, prejudices and bias tending to shine through. This is inevitable, although I have sought sternly to control myself—and, more to the point perhaps, so has my wife. The object is to present, in readable and interesting form, a complete picture, in so far as is possible in the space, of the counties concerned—in this case, Clackmannanshire, Perthshire and Stirlingshire—a picture in depth but with highlights, with every village, town, parish and area described, its position, present-day characteristics, features of interest and brief historical background. This, inevitably, has been a testing and almost alarming task. I thought that I knew my Scotland pretty well, before I agreed to set out on it; I have learned my mistake. Guide-lines are but scanty—for this just has never been done before. Gazetteers, the Statistical Accounts, Ordnance maps, Inventories of Ancient Monuments, parish histories and reference works on specific localities and subjects, have been enormously helpful—although these are often quite out-of-date. But there are vast areas untouched by such, never previously written about in any objective or comprehensive fashion, if at all. It is strange, indeed, for so ancient, exciting and colourful a country, how much has *not* been written up. Personally, I have long and frustratedly recognised the dire need for some comprehensive work such as this. I am both grateful, and ruefully reproachful towards my publishers, Hodder & Stoughton, for asking me to tackle the task. It looks like being something of a life sentence.

My wife has been as deeply involved in it all as have I; for this project could not have been tackled without a collaborator, to map-read during the endless driving, to take volumes of notes, to check for accuracy, remind, bear up and with, and generally assist. Very much a dual-harness task, this volume should undoubtedly read 'by Nigel and May Tranter'.

It is presented for a wide range of readership—the visitor to Scotland, Scots folk themselves, the armchair traveller who can

I

still appreciate without actually visiting, all who love fine country, works of beauty, the story of progress and working out of history, things ancient, even legendary, and the firm footmarks of a people on a land. And it is presented with pride—not in the writing or the labour or the workmanship, to be sure, but in the splendid land it seeks to describe.

NIGEL TRANTER

Aberlady, East Lothian
   August 1970

CLACKMANNANSHIRE

The triumph of quality over mere quantity, the vindication of the Scots proverb that *guid gear gangs in sma' bulk*, is notably demonstrated by Scotland's 'Wee Coonty', the smallest in the land, in the United Kingdom indeed, covering only 34,957 acres. Many Perthshire *parishes* are larger. Moreover, its northern half is wholly empty hill-country. For all that, crammed into the rest is a sufficiency of worth, interest, history and antiquities such as would serve a county many times Clackmannan's size. And people, too; for with 41,000, there are twelve counties in Scotland with fewer.

The inhabited area comprises the lower basins of the Rivers Devon and Black Devon, separated by an intermediate spine of higher ground, and all squeezed in between the Ochil Hills and the Firth of Forth. It is therefore one of the most central counties, and strategically placed, so that it has taken a much greater part in the history of Scotland than its size might suggest. Stirling, only a few miles to the west, inevitably was both the cockpit and the historic centre of the land, and Clackmannan tended to share in its importance. Rich alluvial soil in the Forth plain, the presence of coal and plentiful, fast-flowing and excellent water for the turning of mills and the distilling of spirits, plus ample port facilities and a good road system, all marked out this area for prosperity and development.

Clackmannanshire was in early times inhabited by the Caledonian Damnonii, a Pictish people of which no great deal is known, never truly subdued by the Romans, probably Celts of Cymric rather than Gaelic stock, and Christianised after a fashion in the 6th and 7th centuries traditionally by St. Begha (or Bee) and St. Serf or Servanus. Then, in Clackmannan, was fought the great battle at Baingle Brae, in 844, when the warrior-king of the Dalriadic Scots of the West, Kenneth MacAlpine, defeated the Picts, to initiate the unification of Scotland. Thereafter Clackmannan became a favourite dwelling-place of the Scottish monarchs, who built their royal palace on the summit of the ridge where Clackmannan Tower stands today. David II, 500 years later, Bruce's son, granted the lands to his nephew, so that they ceased to be a royal domain. The Earls of Mar, hereditary keepers of Stirling Castle, and therefore always close to the throne, with the Bruce family, dominated thereafter. The growing power of Holy Church, too, affected the area— for the Church came to own half of the best land in Scotland. Clackmannan was included in that curious and little-known ecclesiastical jurisdiction called Fothrif, comprising all the land west of Collessie in Fife right to Stirling itself, and under the sway of the great Abbey of Dunfermline. So, in this small area we have many castles, manors, towers and ancient churches. The Reformation reduced the Church's interest, but brought only more lairds.

Modern times, of course, brought about industrial exploitation of resources—although, strangely enough, it also allowed the small Forthside harbours to silt up and become unusable. But the essential nature of the land remained. As did the lairds. The Earl of Mar and Kellie still lives in the centre of Alloa, and a Bruce still owns Kennet, at Clackmannan.

Inevitably, perhaps, with the ever-increasing tendency towards centralised control, of the only three burghs, Alloa, which displaced Clackmannan itself as county town in 1822, dominates the rest. A go-ahead and ever-growing place, with a population about one-third of the county's total, it could hardly be otherwise. In some ways, of course, this is of considerable benefit, in local finance and efficiency. Not that the county's rating is thereby reduced—but it can be used to greater advantage than in many wider-spread and less compact communities. Nor for Clackmannanshire are the vast mileages of county roads, expensive of upkeep; the remote schools to be maintained; the far-flung community services of every sort. All is nicely centralised. Results are not hard to perceive, even by the casual visitor. I know of no county where municipal gardening, for instance is so much in evidence, with roadside plots and flower-beds, trimmed verges and tree-planting, tree-preservation. The standard of municipal housing and planning is notably high. Modern schools are a feature. Amenity and recreational facilities flourish. It is all heartening—although centralisation can have its drawbacks also, as not a few county residents will feelingly assert.

In this volume, Clackmannanshire is included with giant Perthshire, and with the large and highly industrialised county of Stirling. It need not shrink back or hide its head, however. Not that it ever did. Although only one-forty-sixth the size of Perth, for instance, its rateable value is fully one-third. Guid gear . . . !

Alloa. Here, 6 miles from Stirling, where the Forth begins to widen from river to firth, is the busy industrial town and metropolis of Scotland's smallest county, with a population of approximately 16,000, an active, well-doing, inspiriting place. But, despite all the bustle and efficiency, the brewing, distilling, glass-making, electronics and other industries, Alloa, like most other Scots communities, is at heart ancient. Its size is new, like its elevation to county town—which took place in 1822, when it superseded neighbouring Clackmannan. But the old burgh which grew up under the shadow of the old grey Tower of Alloa, was modest, narrow of street, authentic as to character, clustered by the banks of the Brathy Burn. Traces of it are still to be discerned, around the Candleriggs, the East Vennel, Kirkgate and Castle Street. But Paton & Baldwin's great mills now cover most of the site. The ruined 17th century church of St. Mungo still stands, with a Dutch-style ogee-roofed bell-tower. Notable is the stone effigy of the saint, somewhat crudely carved, in a niche on the inner face of the gable.

Alloa, or Alloway, as it used to be spelt, like Burns's birthplace in

4

Ayrshire, once had quite an important harbour, Daniel Defoe writing that "a merchant at Alloway may trade to all parts of the world as well as at Leith or at Glasgow". Silting mud-banks and larger ships have changed all that. But Broad Street—which really is broad—and Lime Tree Walk, lead down to The Shore still, and it was here that David Allan, 'the Scottish Hogarth', was born.

Also born at Alloa, one of a long succession of earls, was 'Bobbing John', the famed if blowing-hot-and-cold Jacobite Earl of Mar, leader of the Rising of 1715. He first saw the light of day in the massive ancient grey Tower, which still stands in the middle of the town, a probably 14th century keep with 15th century alterations and walls 10 feet in thickness. The property of Alloa was conferred on Sir Robert Erskine, Great Chamberlain of Scotland, by David II in 1360, conveniently near to the royal castle of Stirling, of which the Erskines of Mar were the keepers. It still belongs to the Earl of Mar and Kellie, and the present earl lives in the burgh, though no longer in the old Tower. It is unusual nowadays for a great noble-man to dwell in an industrial town, however ancestral, a pleasing link with the past. The Tower has had a stormy history. Mary Queen of Scots stayed here; also her son, and his son. Montrose was here the day before he burned Castle Campbell in 1645, and his unruly Highlanders, having nothing particular to do in the evening, spent it looting the town. In gentler vein, in the early 18th century, the Earl of Mar invited the famous Le Nôtre, landscape-gardener to the King of France, to visit Alloa and advise on the lay-out of new gardens and policies, which duly became renowned. He also brought in James Gibbs, the well-known architect, to plan improvement to the town.

Today Alloa is developing hugely, with ambitious and attractive new housing schemes, especially in the area which was formerly the wide parklands of the Erskines. Happily, the trees are being retained where possible. In the north-east corner of that parkland, quite near the Clackmannan road, is an ancient upright monolith, about nine feet high, with a roughly incised cross on either side, on the edge of a grassy amphitheatre. The mound on which it stands is known as Hawkhill, and it is said to be the site of a great Pictish battle, where fell a high-born youth in A.D. 711.

A new shopping centre rises at Shillinghill, with 18 shops, including a supermarket and 24 maisonettes, enhanced by mural sculpture. A very recent and exciting development is the special plant for producing white flint glass-making sand, at Devilla, near Alloa. The deposits, in Forestry Commission land, discovered after a nation-wide search, are being processed at a £500,000 treatment plant, with a 1000-foot conveyor, to meet the needs of an industry so important to Alloa, by a consortium of well-known glass companies. Formerly the sand was imported from the Continent. A new development is the great Lornshill Academy, recently opened, costing £1,150,000, with theatre, closed-circuit T.V., etc.

5

Alva. One of those attractively-placed communities known as the Hillfoots, nestling at the base of the abruptly-rising Ochil Hills, Alva is a modest place to rival neighbouring Tillicoultry as second-largest burgh in the county, with a population of just over 4000. For long a thriving little town of textile mills, that used the power of her rushing streams to process the wool of the Ochils sheep into blankets and tweeds, of late years Alva suffered declension, in the industry's recession, when four of her eight mills closed down. However, necessity and self-help have brought other industries to more than compensate, synthetic fibres, electronics, road transport, and even the hand-making of stringed instruments. Here also has long been based one of the largest quality printing firms outside the great cities, where many a fine book has been produced.

Yet it was something even more romantic, industrially, which made Alva famous. For here silver was once mined, and fine silver at that, in the glen between Middle and Wood Hills. Unfortunately the bonanza did not last long; and the story is of the laird, Sir John Erskine, walking one day with a friend on the hill, and pointing. "From this hole I took £50,000." Then, changing the direction of his walking-stick, he added, "And I put it all into *that* hole!" where a less-rewarding mine-shaft still gaped.

Parallel with that climbing valley is another, Alva Glen itself, now a highly unusual public park, steep, narrow and attractively wooded. Near its foot is the new Academy, very modern in style but delightfully set immediately against the green background of the soaring hillsides, the principal secondary school for the Hillfoots area.

Alva Church has been twice rebuilt, in 1632 and 1815. Its bell is reputed to carry the inscription: *They who me giveth ar David Jenkin William Bell to Alva Kirk cursed be that wretch who preventeth from sacred use or else doth sell. Anno 1633.* The original church here was ancient, dedicated to St. Serf, whose well is also in the neighbourhood.

Alva House, partly designed, with the stable-block, by the Adam brothers, is now a ruin. The lands had belonged to Cambuskenneth Abbey, Stirling, but after the Reformation were granted to a son of the 7th Earl of Mar. Of this line was the aforementioned Sir John Erskine, and he it was to whom the unfortunate Alexander Steuart, found guilty of death for theft at Perth in 1701, was gifted as a 'perpetual servant' according to a brass collar dredged from the Forth at Logie. Sir John's nephew, the judge, Lord Alva, presented two communion cups of the native silver to the church in 1767.

Castle Campbell. Here is one of the most splendidly-sited and dramatic castles in the land, a large and handsome fortalice of the 15th century, with later additions and possibly an earlier nucleus. Now the property of the National Trust for Scotland, to whom it was presented in 1950 by J. E. Kerr of Harviestoun, its tall keep and high curtain-walls soar in magnificent isolation above the rocky

6

Alva from the Ochils. Vast Glenochil Distillery bonded warehouses in middle distance. Forth to the left, Wallace Monument, Stirling, right background

Alloa, the Carse of Forth and the Ochils from the air, with Strathearn beyond to the north

Castle Campbell, Dollar, looking south across plain of Forth

ravines of the Burns of Care and Sorrow, overlooking the little town of Dollar and backed by the steep slopes of the Ochils, today a mecca for visitors.

Various additional buildings, within the walled courtyard, flank the oblong five-storeyed keep, with its parapet and gabled roof. The main entrance to the enclosure is by an arched pend, to the north, above which formerly would be a gatehouse. As is quite usual, the keep's ground-level door admits only to the vaulted basement chamber. A small service stair within the walling now connects with the upper floor; but this is an addition, and formerly the main door opened at first-floor level, reached by a removable timber stair, for security. The Great Hall is on this floor, also vaulted, with an unpleasant pit or prison, reached via a hatch in the floor, down at ground level. The second storey, sleeping accommodation, was not vaulted; but the next floor is, and elaborately. The entire building is well supplied with wall-closets, aumbries and garderobes in the very thick masonry.

Castle Campbell has a history to match its appearance. Its original name was The Gloume. Why is not obvious. All this emphasis on gloom, care and sorrow is hard to account for, sited as the castle is on the sunny, south-facing lap of the Ochils. It was early a stronghold of the Stewarts of Lorne and Innermeath, but was acquired by the Campbells of Argyll, in marriage. In 1489 Colin Campbell, 1st Earl of Argyll, and Chancellor of Scotland for the young James IV, requiring a seat near the royal headquarters of Stirling, made this fortalice his home, much enlarging it. Also, he changed its depressing name, and by Act of Parliament.

"Our Soverane lord of his Riale authoritie at the desire and supplicacioun of his coising and traist Councalor Coline, Erle of Ergile, Lord Campbele and Lorne his chancellour has chengit the name of the castell and place quhilk wes callit the Gloume pertenying to his said coising . . ."

Inevitably, in such hands, the castle was involved in stirring activities. Many of the local people fell at Flodden, with Archibald, 2nd Earl. In 1560 during the Reformation struggles, the Lords of the Congregation found it a refuge.

"and quhene they had comed to Stirling to haif had entres, the frinchemen war in the toune and wald nocht suffer the congregatioun to enter thairin and the lordes retired to Inchcome and castell Campbell quihill the English mens incoming".

Four years earlier John Knox, residing here with the 4th Earl, had dispensed the sacrament of the Lord's Supper on the grassy slope between the castle and the cliff. And in 1645 it was captured by the forces of the Marquis of Montrose, and burned by the Macleans of Montrose's army, who had accounts to settle with the Campbells.

B

It must have been rebuilt speedily, for only nine years later General Monk was reporting it burned again, in a despatch to Cromwell.

Clackmannan. It is perhaps surprising that there is no evident air of regret, reproach, even of wistfulness, about Clackmannan's little town. For if ever an ancient community had reason to be preoccupied with past glories, and status filched from it by the hand of time and more aggressive neighbours, this is it. But not so Clackmannan. Though no longer the county town, no longer even a burgh with its own provost and town council, shorn of its former port on the Forth, and with its fine castle merely an empty ruin, it nevertheless still smiles athwart its ridge, renews its derelict housing with taste, even flair, cocks up both its church and its Tower as landmarks for miles around, and makes no complaint. Also it proudly retains the feature which gives it, and the whole county, its name, the Clach or Stone of Mannan, a pre-Christian sea-god—although this has been removed from the foot of a nearby brae to the south with the evocative name of Lookabootye, to the centre of the old Market Place, beside the Burgh Cross and Tolbooth.

Clackmannan was a royal place in more than its burgh charter. The castle on the hill, itself known as King's Seat Hill, was an early royal residence, with a hunting forest below. Malcolm IV (1141–65) lived here, and gave Dunfermline Abbey "the toft e croft in my town of Clacman". Nearly two hundred years later Robert the Bruce dwelt and hunted here; and it was his son, David II, who transferred the barony to his nephew, another Robert Bruce, son of an illegitimate son of the hero-king. So commenced the Bruce connection with Clackmannan—it was said that a round dozen Bruce castles about the Carse of Stirling could see this Tower's lofty beacon blaze, and take due heed—a connection not entirely severed, since Lord Balfour of Burleigh, whose family name is Bruce, is still a local landowner, and lives at Brucefield, a late 17th century house near by. The last of the actual Bruces of Clackmannan Tower was one of those indomitable ladies of which Scotland produces so many, who ceremonially 'knighted' Robert Burns with her great ancestor's sword, a gesture which did both credit, even if scarcely valid.

Like so many a larger medieval Scots town—Edinburgh itself, Stirling, Jedburgh and others—Clackmannan climbs a long narrow dorsal ridge, rising like a leviathan out of level lands, with its castle crowning the escarpment. Burgh, church and fortalice make an entity. Half-way up is the wide Market Place, still flanked by a few old houses. The Royal Oak Hotel is notable in having curvilinear late 17th century gables, of Dutch type—a reminder of the strong commercial links these Forthside burghs had with the Low Countries. In mid-street is a further reminder, the clock-tower, Dutch-style, of the former Tolbooth, with one crowstepped gable remaining, erected in 1592 at a cost, it is recorded, of £284 Scots. This comprised court-room, prison and jailer's house. Prior to this,

8

it is said, the sheriff-court of the county was held on the steps of the Burgh Cross which stands close by, conjuring up a pleasingly informal scene however unpleasant the verdicts must frequently have been. The Cross shaft is still surmounted by the Bruce arms, and towards its base its stonework is worn by the chains of prisoners attached thereto. The Stone of Mannan also stands near by, raised on top of a monolith itself apparently of no importance. It looks a very ordinary water-rounded boulder to have given its name to a whole county.

A little higher up the hill is the parish church in its large kirkyard. The present building was completed in the year of Waterloo, a handsome edifice rising on the site of an ancient foundation, dedicated to St. Serf—as are others in this area, St. Serf's Abbey of Culross being not many miles away down Forth. In the kirkyard here are a great many of the unusual gravestones peculiar to this district, rectangular and up to six feet long by only some eighteen inches high.

Clackmannan Tower, lording it over all, is a splendid parapeted double-keep of the 14th and 15th centuries, with older nucleus. Although long neglected it is now, fortunately, being taken in hand by the Ministry of Public Buildings and Works.

The Devon Valley. Clackmannanshire is basically the lower basins of two rivers, both oddly enough called Devon. This is not quite so strange when one considers that the Celtic word for river was *abhainn*, pronounced avon, and that there are innumerable streams deriving their names from this source, and not only in Scotland—all the Avons, Avens, Almonds, A'ans, Devons and Deverons. Still, two Devons in one tiny county is confusing, even though the smaller and easternmost is called Black—this because its fall is much less rapid and so its waters are less clear. The larger, "crystal Devon, winding Devon", as Burns wrote of it in his very last and dying lyric, is very different, a lively river that indeed stole the headwaters of a number of other streams in its upper and eastwards course through the Ochils. At Crook of Devon, it emerges from the hills and makes its dramatic bend to flow in the opposite direction. It is its fine valley from there, all the 20 winding miles to where it joins Forth at Cambus, that makes up the major part of this small county. An added oddity; geologists tell us that, because of the swooping Ochils Fault that plunges thousands of feet deeper than the visible 1000-foot drop of the hills to the plain, the river's true bed lies hundreds of feet lower, indeed almost four hundred feet below present sea-level, a dramatic reversal of the usual position.

The abrupt escarpment of the Ochils hems all in to the north; but a fine panoramic and comparatively little-known view of the vale, with its little towns of Dollar, Tillicoultry, Alva, Menstrie and so on, for those lacking the inclination for mountain-climbing, may be obtained from the quite scenic ridge-road (B.9140) which divides the valley from that of the Black Devon and the Forth plain south-

9

wards. This runs from south of Dollar all the way to Tullibody, about eight miles, and touches on the small mid-county villages and hamlets of Sheardale, Coalsnaughton, Coalyland, Fishcross and Sauchie. As the names indicate, coal was worked in this area; but this is not too obvious today. Although the villages themselves are scarcely beautiful, the ridge road is well worth traversing.

The most rewarding feature to visit is the fine 15th century ruined Tower of Sauchie, rather difficult to find amongst the scrub woodland that cloaks old mine-workings north-west of Fishcross. It is a square, well-planned keep of four storeys and a former garret, within a now ruinous courtyard. The hexagonal, conical-roofed caphouse at the stairhead is notable, as are many internal features, advanced for the period, with early examples of labour-saving devices. It was long the seat of the family of Shaw or Schaw, who acquired the property from another named Annand in 1420. The builder of the present tower was probably James Schaw of 'Salquhy', tutor to young King James IV. The Schaws were hereditary Keepers of the King's Wine-cellar, and their arms show three covered cups.

There are plans to set up a local nature reserve at Gartmorn Dam, near New Sauchie, an ambitious project to utilise 140 acres of loch and 80 of scrub woodland as a wildfowl refuge, with nature trails, picnic and parking sites and observation points.

Dollar. Dollar is the Hillfoots town with a difference. Not for Dollar the bustle and industry of its neighbours in Clackmannanshire. Here is an academic oasis, a residential retreat set amongst gardens and trees, dominated by Castle Campbell (noted separately) and presided over by the classical, park-embosomed Academy, one of the most famous schools in the land.

The little town, now developing fast—but still respectably residential—on the steeply-rising ground to the north-east, is douce, discreet, dignified. It grew out of the old village, much of which still stands on the steep hillside below Castle Campbell's glen. Here are a number of traditional houses and cottages, with crowstepped gables, rolled skews and pantiled roofs, with a hump-backed bridge across the burn. The very attractive Burnside, a wide double-street with the burn rushing down the centre and spanned by little bridges, leads down to the lower town, which grew up largely in the early 19th century. Here are several interesting houses of that period, some in fine gardens.

This Georgian development, of course, followed largely the founding of the Academy in 1818. John McNabb, a herd-boy born 1732, left Dollar to make his fortune—borrowing, it is said, $1\frac{1}{2}d.$ to make up his ferry fare to Leith. Died a wealthy London shipowner, he left £74,236 for "the endowment of a charity or school for the poor of the parish of Dollar". The splendid Grecian edifice built by the famous Playfair, with its dependent schoolmasters' houses, perhaps was not exactly what the founder visualised—but it became one of

Scotland's brightest educational lights. A mixed academy for boys and girls, it has both fee-paying and foundationer or free pupils, almost a third of them apt to be from overseas. Inevitably much of Dollar centres round the Academy.

Dollar also has its lovely glen as a park, in the care of the National Trust, dramatic in its overhanging cliffs and mountain-defile atmosphere. There is a strange melancholy about the names here, for the Burns of Care and Sorrow meet just below Castle Campbell— which used to be called The Gloom—and Dollar itself is sometimes alleged to have been once Doleur, although it is much more likely to have derived from the Gaelic *dal-aird*. No one has yet explained to the author this emphasis on the dismal: certainly it is far from applicable, on the face of it, to the neighbourhood.

Inevitably there is history here also. At Dollar was fought, and lost, a great battle by the Scots under King Constantin, Kenneth MacAlpine's son, against the Danes, in 877. And the Vicar of Dollar, Master Thomas Forret, was one of the first martyrs of the Reformation, being burned for heresy in 1538.

Kilbagie and Kennetpans. Kilbagie is a name that used to mean quite a lot in Scotland, as one of the best Scotch whiskies, renowned, the product of a great distillery here, once the largest in Scotland. It was also the site of the first threshing-mill. Later it became a paper-producing centre. Today, tiny place as it is, it still breaks new ground, as site of an office-machinery factory. Yet, despite all this, Kilbagie can hardly be called a village, so small is it. On the very edge of both the flood-plain of the Forth and the county boundary, it lies between Kincardine and Clackmannan, but off the busy main road, to the west.

Small or not, Kilbagie had the distinction of having its own port, a mile away over the green levels, at Kennetpans, with its own railway system between. From here was exported the whisky, mainly to London. Also coal, which was mined early in this neighbourhood. And salt, the pans for which gave the little port its name. Alas, Kennetpans amongst the mud-flats is no longer a hive of export and import; but that formerly it was busy indeed is evidenced by the facts that Kilbagie Distillery used to use as much as 60,000 bolls, or 360,000 bushels, of barley a year, and excise duty even in 1795 was £8000 sterling, greater than all the land-tax revenue of Scotland.

Kilbagie House is a solid square and plain mansion of the late 18th century; but near by is Garlet House, an attractive small laird's house of a century earlier, now somewhat faded as to status, but formerly probably the Dower-house of the Bruces' Kennet estate. It retains its sturdy and pleasing architectural features of steep roofs, crowstepped gables, pilastered doorway and central gablet above, with some pine panelling remaining within.

Kilbagie, nevertheless, is much older than these 17th and 18th century relics. Its name reveals that it was the site of a chapel of that romantic lady, St. Begha, the Christian daughter of an Irish prince, who in the 7th century was taken to Norway to wed the son of the king. She would have none of him, however, and fled back across the North Sea, landing on the Northumbrian coast where she put herself in the care of St. Aidan. From there she moved west, to found the religious house of Kirkby-Bega, or St. Bees, in Cumberland, before heading northwards to the remote shores of Forth, to give her name to this corner of Clackmannanshire.

Menstrie. The westernmost of the Clackmannanshire Hillfoots communities, Menstrie is smaller than the others, and not a burgh, but otherwise fairly similar in character as in situation, beside its rushing burn in the lap of the Ochils.

Oh, Alva's woods are bonny, Tillicoultry's hills are fair;
But when I think o' the braes o' Menstrie, it makes my heart aye sair.

So wrote a one-time miller's wife, alleged to have been spirited off by fairies.

Quite a large village, it has of recent years become something of a show-place because of the restored fame of Menstrie Castle and its Commemoration Room of the Nova Scotia baronets. This attractive late 16th century fortified house stands to the south of the road, now within a modern housing scheme, for which it makes a most delightful centre-piece. Yet for long it was derelict and condemned to demolition. Agitation however enabled the County Council, with the financial aid and encouragement of the Lieutenant-Governor and Premier of Nova Scotia, the Mayor of Halifax there, and the National Trust for Scotland, to save and rehabilitate the building. It is now their mutual pride.

The castle, curiously enough, was the home of the chiefs of the West Country Clan Alister, who came east with that Earl of Argyll who became Chancellor of Scotland in the late 15th century and lived at Castle Campbell. The MacAlisters anglicised their name to Alexander, and in 1567 here was born Sir William Alexander, poet and statesman, who became 1st Earl of Stirling, and was a founder of Nova Scotia. He it was who advised James VI and I to found the Order of Baronets of Nova Scotia, as a money-making scheme to help exploit the new colony. In exchange for considerable hard cash, each new baronet got a grant of 16,000 acres of land in Nova Scotia. Today the Commemoration Room displays the coats-of-arms of all these baronetcies still extant—a highly colourful and romantic exhibition. The L-planned, turreted mansion also now contains four modern flats.

There is another Nova Scotia baronetcy connection with Menstrie. Until fairly recently there was a second laird's house, on the north side of the road, locally known as Windsor Castle or House, the home of a family named Holbourne. A descendant of the Alexanders sold the estate to Sir James Holbourne, a major-general in the Scots army during Cromwell's invasion, in 1649. His grandson was created a baronet of Nova Scotia in 1706. In 1719 most of the Menstrie estate was sold again to Abercromby of Tullibody, whose grandson, Sir Ralph, the hero of Aboukir, was born in the castle in 1734. But the Holbournes kept the smaller mansion—which was probably a dower-house. It was demolished in comparatively recent times, but a Holbourne heraldic panel in stone, from over the door, was preserved and built into the gable of one of the very attractive enclave of Old Folks' Homes erected on the site by the burnside. Its motto, *DECUS MEUM VIRTUS* may still be distinguished. The last of the Holbournes, Miss Mary Anne, of Bath, daughter of the 5th baronet, left an endowment of £8000, in 1882, for the church of Menstrie.

There are a number of 18th century cottages in the village. But Menstrie is not all of the past. Far from it. It had its own woollen and blanket mills. But most important, now, here is sited the vast Glenochil Distillery, of the D.C.L. Its enormous range of bonded warehouses daunts the imagination.

The Ochil Hills. It is not unusual for ranges of hills to display different aspects and characters on different flanks. The Cairngorm Mountains and the Lammermuir Hills are diverse but typical examples. But surely few can rival the Ochils in this split personality? Their south-facing slopes, looking out across the level plain of Forth, are abrupt, dramatic, vigorous, slashed with deep ravines and steep gorges, their sides swooping, without foothills, directly to the flats, in a fashion not seen elsewhere in Scotland—as a consequence of the great Ochils Fault which, the geologists tell us, plunges for further thousands of feet below the now silted up floodplain. On the other hand, their northern and eastern aspects are of gentle rolling braes and smooth grassy ridges, with open valleys; as are most of those facing west, although, facing the Bridge of Earn area there are some steeps. Possibly this dichotomy would account for the general association of the range with Clackmannanshire, where its spectacular face soars in a thousand-foot wall above the Hillfoots towns and villages for a dozen miles—dramatic in more than their steepness, for, because of their slashed and riven contours and south-facing aspect, they are a nearly vertical playground for light and shadow, so that their appearance changes as often as the hours and the clouds. Nevertheless, of their 250 square miles, not 30 are actually in Clackmannanshire. The great majority are in Perthshire, while Kinross-shire, Stirlingshire and even Fife, share the total.

There are some quite major summits, although they are not looked on as 'climbers' hills'. Ben Clach, behind Tillicoultry, reaches 2363 feet—and a young local man once reached the top, at the run, in 49 minutes, and took only 17 to come back. Tarmangie, King's Seat and Whitewisp, a little to the east, are all over 2100. For all that, the best-known peak is probably the comparatively modest (in feet) Dumyat, pronounced Dum-*my*-at, in the extreme western,

Stirlingshire section. Because of its abrupt and commanding lines and its position at the western 'hinge' of the range, standing out from its fellows like a buttress, it offers a view from its summit almost unrivalled in the Lowlands.

The northern flanks are not to be scorned. The vistas across the straths of Allan, Earn and Tay are very fine, and something of the vast extent and richness of southern Perthshire may here be sensed— a scope not always realised. Here are communities, parishes and villages that nestle in the foothills—Dunning, Dron, Forgandenny and Glenfarg. The latter's long, deep and winding cleft is famous for its scenery but infamous for the narrow constriction of the twisting A.90 highway to Perth and the North, a sore frustration to the motoring public. Gleneagles, to the west, is less tortuous and less busy, carrying the A.823 pleasingly through the hills. But to savour the Ochils without leaving the car, take the longer B.934, Yetts of Muckhart—splendid name—to Dunning, 10 miles of unspoiled hill-country without so much as a hamlet, but not a road to hurry over. Who would wish to?

Tillicoultry. Although there is little that looks particularly beautiful—save for its fine Hillfoots setting beneath the steeply-rising green Ochils—or even very ancient, this little burgh's history goes back a long way, though not as a burgh. Tillicoultry consisted formerly of two rural villages, rather than a small town—Earlstoun, or Eastertoun, and Westertoun. But early last century, when industrialisation arrived, it did so with vigour, and soon no fewer than 18 factories had been established, mainly woollen and textile mills to make serges and tartans that became famous throughout Scotland. Copper was mined locally, but like the silver at neighbouring Alva, soon was worked out. It even published its own newspaper, *The Tillicoultry News*. Today it has resiled somewhat from these heights, but with a population of 4270 is still bulks large on the Clackmannanshire scene.

But as long ago as 1199, William the Lion granted to Cambuskenneth Abbey—always a favourite with the early Scottish kings— the lands and revenues of the 'ecclesia Tullicultre', which church was then ancient, and, as was so frequently the case hereabouts, dedicated to St. Serf, or Servanus, the 8th century princeling from the land of Canaan, who reversed the usual programme by first becoming bishop and then turning missionary, crossing the Alps and coming to these islands, to settle eventually at Culross; there to rescue and indeed bring up young Kentigern, whom he nicknamed Mungo, and who in due course became a more famous saint still, and founded the community that grew into Glasgow. At 'Tuligcultrin', St. Serf is alleged to have worked many miracles, including the raising of a widow's two sons "frae ded to lyf". Only relics of the old graveyard near Tillicoultry House remain to indicate the site of his church, a new place of worship being built in 1773, near the main road.

Still older, presumably, were two other local monuments. One was a Caledonian stone circle, 60 feet in diameter, which stood at the south end of the Cuninghar—an eminence, whose name means a rabbit warren—of which only one standing-stone survived, this eventually being removed to the vicinity of the House. The other antiquity is a circular fort, on the hillock known as Castle Craig.

Today, like Alva again, Tillicoultry has its fine glen for a public park, down which rushes the strangely-named Gloomingside or Gannel Burn, producing in rainy weather a splendid waterfall. Not so splendid in 1877, however, when a cloud-burst sent down an enormous cataract of water that burst all bounds and did great damage in the town. Unfortunately a huge quarry is gouging out the face of the hillside here, to no scenic advantage.

Tullibody and Cambus. These neighbouring Devon valley villages, at the west end of Clackmannanshire, have played a seesaw game in relative size and significance. Tullibody is much the more important, however, and after a period of declension, is again dominant, with a particularly fine and landscaped new-housing development, with old trees retained, and including a very modern shopping precinct beside the nucleus of older housing.

Originally it has been a very wide-scattered place—it was its own parish once, of course, until 1600. Its ancient and now ruined parish church is situated on rising ground well to the north of the Stirling road (B.9140); most of its traditional village is south of the road; its laird's house, a substantial early 18th century mansion with graceful bell-curved roof, is sited well over a mile from the kirk, down on the levels of Forth; while Tullibody Inch is actually an island *in* the Forth, half a mile farther south still.

It is claimed that the parish was founded by no less than King Kenneth MacAlpine. In 844 he had won his most significant victory against the Picts, which served to unite Scotland, near by at Baingle Brae. The old kirk was built by David I in 1149, a modest rectangular building with crowstepped gables and belfry. It has twice suffered the indignity of de-roofing; for in 1559 Mary of Guise's French troops took off its stone flags to remake a bridge, demolished by the Lords of the Congregation, across the Devon; and now it is again roofless—although a photograph in a work of 1915 shows it again stone-flagged. Its bell is still preserved near the neighbouring modern church. Not far to the west, the Ordnance map shows the site of the ancient Lady Well, amongst later housing; but the superstructure of this has been removed half a mile to the south, where it admittedly makes a pleasing feature in the excellent new development, however lacking in authenticity as a well. Two old bridges grace the area, one carrying the Menstrie road across the Devon on two segmental arches; the other, at Bridgend, now unused, bore the Stirling road by an extra long carriageway to cover risk of flooding.

The old kirk contains the mausoleum of the famous Abercromby family, of Tullibody House, whose most renowned member was General Sir Ralph, hero of Aboukir. His son was Speaker of the House of Commons in 1835, created Lord Dunfermline.

Cambus village, down where Devon joins Forth, has no such history and antiquity. But it has two distilleries, a former brewery, and when, as once, it had a railway station and also a harbour, it superseded Tullibody for a time in bustle and importance. Today the reverse applies, and apart from the distilleries, the rather pleasing atmosphere of a backwater prevails. There are some 18th century cottages, the old mill and the tree-girt weir, amidst much sound of rushing water and scent of good malt liquor.

PERTHSHIRE

By any standards this is one of the truly great counties. In size it is the fourth largest in Scotland, comprising 1,595,804 acres. In England, for instance, only the West Riding of Yorkshire is larger. But size is not everything; and despite having no large city, it has a much larger population than the other Scots counties which top it in size, Inverness, Argyll and Ross and Cromarty. Yet it has no industrial area, apart from the town of Perth itself. It has its great mountain tracts, of course, including some of the most famous scenery in these islands; but there is an enormous amount of fertile, populous countryside—far more, probably, than is generally realised—its great green straths, or wide open valleys, its especial pride. Contrary, therefore, to frequent pronouncements, the true glory of Perthshire is not its hills and lochs, however fine—for in these it can be excelled by Argyll and Inverness-shire, Ross or Sutherland; it is in its magnificent, age-old settled lowlands, its characterful small towns and its unnumbered villages. Especially the latter. Here are, probably, more ancient and interesting small communities than anywhere else in Scotland—although Aberdeen-shire may run it close.

Basically, Perthshire is the basin and catchment area of the great River Tay; although the south-west section, or Menteith (more properly *Mon*teith) as its name suggests, is the mounth of the Teith, principal tributary of the Forth. But in the main, Perthshire's innumerable and often splendid rivers reach the sea via the silver Tay. The county has another basic feature—the great Highland Fault, which runs across Scotland from the Gareloch to the Tay, most of it in Perthshire. This, because in general it marks the division between Highlands and Lowlands, is important. The county, therefore, inevitably has a split personality.

Owing to its great size and ancient lineage, Perthshire has always been split up into large sub-provinces, with very pronounced characteristics and identities of their own, mainly themselves ancient earldoms—Menteith, Strathearn, Gowrie, Atholl, Breadal-bane, each with its own subdivisions. These, all themselves mighty areas, are the very stuff of Scotland's story, an integral and vital part of our most exciting past. Perthshire is, in fact, an exciting county. Here, indeed, the past can be studied at its earliest, as far as Scotland is concerned, better than most; for it so happened that into Perthshire, Strathearn in especial, came the early Christian missionaries of the Irish Celtic Church, via Iona, the Brethren of Columba, to set up their cells and churches in these lovely valleys. The greatest concentration of early Celtic Church sites are here; also a large number of those quite extraordinary Pictish sculptured stones, with their symbols, things of splendid beauty and work-

17

manship, full of as yet unsolved mystery, which so give the lie to the folly, sedulously propagated by generations of ignorant educationists, that the Picts were a race of savages, painting their bodies and going about half naked. This is a subject which ought to be much more fully researched and studied. Quite clearly these Pictish ancestors of ours, whom the Celtic Church missionaries Christianised, were a highly developed and artistic people, with unique culture. Perthshire is where they can best be studied, probably.

Each town, village and parish of the county is dealt with hereafter in some detail. But perhaps some reference here to the ancient basic divisions would be appropriate and revealing. Menteith is the most southerly, a large area stretching from the Allan Water to Loch Lomond, including the Doune, Callander and Trossachs districts; and of course the parish of Port of Menteith itself and the Lake thereof—no significance about that appellation of lake, despite the nonsense talked by some about it being the only lake in Scotland. It was called Loch of Menteith until well into the last century. The early Celtic Earls of Menteith were a great force in Scotland, for their territory straddled the waist of the country, and, moreover, held the line between Highlands and Lowlands. Their principal castle was on the island of Inch Talla, in the Loch of Menteith, where they kept up princely state, with the Priory of Inchmahome on the next islet; but when Murdoch Stewart, Duke of Albany, James I's cousin, married the heiress in the early 15th century, he found the island-fortress inconvenient, and built a great new castle at Doune, which thereafter became the capital of Menteith. On his execution, for treason, James split up the earldom, as being too powerful for any one subject, giving Doune and the eastern part to another branch of the Stewarts—who still hold it—and the rest, with the earldom itself, to the Grahams. Certain descendants of the Grahams, also, are still landholders here, though the earldom itself was eventually suppressed by Charles I in shameful fashion. Menteith is half Highland, half Lowland, fertile, scenic, nonindustrial, typical indeed of the county as a whole. Being within easy reach of Edinburgh and Glasgow, it is very and deservedly popular with the visitor who has not time to 'do the Highlands properly'.

Strathearn is the next stratum of Perthshire northwards, and even larger. As the name implies, it comprises the very wide and fertile vale of the River Earn, from Lochearnhead right down to the river's confluence with the Tay estuary near Bridge of Earn, with all its feeder glens and flanking territories. Crieff is its largest town, with the more ancient Auchterarder, however, its capital. The sheer extent and rich fairness of this magnificent strath has to be seen to be appreciated—and nowhere is it better observed than from high on the north-facing Ochil Hills that separate it from the Forth plain, above Dunning or Forteviot. From one of the side-road summits up there, on a clear day, Strathearn is a splendid sight indeed, one of the finest in the land—although seldom remarked upon. Some two hundred square miles of Scotland's best is spread out below, great fields, rich pastures, ancient parkland, rolling woodlands, villages, castles and mansions innumerable, all flanking the noble, coiling river, and all contained within the vast bowl of the hills, the green Ochils to the south, the infinity of the Highland giants to the north.

All this splendid heritage was the domain of another line of Celtic earls. The Strathearn earldom, if slightly less strategically placed, was much richer than that of Menteith; and for the same reason, was finally incorporated into the Crown—so that, for instance, one of Queen Victoria's sons was Duke of Connaught and Strathearn. But the place was royal even before the earls, for this was Fortrenn, the Pictish kingdom, with its capital at Forteviot—in the parish church of which there are still sculptured stones dating from that early period. The famous Dupplin Cross near by, too, is one of the finest early Christian monuments in the country. At Forteviot was the palace of Angus MacFergus (A.D. 731–61) of St. Andrew's Cross fame, and a long succession of kings thereafter until Malcolm Canmore. Here died the great Kenneth MacAlpine who, conquering the Picts, finally united the Dalriadic Scots kingdom with that of the Picts to form the Scotland we know. Perhaps, because of these royal origins, the Celtic Earls of Strathearn always styled themselves 'by the Indulgence of God'!

Gowrie is the next great division, and rather less easily delineated. Indeed, not everyone even in Perthshire could tell you what was in Gowrie and what was not. Many think of it merely as the Carse of Gowrie, that level plain between the Sidlaws and the Tay, between Perth and Dundee. But this is not to take into account Blairgowrie, many miles to the north; nor the Gowrie in the Stanley area; nor the fact that the seat and centre of the Earls of Gowrie was at Ruthven, north-*west* of Perth. The name merely means the Plain of the Wild Goats, which is not much help. In fact, Gowrie seems really to have been all eastern Perthshire, from the head of Strathmore and the flanking Grampians down to the Tay estuary, including the western Sidlaws. The city of Perth itself, therefore, is in Gowrie. Also the highly important areas, in previous ages, of Scone, Dunsinane and Inchtuthill—all of which indicates the enduring status of the area, from Roman times onwards. The great family of Ruthven dominated most of it, once, and in 1581 became Earls of Gowrie. The notorious Gowrie Conspiracy, one of the murkiest incidents in Scots history, is linked with their name—but they were the victims of it, not the perpetrators. That shame belongs to James VI, who, owing the young Earl £80,000, organised his murder, and that of his brother, at Perth in 1600; and six weeks later, to clear his own name, had the two dead bodies tried for treason in court at Edinburgh, himself attending. The Murrays of Tullibardine, who had aided the King in this sorry business, were rewarded with large sections of Gowrie, especially in the Stormonth or north-western area. Their representative, the Earl of Mansfield, still holds sway hereabouts from Scone Palace, his eldest son Lord Stormont.

The northern parts of Perthshire are divided between Breadalbane and Atholl, huge tracts both, and largely mountainside. Breadal-bane is the more westerly, stretching from the edge of Argyll, at Strathfillan, Mamlorn and Moor of Rannoch right across the country to Glen Almond, Aberfeldy and Strathtay—braid Alban indeed, the very geographical centre of Scotland. It measures almost a thousand square miles, 33 by 31 miles, according to the gazetteer, and is basically the basin of the upper Tay, including the great Loch of that name and all the catchment area. Aberfeldy is some-times claimed as its capital; certainly it is the largest town and only burgh (population 1469). But Killin, at the other end of Loch Tay, has the better claim, as the original centre, where the Campbell lords had their main seat, at Finlarig Castle. Strangely, although the name is ancient and the area an entity from early times, there were no great Celtic earls or mormaers here. It was not until 1681 that the 11th Campbell of Glenorchy, having by then got rid of the MacGregors who anciently lorded it hereabouts, got himself created Earl of Breadalbane, and by peculiar means. His successors became almost the greatest landowners in Scotland, being able, at one time, to ride from the Atlantic shores to the North Sea on their own land—or so it is said. These territories include some of the most renowned scenery in the Central Highlands, from Glen Ogle to the Tarmachans, from Glen Dochart to Glen Lyon.

Finally there is great Atholl, another 500 square miles, celebrated in song and story—even for a special drink compounded of whisky, eggs and honey, called Atholl Brose—its duke the proud possessor of the only private army still left in these islands, The Atholl High-landers. Everybody knows Dunkeld, Pitlochry, Killiecrankie and Blair Atholl, amongst the most popular tourist areas of the land. Not so well known, however, are the great stretches of Strathardle, of Tilt and Tarf and Edendon, of Errochty and Fincastle, of Craiga-nour and Talla Bheith, mainly far from roads. Atholl was always a semi-royal territory. Indeed it is claimed that there were once Kings of Atholl. But less misty is the fame of Madadh, grandson of King Duncan, Earl of Atholl, whose own grandson Henry, dying in 1210, left only a legitimate daughter—though his illegitimate son, Conon, was the forebear of the Robertsons of Clan Donnachaidh who, next to the earls, were the greatest landholders in Atholl. The Crown bestowed the earldom on one of the sons of Robert III, the second of the Stewart kings, and for long the Stewarts lorded it here. Then, in the early 17th century, the 2nd Murray Earl of Tullibardine married the Stewart heiress, and got Atholl—and have held it ever since, becoming marquises thereof in 1676 and dukes in 1703. Their castle at Blair is a treasure-house, one of the most magnificent in Scotland, with no fewer than 32 rooms, filled with objects of value and interest, open to the public.

The last of Atholl is the lumpish mountain, the Sow thereof, facing the Boar of Badenoch at the Pass of Drumochter, and there-after we are in Inverness-shire.

Perthshire therefore is more like half a dozen counties than one—

and even so, great semi-subdivisions such as Strathallan, Strath-braan, Strathardle, Rannoch, Glen Shee, Stormont and Mamlorn, have scarcely been mentioned, if at all.

Obviously this could not be an industrial county. But Perthshire contributes much to the national economy. Its farms are legion, and many of them in the southern half are rich indeed and highly productive. Fruit-growing, especially in Gowrie, is widespread and profitable. In the Highland parts hydro-electricity is developed on a huge scale—indeed it was here that the first schemes commenced, in the Grampian projects. Forestry has become an ever more important feature of the scene, and a very large area is now under commercial timber. And tourism, of course, flourishes here on a larger and more organised scale than anywhere else in Scotland. But certain rural-type industries there are, such as distilling, the bleaching and dyeing of fabrics, jute and woollen spinning, saw milling. And the salmon fisheries are important.

Sir Walter Scott, that fervent Borderer, yet said: "If an intelligent stranger were asked to describe the most varied and most beautiful province in Scotland, it is probable that he would name the County of Perth." The present author finds no fault with that.

Aberfeldy and Weem. This thriving town of about 1500 people is known as the Capital of Breadalbane, and is pleasantly situated in Strath Tay 7 miles east of the loch, its setting particularly attractive as seen from the swiftly descending A.826 road from Crieff, with the woods of Weem Hill behind and the shapely cone of Schiehallion far to the north-west. Like so many Highland townships, the street scene itself is not particularly beautiful, but the parts which flank the Tay and the incoming Urlar Burn are pleasing.

The latter's banks are now a highly scenic public park, the upper portion, the long Den of Moness, tending nowadays to be known as the Birks of Aberfeldy, after the famous song Burns wrote—even though some shamefully suggest that the poet's memory was at fault, and he was in fact remembering the birches of Abergeldie, on Deeside, when he got home from his Highland haunt to write it. Certainly birch trees are not at all prominent here, although others are. Be that as it may, the attractions of this lovely climbing glen lose nothing, and the Falls of Moness are a famed beauty-spot, in three distinct sections.

The Tay itself contributes much to Aberfeldy's fame, here a broad and handsome river. Indeed, the burgh's Gaelic motto is translated *Swift and Often Rows the Boat to Aberfeldy*, a highly unusual but practical piece of ferry-advertising. For long, however, Wade's famous bridge has spanned the river here, five-arched, and his greatest achievement—even though Dorothy Wordsworth called it ugly. Near by, in a green park, is the towering Black Watch Memorial, a lofty cairn topped by a Highland *duine-uasal* or gentleman volunteer, marked by his single eagle's feather, commemorating the raising of this famous regiment from six Independent Watch Companies in

1739. The fact that the unit was embodied to put down the Highland Jacobites is discreetly disregarded.

Aberfeldy became a centre of wool manufacture in the 19th century and remains so, with dyeing, saw-milling and distilling as added industry. The distillery lies to the east of the town. But it is as a holiday centre that Aberfeldy most flourishes. The Atholl and Breadalbane Agricultural Show, in August, is a popular annual event, combining a cattle, flower and produce show with a Highland gathering.

Across the river, only a mile to the north, is the historic village of Weem, with its tall, whitewashed old inn, and General Wade's portrait hanging outside, for here he dwelt while building his local bridges. Not far away is the splendid 16th century pile of Castle Menzies, with its 19th century additions in the same style, former seat of the chiefs of that clan, long neglected but now being cared for by the clan society. Some of the trees here are reckoned to be the finest in Scotland, individual beech, oak, sycamore, spanish chestnut and ash reaching as high as 95, 80, 104, 80 and 83 feet respectively.

In the village itself is the ancient pre-Reformation church, now used as a burial-place for the Menzies family, a late 15th century structure of some interest, with a number of remarkable monuments and heraldic hatchments within, especially the floridly handsome memorial to Sir Alexander Menzies who died in 1624, and who altered this church for 'reformed' worship in 1609. Near by are two of the famous sanctuary crosses removed from nearby Dull. Up the steep wooded hillside behind is still to be found, amongst the undergrowth, the so-called St. David's Well, thought originally to have been opened by the great St. Cuthbert, who came here as a young man to stay at Dull. The change of name is judged to have come about by the well being restored by a certain laird turned monk, Sir David Menzies, Sir David's Well soon becoming *Saint* David's. The cave which gave the parish its name—*uaimh*, pronounced weem—is not so easily found nowadays on the tangled hillside.

Aberfoyle. This is the most readily accessible truly Highland community, from the south, with Glasgow only 30 miles by road, and Stirling 16. It is consequently highly popular for visitors, and deservedly so—indeed it is today becoming so for 'commuters' also. Itself an attractive area, it is also the gateway to further delights.

There are four distinct sections of Aberfoyle, two of them 2 miles apart—from the Rob Roy Roadhouse area, where the Glasgow and Stirling roads join, to the east, to the Milton on the west, almost at the narrow foot of Loch Ard. The former is most visitors' first sight of Aberfoyle, and here there has always been a mill and cottages also, the mill-wheel still in position. Here too is the golf-course. The other two sections are called the Clachan and the Kirkton— these all being typical old Scots divisions of any community. Now-

Clackmannan. Old Tolbooth, Mercat Cross and Stone of Mannan

Menstrie Castle. Wall of Nova Scotia Baronets' Room

Atholl, from above the Pass of Killiecrankie, looking north-west

Blair Castle and Forest of Atholl

adays the whole village tends to get called the Clachan of Aberfoyle; but this in fact used only to refer to the group of cottages round the famous inn, which lay almost a mile west of the present modern village—an inn haunted by Rob Roy and generations of other MacGregors, coming down from Glen Gyle, Inversnaid and so on. The present Bailie Nicol Jarvie Hotel is the 'descendant' of this inn, though on a more easterly site, and still retains the famed poker, really a plough coulter, with which the doughty bailie laid about him, as in the scene immortalised by Scott in his *Rob Roy*. This modern part of the village is not particularly attractive, despite its fine setting—indeed it grew up round the now-defunct railway station, and rather looks the part. The station has gone, and its yard is now used as a large, necessary but hardly handsome car-park, with facilities. Here are good shops, tea-rooms, craft centres and the like. A little to the east is the Dounans Residential School Camp, of the Scottish National Camps Association.

The Milton, to the west, still retains its old-time atmosphere, despite some modern housing development. The school and modern church are pleasantly placed on the rising ground between.

For antiquities one has to take the road which turns south, at the Bailie Nicol Jarvie. Here is the ancient, hump-backed and famous bridge over the infant Forth, leading to the Kirkton—site of a notable affray in 1671, when, at a christening of all things, the Grahams of nearby Duchray came to blows with followers of their far-out kinsman, the Earl of Airth, in typical Highland feuding fashion. The old parish church, where the christening took place, is a little farther on, and though now a ruin, still retains its belfry. How old it was is uncertain, for it was rebuilt in 1744 and repaired in 1839. It was an appendage of Inchmahome Priory. At the door still are two heavy mort-safes, in the shape of iron coffins, to foil body-snatchers of the Burke and Hare type; and there are many old gravestones, including one, dated 1692, for the Reverend Robert Kirk, who translated the Psalms into Gaelic verse—as well as distinguishing himself in more esoteric ways. In this connection it is interesting to note that, as late as the 1842 Gazetteer, it is declared that "everybody (in the district) understands English, though the Gaelic is chiefly in use". One wonders how many Gaelic-speakers there are in Aberfoyle today?

The road past the kirk is a cul-de-sac, ending in a number of woodland tracks through the great planted Loch Ard Forest which clothes all the foothills to the south—for this area is greatly invaded by the Forestry Commission. Half a mile along, near the fork, on rising ground now used for Forestry housing, is the site of a good stone circle, which had ten stones, with a larger one in the middle. To the east of the Kirkton rises the large modern Covenanters' Inn, a well-known hotel whose name refers to the 20th, not 17th century Covenanters, who met here and drew up the wording of their Scottish Covenant on self-government which attracted over two million signatures, in 1949. Now, this is a great place for pony-trekking—indeed everywhere you go in Aberfoyle area, Highland garrons are in evidence.

The road in the other direction, rising steeply behind the village northwards, A.821 to the Trossachs, is a 'must' for all visitors. A short way up, crowning an isolated knoll, is the magnificently-sited Tea House, a notable piece of modern architecture, circular and pillared all round, providing the most splendid views. Indeed all this road, known as the Duke's Road, and threading the Duke's Pass, gives vistas in all directions—the slate quarries on the left being not too great an eyesore. The Duke, incidentally, was a Graham one, of Montrose, descendant of the Great Marquis. The large Achray Forest, which covers much of the area, diversifies the vistas. Just beyond the highest point, about 800 feet (Aberfoyle is at 65 feet) is seen the oddly named but attractive Loch Drunkie, famous for red-fleshed trout. It is a strange geographical fact that its north-eastern tip is within a quarter-mile of the shore of Loch Vennacher, though with high ground between, and 200 feet higher. The descent, on the north, to the head of Loch Achray in the Trossachs, is fine, the foot of Loch Katrine being only a mile to the west, and the head of Loch Vennacher 2 miles to the east.

Another very attractive road, though a private one, leads from the Kirkton westwards through the Loch Ard Forest to Duchray and beyond, passing by the picturesque wood-girt Lochan Spling. Duchray Castle, nearly three miles along, and actually in Stirlingshire, is a small but interesting tower-house of the late 16th century, with older nucleus, oblong, with a circular stair-tower and angle-turret. Unfortunately someone has 'gothicised' the windows, to ill effect; but the little fortalice is still delightful and kept in good order. In 1528 the laird was Buchanan of that Ilk; but in 1569 it was sold to the Grahams, and remained with that powerful family until modern times. The castle gave shelter to Rob Roy, despite his anti-Graham bias, on an occasion when the two Graham sisters managed to smuggle him out of the back door while entertaining dragoon officers at the front. Earlier, in 1653, Duchray was involved in the Earl of Glencairn's unsuccessful battle against Monk's Cromwellian troops in the Pass of Aberfoyle. After the Forty-five Rising, it was burned; which accounts for the altered roof-line.

The main B.829 road, west of Aberfoyle village, although a dead-end, continues for 15 glorious miles through the mountains, to terminate at Inversnaid on the east shore of Loch Lomond, passing Lochs Ard, Chon, Katrine and Arklet, one of the finest scenic runs in the Southern Highlands. This is dealt with separately.

Abernethy. Although today no very important place, and with appearance to match, Abernethy—not to be confused with the Speyside parish—is a most potent name in Scotland's story. Here was an ancient Pictish capital, and then the ecclesiastical metropolis of the Celtic Church of the Culdees, before St. Andrews, conveniently near to Scone, the one-time royal centre of government only 8 miles away across Tay, as the crow flies. Indeed before that, Abernethy was important, with a Pictish and also Roman fort, port and baths, at Carpow just to the north.

Now little more than a village, Abernethy stands at the foot of its own steeply-climbing Ochils glen, right on the Fife border, looking out across the level carse to the junction of Earn and Tay, just where the latter begins to widen to an estuary, 6 miles south-east of Perth. It is perhaps now most famous for its Celtic Round Tower, one of the only two remaining in Scotland, although there is the stump of another at Iona—the second being at Brechin. These are tall, slender, tapering columns, free-standing and not part of church buildings, although sited in later kirkyards. Abernethy's dates probably from the 9th or 10th century, with 11th century alterations. It is 72 feet high and only 8 feet in interior diameter, with walls 3½ feet thick. There were six stages of timber flooring, and door and windows are in the Irish style. The modern clock is somewhat incongruous. These towers served the Celtic clergy as steeples, watch-towers against Viking invaders and others, and refuges. There are still 76 of them standing in Ireland.

Apart from a few remaining traditional houses, Abernethy village has not a great deal to show the visitor, considering its resounding history—although scarcely resounding perhaps was the sorry day when the great King Malcolm Canmore did homage to William the Conqueror, in 1072, at Abernethy, as evidently the only way to get the Norman and his invading army to go home. It was Malcolm's English Queen Margaret, later sanctified by grateful Rome, who instituted the pro-Romish movement in Scotland which was to oust the Celtic Church not only from Abernethy but from all the land. The place was made a burgh of barony in 1476, under the famous Archibald Bell-the-Cat Douglas, Earl of Angus; and his present-day descendant, the Duke of Hamilton, bears the style of Lord Abernethy amongst his many subsidiary titles. The Douglases had inherited Abernethy by marriage with the heiress of the MacDuff line of Hereditary Abbots of Abernethy, who became secularised as the de Abernethy family. To them, as the second main stem of the great MacDuff house, had passed the right of crowning the Scots monarchs, after the end of the senior stem, Earls of Fife—hence the Duke of Hamilton's presenting to the present Queen her Scottish crown at St. Giles Cathedral in 1953, at that significant ceremony.

About two miles east of the village, and actually over the Fife border, are the remains of MacDuff's Cross, where once all man-slayers to within the 9th degree of consanguinity with the Earls of Fife or Lords Abernethy, could claim sanctuary and gain remission of penalty other than the payment of a fixed indemnity to the victim's family—a most useful inheritance in otherwise lawless days.

To the other side of the village, high on a shoulder of Castle Law hill to the south-west, is the site of a famous Scots hill-fort, massively built of dry-stone walling with binding timber beaming, a type of construction noted by Julius Caesar. These forts were roughly contemporary with the Roman invasions. It was in A.D. 80 that the celebrated Agricola "opened up new nations, for the territory of tribes as far as the estuary named Tanous (Tay) was ravaged", according to the Consul's son-in-law Tacitus. The Carpow Roman fort's site, unlike the Pictish one, is on low ground near the Tay. Near by is Carpow House, and the scanty remains of Old Capow. Hear was the ancient seat of the Lords of Abernethy. A Pictish symbol-stone stands near the Round Tower.

Abernyte and Rossie. The South Sidlaws village and parish of Abernyte is not so well known as it deserves to be, sitting in its wide, south-facing, hanging valley between the Carse of Gowrie and Strathmore, 9 miles west of Dundee and 2 north-west of Inchture. It is a pleasant place—but to call it a village is almost a misnomer. One gets the impression that the Abernyters are notably fond of walking. For its various sections are all so wide apart as to be extraordinary, scattered over a network of side-roads in the laps of the green hills. All, however, have fine and extensive views, especially south-eastwards through the gap in the hills to the carse and the open sea at the mouth of the Firth of Tay. King's Seat is in this parish, and presides over all, at 1236 feet the highest point of the South Sidlaws, with an ancient chambered cairn and enclosure at its summit.

The major parts of scattered Abernyte lie dotted along the B.953 Inchture to Balbeggie road, threading the very attractive fertile glen, shut in on three sides by green hills. The first we come to, from the south, is the former Free Church and manse, now converted into a large garage establishment, and seeming as odd as must have been the church to be isolated thus. Then, half a mile on, at a road junction, is the Milton and school with some cottages; and a little way farther up still, another group of houses as a crossroads. A quarter-mile on, built on higher ground, is the largest section of the village, still growing with modern houses. Then, away more than another half-mile to the east, passing Abernyte House and its rather strangely set-down walled garden, is the very detached Kirkton, with the parish church and a large, whitewashed and fine-looking manse facing out over the sinking braesides to the south, all under the wooded craigs of Rossie Hill.

The church is an old foundation rebuilt in 1736. There is a parish record declaring: "December 4 1664, the whilk day Mr. Andrew Shippert was admitted minister of Aberneit, by Mr. Robert White, minister at Instur, being authorized by my Lord Bishop of Dunkelden to that effect. Collected that day 7 shillings two pennies." The said bishop was himself contemporaneously minister of St. Madoes parish, along the Carse, nimbly straddling circumstances. There are some old tombs in the graveyard.

Abernyte parish boasts sundry antiquities. There are not a few cairns, one of which used to stand in the manse glebe, with bones found under it. These were said to commemorate a battle between the Grays of Fowlis and the Boyds of Pitkindie, just up the road—though it seems much more likely that they are of prehistoric origin. On a hill called Glenny Law, as well as cairns, is said to be a stone circle of seven stones; and at Stockmuir, one of nine. On an ancient map north of Ballairdie, were marked the remains of a castle named Carquhannan, though locally called Balchuinnie, with a spring near by designated the King's Well. This may well have been Scotland's only King Edgar, for a mile or so down the road southwards is the rather unusual hamlet of Baledgarno—pronounced Bal-egger-ny—bearing the name of Edgar, 4th son of Malcolm Canmore, anointed king in 1001, and who built a castle on the hill just above here, still called Castlehill. Boethius declares it was "foundit by Edgar in Gowry, wha gat certane landis fra the Erle of Gowry, and annexit his name to the castle".

Baledgarno, however, as a village, only dates from the early 19th century; and an attractive place it is, lying on either side of a falling burn just to the west of the policy wall of the Rossie Priory estate. But this hamlet did not grow; it was made. The 8th Lord Kinnaird decided to leave Drimmie House, down near the present A.85 road, and build a great new mansion up on a terrace in his splendid parkland, under Rossie Hill—this in 1807. Unfortunately the old village of Rossie seems to have offended his sensibilities. Not that it cluttered the site, being fully half a mile away to the east, and not very evident from the new palace. But these were the days of great lords and large gestures, and for better or worse the village was bodily removed a mile to the west. Oddly enough, the old market cross was left behind, and still stands in lonely splendour by its burnside in the open parkland, with the former village church, now the family burial-chapel, on the yew-clad hillock behind. The cross has a four-stepped plinth, and on top of its shaft is a highly unusual finial in the form of four lions and unicorns back-to-back, beneath inscribed R.H. and K.G. 1746. The significance of these initials is not clear. A single standing-stone projects from the turf a few yards to the west, which also must have been in the village street. The Kinnairds' chapel is kept in good repair, and within, amongst the memorials of the family, is a splendid Celtic cross-slab, highly decorative, with horsemen, animals and intricate ribbon ornamentation. These cross-slabs, another of which stands at St. Madoes Church 9 miles to the south-west, date from the period A.D. 800–1000, it is thought, and are of Celtic–Pictish origin.

Rossie Priory itself, standing in a magnificent position in finely-rising parkland, is still a most handsome mansion although greatly reduced in size in recent years. It contains many treasures, and remains the seat of the Lords Kinnaird. Highly unusual is the pend which passes through the middle of the house, so that a visitor may drive right through from one side and driveway to another. The predecessor of this great house and Drimmie also, is the red-stone, late 16th century castle of Moncur, which still stands in a ruinous state, within the estate, about a mile to the south, near an attractive pond and visible from the main A.85 road. It has been a fine fortalice, liberally equipped with gun-loops, built on the Z-plan, with a notable hall fireplace and great chimney-stack therefor.

To the east of Rossie, in a field, is another monolith called the Falcon Stone, allegedly one more of those landmarks which the Hay's hawk alighted upon, after the Battle of Luncarty in 990, in its over-flying of the lands the Hays were to gain as reward for their part in the battle—an active and useful bird. Probably, however, the stone has a much earlier significance.

Behind wooded Rossie Hill is the estate hamlet of Knapp, tucked away in a quite secret valley threaded by a side-road. Here is an unusual feature—a 17th century doocote turned into a cottage. Farther north, on the high ground of Dron, is a Pictish fort on the hilltop. And to the east, at the farm of Dron, are the ruins of a 12th century chapel, formerly attached to Coupar Angus Abbey. Only two gables remain, by the burnside, but that to the west has a fine, tall pointed archway.

North of this point, the land climbs to a high and lonely moorland plateau area, part of Longforgan parish, around the 650-foot contour, scattered with ancient Scots pines and other wind-blown trees, gorse and heather. In its remote centre is the small loch of Redmyre. It is hard to believe that this lofty wilderness is only 7 miles from busy Dundee.

Aberuthven. Once a separate parish, and a place of some standing, a hand-loom weaving centre with its own cattle fairs, Aberuthven is now just a village on the busy A.9, $2\frac{1}{2}$ miles north-east of Auchterarder, with raspberry-growing its chief preoccupation. Despite its name, it stands some distance from the confluence of the Ruthven Water, which flows close by, and the Earn, in a pleasing pastoral setting, looking north to the Highland Line and south to the characterful Ochil hills of Rossie Law and Craigrossie—the former with a large earthwork, or prehistoric fort on its brow, the latter sporting two such, one on either side of the picturesque glen of the Pairney Burn which divides the hill's corrie. At the north-eastern base of Craigrossie, also, is the curious and interesting broom-grown mound, shaped like a great ship and called Ternavie—a suggested corruption of *Terraenavis*, meaning the ground of the ship, and thought to be a Viking burial-ground. This is readily seen from the very attractive back road to Dunning, a scenic route with splendid prospects.

A little to the south-west of the village itself is the ruined pre-Reformation chapel of St. Kattans, set amongst trees at the roadside, and better preserved than some, once the church of the former parish of Aberuthven. Built in the Norman First Pointed style, it retains two ogee-headed slit windows in its east gable, with a belfry surmounting that to the west. Alongside is the Montrose Aisle, an urn-topped mausoleum of the Dukes of Montrose, dated 1736, in classical style. Another senior branch of the Graham family also used St. Kattans as burial-place, that of Inchbrakie, whose castle, about six miles to the north-west, was demolished by Cromwell in 1651 for the laird's strong adherence to the royal cause.

Alyth. This small red-stone burgh—pronounced Ay-lith, *aileadh* meaning ascent—with under 2000 inhabitants, stands at the eastern extremity of Perthshire, in the Grampian foothills overlooking Strathmore, 5 miles east of Blairgowrie, backed by and partly climbing the Hill of Alyth, behind which lies the great treeless Forest of Alyth, once a royal hunting-ground. It is an attractive place on two levels, grouped round a pleasing Market Square through which runs a hurrying burn confined within walling, little bridges connecting the riverside streets. The Auld Brig dates from the 16th century. Flanking the Square is a marble obelisk commemorating 'Three Brave Men'—the 9th Earl of Airlie, Nigel Neis Ramsay, Younger of Bamff, and Charles Ogilvy, Younger of Ruthven, heroes of the South African War. Their names tend to sum up Alyth's story, for the area has always been dominated by the Ogilvys of Airlie and the Bamff Ramsays. It became a burgh of barony in 1488 and a police burgh in 1875.

Its earliest origins, however, were connected with the royal forest, and a 1377 charter appoints a Justiciary therefor, with the royal castle of Inverqueich to the east. Alyth developed as a linen-weaving centre, which manufacture still continues. There is also a carpet mill.

The present parish church, a large and handsome Gothic edifice of 1839, stands high, like its predecessor, overlooking the town. Its vestibule contains the Alyth Stone, a Pictish cross-slab with double-disc and Z-rod symbols. Within is a remarkable heraldic hatchment commemorating Sir George Ramsay of Bamff, killed in a duel 1790. The old ruined church of St. Moluag, or Malachi, in its ancient graveyard, stands a little to the east, remarkable architecturally. The aisle known locally as 'The Arches' was a post-Reformation enlargement. In the chancel is an aumbry and piscina, and a memorial to a minister and wife dying simultaneously in 1636, and interred in the same grave. Outside lie the Ramsays of Bamff.

Farther east, at a braehead below the manse garden, is re-erected the old Mercat Cross, dated 1670, 8 feet high with a quadrangular finial.

Bamff House lies within a large estate behind Alyth Hill, a fairly plain but interesting mansion, grown from an early nucleus and from a free-standing 16th century tower, with splayed gunloops and four storeys above a vaulted basement. Sir Neis Ramsay is 12th Baronet; but the Ramsays were here long before baronetcies were invented, for in 1232 the first Neis, or Nessus de Ramsay of Bamff, was physician to Alexander II.

Directly behind Alyth are also the Hills of Loyal and Barry. The romantically-named Lands of Loyal House, former Ogilvy laird-ship, is now a hotel. Barry Hill (681 feet) at its steep summit has the remains of a large vitrified Pictish fort, 450 feet in circumference, with ramparts, plus a resounding legend. Allegedly it was the prison of Guinevere, or Vanora, King Arthur's erring queen, who had relations with the local Pictish chief.

Farther east still, passing a standing-stone below the road, on lower ground where the Alyth Burn joins Isla at the Angus border, is the aforementioned ruined castle of Inverqueich, with walling and enclosure, strongly sited above a ravine. Robert II granted the keeping of 'the King's Castle of Inucuyth' to his nephew James de Lyndesay, 1394. Edward I had slept here in July 1296. A pic-turesque mill still works near by. At Bruceton, 2 miles east, in a field below the road, is another weather-worn Pictish symbol-stone, with Celtic beast still to be discerned. At the neighbouring farm westwards, Shanzie, is a group of five standing-stones crowning a knoll.

The hamlet of New Alyth lies a mile south-west of the town, on the A.926.

Alyth session records have many references to the religious troubles of the 17th century, being particularly critical of the great Montrose—or at least his army, which was stationed here for 6 months in 1646, and seems to have behaved as idle armies do. In 1651 there was actually a parliament, or meeting of the Estates, at Alyth, while Monk was besieging Dundee—but unhappily it was caught napping by a detachment of Englishmen and its notables—including the commander-in-chief, Leslie, Earl of Leven, sent prisoners to London.

Amulree and Glen Quaich. The village of Amulree is a long way from anywhere, remotely set on the high, bare uplands between the valleys of Tay and Almond, 12 miles north of Crieff, an equal distance south of Aberfeldy, and 10 miles west of Dunkeld. Although it does not give that impression on approach from either side, it is however at the foot of a glen of its own, the high Glen Quaich, and indeed in the admittedly very shallow valley of upper Strathbraan. From the A.822 highway there would appear to be little call or sustenance for a village here, with miles of empty moorland all around; but hidden Glen Quaich and the upper Braan are more populous than appears, and this is their centre. Not that Amulree is any metropolis. There is a fairly large hotel, at whose predecessor Dorothy and William Wordsworth once stopped; a church and manse, and graveyard with some old stones; a school, a post office and two petrol-stations. For the Highlands that represents a basic centre.

And it is certainly very central, plumb in the very centre of Scotland in fact. Perhaps that is why it was here that, in 1715, the clans assembled and were armed for that Jacobite rising. Amulree is, in fact, mentioned in the Jacobite song, *The Piper o' Dundee*. Fairs once were held here, twice a year, for cattle and sheep, but those days are long past.

Glen Quaich, so little known because unseen from the main road, is really the *raison d'être* for Amulree. It is quite a charming valley, and deserves greater fame. It is in fact something of a hanging valley, lying at almost the thousand-foot contour, and running nearly seven miles westwards into the great hill mass of South Breadalbane, embosoming towards its east end the pleasant sheet of Loch Freuchie, 2 miles long and a quarter that wide. It is all more mellow and sheltered than might be expected from the rather bleak and bare heather moors surrounding, and there are in fact no fewer than ten farms, a shooting-lodge and a small laird's house therein. At the far west end, a very rough and extremely steep extension of the road climbs as high as 1670 feet by numerous alarming bends, and down to Loch Tay-side, at Kenmore, scarcely to be recommended to the nervous motorist. The normal A.822 highway goes north by way of Glen Cochill and across the rather dreich moorland, past the lonely Loch na Craige, following the line of Wade's road, to the Tay at Aberfeldy.

Atholl. Atholl is one of the most ancient and important divisions of old Scotland, one of the original Seven Earldoms into which the country was split up, arising out of the early mormaorships, a name as renowned as Fife, Mar, Lennox or Lothian. In sheer size, as in scenery, it is notable, however lacking nowadays in population, comprising about 500 square miles, larger than the counties of East Lothian or Peebles-shire, and five times as large as Clackmannan. It includes a large part of the Central Highland massif, and much of northern Perthshire. It marches with Badenoch, to the north, where Perthshire joins Inverness-shire, and here two great lumpish mountains face one another, above the A.9 highway, the Sow of Atholl and the Boar of Badenoch. Innumerable lofty and heather-clad summits rise in Atholl, mainly of rounded rather than peaked formation, amongst the highest being Ben-y-Gloe (3671 feet) Ben Iutharn Mhor (3424) Glas Tulachean (3445) Ben Dearg (3304) Ben Udalain (3306) and An Sgarsoch (3300). Great rivers drain the uplands, including the Tilt, Bruar, Errochty, Edendon and of course the Garry. Strangely, the area is sparse in great lochs, there being only Garry itself, with Ericht on the northern boundary; but there are hundreds of small ones. The Forest of Atholl is one of the largest deer-forests in the land, and great herds of stags may sometimes be seen, even from the main road.

Lords of all this, from earliest times, have been the Earls, now Dukes, of Atholl. The present Duke combines in his person the chiefship of the Stewarts of Atholl and the Murrays of Tullibardine, both of which lines have played major parts in Scots history. Their main seat has always been Blair Castle, set in its vast estate at Blair Atholl, a huge whitewashed pile, much altered down the centuries but containing a 13th century nucleus, Comyn's Tower. It has seen great excitements, inevitably; indeed it was the last castle in Britain to have withstood a siege—and, oddly enough, from one of its own people, Lord George Murray, Prince Charles's lieutenant-general, who besieged a government force in his old home for 17 days, in 1746. The castle is open daily to the public, and is an almost overwhelming storehouse of treasures to be inspected, no fewer than 32 rooms being on view, filled with a vast variety of furnishings, pictures, arms, uniforms, trophies, china, needlework, documents and so on. Here is an embarrassment of riches that demands a whole day to view. For a wet day in the Highlands, nothing better could be suggested.

The village of Blair-in-Atholl—to give its proper name—lies at the castle gates, where the rushing Tilt joins the Garry, and is a pleasant place. Old Blair, the former Castleton, lies to the north, within the estate—the old road crossed at Bridge of Tilt, higher up; and here, at the old St. Bride's Kirk, lies buried Bonnie Dundee, slain at Killiecrankie in 1689. Blair is, of course, the headquarters of the only private regiment still permitted to be maintained in Britain, the Atholl Highlanders—even if today they are only a very token force. The War Memorial here, erected after the First World War, is notably effective and suitable—merely a great rough boulder, reared up in traditional fashion as a standing-stone, with the figures 1914 and 1918 inscribed thereon.

Glen Tilt, which strikes north for 16 miles, to the small Loch Tilt only about five miles from the Aberdeenshire border, is an exciting and truly Highland valley, narrow, overhung by huge mountains, threaded by a splendid torrent. Bridge of Tilt, a little way up, is really a separate village from Blair, set in a delightfully wooded ravine; and near by are the triple Falls of Fender, where that river comes in out of Glen Fender, from the north-east. This glen drains the area called Lude, an ancient lairdship, and the remains of its old church lie some two miles up. From Bridge of Tilt northwards the main valley is almost a distinct, elongated world of its own. Through it runs a track which leads on over the high watershed to Mar and Dee—a walker's marathon of delight. The Witch's Rock hangs above the river, *en route*. About fourteen miles up are the multiple Falls of Tarf, where a major tributary comes cascading in from the remote fastnesses of Gaick Forest on the southern flanks of Glen Feshie and the Cairngorms. Tilt in its upper reaches is certainly unspoilt, but lonely nowadays. It was not always so, for this was an important route into the north-east—even Bruce is said to have used it on his way to Mar. Its importance is verified in that we read that the brother of the great Ranald of the Isles was one Eugenius, Thane of Glentilt. Its traverse today makes one of the finest hilltramps in Scotland—but only for the tough and seasoned walker.

Across the Garry, the scar of the great limestone quarries near Glackmore is unsightly, but is industrially important. From Blair

Atholl in the days of steam, extra engines were attached to help push the trains over the Drumochter Pass, at 1506 feet the highest point reached in any railway in Britain.

Auchterarder. The Royal Burgh of Auchterarder looks modern enough, stringing the busy A.9 highway for more than a mile midway between Stirling and Perth, above the pleasant vale of the Ruthven Water which flows out of Glen Eagles; but it is very ancient, having been the head burgh of the great and influential earldom of Strathearn, before it became a royal burgh. Its modern look is partly accounted for by the fact that, like other communities in this area, it was burned by Bobbing John, Earl of Mar, in his retreat after the defeat of Sheriffmuir near by, in 1715. Though so 'lang a toun' it is in the main only one street thick, and its population no more than 2425. But it is a convenient centre for visitors to Strathearn, as is indicated by its no fewer than 8 hotels. Large cattle fairs used to be held here, preparatory to the famed Falkirk Trysts.

The long main street, steadily sloping northwards, is not perhaps notable for architectural merit. Nevertheless it was used by that pawky but shrewd monarch, James VI and I, as illustration to confound some of his superior London subjects. One of them had been boasting of the magnificence of some walled English city, with its many drawbridges, and King Jamie assured the company that he could take them to a modest Scots burgh, which they considered little more than a village, yet with no fewer that 50 drawbridges. He did not add that these were the little removable planks which the burghers and cottagers put out to bridge the open burn and gutter running down the centre of this long street. Today things are better than that. Next to the Town-hall is a building called the Girnel House—girnel the Scots word for granary—founded by the famous judge, Lord Kames, in 1790. It is now an institute, with hall, library and so on. Near by is the attractive War Memorial Gate, forming an entrance into the old churchyard. Here stands only the tower of the earlier church, a good square edifice of the 17th century, with vaulted basement and sundial.

Auchterarder again attained fame, in 1834, when it became the scene of the first struggles on doctrine and church government within the established Church, which led to the great Disruption.

In the near vicinity are three features of interest. Half a mile to the west, at the side of the Tullibardine road, near the Gallowhill, are two standing-stones. To the north, and nearer, in the yard of Castleton farm, are the scanty relics of the once-important castle of Auchterarder. Only a fragment of early walling remains, with some more modern reconstruction work at the east, into which two 16th century shot-holes have been built; but traces of the original moat may be seen in the garden to the south. This was a favourite hunting-seat of King Malcolm Canmore (1052–93). Edward,

33

Hammer of the Scots, rested here on one of his invasions of Scotland, and issued edicts. There was even a Treaty of Auchterarder signed here, between the Regent, Mary of Guise, widow of James V, and the Protestant Lords of the Congregation, granting free worship— forerunner of the Reformation. Lastly, the pre-Reformation church —as distinct from the first post-Reformation one, whose tower has been mentioned—lies nearly a mile to the north-east, off the B.8062 road to Kinkell, in a sorry state of neglect. It was a shrine dedicated to St. Mackessock, its founder, Gilbert, Earl of Strathearn, granting its revenues to the Abbey of Inchaffray in 1200. Today there are only tumbled ruins in a neglected overgrown graveyard, with sheep in possession. Most countries, one would imagine, that had monuments dating from 1200, would be apt to cherish them.

Ballinluig Station and Tullymet. There are two Ballinluigs within 5 miles, a source of confusion. The older and less well known is a village of Strathtay, on the south bank of the river, 5 miles east of Aberfeldy. The other, with which we are concerned here, is on the main A.9, near the meeting of Tummel and Tay, 5 miles south of Pitlochry. Here is Ballinluig Station, formerly Junction. The name merely means the village in the hollow—so who knows which came first?

This stretch of the east bank of the Tay valley is remarkable for its two levels. Everyone knows that which lies along the river, where runs the A.9 and the railway to Inverness. But the high, wide and fertile shelf above, probably few visitors realise exists, though it runs, a mile wide, all the way from the Pass of Dunkeld to Moulin at Pitlochry, threaded by its own winding road. This is mainly a part of the parish of Dowally, but it is convenient to deal here with the northern section.

Ballinluig itself is on the low ground, of course, and is not particularly interesting. It comprises a scattered village, not very large, with a hotel and the railway station. It was not in existence as a village in 1843, when the New Statistical Account was written. Here the A.827, like the former railway-line, branches off for Aberfeldy, crossing the river by a long modern bridge. Two miles to the south, in the Haugh of Kilmorich, is the *Clach Glas*, the Grey Stone, of uncertain significance; with a standing-stone near by on the other side of the road. On the higher ground, in the same area, is the site of St. Muireach's Well; also the former distillery of Kilmorich—*cill Muireach*, meaning the Chapel of Mary. One mile to the north of Ballinluig is a stone circle; and in another mile, the former hamlet of Moulinearn, once with its importance, where the Lochbroom Burn, flowing out of the quite large and troutful Loch Broom away to the north, joins Tummel.

The higher shelf of land is of greater interest, perhaps. Here were two ancient baronies, Dalcapon and Tullymet. On the former, to the north, remains the ruinous little laird's house of Pitcastle, dating probably from the 17th century, and unusual in that it represents

34

a different tradition from the typical tall tower-house—a purely Highland tradition. It has been a modest, primitive house of only four rooms, with no other defensive feature than a draw-bar-socket at the chamfered doorway. There has been a large fireplace in the main ground-floor chamber, and a small inside stairway up to the laird's bedroom. The other upper room appears to have been reached by a stone outside forestair, now collapsed—but this may have been a later access. Painted panelling and a nail-studded door were removed to Blair Castle for preservation. Pitcastle, despite its rough and tiny proportions, was the seat of chieftains of a branch of Clan Donnachaidh, the Robertsons of Pitcastle, who claimed royal descent.

The other barony, Tullymet, still has its large estate, with a plain mid-18th century mansion set on remarkably high ground. This was the seat of the Dicks of Tullymet, one of whom, Dr. William Dick, was an eminent physician of the East India Company, whom Sir Walter Scott credited with saving his life from a liver complaint —and presented with a silver, engraved inkstand to prove it. General Sir Robert Dick of Tullymet met a hero's death at Sobraon in 1846. There is a scattered hamlet, and a number of farms. Also, on a small mound, the ruins of a very ancient chapel, with broken gravestones and a yew tree, all now completely neglected. Close by is the somewhat better preserved private burial-place of the Tully-met family, and an abandoned house. Here Scott's Doctor Dick is buried.

This shelf is a pleasant place, detached and remote-seeming. It is hard to realise, looking across to the hills to the west, that the great valley of Tay, and the busy A.9, lie between.

Balquhidder. This is a famous name, but like its neighbour Strathyre, misleading. Nowadays the name is given to the whole 15-miles-long glen, although the word means the township in the back-country. Some claim that the glen itself ought to be called Lochlarig—though this again is scarcely descriptive. It contains the Lochs Voil and Doine, meaning respectively muddy and deep, with a long stretch at the head flanked by very high hills, Ben Chabhair, Ben a' Chroin, Ben Tulaichean, Stob a Choin and so on, respectively 3055, 3104, 3088 and 2839 feet. A feature of this great glen is the number of deep and impressive side glens coming down on both sides, but especially on the north through what are known as the Braes of Balquhidder—the glens being named, east to west, the Kirkton, Crotha, Monachyle, Carnaig, Inverlochlarig and Ishag, some of them providing passes over to Glen Dochart through the Ben More–Stobinean massif; those on the south leading to the Trossachs–Loch Katrine area. All were once much used by the MacGregors for the droving of cattle—for this, of course, was their heartland, and Rob Roy's favourite stamping-ground. Monachyle Tuarach was Rob's first farm; and he died at Inverlochlarig, to be buried in Balquhidder kirkyard in 1734.

There is no through road, and the public road ends at the ford below Inverlochlarig, so all travellers approach the valley from the east, at Kingshouse on the A.84. It is convenient to describe Balquhidder from there onwards. A mile along is the scattered hamlet of Achtoo, on the slope of the first of the green Braes of Balquhidder. At the roadside is a somewhat neglected mausoleum for the MacGregor chiefs, who now live at Edinchip 2 miles to the north-east, the present and 23rd chief being Colonel Sir Gregor MacGregor of MacGregor. A mile west of Achtoo is the main centre of interest in the glen, the Kirkton of Balquhidder with, in between, below the road in rough pasture, a single standing-stone known as Clach Puidrac, unusual in having two triangular nicks cut out of its south-west corner, similar to those on some old sundials.

At Kirkton have been four different churches; the original Celtic cell of St. Angus or Aeneas, its site in the field below the later buildings; the 13th century pre-Reformation church known as Eaglais Beag, or the Little Church, foundations of which are still to be made out beside Rob Roy's grave; the ruined post-Reformation kirk of 1631, built partly on top of the other; and the modern parish church of 1855—all a great place of pilgrimage for visitors. In the modern building are preserved sundry relics. There is Clach Aeneas, or the St. Angus Stone, a tall, coffin-shaped slab incised with a saint bearing the cup of salvation; but it appears to be an early medieval rather than a Celtic stone—though Angus was one of the Celtic Church missionaries. It formerly lay before the altar in the old church, where people marrying stood on it; and was set up here in 1917. Also a massive ancient font dug out of a boulder, which may be earlier. There is the bell of the 17th century church, cracked. The still earlier bell of the pre-Reformation foundation, contained within the iron-bound session-chest—this having been transported by Rob Roy to Acharn on Loch Tay-side, and brought back only in 1930. There is the Irish Gaelic Testament known as Bishop Bedell's Bible; and the Scottish one translated therefrom by the Balquhidder incumbent, Master Robert Kirk, in 1685. This Master Kirk was a famous character, renowned not only for his scholarship and Gaelic translations but for his studies, and more than studies, into fairy-lore and second sight. Many are the stories told of him. He has been mentioned already under Aberfoyle.

In the kirkyard are many items of interest. Rob Roy's grave is supreme, not only on its own account; for of the three tombstones used to mark it, two are far more ancient. The one on Rob's own grave is in fact a Pictish sculptured stone, with typical symbols and decoration, on which has later been incised a broad two-handed sword. Another stone with an incised sword covers the grave of Rob's son Coll; but this has no other carvings visible. The stone over Rob's wife, Mary MacGregor of Comar—whom for some reason Scott misnamed Helen, and which here has the cast-iron notice with Helen in brackets before the Mary—has just an ordinary gravestone of the 18th century. There are many other interesting stones. At the far side of the ruined kirk there are many recumbent McLaren stones; and elsewhere a memorial to the McLaren chiefs. Kenneth MacAlpine granted Balquhidder to the McLarens, and for long they were so pre-eminent in the glen that no one otherwise named was allowed to enter the church until all the McLarens were inside. This produced many unseemly Sabbath fights, in one of which was murdered the McLaren vicar. One flat stone on the bank above the west gate was carved by Master Kirk himself, in his wife's memory—surely a unique memorial. From the kirkyard, an attractive little woodland path leads up a wooded dean to a water-fall.

The Kirkton of Balquhidder is a pleasant place, scattered on both sides of a fine four-arched old bridge across the Balvaig, overlooked by thrusting mountain shoulders. James IV visited here on many occasions. And here took place the famous oath of the MacGregors, which resulted in the ghastly murder of Drummond of Drummond-Earnoch, in Glen Artney.

Directly to the north of the Kirkton rises its own steep glen, really a hanging valley. Very different is that to the south, Glen Buckie, up which a delightful road probes for nearly three miles, through woodland and heather. The views northwards from this glen are very fine. It was a Stewart glen, and the last Stewart of Glenbuckie is commemorated by a stone within the ruined church. In the flats between Glen Buckie and Achtoo was fought a bloody battle in the 13th century, between McLarens and Buchanans of Leny. It is alleged that there was a hospice for victims of the plague, in Glen Buckie; but where is not known. To the west of the arched bridge, and above the foot of Loch Voil, is the former mansion of Stronvar, now a Youth Hostel, with caravan sites around.

Loch Voil is 4 miles long, very attractive with wooded braesides flanking. At the head it is separated from Loch Doine by only a few hundred yards of isthmus. Here the Monachyle Glen comes in from the north, the greatest of the side-glens, with Monachyle House at the foot. Across the isthmus is Monachyle Tuarach, the small farm in which Rob's father set him up as a young man. Loch Doine is only a mile long, with at its head a small overgrown burial-ground within a high wall. Only one or two indecipherable grave-stones remain amongst rowans and bracken.

Inverlochlarig, where Rob died, lies another 2 miles up; but the house he occupied has been superseded, and nothing old remains. There are no houses in the 7 miles farther up the glen; but there was once a much-used pass over to Glen Gyle, where Rob's father, Colonel MacGregor of Glengyle, was laird and chieftain, at the head of Loch Katrine. Still another pass, at the extreme west, led over to the head of Loch Lomond. Small wonder that the freebooter-hero was for so long able to defy the government of his day.

Bankfoot and Auchtergaven. Bankfoot sounds a very modern and humdrum name for an ancient Perthshire community. It should in fact be called the Bank-foot of Auchtergaven, there being a distinct bank here, with the modern parts of the village below it, and the parish church of Auchtergaven and the old village just above it. To further confuse the issue, the upper village also rejoices in the name of Cairniehill. This red-sandstone village, quite large, lies athwart the main A.9 road 9 miles north of Perth, in pleasing rural country rising to the skirts of the Highlands.

The village falls into three parts. The modern roadside section is quite lengthy and not unattractive, with shops and hotels—though not with the 26 public-houses complained of in 1838! One hotel at the south end is notable for having a complete phaeton, or light carriage, surmounting its porch. The large church, with its clock-tower a landmark, is sited on the brow of the hill, with splendid views, and dates from 1812. It seats 1200, is fairly plain, and unusual in having galleries all round. There are several 18th century tomb-stones in the kirkyard, two built into the walling to the east, which had evidently been the west wall of the original church. One is dated 1665, to a former minister. There is another stone, to the north, and sadly inscribed:

> For us they sicken and for us they die.

The old village climbs on up the ridge, picturesque amongst the raspberry-cane fields. Up here is a plateau which stretches for some four miles eastwards to the Tay, referred to hereafter. Below the main road, the third section of Bankfoot is the 'suburb' of Prieston, old also, but now spreading fast in council housing. This however leads abruptly to an artist's picture of the burnside community of Arleywight, formerly Arlewhat, where an old red-stone farmhouse of 1784 presides benignly over the rural scene. Past the mansion of the same name, and where once was a linen-weaving works, the most northerly of three spoke-like roads leads up into the hill-skirts, following the Garry Burn for 3 miles, eventually to Upper Obney farm. The deep Glen Garr opens ahead, really only a major corrie in what are called the Obney Hills, outliers of the Grampians, and through which a footpath leads to Strath Braan.

Back at Prieston, the middle spoke-road leads 3 similar miles to end at Tully beagles Lodge, the site of a former barony, where were former slate quarries and stone circles. On the hill of Craig Gibbon behind is a tall obelisk. This, oddly, was erected *by* Colonel Mercer of Meikleour, not to him, in order that he might distinguish his own hill from faraway Meikleour! The name eagles in any Scots place-name is almost certain to imply a church, *eaglais* so meaning; and sure enough, near the farm of Balquharn is the site of an old chapel, where coins were dug up.

The third of these roads is the most interesting. After passing a standing-stone half a mile up on the left, it dips, and opposite where a farm road goes off to the former mill of Balmacollie, a few yards up the hedge-side in the field is a cattle-trough, all that is left of the Holy Well of St. Bride, once the *raison d'être* for a whole parish

Birnam in its woods across Tay, from tower of Dunkeld Cathedral

Balquhidder. Rob Roy's grave. Ben Vorlich in background

Clunie. Parish Kirk, Manse and Loch Clunie encircle The Ward, the mound
on which stood King Malcolm Canmore's summer palace

suppressed in the 17th century. It still produces ice-cold excellent water. A little farther is the little old graveyard of the parish church, which grew up in connection with the Well. Nothing of the church survives; but the kirkyard wall is kept in good repair, however neglected the interior. Here is a memorial, erected in 1828 by parishioners in faraway Stromness, in Orkney, to their beloved minister, the Reverend Andrew Wylie, born here in Logiebride in 1783—a touching demonstration of appreciation. The farm near by is still called Logiebride. Behind the next farm of Tullybelton is another obelisk, to the memory of Robert Nicoll, a young poet of great promise, sometimes called 'Scotland's Second Burns', who died aged 23. One of his songs is *The Fouk o' Ouchtergaen*. Scotland has always been good at venerating her poets—once they are safely dead. Another farm road here climbs to Berryhill where, in a field still called Chapel-park, was another church, graveyard and holy well, by the Ordie Burn, to which folk used to repair on the first Sunday in May to drink the water. Now only a wet apron in the grass remains. In the lower ground is the old estate of Tullybelton, to the former mansion of which, owned by his friend and kinsman Black Pate Graham of Inchbrakie, came the great Montrose, in disguise, to commence his famous campaign of 1644–45.

Another road leads back, south-easterly, to the A.9, 3 miles down what used to be called Strathord—and is once again being so named by the Forestry Commission, busy here. The Nairnes were Lairds of Strathord before they attained the peerage. Their original House of Nairne was at Loak, where their Court-hill still stands, with a standing-stone near by. Nothing now remains of what was described as one of the finest seats of the Scots nobility, where Prince Charles was entertained. It had just been rebuilt, by the 3rd Lord Nairne, when, assembling his clan at Loak, he marched off to join the Prince at Perth. He was forfeited, and the Duke of Atholl, on the winning side, purchased the property and demolished his son's house. For it *was* his own fourth son, the Lord William Murray having married the Nairne heiress and obtained the Nairne peerage by special remainder.

At the other side of Bankfoot is the aforementioned plateau area of some fifteen square miles, comprising the former wastes of Cairnleith Moss and Muir of Thorn. The Moss is drained and the Muir is now a forest, and what was called a dismal and dangerous scene, the haunt of robbers, is now a fair tableland with glorious vistas all around, which Scott described as "one of the loveliest and richest views in Scotland, the mouth of Strathmore". In the middle of it all is the decaying village of Airntully, once an important barony, now mouldering into picturesque degeneracy, its little church abandoned like many of its cottages. But still children play and laugh here. Near by is the tall modern tower of a farm called Stewart Tower, site no doubt of the original fortalice of the barony. This was very much a Stewart place, granted to the youngest natural son of Robert II. In 1560, the Regent Moray, natural son of a king himself,

D

commanded Sir John Stewart of Airntully to 'cast down the images' in Dunkeld Cathedral, Reformation in progress. These lands are still owned by descendants, the Steuart-Fotheringhams of Murthly. The loch of the King's Myre, embosomed in forest, is near by.

Two miles north of Bankfoot, on the main road, is the hamlet of Waterloo, well known by travellers to the north. It was erected as a new weaving village of 100 inhabitants just after the Battle of Waterloo. Some of its houses are abandoned, but others are restored and flourishing. The site is attractive—but the traffic must be most trying.

Bendochy. It would be safe to say that not one person in ten, perhaps even in Perthshire, has ever heard of Bendochy; or, if so, could say where and what it is. This is one of those hidden, modest, yet surprisingly rewarding areas, for those with eyes to see and enquiring minds. There is no village, nor even a hamlet of the name; and even its parish church is not marked as such on the Ordnance Map; but it is in fact quite a large parish, of nearly 10,000 acres, in two inconveniently detached portions, situated partly in the flood-plain of the Isla south-east of Blairgowrie; and partly in the empty hills that rise up to Glen Shee, from eight to thirteen miles to the north-west. This northern portion is more conveniently dealt with under Bridge of Cally and Drimmie.

The parish ministers over the centuries must have bewailed the ridiculously inconvenient site of their church and manse; for these are placed down on the Isla's green bank, on the very southern verge of the parish, not even on a main road. But if it makes an impossible centre for worship in a far-flung parish, this can have been the clergymen's only complaint: for it is a lovely and peaceful spot, an interesting and historic church and a fine manse. Oddly enough, despite its seeming remoteness, it is only a mile due north of Coupar Angus—though on the other side of the broad river.

The church, on low ground below the side-road and the manse, is long, low and 700 years old, though restored in 1885, and stands in an ancient graveyard. It has many interesting features. Being close to the important Abbey of Coupar, and lying between it and its main farms, one of which is still called Coupar Grange, it had importance in pre-Reformation times. There are notable memorials within. One, a slab set upright in the walling, shows a knight in armour, the carved work meticulous even to the studs in the plating, feet resting on a dog whose tail curves over the left foot. This represents John Comyn, or Cumming, of Couttie, who died 1606. Another, probably once over a doorway, heraldically commemorates Leonard Leslie, Commendator of Coupar—that is, lay lord of the forfeited Church lands—styled here Dominus de Cupro, who died 1605 aged 81. The other two stones refer to Abbot Donald Campbell, nephew of the Earl of Argyll, of the Abbey of Coupar at the Reformation period, who died 1587—after he had handsomely provided for his five illegitimate sons by settling on them the rich

Abbey estates of Keithock, Balgersho, Denhead, Cronan and Arthurstone—a fairly typical proceeding. There are other items of interest in this little church, including an aumbry in the walling near the pulpit. In the manse garden stands the former belfry.

The surrounding country is very fertile and has been farmed from a very early date, thanks to the Abbey monks. There is a hamlet at Coupar Grange Farm, set amidst a sea of grain-lands. The Monk and Hare Myres, and Stormont Loch lie in this plain, with the very minor mount of Rosemount rising perhaps fifty feet above all. To the north-east, beside the large modern sand quarries of the East Rattray area, is a whaleback wooded mound crowned by the remains of fortifications, merely marked 'castle' on the map. North-west of this, just above the A.926 road to Alyth, a standing-stone rises in a field of raspberry-canes. And on the high ground, north-east again, at the farm of St. Fink, are the tiny remains of a burial-ground belonging to the former pre-Reformation Chapel of St. Phink, of the odd name. There was a common at the Hill of St. Fink, of about two hundred acres, divided up and enclosed about 1810, indicative of at least a large village, though not even a hamlet survives. Fink was Findoca, one of the daughters of St. Donevald.

Birnam. Birnam is an unusual place in many ways—not least in that, despite its renown, it was until little more than a century ago only a famous wood, a hill, an estate; and of course, an idea. The comparatively modern village of Birnam, really only a suburb of Dunkeld across the Tay, should in fact properly be called Little Dunkeld.

Little Dunkeld, to distinguish it from Meikle Dunkeld, the cathedral town and parish across the famous Telford bridge, is a large parish—larger than the other, actually—with its church near the riverside, now surrounded by the council housing of Birnam and the well-known Dunkeld Royal School, also in modern premises although allegedly founded by James VI in 1567 (the King was one year old at this time—so somebody close to him must have had an interest in Dunkeld). The church, built in 1798, is plain, substantial and yellow-washed, a modest place compared with its magnificent neighbour some hundreds of yards to the north-west, across Tay. There is an old graveyard, but few ancient stones remain. Buried here is John Stewart, first of Dalguise, who in 1576 was commanded by the Regent Moray to 'deface the images' at the cathedral—so that his true memorial is the ruins across the water.

The impressive part of Birnam—apart, of course, from the setting of magnificent and steep wooded hills close on every side—is of Victorian erection. There is an enormous 'Saxon-Gothic' hotel; a highly ambitious gateway to the 3-mile driveway to Murthly Castle; many ornate and substantial villas—two of which the painter Millais rented; and the sort of rustic railway station amongst trees, beloved of the old Queen herself, all in the heavily romantic taste

41

of the period. We must admit, however, that it was a period which certainly got things done. Birnam Hotel is almost overpowering, with an enormous Baronial Hall, now the dining-room, which accommodates 200 and, at the time, was reputed to be one of the finest in the country. Yet, despite all this grandeur, the hotel is pleasant, and seeks to offer a more homely welcome than its architecture would suggest. There is everywhere an air of space as well as substantiality—even the road up to the station is twice as wide as Dunkeld main street. Here is a sign of these later times—a small ski factory.

Down at the riverside is what is called The Oaks, a delightful walk amongst some of the ancient survivors of the famed Birnam Wood of MacBeth's day, sycamores as well as oaks. Birnam Wood is an enduring, living thing, clothing all these hillsides, right to their tops. Birnam Hill itself reaches 1324 feet, its former slate quarries fortunately largely screened by the trees. Burns climbed here on his Highland Tour of 1787. High on the east face of the hill, in a most inaccessible position, are the extraordinarily-sited remains of Rohallion Castle, a small, Z-shaped fortalice apparently of the 16th century. Why anyone should build it in such a situation is beyond comprehension—unless there was some now-defunct drove-road, or pass, over the steep hill here, for a robber-baron to prey upon. Near by are cup-marked stones. The entire wooded estate of Rohallion, flanking this south-west side of the Tay's gorge, is interesting as well as highly attractive. Crowning another rocky summit, at 659 feet, are the vestiges of the round fort of King Duncan's Camp, again suitably inaccessible. Even more so, oddly enough, high on the side of Buffalo Hill, is Allan's Bridge, a handsome arched structure of stone over a small gorge, allegedly built by a butler named Allan from Rohallion House, from the windows of which it is visible—apparently for no better reason than that he wanted to do so. Buffalo Hill, soaring above the tree-girt lochs of Rohallion, gets its name from the buffalo imported here by the mid-19th century laird Sir William Drummond Stewart of Murthly, after an adventurous time pioneering in Canada. He brought some Red Indians to look after the animals, too—but unfortunately they all died of pneumonia, while the buffalo throve mightily, and proliferated, to terrorise the neighbourhood for some thirty years before the last was disposed of.

While Little Dunkeld was only a kirkton around its church, and Birnam was still only a wood, there was a community here, at Inver, near where the Braan River joins Tay from the west. This is famous as the birthplace of Neil Gow (1727–1807) the master-violinist, whose house Queen Victoria visited, and heard play his son, Nathaniel, also a master. There is still an attractive little hamlet here, with a large caravan-park in the haughland to the east. From Inver are reached the renowned Hermitage, Ossian's Hall and Falls of Braan, described under Strathbraan.

Blackford. This is one of those modern-seeming villages on a busy highway which, at first glance, appears to have little to attract the visitor, but which will repay closer scrutiny. It lies on the main A.9 Perth road, in the vale of the Allan Water, 10 miles north-east of Dunblane and 4 west of Auchterarder, a sizeable place, boasting the Tullibardine Distillery as well as other industry. Parallel to its traffic-dominated main street, to the south, is another quiet street of older houses, which was once the principal thoroughfare apparently, and still gives a much better impression of the old Blackford. But not the oldest, for this was another of the villages burned by Mar after Sheriffmuir in 1715, in the Jacobite retreat.

At the extreme north end of the village, over the main-line level-crossing—a sorry anachronism, on the A.9—rises an isolated hillock crowned by the old ruined church of Blackford, in its graveyard, its lych-gate prominent against the skyline. This is another long, low kirk with a belfry, like so many hereabouts; but in fact it is of later date than appears, a *post*-Reformation building. The original parish church was far away, at Strageath, north of Muthill—for this was, and still is, a large parish. It was moved to Blackford at the Reformation, and built here in 1617. As well as its dramatic site, it is unusual in that it was a two-storeyed building, the massive corbels for the upper floor projecting from the walling, and the forestair still standing, to the west. Presumably it was this upper floor which was used as the village school, and which in 1738 caused the whole kirk to be burned down, when some scholars, in the absence of the dominie, began tossing about burning peats from the fire. It was rebuilt, however, and it was not until the early 19th century that it was abandoned and a new and more conveniently-placed church erected at the east end of the village. In the kirkyard is an octagonal mort-house. The lych-gate has a stone shelf on which to rest coffins after the steep climb. The views from this eminence are fine, up and down Strathallan and Strathearn.

About a mile to the south-west are the remains of Ogilvie Castle, in a strong position above a ravine amongst the Braes of Ogilvie, foothills of the Ochils, a former fortalice of the Grahams of Montrose. It is strange to find the name Ogilvie hereabouts, so far from Angus and the north-east.

The name Blackford itself has an ancient if semi-legendary origin. There was a ford of the River Allan near by, and one of the early Caledonian kings, name unspecified, lost his Queen Helen here, carried away by the river in spate. The bereaved monarch is said to have drained the whole strath—presumably much flooded in those days—to recover the body. The queen's burial-place is still identified as a solitary knoll on the river-bank some way below the village. Be this as it may, Blackford features early in history. Wallace met a party of English here, after taking the Peel of Gargunnock, and threw the bodies into the river. In 1488 young James IV, returning to Stirling from his coronation at Scone, halted here for refreshment, the Lord Treasurer duly noting: "Item—

quhen the King cum forth to Sanct Johnston (Perth) for a barrel of Ayll at the Blackfurd, xlj s."

Near by, to the west across the Allan, is the famous Carsebreck curling pond, where the annual match between North and South Scotland used to take place.

Blair Drummond and Kincardine-in-Menteith. Neither of these places bulks large as population centre, though on the map they tend to look more impressive. One is a large estate, an associated hamlet, and an eastern section of the great Flanders Moss; the other is a parish of South Perthshire, one of the many Kincardines of Scotland—there are two others within 20 miles. It is quite a large parish, lying between the Forth and the Teith, but it has no village of the name, only a parish church—though this is large also, with sittings for 770. The hamlet of Blair Drummond lies close by, picturesque in its rural setting, with smiddy and estate cottages. But despite all this modesty, these names have resounded quite loudly in the past—and look like doing so again.

The estate of Blair Drummond lies 6 miles north-west of Stirling and 2 south of Doune, its hamlet at the fork of the A.84 Stirling–Doune road and the A.873 to Thornhill and Menteith. Although the present large mansion is Victorian Scottish-baronial, the property itself is ancient, long a Drummond lairdship, passing to the Drummond-Morays of Abercairney. There are relics of antiquity on the estate. It has become notable in recent years; first for the holding here of the annual Game Fair; and now for the establishment of Scotland's first Safari Park, a wild-animal reserve wherein lions (3 of them), giraffes, eland, baboons (100) and other creatures, fierce and/or beautiful, roam in the 100 acres of wooded parkland, to which visitors are admitted at a charge, with game wardens in control. This adventurous project is on the joint initiative of the present laird, Sir John Muir, another neighbouring laird, and the proprietors of Chipperfield's Circus. It certainly draws large numbers of people to Blair Drummond.

Almost as revolutionary, though less immediately dramatic, was the initiative of an earlier laird, which put Blair Drummond on the map in the second half of the 18th century. In 1741 Henry Home, Lord Kames, celebrated judge, married the Drummond heiress, and saw the possibilities of turning the great moss near by into valuable arable land. When, in 1767, his wife inherited, he instituted a most ingenious scheme, first of draining the marshland, then of cutting off the deep peat top layer and getting rid of it by floating it down the Forth into the sea. This quite enormous task was done by digging a system of canals and sluices, and the construction of an outsize water-wheel, 30 foot high, at the Mill of Torr which, at a given signal could send a great flow of dammed-up water from the Teith down one or other of the canals, to wash away the cut peat gathered by horse-sleds and dumped into the outlets of the canals. Using for labour needy families from the Balquhidder areas, largely Mac-

44

Gregors left leaderless by the collapse of the clan system after the Jacobite risings, he succeeded in turning some one thousand five hundred acres of sodden wilderness into excellent arable; and settled his workers thereon as agriculturalists. These attracted the part-mocking title of the Moss Lairds; but today their successors farm as fine land as you will see in all Central Scotland. In the reclamations, a stretch of corduroy Roman road was uncovered, some relics, very early wooden wheels, and the skeleton of a whale, indication that the Forth estuary once came greatly farther west.

The Mill of Torr, picturesquely situated at the east side of the estate, is notable also for having a tumulus near by, known for reasons not clear as Wallace's Trench, 190 feet in circumference. There are two other tumuli within the estate, a motte to the west, and a standing-stone on Borland Hill to the north.

The church of Kincardine-in-Menteith is attractively sited near Blair Drummond hamlet, a handsome building in the Perpendicular style, which replaced an earlier foundation belonging to Cambus-kenneth Abbey. A panel over the door, dated 1814, declares in Latin that it was reconstructed by G. Home Drummond, who would be Lord Kames's son.

Blairgowrie and Rattray. This pleasant red-sandstone burgh at the head of the great Vale of Strathmore, is very much a dual-personality town. It is really two communities, divided by the rushing River Ericht, Blairgowrie itself to the west, Rattray to the east—although Rattray itself is two distinct villages, Old and New. In Perthshire, its affinities seem to lie rather with Angus and the rest of Strathmore, the county boundary being not far off. It is the fruit-growing—especially raspberry and strawberry—'capital', which gives it a notably rural atmosphere; but it is also an industrial town in a small way, with auction-marts and jute mills—although these are discreetly hidden in the deep wooded cleft of the Ericht. It has a population of 6500, but was not much more than a village at the beginning of the century—though a burgh of barony since 1634 and a police burgh since 1864.

The site is attractive, very much a hillside town on the skirts of the Grampians, looking southwards over the Vale to the Sidlaws, many of its streets steep, its housing terraced. There is a central sloping square—really more of a triangle—with gardens, near the Brig o' Blair. This carries the main A.926 over into Rattray, affording pleasing views of the turbulent river in its rocky glen, with waterside walks and gardens. It is the shopping centre for a wide area, and a notable road junction, with routes radiating to Perth, Forfar, Kirriemuir, Coupar Angus, Dunkeld and Braemar (via Glen Shee).

There are also two parishes here, Rattray having its own parish church. Blairgowrie's is an unprepossessing building, externally, of 1824, set prominently on high ground, which must tax the faith and lungs of its more senior worshippers. Its site is more like that of a fortified strength, with an ancient graveyard clinging to steep slopes.

Donald Cargill, the martyr, was the son of a Laird of Hatton in this parish, and was hanged at Edinburgh in 1680 for high treason, because of his Covenanting principles. Cargill's Leap is still pointed out, where on one occasion in his career as field preacher, after being banished from the Barony Church in Glasgow, he escaped his pursuers by jumping over the fearsome rock-bound cascade of the Ericht. His dying words are famous, as he mounted the scaffold. "The Lord knows that I go on this ladder with less fear and perturbation of mind than ever I entered the pulpit to preach!" Rattray parish church is not much more handsome than its neighbour, standing off the main street and dating from four years earlier. Vast numbers of churches seem to have been built in Scotland in the 1820s. Its graveyard contains the burial-place of the Rattrays of that Ilk, as Blairgowrie's does that of the Macphersons, holders of that barony and superiors of the town—who even have their own private entrance, dated 1789.

These two families have dominated the area for long. Blairgowrie is unusual in having its laird's castle actually within the burgh, although it is highly placed, even higher than the church, looking out over all. Newton Castle is a most interesting, tall, whitewashed fortalice in a pleasant garden, built on the Z-plan and dating from the early 17th century, although on older foundations. Cromwell sought to burn it down, and it is recounted that a number of local gentlemen who had been aiding in the defence took refuge in one of the semi-subterranean vaults—to emerge unscathed after the fire was over. It was then the seat of a branch of the Drummond family, one of whose members was famed as being no less than six times Lord Provost of Edinburgh, and who helped to found the great Royal Infirmary there. The castle is unusual in harbouring two distinct ghosts!

Craighall-Rattray, the seat of the present Rattray of that Ilk, stands, much more dramatically, within the jaws of the deep and rocky ravine 2 miles north of the town, perched dizzily on a narrow shelf above the tremendous chasm. It must be one of the most extraordinarily-placed mansions in the land. Although it has ancient foundations, the present building was wholly remodelled in 1832, though clinging to the same precarious site. It was the model for Scott's Tullyveolan, in *Waverley*. The Rattrays have been here since before recorded times, no other owners having been known. The site of their original Pictish *rath-tref*, or fort-dwelling, is pointed out, nearer the town, on a serpent-shaped mound; and serpents, a Pictish symbol, are still the Rattrays' heraldic supporters.

The Rattray part of the burgh, although more modest as regards shops, offices, hotels and so on, can in fact show the most advanced ultra-modern housing development, very fine, even including a central television mast for 'piped' TV. There is a supermarket, and a large caravan site. The deep and rocky river valley between the two parts of the town is a great asset—although it has provided dangers for generations of too-adventurous children. The linns and cascades are highly picturesque, for the Ericht is a headlong river which can rise alarmingly, and there have been some devastating floods, one in 1847 doing great damage. Interesting are the mill-lades, cut in the solid rock on either side, to lead water-power to the mills, these producing their own waterfalls. An unmetalled road leads up the west side of the glen, to the partially deserted milling village of Lornty, where that tributary comes in, and weirs proliferate, a pleasant walk. From the high ground of the upper Lornty area the views are fine.

To the south of the town is the detached suburb, really its own village, of Rosemount, a peaceful, mellow place of larger houses amongst old trees, flanking the A.923 Coupar Angus road, and the golf-course. Near by is the quite large Stormont Loch, with the smaller Fingask and Black Lochs, and the Hare and Monk Myres, which add variety and character to the level flood-plain of the Isla.

Blairgowrie has another claim to fame. Here is held, each August, a Festival of Traditional Music, really a folk-music festival, and very popular.

Braco, Ardoch and Greenloaning. Braco and Greenloaning are two villages, not much more than a mile apart, in the parish of Ardoch, 5 and 6 miles north-east of Dunblane, where the Knaik Water joins the Allan, in a pleasant and notably historic area below the eastern extensions of the Braes of Doune, famed for the Roman remains.

Braco is much the larger village, astride the A.822 to Crieff. Despite all the antiquities, the village itself is not ancient, feud out only in 1815. Even the parish was erected not long before, the present parish church, whitewashed and attractive, being built as a chapel-of-ease (a convenience to save travel to Muthill) in 1780. Braco is a neat place, on level land, strung along two roads joining at an angle, the B.8033 coming in here from Cromlix and Kinbuck. Despite its comparative modernity, it is unusual in having two graveyards, one round the parish kirk and the other round what was the Free church, to the south-west. Only the clock-tower of the latter remains, erected 1845. This part of the village is more picturesque than the long main street along A.822. Cattle fairs used to be held here.

To the north the main road takes a sharp bend to cross the Knaik by a bridge originally erected by Bishop Ochiltree in the 15th century. Here is the entrance to Ardoch estate, wherein are the Roman remains. The House itself, a Georgian mansion, is now a roofless ruin; and the Roman sites are overgrown and uncared-for. It seems scarcely believable that ancient monuments of such calibre should be so neglected, a national heritage. Few other countries, surely, would allow it. The complex consists of a large fort, a smaller fort, a great camp and sections of Agricola's military way. No detailed description can be given here. Experts declare Ardoch the most impressive Roman fort in Scotland. It seems that the invaders utilised an already existing town of the Damnonii, called Lindum; and there are still traces of the Caledonian earthworks. No Roman masonry remains above ground, but the concentric rows of huge, grass-covered embankments show that here the Legions really had to fight to maintain a hold. Tacitus describes the scene here when the Caledonians (Picts) attacked Agricola's Ninth Legion, striking panic into the sleeping camp. The size of this camp is extraordinary, accommodating 26,000 men it is calculated. The strongly fortified procestrium, 1060 feet by 900, held 4000; the central citadel and praetorium, 420 feet by 375, with five deep ditches and six ramparts, held 1200. The small camp to the west, probably constructed later, when the large ceased to be used, accommodated 12,000. By any standards, this was an immense establishment; and, properly exhibited, should be a mecca for visitors from all over the world.

Braco Castle lies in a large estate 2 miles north of the village, a tall, rather stark building of four periods, grown from probably a 16th century nucleus. Much of the old work remains visible inside and out, although there have been many alterations as well as additions and sham castellations. It was a Graham possession, the second son of the 3rd Earl of Montrose—and therefore the great Marquis's uncle—being created baronet of Braco in 1625. He no doubt built the 17th century extensions. A later 18th century extension has a sad story. The then laird was equerry to George III. Hopeful of a visit to Scotland by his royal master, he built an enormous addition, to house the King's train—which in fact never came. His latter-day successors have not blessed him for this.

Greenloaning lies a long straight mile south of Braco, beside the railway and A.9. It is a scattered community rather than a village, less attractive than its evocative name, with an old inn, a hotel, a small plain church used once a month, a farm and sundry houses. Across A.9, to the south, is a circular motte, the tree-grown mound of a former timber castle, called The Roundel.

On the B.8033 south-west of Braco is the Feddal estate, now somewhat decayed. Feddal House, ruinous, has old work in it, although much 'gothicised'. A Stewart-Falconer house, it stands on the edge of a ravine, and bears a panel dated 1683.

North-west of Braco there is an extensive and comparatively little-known area of high ground, on the way to Comrie by B.827, interesting and attractive, mainly the valley and watershed of the Knaik Water. The road branches off A.822 half a mile from Braco, swinging westwards and climbing from 440 to 750 feet, passing on the way a remotely-placed spring called Titus' Well. Was he one of the Romans? Across the valley are fine views of the heather hillsides dotted with the dark authentic Scots pines of one more relic of the ancient Caledonian Forest. For four or five miles the road crosses the empty high moorlands, used on the west side by the army as a firing range. This area is full of prehistoric signs and relics. Ben Clach, the Mountain of the Stone, is on the left, and on it is Coire a' Chroisg, the Corrie of the Cross. Near the roadside, a half-mile south of Tighnablair farm, is what appears to be a smallish cromlech, of one oddly-shaped boulder raised on two others—although this could be the work of glaciation, as at Craigmaddie in Stirlingshire. Across the road a mile farther is St. Patrick's Well, where there was formerly a chapel. Near by is a cross-roads, and the narrow road striking off eastwards for Muthill is well worth exploring, especially on foot. It winds between low hills, Dunruchan to the south (the dun possibly indicating an ancient fortress) and Lurgan Hill and wooded Torlum on the north. Actually this is the upper valley of the Machany Water, which joins the Earn at Kinkell Bridge, and is a most pleasing tract, of interesting geological formations and escarpments, dotted with clumps of juniper—unusual so far south—broom and whin. It is particularly rich in standing stones. There is one at Craigneich farm, and a scattered group on high ground opposite. Two miles on there is a tall one north of Dalchirla farm; and to the east of it a stone circle of three, one large and upright. The road runs on, past Drummond Castle policies, to Muthill. A branch strikes off northwards for Crieff, threading the little wooded pass of Balloch (which *means* pass) with its round loch, under the great Torlum Wood on the left.

Bridge of Cally and Drimmie. Fewer travellers use the A.93 than any other main road into the north of Scotland; which may seem strange, since it is a notably attractive one, and fairly direct, especially to Deeside. But it does have the notorious Devil's Elbow to climb, north of Spittal of Glenshee; and this, especially in winter, tends to put people off. But not the skiers. So the road up the Ericht, north of Blairgowrie, is less well known than it might be. And that which forks left therefrom 6 miles up, at Bridge of Cally, A.924 up Strathardle to Kirkmichael and Pitlochry, less used still. But, thanks to the boom in skiing, becoming more so.

From the Rattray side of Blairgowrie, the road winds up the deep and dramatic glen of the Ericht, rising high, to pass near the excitingly-placed mansion of Craighall-Rattray on its cliff. It crosses the rushing river near Easter Mause, but, before this, has sent off a branch to follow the eastern bank of the great ravine. The two roads join again at Bridge of Cally, the eastern one having risen to over 800 feet in the meantime. They make a delightful round trip from Blairgowrie.

Soon after passing Craighall, the A.93 emerges quite suddenly from the pass-like gorge into open, green hilly country with wide vistas of the Grampians. There is little of interest save the views, here, for this section is really passing over the skirts of the Muir of Drumlochy, high above the river. It drops again to the hamlet of Bridge of Cally, where the River Ardle and the Black Water of Glen Shee join to form the Ericht. This is a scattered community clustered in the wooded valleys-meeting, around the two bridges, an attractive place with hotels and guest-houses. To the left,

49

A.924 goes off up Strathardle, and is dealt with under Kirkmichael. In front, A.93 continues up Glen Shee—which see. And to the right, the pleasant side-road leads down over Strone of Cally bridge, to climb the Braes of Drimmie, to send out an adventurous feeler to Alyth across the hills, and itself to return in roundabout fashion to Rattray, serving the many small local communities.

At Netherton, just over Strone bridge, is a small church, with the fine river plunging over rocks below, and a mill alongside, with pleasant cottages. Thereafter the road rises steeply to the east, into the Drimmie area, a highly-placed, wide-scattered farming community without villages. That it has been occupied from earliest times is evidenced by the large number of stone circles and standing-stones. Here the fields rise to the heather, bracken and ancient Caledonian pines, with open vistas, great skies and the calling of curlews. Near Rannagulzion House is a school and schoolhouse of unusual type, on the open moorland, erected to the memory of Professor Ramsay of Rannagulzion. This area has long been the territory of the ancient baronet family of Ramsay of Bamff, near Alyth. Here the hill-road strikes off across the Forest of Alyth to Strathmore again, a lonely route with more stone circles. Rannagulzion was a summer-house of the Abbots of Couper.

Proceeding southwards round the wide flanks of Hill of Drimmie, the attractive Rattray road descends to Courthill, now a farm and once the seat of justice of the Rattrays. Here is a standing-stone and another stone circle, quite close together, on the east side of the road. Two miles farther and the visitor is back at Blairgowrie.

Bridge of Earn. Well known to travellers, half-way between Glen Farg and Perth, Bridge of Earn lies in the level, fertile plain at the southern base of Moncreiffe Hill, 4 miles west of the Earn's confluence with Tay. Although the setting is excellent, the village itself is not particularly attractive today, with little of character and antiquity apparent. It is best known, probably, for its great modern hospital, half a mile to the east. Part of the original medieval bridge is still to be seen, with some of the older houses nearby.

The community which grew up round the ancient bridge has had three main periods of growth. In 1769 leases of 99 years were feud out, in an unusual early development scheme. This was just before the mineral waters of the nearby Pitkeathly Wells became scientifically noticed, and exploited as a spa and medication centre, in 1772; but they had been locally famous from earliest times, and no doubt the first Bridge of Earn development was connected therewith. The second certainly was, for in 1832 the village, only a mile north-east of Pitkeathly, was symmetrically enlarged as a resort for the accommodation of visitors and invalids, water from the wells being brought in daily. So Bridge of Earn's connection with the healing arts is not new, whatever the modern hospital authorities may think of their predecessors.

The village is a notable road junction also, and therefore a centre for exploring lower Strathearn. No fewer than six roads join the main A.90 highway here, linking Abernethy and the North Fife road, Dron, Kintillo, Pitkeathly, Forgandenny, Aberdalgie, Moncreiffe, Rhynd and Elcho. Perth is only 4 miles to the north-west.

Butterstone and Loch of Lowes. The Lunan Burn, in the district of Stormont, east of Dunkeld, is a quite extraordinary stream. Rising high in the Grampians north of Dunkeld, on its 14-mile descent to the Isla near Meikleour it forms, or passes through, a notable series of lochs. Omitting those high amongst the hills, it reaches comparatively low ground beside the A.923 Dunkeld–Blairgowrie road, and opens out into the Loch of Craiglush, half a mile long by a quarter broad. This is separated only by a narrow isthmus from the larger Loch of Lowes, to the south; and this again by another narrow belt of wooded land from Butterstone Loch to the east. Then there is a 4-mile gap till Loch of Clunie; then Marlee Loch, Rae Loch, Fingask Loch, and so down to the Isla, a unique sequence for so modest a stream.

Butterstone is a pretty hamlet, amongst the wooded foothills, where another south-flowing stream, the Buckny Burn, comes down its wooded glen to join Lunan just east of Butterstone Loch. Remotely placed, over 3 miles up this glen, near Crueshill (Cross Hill) and Reimore Lodge, is the holy well of Sancta Crux, an indication that these lonely tracts were once considerably more populous. Butterstone House itself is now a school. Butter is an ancient Perthshire surname, the Butters of Gormack (near here) and Pitlochry and Faskally, having been established since the 15th century. This Butterstone Loch came into prominence recently with the arrival here of a pair of ospreys or fish-hawks, nesting in the area—a great attraction. The neighbouring Loch of Lowes—not to be confused with the more famous Border Loch of the Lowes, in Ettrick—also embosomed in trees, has now a nature reserve maintained by the Scottish Wildlife Trust, at the west end. The coming of the ospreys near by was a major bonus to this new establishment. Queen Victoria much admired this sheet of water—indeed the entire attractive area. There are a number of fine tracks for walkers up into the loch-scattered hills to the north, from this A.923 road.

The ancient estate of Cardney lies to the north of the road between the lochs, now a MacGregor house. It was long a seat of a branch of the Stewarts. Sir Robert Stewart of Cardney was the youngest natural son of Robert II, by Marion de Cardney of that Ilk. She was a sister of Robert Cardney, Bishop of Dunkeld, whose effigy is still in the Cathedral. He was one of the hostages sent to England to redeem the captured James I who was his sister's brother-in-law. The Stewarts of Airntully, Dalguise and Murthly stem from the Cardney line.

Callander. This is not one of Perthshire's ancient burghs, having reached that status only in 1859. It is not a large community either, with a population of 1761. But it is famous, vying with Crieff and

Pitlochry as a gateway to the Highlands. The tradition is that Callander owes its rise from a small village in part to the settlement here of discharged soldiers from the Seven Years War, in 1763; and thereafter to the publicity given the area by Sir Walter Scott in *The Lady of the Lake*, *Waverley*, *Rob Roy* and so on. But, in fact, it was always an important strategic community at the junction of vital South Highland valleys in the land of Monteith, became an earldom in the 17th century, and was the centre of a large parish of 54,000 acres. The church was founded in 1238 and was an appendage of the Priory of Inchmahome, belonging to the Earls of Menteith. But even before all this, there was a Roman camp here, at Kilmahog, at the junction of the Leny and Teith.

Today, of course, Callander is one of the busiest tourist towns in Scotland, full of hotels, guest-houses, catering establishments and shops to tempt the visitor. And of recent years it has gained a new fame and attraction as the prototype of Tannochbrae in the *Dr. Finlay's Casebook* TV series, scene of most of the non-studio shots, site of 'Arden House' and so on.

Most travellers from Edinburgh to the West Highlands pass through Callander, and may tend to think of it as no more than a long main street, wide but traffic-thronged. But the attractive parts of the town are in its flanks, up the hillside under the lofty wooded 1000-foot Callander Craig, with its medicinal Red Well, to the north; and down by the wide, tree-lined Teith to the south. The best views of the place are from here, one notably well known as the opening scene of many a *Dr. Finlay* episode.

The parish church of St. Kessog, one of the Columban missionaries (520–56) stands centrally in the attractive Ancaster Square, dating from 1773 but re-built 1881, and is a fine spacious place of worship, with handsome carved pulpit, and stained-glass by Strachan. Its predecessor stood at the little hill of Tom-na-Chessaig, nearer the river, with an old burial-ground. A market held here annually in March used to be called the Feill na Chessaig. The Manse is some distance from both, across the river on the south bank, built on the site of the old castle of Callander—not apparently a strong site, but no doubt once protected by marshland and moat. This was the seat of the Livingstones, Earls of Callander, and of Linlithgow. A stone from the castle is inserted above the manse doorway, inscribed A.L. E.H. 1596, for Alexander Livingstone, 1st Earl of Linlithgow, and his wife Lady Elizabeth Hay, daughter of the 9th Earl of Erroll. This first Earl was a friend of James VI who indeed entrusted to his keeping his little daughter, the Princess Elizabeth, when he went off to London in 1603; the child to become the Winter Queen of Bohemia, was partly brought up at Callander. A fragment of the ancient masonry survives in the manse garden. Near by, on this southern approach to the town, on the Glasgow road, is the large, modern building housing the well-known McLaren High School; and near by, the well-designed new private housing estate of Molland.

52

In the more central part of the town, amongst the very many hotels, is that known as the Roman Camp, associated with J. M. Barrie amongst others. The serpentine mound from which it takes its name, near the river, is in fact a natural feature, not Roman as was long thought; the true Roman camp lies nearly two miles to the west, below Bochastle Hill, near Kilmahog. At the foot of South Church Street, near the footbridge over the river, is a pedestal sundial, dated 1753, presented by Viscount Esher. Near by is the very pleasing modern police-station complex in a leafy waterside setting.

Callander, of course, is the notable centre for touring the Trossachs and other areas of the Southern Highlands. But there is much of interest within walking distance of the town. On the hill-skirts of the Craig, to the north, the 18-hole golf-course is renowned. Above this, a track leads over open scrub-covered hillside to the spectacular Brackland Falls on the Keltie Water. Here are a series of cascades in a rocky, tree-lined chasm, immortalised by Scott, whose character Roderick Dhu was "brave but wild as Bracklinn's thundering wave". It is extraordinary how Scott has managed to link his purely imaginary characters with local topography, all over Scotland. Some of the falls here are over 50 feet high; and there is a narrow footbridge above—which Scott once rode over on a pony, for a wager, to alarm his companions. Also here, in 1844, a foolhardy couple 'frolicking' fell to their deaths. The Keltie Water's glen probes far back into the Glen Artney hills, wherein it has been dammed to form a reservoir. A walking track up it goes on, under Ben Each and Stuc a Chroin (3189 feet) and then over the watershed below Ben Vorlich (3224 feet), to Loch Earn at Ardvorlich, about 14 miles. There are shorter routes to climb these mountains, however.

To the east of Callander, towards the Braes of Doune area, near the farm of Dalvey, is the ruined former fortalice of Auchleshie, a stronghold of the Buchanans. The district beyond is described under Kilmadock and Doune. To the west, is the interesting area of Leny, and Kilmahog. Leny is probably most famed for its Pass and Falls, below Loch Lubnaig, a series of foaming rapids favoured by visitors and photographers. But the large estate of Leny has its own attractions, with a little glen and falls immediately to the north. Its mansion has grown from the ancient nucleus of an L-shaped fortalice of probably the late 16th century, its east front surviving more or less as originally, with crowstepped gable, steep roofs and vaulted basement. This was the seat of a line of Buchanan lairds, close to the chiefs, until comparatively recently, and some of their heraldry survives. Near the walled-garden is an interesting obelisk-type sundial of probably the early 18th century. At Little Leny, down near the haugh of the Teith, and the Trossachs road-end, is an ancient burial-ground of the Buchanans, and the site of a pre-Reformation church. There is a renewed archway entrance, to hold the old bell, and a watch-house, with many old gravestones.

Here is interred Dugald Buchanan, the Gaelic poet and scholar, from Strathyre.

Near by, on the main road, is the pretty, milling hamlet of Kilmahog, where the picturesque old mill-wheel is still maintained in working order, its lade now a sort of wishing-well, with the votive offerings going to the war-blinded. The mill premises are now a thriving woollen and tartan warehouse and saleroom, highly popular with tourists. Next door is a small factory for making fishing-rods. Above all rears Ben Ledi, The Mountain of God, a shapely peak 2873 feet high. There are interesting features on its northern flanks, described under The Trossachs.

Across the river haughs from Kilmahog, south-eastwards, on the A.892, is the modern development of the Callander Holiday Park, in what was formerly the Hydropathic grounds, a large and imaginative project of permanent caravan sites and amenities. This wooded road is an attractive one. Callander is notably well provided with caravan sites, private and municipal.

Altogether, here is a scenic and readily accessible area that sets itself out to attract, and succeeds admirably.

Clunie, Kinloch and Lethendy. Immediately to the west of Blairgowrie is a delightful stretch of rural country, comprising the foothills of the Grampian outliers, the wide valley of the strange loch-forming Lunan Burn, and the wooded hillocky lands between that and the Tay valley to the south. The lochs tend to dominate the scene—Clunie, the most interesting; Drumellie or Marlee the largest; and Fingask and Rae, smaller to the east. The area is fertile as well as wooded, and dotted with fine old estates, three of them running to castles. There is no actual village, but there are hamlets at Kinloch, Craigie, Concraigie, Clunie, Forneth, Kincairney and Kirkton of Lethendy. Raspberry fields clothe the lower braes.

Clunie, 4 miles west of Blairgowrie is pleasant, a rewarding place. The wood-girt loch is roughly triangular, with half-mile sides. Towards the south end is a small island on which rises the only recently-ruined Castle of Clunie, a picturesque place seemingly of the 16th century, though said to have been built between 1485 and 1514 by the famous Bishop Brown of Dunkeld. It is L-shaped, with a very wide circular stair-tower in the angle. Bishop Brown's successor, Bishop Crichton, at the Reformation, sold the lands to his kinsman, Lord Advocate Crichton of Elliock, in 1562, on condition that they came back to the Church if the Reformation collapsed—quite a common device. This was the father of the famous Admirable Crichton, who spent much of his boyhood here.

On the mainland, near the castle to the west, rises a green eminence known as The Ward. Crowning this are the quite extensive remains of the summer palace of Malcolm Canmore, a lovely spot on the green terraced hill above the loch, now bowered in peace. There are traces of a large walled enclosure, and substantial masses

54

Dunblane Cathedral

Dunblane Cathedral, interior

Dunkeld Cathedral

Dunning.
Celtic tower of parish kirk of
St. Serf

of masonry—a place which should be made much of. The mansion of Forneth sits prominently on a terrace to the north.

Near by is the parish church of Clunie, also delightfully sited, with its manse and ancient graveyard. The building dates only from 1840, in the Gothic style, with typical pulpit-prominence and galleries; but in the kirkyard is preserved the splendid red-sandstone arched doorway of the former pre-Reformation church, with highly decorated lintel. There are many old gravestones. Inside the church is some fine old pewter, and a small old kist; also two ancient Bibles, one dated 1616. At the gate is the inscription *KEEP THY FOOT WHEN THOU GOEST TO THE HOUSE OF GOD 1672*.

To the south-east is the pleasant hamlet of Craigie, on the hill-slopes above the loch; and farther west, on the way to the main road at Forneth, is another hamlet amongst green braes—Concraigie. At Kincairney hamlet to the south again, is the former Free Church of Caputh, now a tractor-shed, its belfry and one stained-glass window rather pathetic. Between here and the Lethendy area, nearer Blairgowrie, is Gourdie, where there in a fine old white-washed mansion on a green terraced site, built by the Kinloch family. Also the site of a Roman fort, 2 miles north of Inchtuthill.

Lethendy was a small parish of its own until 1806, when it was united with Kinloch; it had three churches nevertheless, the parish at Kirkton, a Free, and a United Presbyterian establishment. The estate is large and finely maintained, the great red-sandstone mansion-house typical of the late Victorian Scottish-baronial era. But, tucked in at the side, is the authentic if much more modest late 16th or early 17th century Tower of Lethendy, an L-planned, vaulted house with sundry interesting features, including two large buttresses to the south, a gunloop defending the old doorway and a heraldic panel bearing the arms of Heron, dated 1678. From a daughter of Heron of Lethendy was descended Graham of Claver-house, Bonnie Dundee. The road to Lethendy from Blairgowrie, B.948, passes right through a stone circle, a mile from the town, the monoliths neatly flanking it.

Kinloch, not to be confused with another estate of that name only 8 miles away at Meigle, lies on the main A.923 road 2 miles west of Blairgowrie and north of the large loch of Drumellie or Marlee. Why the loch should have two names is not clear; Drumellie seems to be the original, but the mansion of Marlee nearby appears to date from the late 17th century, a modest E-shaped building. The loch, over a mile long, is shallow, and open compared with its wooded neighbours. There is a burial cairn between road and north shore. The hamlet of Kinloch stands north of the road, where the land begins to rise steeply to the foothills. Here is the parish church, small, yellow-washed and plain, with a gallery, in an old graveyard with stones as old as the 17th century. The school adjoins; also a hotel, formerly an inn. Kinloch House itself is now a large hotel. The parish of Kinloch, like neighbouring Lethendy, was small; indeed in 1842 the combined populations were 656.

E

A mile to the east, readily seen from the road, is the most interesting and attractive Ardblair Castle, whitewashed amongst old trees, a 17th century L-planned vaulted fortalice, with courtyard, curtain-walling and arched gateway. There is a slender stair-turret with a gunloop below, and internal panelling. The Blairs of Balthayock, in the Carse of Gowrie, got these lands from David II; a turbulent family who kept the neighbourhood in a stir. Patrick Blair of Ardblair was beheaded for his part in the murder of Drummond of Ledcrieff in 1554. The estate passed by marriage to the Oliphants of Gask, the famous Jacobite family; and many relics of the period came to Ardblair.

The hill-country to the north has its own charm and interest, the major Lornty Burn traversing it by a wide but remote valley, on its way to the Ericht near Blairgowrie. On these higher and more open lands are a great number of cairns and hut circles, indicative of early population when the lower levels were undrained and scrub-covered. At the farm of Chapelton, north-west of Kinloch House, is the site of a pre-Reformation church. And in the Lornty valley farther north are the ruins of two castles, not far apart; Glasclune and Drumlochy, neither now readily approachable. Glasclune has been a strongly-placed fortalice of the 16th century, set above a steep ravine, its remains still impressive. It was another seat of the Blairs. Drumlochy, with less surviving, was too close by for comfort, and constant feuding went on between its Heron lairds and the Blairs of Glasclune.

The quite long and wide valley of the Lornty, oddly enough, lacks a public road. There is a village of Lornty, a milling place, down near the junction with the Ericht, now really a northern suburb of Blairgowrie.

Collace and Kinrossie. The Perthshire section of Strathmore, between the Highland foothills and the western Sidlaws, is a wide and undulating plain of much fertility and many villages, criss-crossed by many roads, notably the A.93 and A.94. But some of the most attractive villages lie well away from the major roads. Two of these are Collace and Kinrossie, midway between Perth and Coupar Angus, lying below the famed Dunsinane Hill, and only a mile apart as the crow flies. Collace, although the smaller and more scattered, is the older, and the parish seat. Both are pleasingly rural and unspoiled.

Collace, oddly, is in two parts, and not even on the same road. The main village, of both old and new houses, is prettily set at the foot of the hill, on the way to a little high pass between the Dunsinane Hills, and so to the Carse of Gowrie. Kirkton of Collace, to the south-west, half a mile away—but a lot more by road—as implied, contains the parish church, a Gothic structure of 1813, with a square tower, set in an old kirkyard; which also contains the remains of the original pre-Reformation church, including a fine arched door-way with dog-tooth moulding. This older building was converted into a mausoleum for the Nairne of Dunsinnan family; and here is buried the last baronet, the famous judge, Lord Dunsinnan, died 1812. Dunsinnan House, mentioned under St. Martins, is a large mansion lying 2 miles to the west. At Kirkton of Collace also is the school; most of the scholars will grow into good walkers, presumably.

Kinrossie village is quite otherwise, a compact smiling place, consisting of a regular street of cottages widely spaced, with green grass in front, apparently all built to a plan. There is a Mercat Cross on a three-step plinth, with rounded shaft and ball-finial. Also a village pump. The former church, round the back, is now a hall. It is a trim community islanded amongst the fields.

Between Kinrossie and Collace, at a road junction, lies the hamlet of Saucher, remote amidst the rows of raspberry-canes, for this is a great fruit-growing area. It is likewise an area of seeming abiding peace. Once, however, placed between the warlike MacBeth's castle of Dunsinane and his Law, or seat of justice at Lawton, to the north, it must have been much otherwise. For a brief period at least, in the 11th century, this patch of Strathmore must have been the throbbing heart of Scotland.

Comrie. Comrie, really *conhruith*, the confluence of streams, is well named. Here, 6 miles west of Crieff, the Lednock comes in from its glen on the north-west, and the Water of Ruchill from Glen Artney on the south-west, to join the Earn 5 miles from the foot of that loch. At this junction of waters, and also roads, a little town has grown up, over the centuries, a place of character in fine country, latterly a resort and admirable centre for the visitor.

The little town of nearly two thousand, which became a burgh of barony under the powerful Dundas family, has two faces—the main street lying east and west along the A.85 highway, with its shops and sharp right-angled bend half-way, provided with a large mirror for traffic to see what is round the corner; and another, more attractive, older part, stretching southwards along the B.827, across the Earn towards Dalginross, less close-knit, with trees and gardens and space. And, all around, the wooded hills tower.

Very prominent is the old parish church, with its white tower and steeple; but this building, dating from 1804, is now a youth centre, scene of lively activities. The former United Free church, a fine French-Gothic style building farther west, is now the church of Comrie and Strowan parishes, with interesting painted notice-boards depicting the Loaves and Fishes story. An older centre of worship was dedicated to St. Kessog, one of the Celtic missionaries, whose name is still commemorated by the hill of Tom-na-Chessaig and the Freemasons' Lodge of St. Kessock.

Comrie has two 'suburbs'—Ross, to the south-west, a former tartan-weaving clachan of the 17th century; and Dalginross, larger, now growing with modern housing, on the plain of the Ruchill towards the mouth of Glen Artney, famous as the site of a prominent Roman fort and camps, and a possible location of the renowned

Battle of Mons Grampius between Romans and Caledonians. Few traces of the Romans remain—though the two camps are said to have accommodated 10,000 men; but there are standing stones of a still earlier civilisation, one a round boulder with cup-marks. There is another kind of camp to the south, now—Cultybraggan, a modern army training-camp, with firing-ranges covering much hill-land to the south. The old bridge of Dalginross was built in 1756, costing £230.

There are more standing-stones on the flats of Tullybannocher and near Dunira East Lodge, both to the west.

Comrie is, of course, famous for its earthquakes. Lying on the Highland Fault it has more recorded tremors than anywhere else in Britain. Not that these tend to be serious. The worst were in 1839 and 1876, and the last substantial shock in 1965. Sometimes there have been as many as 20 slight shocks in 24 hours. In 1869 a small Earthquake House was erected here, with seismographic instruments, an object of scientific interest.

Glens Lednock and Artney are dealt with separately; but the Devil's Cauldron in the ravine, and the Melville Monument above on the top of Dunmore Hill, are both only a mile up Lednock, and should perhaps be mentioned in this context. Henry Dundas, Viscount Melville (1742–1811), scarcely the most reputable of Scottish statesmen, came of a Lothian family; but his seat of Dunira lies in a wooded estate 3 miles to the west, the mansion now roofless but the property otherwise maintained. On this, at Drumnakyl, the Ridge of the Chapel, is an ancient burial-ground.

Across road and river rises the impressive peak of Mor Bheinn and Ben Halton (2033 feet) with the area of Dundurn below—Dun of the Earn or Eireannach. This used to be an important ancient parish, stemming from the cell of St. Fillan. There is still a Dundurn House and Wood, and the Hill of Dundurn itself, with ancient fort and ruined chapel—but these are better dealt with under St. Fillans. Nearer Comrie, at Kindrochat, is the site of a long chambered cairn, tree-grown and part levelled, excavated in 1929, built on top of earlier burial cists, and 135 feet long by 36 wide. Only relic found was a flint arrow-head.

A 2-mile loop road from Ross follows the south side of the Earn, rejoining the A.85 near Dalchonzie House. This gives access to the old estate of Aberuchill, becoming in 1596 a possession of the Campbells, branch of Lawers. The castle, dated 1607, rises out of a much more modern mansion, a whitewashed tower-house with angle-turrets and circular stair-tower. Sir Colin Campbell of Aberuchill and Kilbryde (near Dunblane), created baronet in 1667, was Lord Justice Clerk. He lost £17,201 (Scots) from the depredations of the Highland army under Dundee, so he alleged, and was granted compensation by Act of Parliament—but never received the money. Moreover, he had to pay blackmail to Rob Roy—a sad situation for a Campbell.

No account of Comrie should omit reference to the Flambeaux procession at New Year, an ancient custom still maintained, with a torchlight parade round the town, and dancing round a bonfire—all to scare away evil spirits; perhaps not unconnected originally with the earthquake tremors.

Coupar-Angus. This small but quite famous Perthshire town was once important in Scotland, on account of its great and influential abbey. To many it comes as a surprise to learn that it is in Perthshire at all; but at one time at least part of the town was in Angus, and the county boundary is still only half a mile to the east. It lies near the head of the great valley of Strathmore, in the centre of the fertile fruit-growing district 5 miles south of Blairgowrie, and on the main Perth–Forfar road, A.94, where crossed by A.923, Dundee to Blairgowrie.

Today, though seeming busy because of its roads, it has a population of only 2000, and there is not a lot to be seen therein. The Abbey remains, down the Dundee road, are very scanty indeed, consisting only of a tiny fragment of red-stone walling with a gateway arch, and the recently-cut inscription: *This Abbey was founded by Malcolm the Fourth in the year 1103*—which is not the usual date given. Two stone coffins lie alongside, and all is surrounded by the large graveyard of the modern parish church. The church is largely built out of the abbey masonry, and on the site, dating from 1681 but wholly remodelled in 1857. Across the road, part of the former precincts are indicated by masonry built into a house wall, showing a coronet above a very weatherworn shield. Close by are Precinct Street, Candlehouse Lane and other quiet back-streets. Nearer the cross-roads centre rises the square Town Steeple, of 1762, on the site of the old tolbooth and the prison of the Court of Regality when Coupar was a Royal Burgh.

East of the town, beyond the churchyard and right on the county boundary, is the site of a Roman camp. It is reputed to have been a square of 1200 feet, with strong double ramparts and wide ditches, the work of Lollius Urbicus. Another similar camp lies 2 miles to the south, at Lintrose over the Angus border.

The most pleasant view of Coupar is that from the north, where it can be seen as on a slight plateau which drops quite sharply to the green haughs of the winding Isla. Here, a mile north, the A.923, crosses by the Bridge of Couttie, of 1766. Formerly there was only a ford, and stones still called the Riding and Wading Stones mark the lines for travellers. Once there was a hamlet at this busy spot—for there would be much traffic here, the Abbey's rich granges lying mainly across the Isla in what is now the parish of Bendochy. Farms are still here bearing names such as Coupar Grange, Grange of Aberbothrie and Grangemount; while Monk Myre lies to the west. Donald Campbell, the last Abbot of Coupar, dying 1587, lies buried with his illegitimate sons—whom he made rich landowners out of church lands—in Bendochy Church near by.

Coupar's fame rested almost entirely on the Abbey, a Cistercian foundation. Wynton's Chronicle declares:

A thowsand a hundyre and sexty yhere and fowre,
Malcolme, Kyng of Scotland, and pesybly in it regnand,
De elevynd yhere of his crowne, mad the fundatyowne
Of the Abbay of Culpyre-in-Angus, and dowyt it wyth his almws,
In honoure of the may kles may relygyws munkis there dwellis ay,
All lyk to Cystwys in habyt, we oys to call thame mwnkys qwhyt.

It was a rich place, endowed by many Scots kings. Robert the Bruce provided a candle and lamp to burn perpetually here in honour (or placation) of the Blessed Saint Malachy O'Moore or Moluag—who had cursed the Bruce family in 1140.

Crianlarich, Strathfillan and Glen Dochart. We are here at the very westernmost limits of the great county of Perth, and quite close to the borders of Argyll, Dunbartonshire and Stirlingshire. Crianlarich is a mainly modern village which has grown up at an important hub of valleys and their roads, and also formerly a railway junction. Here meet Glen Falloch from Loch Lomondside and the south, Glen Dochart from the east, and Strathfillan from the west. Great mountain masses surround it; the Forest of Mamlorn to the north, Ben More and Stobinian to the east, and the Bens Dubh Chraig–Oss–Lui group to the west. On every side the scenery is splendid. Because of all this, Crianlarich is also important as a centre for climbing, touring and winter sports, and a youth hostel partners hotel and eating-place facilities. Moreover, although the closure of the Stirling–Dochart railway leaves only the main Glasgow–Fort William line to run through, nevertheless the erection of the great pulp-mill at Fort William, within good rail access, has made Crianlarich a convenient marshalling-yard and assembly-point for trainloads of timber from the spreading forestry plantations over a great area.

Strathfillan, stretching some five miles to the west, and threaded by the Fillan Water, is a wide green valley which has long been important in the Scots story. Here was established, by St. Fillan, an ancient abbey of the Celtic or Culdee Church, with its five precious relics, each in the care of a hereditary custodian, called a Dewar. Bruce was indebted to two of these during his days as a fugitive hereabouts, and after his victory at Bannockburn, in 1314, founded an Augustinian abbey. The scanty remains of its chapel are still to be seen on the north side of road and river about half-way up the strath. St. Fillan's bell, from here, is now in the Museum of Antiquities at Edinburgh. Near by, at the roadside, is the modern Strathfillan Kirk, central for the valley but remote from any village. Farther west, to the south of the road, stretches an attractive relic of the old Caledonian Forest, the pinewoods of Cononish, with Ben Lui in the background. Still farther up the valley, nearer Tyndrum, is Dalrigh, or the Field of the King, site of Bruce's second defeat, after his coronation, at the hands of MacDougall of Lorne, the occasion when the King's cloak was wrenched off by a clansman, and its jewelled clasp with it—the famous Brooch of Lorne, which has remained the treasured possession of the Chiefs of MacDougall ever since.

The Fillan flows into Loch Dochart, east of Crianlarich, a moderate-sized and gentle sheet of water, with, nevertheless, a ruined MacNab castle on a wooded islet. It lies beneath the soaring twin mountains of Ben More and Stobinian (3843 and 3821 feet), favourites of climbers, its shore being a popular picnic-place for motorists. Almost joined, to the east, is slightly larger and more wooded Loch Iubhair. The River Dochart flows out, traversing another green and fertile valley for 13 miles eastwards to join Loch Tay at Killin, via the Falls of Dochart. A number of old MacNab and Campbell lairdships dot the valley, with the hamlet of Luib and its hotel midway, the whole making a pleasant pastoral upland scene, backed by the high heather hills. The ruin marked on the maps as Rob Roy's Castle, was never in fact a fortalice; merely a cottage where the noted freebooter took refuge at one stage of his exciting career.

Glen Falloch is different, a narrower, steeper valley famed for its romantic scenery, reaching southwards from Crianlarich for 8 miles to open into Loch Lomond at Ardlui. It is well wooded towards the south end, and the impressive mass of Cruach Ardrain (3428 feet) rises to the east, while Ben Oss and Ben Dubh Chraig guard the west (3374 and 3204 feet). Half-way down, the Falls of Falloch are noteworthy. This is all Rob Roy MacGregor country, and vivid with tales of that colourful character.

Crieff. The burgh of Crieff greets travellers with the sign *Welcome to the Holiday Town*. And certainly it gives the impression of living for and by the visitor and tourist. Probably only Pitlochry rivals it in this, in Perthshire. Its hotels are legion, every other house seems to show a bed-and-breakfast sign, its shops are very much geared to the holiday-maker, and sporting and recreational facilities abound. Yet the town has character, with nothing of the tawdry miniature-Blackpool atmosphere. There is little that is ancient about the appearance of Crieff, admittedly—for the Jacobite army burned it comprehensively in 1715, and there are no really interesting buildings; yet the place is in fact very old. Earl Gilbert of Strathearn signed a charter at 'Crefe die Sancta Ambrosii' in 1218; and Robert, Steward of Scotland, later the first Stewart king, held court here in 1358.

The situation of the town is very fine, lying 17 miles west of Perth, climbing the wooded slopes of the Highland Line above the fertile plain of Upper Strathearn, backed by the steep Knock, flanked by the ranked mountains, but facing south with wide prospects over a lovely and sylvan scene. This is the second town of Perthshire as to size—population 5700; but it is not capital of Strathearn; Auchterarder, less than half its size, is the head-town of the former ancient earldom, having that honour. Yet it was in Crieff's vicinity that those important magnates of old Scotland mainly used to dwell—first on the top of Tom a Chasteal to the west, and then at the Castleton of Fowlis Wester to the east. And it was here that the subsequent royal stewartry of Strathearn had its judgment seat.

But that was all a long time ago, for the mighty Celtic earldom was finally suppressed and incorporated in the Crown—so that, for instance, Queen Victoria's father was Duke of Kent and Strathearn, and her son Duke of Connaught and Strathearn; and the royal stewartry thereof came to be administered by the great family of Drummond, whose Drummond Castle lies only 2 miles to the south, near Muthill. So Crieff became very much a Drummond town, under the sway of the Earls and Dukes of Perth—that is, until the Drummonds were forfeited for their Jacobite sympathies. One of the only two true relics of antiquity in Crieff is the Cross of the Regality of Drummond, which stands under a canopy below the town's clock-tower in the main street, a tall, cylindrical shaft 10 feet high with a mutilated fleur-de-lys as finial. The building beside it is not old, having replaced the Old Tolbooth and jail of 1665, demolished in 1842—although a stone with the earlier date is built in above the cross. At the foot is preserved also the iron stocks for shackling offenders. Across the street and 100 yards farther up is another cross under a canopy—this time known as the Cross of Crieff itself. But it is no market cross. It is a typical ecclesiastical cross-slab of the early Celtic Church, probably of the 10th century, highly carved with tracery and design. It is thought to have come from the old St. Ronan's Church of Strowan, 3 miles to the west.

The main street of Crieff is rather dull—which is a pity, for the approaches are quite attractive and the climbing streets and avenues behind are pleasing. There is a central square—very notably on the slope, from north to south, as is all the town—and a row of hotels flanks its upper side. The best known is the Drummond Arms, not itself an ancient building but built on the site of an earlier inn of that name, wherein Prince Charles Edward held a stormy council-of-war on 3rd February 1746. Across from it, in mid-square, is the Murray Fountain, erected by the townsfolk *in recognition of the many benefits received from the Murrays of Ochtertyre*—a pleasing acknow-ledgment from citizens to lairds. This could be called the successor of the town's Well of St. Thomas, Crieff's tutelary saint—which makes the above reference to 'Crefe die Santa Ambrosii' a little difficult to fathom.

If Crieff has no ancient buildings, it has some notable modern ones. The extensive and substantial Morison's Academy, higher up the hillside, within its lofty wall, is a renowned school. Endowed by Thomas Morison, an Edinburgh builder who left £20,000 for the purpose in 1826, it was established here almost by accident, for the founder intended it to be erected at his native Muthill—but no suitable site there could be obtained. Equally well known, and still higher-placed, is the famous Crieff Hydro, more properly called Strathearn House Hotel, a huge establishment of over 200 bedrooms, in an estate of some 650 acres, with its own farm, woodlands and gardens, golf-course, tennis, badminton, squash, croquet, riding, swimming and other facilities—even its own cinema—a deservedly popular place that is unusual in especially catering for children.

Crieff is peculiar in having no ancient church as centre-piece. Places of worship abound, and fine ones; but not the normal and original parish church. This is because the early Kirk of St. Thomas was demolished in 1787, and the parish split into two. At the demolition a hoard of 40 gold coins of Robert the Bruce were uncovered in the walling. One of Crieff's many churches today, towards the west end, is St. Ninians, converted into an ecumenical Residential Training Centre.

Down at the riverside, Crieff Bridge, of 1690, spans the Earn, a fine structure of four arches, still carrying all the traffic from the south. The southernmost arch was demolished by the retreating Jacobite forces in 1715, to hinder their enemies, and rebuilt slightly higher. There is a suburb here, almost a separate village, of Bridgend. Near by, on the Muthill road, are some small but well-designed modern factories, far from spoiling the amenity, one housing, for instance, the Strathearn Glass project. To the south of this, in a field, is a large standing-stone. Still farther south, near Drummond Castle gates, where 'Smithy' is marked on the map, is in fact now a workshop and showroom for ornamental ironwork, an interesting development of the traditional smithy. Near by can be seen a remarkable geological formation, a trap-dike of greenstone, like a long, low cliff rising out of the fields, called Concraig. It gave the early name to the property on which Drummond Castle was built; and there is still a farm of that name.

A little way above the Strowan road from Bridgend, to the south-west, on the farm of Alichmore, is the long cairn of Rottenreoch, between farmhouse and rifle range, an elongated mound of around a hundred and twenty feet, in a field, with trees on top. The view of Crieff from here, across the Earn's fertile vale, is notable. At the other side of Bridgend, to the south-east on the estate of The Broich, is the circular site of the former outdoor court of the Stewarty of Strathearn, where so many victims, especially Highlanders, were despatched to the famous 'kindly gallows of Crieff', on the Gallows Hill.

There are many features of interest in the Crieff neighbourhood dealt with under their own village and parish articles—Muthill, Monzie, Monzievaird and Strowan, Fowlis Wester and so on. In Crieff parish itself, mention should be made of the Knock, or *Crubha Cnoic*, the crouching eminence, the high wooded hill (911 feet) dominating the town to the north. At the far end of this, overlooking the little Vale of Monzie, is Kate McNieven's Craig, where tradition has it that one of the last alleged witches was burned, in Scotland. There are doubts about this, for one account has it that the burning was in 1563—which was, of course, *before* the witch-hunting craze started; and another alleges that she was actually burned at St. Andrews. As confusing is the statement that she was accused by the Graham laird of Inchbrakie, in whose employ she was as nursemaid, as having buzzed round his head in form of a bee; whereas it is also stated that Inchbrakie did his best to save her from the pyre, in consequence of which Kate spat out a blue stone at him, asserting that so long as the Grahams kept it, their line would be secure. More straightforward is the statement that the last 'fruit' to hang on Crieff's famed gallows on Gallows Hill, to the west of the town, was the Reverend Richard Duncan, of Kinkell, in 1682, condemned for child-murder—although, even here, Muthill contests the honour of the hanging. Also on the Knock, to the south, is the Cradle Stone, a huge granite boulder, 30 feet in diameter, split by lightning.

The estate of Ferntower, lying to the east of the town—formerly the seat of 'Oor Davie', the heroic Sir David Baird, of Seringapatam (1757–1829) whose obelisk crowns the hill of Tom a Chasteal—is now Crieff Golf Club's fine course. On it is a standing-stone, the remains of a stone circle, and Cope's Well—Sir John Cope, the unfortunate government general of the Forty-Five having encamped his troops here.

Even this very brief account of Crieff should not close without mention of the famous Crieff Trysts, the great cattle sales held here, the largest in Scotland until, in 1770, they were transferred to Falkirk, and wherein the bovine harvest of a vast area of the Highlands were brought for sale to lowland and English dealers—amidst stirring scenes. Even in 1723, after the heyday of the clan system, 30,000 beasts were sold at one tryst—for approximately 30,000 guineas! If Crieff is a town of hotels and so on today, it was not lacking in places of refreshment in those days either—for it still had 48 alehouses in 1838.

Cromlix, Kinbuck and Ashfield. About a mile north of Dunblane, beside the great Queen Victoria School, the A.9 sends off a branch due northwards, B.8033. This leads up the green Allan Water valley, mainly on the west side, to Braco, about seven miles, a pleasant quiet road in marked distinction to the rushing, lorry-dominated A.9, which can be seen frequently across the river. A mile up this, a side-road strikes off on the left to an unusual community, scarcely to be seen from the road because it lies in the trough of the Allan. This is Ashfield, a quite large industrial village which has grown up solely round the dyeworks here, formerly of Pullars of Perth, now of the British Silk Dyeing Company. Wholly functional and making no claims to beauty of any sort, it yet lies in pleasing rural country, strangely isolated, with fine views over the Braes of Doune.

A mile on is Kinbuck, also by the riverside. This is a more conventional village, with shops and school, that has grown, not been set down all at once, with the highway running through. Without any particular charm, it is also attractively placed. There was a dyeworks here too, but it is now a Ferranti factory for electrical components. A large sand-and-gravel pit operates close by—all this area around Dunblane is dotted with such, indicative of the moraine deposits of glaciation in these foothills—hence, indeed, the Braes of Doune.

A little to the north, the road crosses to the other side of the Allan by an old bridge of two arches, quite high. This vicinity was important in the Battle of Sheriffmuir, in 1715, the Jacobite right wing being based on the Allan, and this bridge vital. Their army had camped the previous night between Balhaldies (on the A.9 line) and Kinbuck, and quite a sharp tussle took place in Kinbuck village itself. It was near here that Rob Roy, with his 200 MacGregors, returning from an errand to inspect the Fords of Frew and a possible outflanking of Argyll's government army thereby, rejoined Mar's force late in the day, and refused to throw away his MacGregor clansmen on what was obviously a hopelessly bungled contest, preferring to hold this west side of the river, to allow the fleeing Highlanders to escape—an action for which he has been wrongly accused of cowardice and treachery, even by Walter Scott.

A little farther north, on this road, is the Cromlix area, where is Cromlix House estate, Cromlix Lodge, Home Farm and Crofts of Cromlix, a country of foothills and woodlands. This was an important entity once, for it was the episcopal barony of the Bishops of Dunblane. It passed to the Drummond Viscounts of Strathallan at the Reformation, and thereafter was inherited by the Drummond-Hay Earls of Kinnoull, who, in a fashion, ruled Dunblane after the bishops' days, the town being made a burgh of barony under Cromlix, with a baron-bailie to oversee the councillors' activities. Mineral wells were discovered here. The estate of Cromlix lies high on the green, south-facing braes of the great hills, really an extension of the Braes of Doune, looking across the vale of Strathallan to the Ochils.

Dalguise and Craigvinean. It is a good idea, if the traveller has a little time to spare when heading north or south in the mid-Tay valley, to take the road B.898, along the west side of the river instead of the A.9. It is attractive and gives a much finer aspect of a very worth-while stretch of country. Going north, take the left fork at the Birnam end of Dunkeld bridge—that is, the Strathbraan road, A.822—and then quickly fork right, by Inver, Neil Gow's birthplace. The road twists and turns picturesquely under soaring Craig Vinean, thickly wooded. This great forest of Craigvinean stretches up this side of Tay for over six miles, rising well over the 1500-foot contour; and its many footpaths provide magnificent walks, other than the well-known one which follows the Braan up by the famed Hermitage. A one-inch Ordnance Map shows many of these tracks.

There are only occasional scattered houses along this road until, 5 miles up, Dalguise is reached. This itself is only a scattered hamlet, though pleasing; but it was once an important clerical community, becoming a powerful lairdship. The present air of settled peace is partly accounted for by the prevalence of old fruit trees; for this part of the great parish of Little Dunkeld was famous for its orchards, and was known as The Bishopric, being part of the prelates' own lands. At the Reformation, of course, all changed; and Dalguise was given to a son of Stewart of Airntully, near Murthly in 1543—very early in that great land carve-up. Bailie of the new Regality of Dunkeld, he was commanded by the Regent Moray to destroy the 'idolatrous works and images' of Dunkeld Cathedral; which he did all too thoroughly. Dalguise House, whitewashed and pleasant amongst lawns and woodland, dates from the late 17th and early 18th centuries, with later additions, and shows the Stewart arms, dated 1753, and initials J.S. and R.M. separated by a heart. It is now the property of the Scottish Association of Boys' Clubs, and runs as a training-centre for outdoor pursuits. At Easter Dalguise, standing high on a shoulder of hill above the road, is a little church, still in use, demanding of stout leg muscles in its worshippers.

Only walkers will discover another interesting place here, high in the forest above Dalguise—the former mansion of Stewartfield, built most inaccessibly in 1821. It has been more than any mere shooting-lodge, for here is a walled garden and all the offices of a large mansion—now all lost in trees and undergrowth. The local story is that one of the Dalguise lairds got so tired of his womenfolks' tongues that he erected this inaccessible place to escape to—or, alternatively to banish the ladies to. Perhaps!

Two miles beyond Dalguise is the fine 18th century mansion of Kinnaird, another Stewart house. A son of the first Laird of Dalguise married the Stewart heiress here. He was a man of note, called Ian Mor MacAlastair, and fought for Montrose. He was Chamberlain for the Reformed Bishops of Dunkeld.

This pleasant road comes to Balnagard in another 3 miles, an agreeable village of cottages set amongst banks and braes in the mouth of Strathtay, almost opposite Logierait. Here a wooded ravine comes in from the south, containing the Falls of Balnagard. There is a standing-stone in a field below the road. A further 2½ miles, and B.898 joins the main Strathtay–Aberfeldy A.827, at Ballinluig (the original village, not the modern station-place on A.9) where there is the first road-bridge across Tay since Dunkeld. This area is dealt with under Strathtay and Grandtully.

Doune. The little burgh of Doune is a proud place, and worthily so. It is the capital of Menteith, more properly *Mon*teith, the mounth of the River Teith, which was once one of the great earldoms and divisions of ancient Scotland. Near by stands one of the finest castles in this, or any other, land. Doune had, inevitably, a stirring history. And it is an attractive place, attractively sited, old-fashioned admittedly, but authentic. And despite all this, it has a population of less than 800.

The town stands where the Ardoch Burn comes down from the northern heights to join the Teith, 4 miles west of Dunblane and

8 south-east of Callander, where the A.84 and A.820 also join; and behind it, the Braes of Doune—not to be confused with the "banks and braes of bonnie Doon", in Ayrshire—rise in great folds to the high heather hills of the Ben Vorlich and Forest of Glenartney range. The Teith, rushing down from its double sources in the Trossachs and Lubnaig areas, has formed here a great and wooded valley through the foothills, so that Doune is a comparatively hilly place. The main street is picturesque at both ends, but in the centre, around the great, gaunt parish church of 1822, with its 1150 sittings, tall tower and shamefully neglected graveyard, it is much spoiled. At the west end, is the little triangular market place, with its typical old Mercat Cross in the centre, relic of the days when cattle and sheep fairs, authorised by special Act of Parliament in 1665, made Doune a busy place. To the south from here, the main road crosses the Teith by a fine two-arched bridge, later widened, but first built in 1535 by Robert Spittal, the Stirling tailor of James IV's widow, Margaret Tudor—the same who founded Spittal's Hospital, Stirling, and built also the bridge at Bannockburn. He was a great public benefactor—but the story of this bridge shows a less noble side of the man; for it is said that he erected it to spite the ferry-man here, who had refused the wealthy tailor passage because he had no money about his person at the time. It was built, therefore, to do the other out of a living—though no doubt to the great advantage of the good folk of Doune.

The town used to be greatly famed for the manufacture of Highland pistols by its craftsmen—and indeed the burgh sign still shows two pairs of crossed pistols on either side of the Mercat Cross. Nowadays Doune pistols are almost worth their weight in gold. Sporrans also were made here. But when, after the Forty-Five, the Proscription Acts from London banned the wearing of Highland dress, and pacification was the order of the day, a different kind of manufacture came to replace these—cotton-milling at the Deanston Mills, by the Teithside half a mile to the west of the town. There is also Deanston Distillery and a large modern village. At one time there were no fewer than five churches in the little town—the Parish, the Free, the United Presbyterian, the Roman Catholic and the Episcopalian—something of a plethora, surely, for a population which could not even fill the first. Though, of course, a century ago, the population was almost double its present numbers.

Doune Castle is not readily glimpsed from the town itself, strangely enough lying in a low but strong position at the junction of Ardoch and Teith. It is a large and magnificent courtyard-type castle of the late 14th and early 15th centuries, and its splendours and exciting history may only be hinted at here. It consists of two great and tall keeps, linked by a lower range of building containing a notable Great Hall with centre-of-the-floor fireplace, to form the north side of a quadrangular court, the other three sides being enclosed by a tremendous 40-feet-high curtain-wall, 8 feet thick and topped by a parapet and wall-walk. Of the two keeps, the older and higher is to the north-east, with the doorway pend driving through. Although undoubtedly there was an older nucleus, most of the present castle was built by Robert, Duke of Albany, brother of Robert III, who had married the heiress Countess of Menteith, and by his son, Murdoch, 2nd Duke, both Regents of Scotland during young James I's enforced exile in England—for which exile, in due course, the said James had off Duke Murdoch's head. The original principal messuage-place of this ancient Celtic earldom was the castle on the island of Inch Talla, in the Lake of Menteith; but this proving an inconvenient place when times grew a little more settled, it was moved to Doune—which really should be called the Doune, or Dun of Monteith. After the execution of Murdoch Stewart and his sons, the castle and earldom was merged with the Crown, until James IV settled it on his English queen, Margaret Tudor—who, in 1525 passed it to her third husband, Henry Stewart, Lord Methven, actually a descendant of Albany. James V granted it to another of the same Stewart line, who became Lord Doune and whose grandson married the Regent Moray's daughter, to become himself the famed Bonnie Earl of Moray of the ballad. Their descendant is still the owner; and though the castle fell into partial ruin, the then Earl of Moray restored it in 1883. It is, naturally, a magnet for visitors, and is open from 9 to 6 daily, or dusk if earlier. Here stayed Mary Queen of Scots, and many another royal figure. Rob Roy's nephew, Gregor MacGregor of Glengyle, garrisoned it for Prince Charles Edward in 1745—during which siege one of the prisoners was the young Reverend John Home, of Athelstaneford, captured while fighting for the government at the Battle of Falkirk. He managed to lower himself from a window by a blanket-rope and made his escape. An exciting episode for a clergyman, a poet and the author of the *Douglas* tragedy—for which last flirtation with the theatrical he aroused the wrath of the Presbytery of Edinburgh and had to vacate his pulpit.

Not far to the east of Doune Castle, on higher ground, is the most attractive late 16th century lesser laird's house of Newton Doune, a small L-planned fortalice, harled and pink-washed, unusual in that its wing has a rounded not a square gable. It was the residence of a branch of the Edmonstone of Duntreath family, who became hereditary captains of the great castle close by, for the Earls of Moray. Like their masters, they remained loyal to the royal house of Stewart, and in 1708 the Edmonstone Laird of Newton was one of the five Perthshire lairds arrested in an abortive Jacobite attempt. It is interesting to note that, in September 1745, Prince Charlie 'pree'd the mou'—kissed the mouth—of Miss Robina Edmonstone, at Doune Lodge, near by—although this house was then called Cambuswallace. It is a handsome white mansion, standing pleasingly on a green terrace above parkland, just over a mile west of the town, and is now the seat of the Earl of Moray's heir, Lord Doune. The Doune Car Museum is established here.

About two miles to the other side, east of Doune, a fine circle of standing-stones lies in a field to the north of the B.824 road from Keir.

Dowally, Guay and Kindallachan. North of Dunkeld, on the east side of Tay, there is no sizeable centre of population until Pitlochry, nearly thirteen miles on. But there are a number of hamlets, and more population than might be expected; for there is a higher shelf of land to the east, not perceived from the main highway, a terrace of good land on the skirts of the mountains. This has already been described under Ballinluig and Tullymet, the northern section of this area. It is all part of the large parish of Dunkeld and Dowally; and the southern communities thereof cluster round the hamlets of Dowally itself, Guay and Kindallachan, all sited down at or near the A.9 road.

Dowally had a strange genesis. During the great plague which ravaged Scotland in 1500, there was a touching belief that the holy city of Dunkeld was immune from the dread pestilence on account of the virtues of its founder, St. Columba. So refugees flocked hither—and Bishop George Brown of Dunkeld, not to have his town over-run, settled them in the haugh of Dowally, 5 miles to the north. That these people, who evidently came prepared to stay, should not lack religious attention, the Bishop erected Dowally into a parish, the latest original to be founded in Perthshire, with its own church. This was allegedly a 'long, narrow and inelegant structure', dedicated to St. Anne. The present church, built on the site in 1818, is quite attractive, in the midst of its older graveyard. There are two very old stones. Built into the east wall are the arms of Bishop Brown, from the earlier church; and also therefrom are the iron jougs, hanging outside the modern porch.

The hamlet stands back from the road, like the church, in the mouth of the little glen of the Dowally Burn which comes down from a series of lochs set high to the north-east—Dowally, Rotmell and the quite large Ordie. It is a picturesque spot, unspoiled, with a mill, farm and cottages. Across the main A.9, at the roadside, are two standing-stones, one fallen. A little to the west is the site of a cairn, 30 feet in diameter, from which stone coffins were extracted when the road was being driven through this haugh. The local people were very loath to allow this, claiming that the pestilence itself was buried in this cairn, and that any disturbance might renew the calamity. There was also a holy well dedicated to St. Anne near by. St. Columba's name also is perpetuated in St. Colme's, a large model farm up on the high ground half a mile to the southeast, at Rotmell, established by a former Duchess of Atholl. There was once a royal castle of Rotmell, demolished in 1810.

A mile north of Dowally is Guay, another hamlet which stands back from the main road on the fairly steep slopes up to the aforementioned shelf. There is a school here, and a former inn. This had very ancient origins, for in 1340 the then Bishop of Dunkeld erected a house here for travellers and visitors. It was renewed by the good Bishop Brown in 1490, but abandoned at the Reformation.

In less than a mile is the third hamlet, Kindallachan, a scatter of cottages on and near the A.9. Once it boasted its own sheep market. Just behind is the district of Kilmorich, meaning the Chapel of Mary, where there was once a Culdee cell; and more recently a distillery. The Haugh of Kilmorich extends along Tayside between Kindallachan and Ballinluig Station. The back-road, some hundreds of feet higher on the terrace, makes a pleasant change from the rush of the main highway, with much wider views on all sides. Up on these hill-skirts are many caves, reputed to have been tenanted, for long after Culloden, by Jacobite refugees.

Dull. This strange and strangely-named hamlet tucked away on the hillside overlooking the Tay 3 miles west of Weem, has cut an unexpectedly wide swathe in Scotland's story. For here, when the world was younger, was one of the land's foremost educational establishments, the College of Dull, renowned for learning and piety. It was an ecclesiastical foundation of course—all colleges were—but this was one of the ancient Culdee centres, part of the original Columban church, before Rome took over Scotland's faith. The tradition is that St. Cuthbert, who later shed his lustre at Lindisfarne, came here as a young man, and built an oratory of wood. He also founded the well at 'Doilweme', mentioned under Weem. His stay was not long, and seventeen years later St. Adamnan arrived from Iona, aged Abbot thereof and biographer of Columba. He it was who established the College, allegedly in 687, and here he is supposed to have been buried. A later abbot was the famous Crinan, also Abbot of Dunkeld, who married the elder daughter of Malcolm II and so became father of King Duncan, slain by MacBeth, and progenitor of the succeeding royal line of Scotland. Marriage was not prohibited for Culdee clerics. It is interesting to note that before the Reformation, Dull's college was moved to the ecclesiastical metropolis, St. Andrews; and the parish minister here still receives a contribution to his stipend from St. Andrews.

At the side of the B.846 highway, below Dull, is a group of standing-stones. And a little farther west are two tumuli, between road and river. Dull was always a place of veneration, it seems.

The wide flat of the Tay here is known as the Appin of Dull, and the Strath of Appin strikes off to the north—not to be confused with the Appin in Argyll. Appin, in fact, is just a corruption of the Gaelic *abthania*, meaning abbatical lands. Here are the little communities of Keltneyburn and Coshieville. Near the former, just across the bridge over the River Lyon, which here joins Tay, is the small 16th century castle of Comrie, now much ruined but with interesting features surviving. It was a former Menzies stronghold. Here also is a Scottish Wildlife Trust nature reserve of 13 acres, specialising in orchids.

Elcho Castle

Drummond Castle and gardens, Crieff

Glen Lyon. Bridge of Balgie

Coshieville, at the foot of the Strath of Appin, is a strange name to find in the Gaelic Highlands—no doubt a corruption. There is another of the same name, near Grandtully. There is a hotel here. And 2 miles to the west is Garth House, the mansion in the fine estate now a splendid Youth Hostel. From Coshieville the B.846 begins to climb steeply up the Strath, rising eventually to over 1200 feet, near White Bridge, on its way to Tummel, following General Wade's road. But up the other side of the Keltney Burn a much rougher and presently private road leads to the ancient Garth Castle, a stark, stern 14th century keep, recently excellently restored, which stands in a strong position above the junction of two steep ravines. This was built by that notorious royal free-booter, Alexander Stewart, better known as the Wolf of Badenoch, third son of Robert II, and therefore great-grandson of The Bruce, one of the most disreputable though picturesque soundrels to decorate even Scots history. He died here in 1396. His successors, the Stewarts of Garth tended to be little improvement, one, Nigel Stewart, burning the predecessor of Castle Menzies and immuring its laird, Sir Robert Menzies, in the dungeon at Garth without food until he signed away sundry rights. Later he arranged the murder of his own wife by having one of his followers kill her in the burn below the castle 'negligently, by the blow of a stone'. Mercifully he was kept imprisoned in his own tower, thereafter, for nine years, till death in 1554.

Dunblane. Dunblane is a splendid illustration of the fact that quantity and quality, size and excellence, have little mutual relevance. It is a small burgh of less than 3500 souls—though it delights to call itself the Burgh and City of Dunblane—yet it contains more of delight and interest than many a large community. Because of its position, its history is almost that of Scotland.

Lying in the valley of the Allan Water, 4 miles north of Stirling and the Forth, it of course centres round and enshrines its ancient cathedral. The busy A.9 highway used to run through, but happily it now by-passes the little town to the east. Less happily, there are plans for new road developments which could endanger amenity—being strenuously resisted. The old parts lie along the east bank of the Allan, on a terrace above the river, and the old single-arched bridge thereto, built by Bishop Finlay Dermoch in the 15th century, is still visible, though incorporated in a wider, modern structure. The narrow main street is short and rather attractive, leading up to the open cathedral yard or Square. Here are some interesting houses, including two of the old canons' manses; Bishop Leighton's Library, a crowstepped-gabled house of 1687, with forestair and the Bishop's arms; the Dean's House, dated 1624, now a museum; and to the north and east the picturesque complex of Kirk Street and Sinclairs Street, now restored by the Society of the Friends of Dunblane Cathedral, as the Scottish Churches House, an ecumenical centre for all Scotland. It has an exciting underground vaulted chapel. This society, the first of its kind, was formed in 1929, and has done much to preserve and beautify this ancient shrine.

Dunblane was the smallest of Scotland's 13 dioceses, administering only 43 parishes; but it was one of the most ancient. Founded, in the Celtic polity by St. Blane about A.D. 600—who came from Kingarth in Bute and whose mother was a daughter of King Aidan of Dalriada—the lower four storeys of its red-stone tower are all that remains of the early Celtic church with its own rough symbol-stone —which has obviously been very similar to those of Dunning and Muthill not far off. This tower fits but awkwardly into the later fabric. In 1140, after the reduction of the Celtic or Culdee Church by the Romish polity, largely at the instance of Malcolm Canmore's Queen Margaret, her son David I erected the see of Dunblane. But it was Bishop Clement (1233–58) who built most of the present work, though a Celtic Earl of Strathearn had been busy before that. First came the Lady Chapel, also called the Chapter House, in early pointed style, with its fine groined roof, reached now from the Choir by an arched doorway with aperture at the head, allegedly to admit a tall bishop's mitre. This chapel is notable for its floor of Purbeck marble, its fine War Memorial windows and oak panelling. The Choir itself is very fine, and under three blue slabs in its floor are buried Margaret Drummond and her two sisters, daughters of the first Lord Drummond, who died of poison one breakfast—almost certainly administered to make sure that King James IV did not make Margaret his queen (to whom he was probably secretly married) in place of Henry VIII's sister Margaret Tudor—an ancient but grievous story. Here is also the effigy of a bishop, probably the aforementioned builder, Clement. The wood carved work is magnificent, both early and modern, and though irreplaceable, is insured for £500,000. The modern stalls, completed in 1913, are quite superlative in their beauty and variety. The stained glass windows here, also, are very wonderful, of unusual richness.

The Nave, measuring 130 by 57 feet, of eight pillared bays with clerestory, is of mid-14th century date, the entrance thereto, the West Door, being of great excellence. Above is the tremendous West Window, portraying the Tree of Jesse, with the Baptismal Window near by, with fine font beneath and entrance to the Clement Chapel. It is quite impossible to do justice to Dunblane Cathedral in the space here available, so full of beauty, treasure and splendour is it. Let it suffice to quote Ruskin, speaking in Edinburgh: "He was no common man who designed the Cathedral of Dunblane. I know not anything so perfect in its simplicity, and so beautiful, as far as it reaches, in all the Gothic with which I am acquainted . . ."

The cathedral is still the parish church.

Between cathedral and river, the remains of the former bishops' palace are still to be seen in walling and vaulting, on the steeply-sloping site. Below is a pleasant riverside walk, and a bleaching green given, as a pillar records, by H.M. Commissioners in 1842.

The Leighton Library has been mentioned. That saintly bishop (1613–84), later translated to the archbishopric of Glasgow, who tried so hard to reconcile the opposing sides during the religious wars of that century, bequeathed his collection of 1400 books for the use of the clergy of the diocese; and his nephew built the house to contain them, and provided an endowment. Books have been added through the centuries.

The modern parts of Dunblane are like the curate's egg. The area across the river is depressing and unworthy of the town, typical industrial expansion. But higher up the hill to the west things improve, with more up-to-date housing. On the other side of the valley, too, beyond the A.9, there is excellent development. Up here, amongst the very modern houses, stands an unusual doocote, circular with a parapet and roof apertures for the birds; it belonged to the Kippendavie estate which lies near by. This prefix 'kippen' in this area is notable. There is the other old lairdship of Kippenross a mile to the south, as well as Kippenrait Glen and farm. The Stirlings of Kippendavie and Kippenross are branches of Keir, all in this vicinity.

To the north of Dunblane is the rather quaint little village of Ramoyle, now absorbed as a suburb and expanded with modern housing, but still retaining its own post office in its old, narrow village street. There was a mineral well, some say two, discovered here, which at one time was hoped would turn Dunblane into a spa to rival Bridge of Allan down the road—the great hydropathic hotel, built in 1878, being still very much to the fore, and a noted centre for conferences and events. Whether this well was the same as the Bishop's Well sometimes referred to, is not clear. Beyond Ramoyle, the A.9 sends off a branch at Duthieston, leading to Kinbuck and Cromlix; and at this fork is the great Queen Victoria School for the sons of soldiers, sailors and airmen, a famous military educational establishment with its own chapel and playing-fields.

Dunblane has had a chequered story. It was burned by Kenneth MacAlpine, by the Britons of Strathclyde and by Danish pirates. Its bishops included Nicholas Balmyle, Chancellor of Scotland and a helper of Bruce, who was succeeded by Abbot Maurice of Inchaffray, the hero-king's friend, who dispensed communion before taking active part in the Battle of Bannockburn. Also three Chisholms of Cromlix, the middle one said to be a robber and fornicator! Much involved in the Jacobite struggles, Dunblane saw stirring scenes when Sheriffmuir was fought on its doorstep in 1715. And thirty years later Prince Charles held a levee at old Balhaldies House, the house of the then chief of MacGregor. For some odd reason, Charles II conferred on the heir of the English Duke of Leeds, Peregrine Osborne, the title of Viscount Dunblane, in 1675.

Today the little town is a place well worth visiting, rather than bypassing—even though in 1658 the English traveller Richard Franck declared: "Dirty Dunblane—let us pass it by and not cumber our discourse with so inconsiderable a corporation." Eloquent Mr. Franck!

Dunkeld. This famous town, although so small, little larger than a modest village, has a name which has resounded loudly in Scots history, as the seat of one of its most ancient and influential bishoprics. If it appears remote from the main stream of Scottish life today, it was not always so; for it lies only 12 miles north-west of Scone, as the crow flies, where, after the merging of the Pictish and Scottish kingdoms, was the capital. Moreover, it is set immediately at the southern throat of the narrow and steep Pass of Dunkeld, where the Tay breaks out of the true Highlands, so that it was always a strategic place. It was not until General Wade built his military road that there was anything such north of here; and we read that the Duke of Atholl, from Dunkeld House, took 13 hours by sedan-chair, to reach his main seat at Blair Atholl only 17 miles north, so rough was the going. So it was always a frontier town. It is claimed as the site of Pictish Orrea, one of their five original cities. Its name is thought to derive either from the dun of the Caledonians, or the dun of the Keledi or Culdees—which dun, or stronghold, was perched on the top of the isolated hillock of King's Seat, now within the grounds of Dunkeld House Hotel. There are the remains of another hilltop fort a little to the east of this.

What seems certain is that King Conal of the Picts built a monastery here in 570, for St. Columba, who preached for six months in the neighbourhood, and whose St. Colme's Well is still pointed out in the mouth of the Pass. This became the foremost ecclesiastical establishment in the land, and a long line of Culdee abbots ruled in the Celtic Church. At least one, Mathal MacFergus, is referred to also as Archbishop of Fortrenn; but archbishop was not a title used by the Celtic hierarchy, which was basically monastic rather than secular. One, most famous, was Crinan the Seneschal (killed A.D. 1045) who married Bethoc, daughter of Malcolm II, and whose son became King Duncan, murdered by MacBeth, when nearby Birnam Wood marched to Dunsinane. In 1127 the Romish episcopate of Dunkeld superseded the old Celtic polity, and a new series of powerful bishops followed. These included Bishop Sinclair, 'Bruce's own bishop', who built the choir of the cathedral in 1318; Bishop de Cardney, who built the nave in 1406; and Bishop Lauder, responsible for the Great Tower, in 1469. This splendid cathedral was wrecked, by command of the Regent Moray, at the Reformation, so that the seven-bayed nave, to the west, became a roofless ruin. But the four-bayed choir was re-roofed in 1600, and has long been used as the parish church. The whole building is very fine, and most charmingly set in attractive ancient woodland at the riverside, excellently cared for. The place is full of interest. There is a Pictish Apostles' Stone, depicting the miracle of the Loaves and Fishes, and another red-stone cross-slab; a Lepers' Squint; a whipping pillar; the great 'She' Bible of 1611—so called because of the correction of a misprint; the decapitated effigy of Bishop Sinclair; and, grimly amusing, the magnificent tomb of that prince of scoundrels and Prince of Scotland, the Wolf of Badenoch, whose larger-than-life effigy lies behind the handsome modern carved oak screen designed by Sir Robert Lorimer. He never failed to assail the Church during his savage career, sacking and burning Elgin Cathedral—yet here he lies enshrined in holy pomp with laudatory inscriptions, and even a lion at his foot, the mark of a Crusader! Apt it is that it was Sir Donald Currie, the shipowner, who in 1908 restored the choir and presented the great stained-glass window— for he was the modern laird of Garth Castle, built by the said Wolf to terrorise this area. There are two fine tempera paintings in the base of the Tower.

The palace of the bishops—or one of them, for they had three others at Cluny, Perth and Edinburgh—stood just to the south-west, but is now gone.

The old town of Dunkeld clustered round the cathedral; but it was burned, all but three houses, in 1689, when, after Killiecrankie, the victorious Jacobite Highlanders besieged the cathedral which Colonel Cleland of the Cameronians held against them. He died there—but not before his men set fire to the town, to drive out the Highlanders who sniped at them from the houses. Dunkeld was rebuilt next year on the present site, to the east. These houses have been saved and handsomely restored by the National Trust for Scotland. There are no fewer than 20 of them renewed, and a delightful sequestered but vital group they form, in the former Chanonry. In the centre, the Town Cross, 20 feet high and with four jougs attached, was replaced by a fountain in memory of a Duke of Atholl in 1864. But on one of the houses, the standard ell measurement, in iron, still survives, set up here by the Chapman Society. Near by is the Scottish Horse Regimental Museum. There is a National Trust Information Centre. Behind the houses, to the north, is the artificial mound known as Stanley Hill, now part of a park—not ancient but thrown up as a pleasaunce in 1730 by the same Duke of Atholl who named the village of Stanley after his English wife.

The remainder of the little town tends to be dominated by hotels —and by the rush of traffic on the busy A.9 highway which threads its narrow street. But it is delightfully set amidst lofty wooded hills, and makes a good centre for visiting Northern Perthshire. The fine seven-arched bridge over the Tay was built in 1809, by Telford, mainly at the expense of the much-loved 4th Duke, at a cost of £33,000. For long, one of its land-based arches was used as the town gaol.

Dunkeld House, the former ducal seat, lies to the north-west, in a great wooded estate. The mansion itself, now a hotel, is surprisingly modest in style, considering, and of no great antiquity. A former, greater house lay to the east. It is all very pleasant. Near by are two great larch trees, imported from the Tyrol by Menzies of Culdares in 1738, alleged to be the original progenitors of all the Scottish larches—though this is contested by Dawick in Peeblesshire, which claims an earlier importation of 1725. One, just behind

75

the hotel, has astonishingly contorted roots. A standing-stone known as *Poll nan Gobhair*, near the north lodge-house, is said to be the grave of a Highland chieftain—though the name means the hole or pit of the goat! Behind rears the great precipitous hill of Craig-y-Barns, above the King's Pass, beloved of rock-climbers. On top is a rocking-stone, supported on three fragments; and there are caves below. A small vein of copper was discovered here, but not worked.

In the vicinity of Dunkeld is much of interest, but this is dealt with under Birnam, Dowally, Strathbraan etc. The Dunkeld Royal School, founded in 1567, is now situated in modern premises at Birnam. And at Newtyle, 2 miles along the wooded road to Caputh, are two standing-stones, alleged to relate to two 10th century Danish warriors killed here. At Newtyle, too, the burghers of Dunkeld were granted the right to quarry stone from the Duke's hillside!

Dunning. Dunning must be one of those places, in Central Scotland, most frequently signposted and infrequently visited. Large numbers of finger-posts beckon the traveller towards Dunning from many main roads north and south of the Ochils; and indeed it is itself a very hub of roads, but small and unhurrying ones, not main roads. For it is not on the road to anywhere special, and remains sequestered and but little visited, nestling in the northern lap of the hills.

There is much to see here. The village, although not a burgh, is a quaint brown-stone place of some size and character which gives an excellent impression of the Scots country burgh of the past. Although an ancient community, and looking it, nevertheless there are no buildings of great age; for it was one of those burned by the Earl of Mar after the Jacobite defeat at Sheriffmuir in 1715, all but one house being destroyed. The thorn-tree planted to commemorate this event, in the centre of the village, survived until 1936; but was replaced by another a year later to celebrate the Coronation of George VI and Queen Elizabeth.

Fortunately the church of St. Serf, or Servanus, was spared; and it is both very fine and disappointing. Its tower is splendid, one of a small group of similar edifices, of which Muthill is another, dating from the 12th century, rising in three unequal stages to a saddle-roof 75 feet high. Unfortunately the large church itself, replacing an earlier work in 1810, is plain and dull, also not made the most of. And the tower is not kept in the best of repair. A very fine Norman arch, with dog-toothed ornamentation, which had been bricked up and buried at the foot of the tower, was discovered during a repair. An old Celtic cross-slab stands internally near by, scarcely to be seen in a dark corner. There are two hog-backed gravestones. Outside the kirkyard gate, in Tron Square, is what appears to be the shaft of a market-cross, built into the wall, to which is still attached the chain for a jougs-collar, the collar itself having only gone within living memory.

Just to the north of the village is the Park, which pleasingly commemorates Dunning village's links with its lord. An inscribed stone, under the Rollo crest, describes how this park was presented to the parish by John, 12th Lord Rollo of Duncrub, in 1946, to emphasise over 550 years of friendship between the families of Dunning and that of Duncrub—which latter obtained the barony in 1380, and is still in possession. Duncrub House has recently been demolished, its walled-garden is now a commercial rose-nursery, and the episcopal chapel, though still standing, is now a store; but Lord Rollo still lives in the Dunning 'suburb' of Newton of Pitcairn, to the south-east. Not far from the Park is a standing-stone alleged to mark the site of the ancient Battle of Duncrub.

As indicated, roads radiate from Dunning like spokes of a wheel. That to the west, B.8062, flanking Duncrub, leads, after a mile, to the small, wooded estate of Keltie Castle, lying snugly under Rossie Law. This is a most attractive and sturdy laird's house of the late 16th century, on the L-plan, with an older nucleus. It has a most unusual angle-turret corbelled out above first-floor level at one corner, a defensive feature containing no fewer than five shot-holes. In 1454 William Bonar de Keltie witnessed a charter in which a perpetual liberty to fish for eels, in a pool called Polpeffray, was granted to the Abbot of Inchaffray, on condition that he prayed constantly for the souls of the granter, his wife and son. In 1692 Keltie was bought by a scion of the Drummonds of Culdees. Near its gateway, at the roadside, is a cairn to one Maggie Wall, who was burnt here, as a witch, in 1657. Local ladies still take turns at the duty of whitening-in the lettering of this sad memorial.

One of the roads southwards is the picturesque route, B.934, to Yetts of Muckhart, which climbs over Dunning Common—at over a thousand feet higher and 4 miles distance, a rather inconvenient public amenity for the villagers. It rises by the side of a deep dell, and about half-way up, after passing the Victorian sham castle of Kippen, out on the braeside of the Black Hill of Kippen is the Gray Stone, or locally, The Old Man, an oddly-shaped, isolated monolith. Whatever this commemorates, the view from this point is quite magnificent. Another of these spoke-like roads runs eastwards to Invermay, and about a mile along, in the estate of Garvock House, are the scanty grass-grown remains of Ha' Towers, oddly-named former castellated seat of the Grahams. Still another road is perhaps the most adventurous of all, that past Pitcairns and leading up into the remote, hidden Ochils valleys of Condie and Struie. This rises from 160 to 823 feet in not much over a mile, but in most attractive scenery with fine vistas. Once on the high ground, it continues pleasantly down the Binzean Burn, eventually dropping, by a dramatic hairpin bend, to Path Struie hamlet deep in its little glen. Here one exciting route probes, by more testing gradients, by Path of Condie and Stronachie Distillery, to Milnathort in Kinross-shire; and another climbs on eastwards to Glenfarg and also Milnathort. The remains of Struie Castle, in the garden of Mains farmhouse, show only a circular stair-tower with shot-holes.

Errol. This is a famous name, largely because of the great part played in Scottish history by the Earls of Erroll (spelt with an extra l), hereditary Lord High Constables of Scotland, and chiefs of Clan Hay. Errol itself is a large village, almost a little town, in the centre of the Carse of Gowrie, surrounded by its own parish. The village is attractive, standing on a discernible ridge in the level carselands, and retains an old-fashioned and unspoiled air. Many of the houses, which tend to be set down rather at random, are pleasingly colour-washed, while the orchards of fruit trees are notable. There is a small triangular market-place—fairs used to be held in July and October—and though the cross in the centre is in fact only a drinking-fountain erected to celebrate Queen Victoria's jubilee, it is built in the traditional style, and looks well.

There is a large and ambitious Gothic parish church, of 1831, designed by the well-known Gillespie Graham, having a lofty square tower and seating for no fewer than 1450. The earlier church is now gone, but its graveyard survives, across the street, to the south, with a central burial-vault of the Errol Park families, which probably represents the site of the original chapel. Here are many ancient gravestones, including a fine but very weather-worn heraldic memorial against the west wall. To the east adjoins what was formerly the Free church, now, suitably or otherwise, a coffin factory and joinery works. Further to the medieval castleton, the village developed as a settlement of Flemish weavers, flax having been grown extensively in the surrounding carselands.

Dominating the head or western end of the village, is the large wooded estate of Errol Park, with its great mansion, rebuilt after a disastrous fire in 1874. This property was historically granted, about 1160, by William the Lyon to William de la Haye, his Butler. who became ambassador to England in 1199. But legend has it that the Hays were here much earlier, long before these Norman barons. The story goes that at the Battle of Luncarty, in 990, the peasant ancestor of the line turned up unexpectedly and saved the day for King Kenneth III, he and his sons and followers laying about them with ox-yokes to such effect that the Danes were quite demoralised. In reward for which the King gave the Hays all the land that their hawk might fly over at one flight. Which is the reason for the various Hawk and Falcon Stones in the Carse—and why the present Countess's sons are called Merlin and Peregrine. Be that as it may, in the Wars of Independence, Sir Gilbert Hay of Errol was one of the Bruce's staunchest supporters and was made High Constable hereditarily. William, Lord Hay, 9th chief, was created Earl of Erroll in 1452; and Diana, Countess of Erroll in her own right is now 23rd holder of the earldom and *Mac Garaidh Mor*, 31st chief of Clan Hay, High Constable. But though the titles remain, the Hays parted with the property in 1634—though they left descendants in other properties in the Carse. Whereafter the barony of Errol passed through a large number of hands. There is a traditional reason. Allegedly, one of the lairds was cursed at the burning of a witch, to the effect that the property would not pass from father to son thereafter—a favourite sentence. One of these short-time lairds was J. P. Allen, buried in the graveyard vault, who did much to bring industry to the area. Amongst other activities, he reclaimed a large acreage from the Tay by building enclosing embankments; and here he founded a harbour, still called Port Allen, although now only the farm, one other house, and various vestiges remain, at the end of a mile-long straight road south of the village. Here woven goods, tiles and fine sandstone from Clashbennie quarries were exported; and lime and coal was imported; and there was a daily ferry across to Newburgh in Fife. The harbour works included a sluice contrivance, still there, to counter the effect of the tide; and the bed of the creek is slabbed with sandstone, under the mud. Iron rings for tying vessels to remain amongst the grass.

Near by, to the north-east, is the former estate of Murie, of which only the walled gardens remain, with a modern cemetery for the area set in unusual style in these rural surroundings. There is a tree-grown mound, 20 feet high, on the property, known as the Law Knoll, with an avenue of oaks leading thereto, said to be the ancient justice seat of the barony. This is the highest point in the parish. A mile farther north-east, in lower ground, is the thriving tile-works of Inchcoonans. This area of good clay has long been famed for its tiles and field drain-pipes. Another inch, Inchmartine lies at the north-east extremity of the parish, with an estate, and an ancient ruined chapel, which belonged to Coupar Angus Abbey, called the Church of the Blessed Virgin of Inchmartine, with old burial-ground. Still another inch lies between Errol and Inchmartine—Inchmichael, where there is now a garage and filling-station on the busy A.85 highway. These inches were islands, when all the carse was undrained and largely under water.

Errol is well worth visiting, the 'capital' of the Carse still—even though it cannot now rise to the eleven houses for the sale of intoxicating liquors which it boasted in 1837.

Forgandenny, Dunbarney and Dron. These rural communities lie south of the Earn, nearing its junction with Tay, below the northern slopes of the Ochils. Forgandenny is the largest and western-most, a pleasant village and a parish, 3 miles west of Bridge of Earn. Although now fertile and fair, much of the land has been reclaimed from waste and the Earn flood-plain. The village has an attractive older street to the north of that flanking the B.935, and here a good enclave of modern housing has been erected. Nearby is the very interesting parish church, still basically of pre-Reformation architecture, long and low, but most pleasingly decorated and furnished within. It has an additional 18th century wing, used as an organ-loft in memory of the Lords Ruthven of

Freeland. In the porch is a memorial stone to Andrew Brodie, one of the Covenanting martyrs, shot in 1678. There are various heraldic stones, and some old tombs in the kirkyard. A notable succession of immediately post-Reformation ministers called Row officiated here for a century.

The large estate of Freeland to the north and east of the village, is now the well-known Strathallan School—a rather confusing name, since it is a long way from the Allan Water. But it is a very fine establishment, with some notable modern buildings, as well as the former mansion of the Ruthvens, which contains a nucleus of old work. On the other side of the village, the former large Oliphant estate of Rossie had suffered an eclipse, its mansion a ruin, although the impressive walled-garden remains. The Oliphants, sprung from nearby Gask, were a great family in this area, settled in Strathearn by Bruce. Rossie Ochil, and Condie, up in the hills to the south, were also Oliphant estates.

Farther to the east is Dunbarney, another parish, now without a village of the name although once there was such. It was in the vicinity of Dunbarney House, where its ancient burial-ground and site of its church may still be seen. The latter was moved nearer to Bridge of Earn in 1684—no doubt for the laird's convenience rather than the villagers'. About half a mile to the south-east are the remains of an old stone windmill, apparently of the 17th century. Not many of these survive in Scotland; the growth of plantations of tall trees in estates, however good for amenity, tended to interfere with the steady breezes required to work the sails, and water-mills took over:

> Blaw wind, blaw, and let me mak my bread:
> For whan ye are awa, it's hungry I maun bide.

South of the B.935 road, 2 miles east of Forgandenny, is the interesting community called Pitkeathly Wells, sometimes spelt Pitcaithly. There is a loch of this name high in the Ochils 3 miles to the south; but the wells are not far down a side-road. There were five of these springs, known as East, West, the Spout, Dunbarney and Southpark Wells, renowned from time immemorial for their medicinal properties, especially for skin ailments. They became so popular that, in 1832, the village of Bridge of Earn was much enlarged to accommodate the visitors. Two of the saline wells were still in use until comparatively recently; indeed the renowned firm of Schweppes took them over in connection with its own mineral-water production. Schweppes are still there, seeming strange in these rural surroundings, but their production has ceased, and one of the wells with its bath-house has been converted into a private house.

A mile farther south, within the modern estate of Glenearn, are the chapel and fortified house of the extraordinarily-named Ecclesiamagirdle—pronounced locally Exmagriddle—a corruption of the Gaelic, meaning the church of St. Grill or Grillon, said to have been one of the twelve harpers of Columba. The chapel was a dependency of the Abbey of Lindores in the 12th century, and its remains are in a grove of yews, the graveyard containing another Covenanting memorial to one, Thomas Small, 'who died for Religion, Covenant, King and Cuntrie 18the September 1645'. The 17th century laird's house is picturesquely situated near by on the edge of a lochan in woodland, a quite small but most attractive T-planned fortalice, with the usual crowstepped gables, stair-turret and watch-chamber, recently restored as dwelling-house after a period of neglect. After the Reformation, the church-lands were erected into a temporal lordship, and Carmichael of Balmedie built the house in 1629.

Another 2 miles eastwards is the foothills hamlet of Dron, also a parish on its own, a pleasant retired place amongst the swelling green Ochils which cluster round Glenfarg. The church was built in 1826, but the site is ancient, and there are more Covenanting graves here. Just behind is the imposing tall tower-house of Balmanno Castle, rising whitewashed amongst its old trees, a late 16th century stronghold of the Murray family, restored by the famous architect Sir Robert Lorimer—who, for once, rather spoiled the effect by adding an over-high caphouse, with ogee-roof, to the already tall stair-tower. There was once a family of Balmanno of that Ilk. High on Balmanno Hill is a great rocking-stone, 10 feet by 7, readily moved by hand pressure. There was once another pre-Reformation chapel in the parish, where later was the Mill of Pottie, at the mouth of Glenfarg, but this has now disappeared.

Forteviot, Dupplin and Aberdalgie.

Forteviot is a resounding name, from the days when Scotland was young. This was capital of the Pictish kingdom of Fortrenn. Here was the palace of Angus MacFergus (731–61) and a succession of kings until MacBeth and Malcolm III. Here died the great Kenneth MacAlpine. From being a capital it declined to a royal hunting-seat—but still great things were done here. Today it is a small, quiet village, of mainly modern housing, depending on the great estate of Dupplin Castle, picturesquely situated in the green haughlands where the Water of May joins the winding Earn, some six miles south-east of Perth.

There is little enough to speak of the colourful past. At the east end is the attractively-sited parish church, erected in 1778 but modernised, in an old kirkyard; this succeeded the church which Angus MacFergus dedicated to St. Andrew. He it was who, with Achaius, King of Scots, took part in the great battle with Athelstan (or so it is said) in East Lothian, perceived the white cloud in the blue sky, shaped like St. Andrew's Cross, and both vowed, if given the victory over the English invader, to adopt Andrew as patron of their realms. In the present church is a typical Celtic saint's bell, though lacking its clapper; which saint it belonged to does not seem to be known. Also an old font, heraldically decorated; and in the porch, are six fragments of the former Celtic cross-slab of Dronachty, the largest portion showing a spirited rendering of a bull tossing a victim. There is, too, a bowl-like piscina. Other Pictish ornamental stones from Forteviot are now in the Museum of Antiquities, Edinburgh, including the fine sculptured arched lintel from the ancient palace.

This palace stood, it is believed, on the slight mound at the east of the village, opposite the church, and named the Halyhill, now grown with conifers. Near by is the Miller's Acre, or Milton. There is a tradition that King Malcolm Canmore, slayer of MacBeth, was an illegitimate son of King Duncan by the miller of Forteviot's daughter. This was certainly a favourite residence of that monarch. In the Miller's Acre Edward Baliol, puppet-King of Scots, camped with his army before the shameful Battle of Dupplin.

The parish of Forteviot is scattered in three separate sections, one of which used to be the distinct parish of Muckersie. To the north, across Earn, is the long ridge of Dupplin, actually in Aberdalgie parish, dominated by its great estate, now the property of Lord Forteviot, of the Perth whisky family of Dewar. From this ridge the views over Strathearn are superb. Here Baliol's quite small army defeated the vastly larger Scots force under the Regent Mar in 1332, three years after Bruce's death. A fine stone cross stands on the open hillside west of the farm of Bankhead, often erroneously said to commemorate the battle. It is in fact a much earlier handsome Celtic Church ecclesiastical cross, elaborately carved.

Aberdalgie and Dupplin parishes were united in 1618. Even so this is a small parish, lying between Perth and the Earn, with no real village, only the hamlet of the Kirkton; but it is a most pleasantly rural area, with fine vistas. The parish church was built in 1773, and is the burial-place of the Earl of Kinnoull's family, Hays, Viscounts of Dupplin, who formerly owned the estate.

Not to be confused with Aberdalgie is Ardargie, at the other, southern, side of Forteviot, in the attractive glen of the Water of May. This is very different country, with steep, narrow, wooded foothill valleys. Ardargie itself is a former mansion, now a hotel. Near by is the large estate of Invermay, associated with Scott's *Redgauntlet*. There is a large Georgian mansion; but standing beside it, and still kept in repair, is an attractive, small late 16th century fortalice, L-planned and added to in 1633, its stair-tower surmounted by a neat little watch-chamber reached by a tiny stair turret. The Belshes, formerly of Invermay, though a small family, played a not inconsiderable part in history. They stemmed from the Norman Ralf Belasyse, whose descendants arrived here in the 16th century, on marrying a Murray heiress. They were buried in the little churchyard of Muckersie, the old ruined and former parish church standing in a wood above the farm of the same name. *The Birks of Invermay* is quite a well-known lyric, adapted by David Mallet.

From Ardargie two interesting hill-roads climb southwards and south-eastwards over the Ochils to Glenfarg and Milnathort respectively, by lonely hill farms, deep hidden valleys, and with magnificent views back over Strathearn. That to Milnathort is dealt with under Dunning; that to Glenfarg makes a most attractive run, passing the remote property of Rossie Ochil, and reaching 859 feet above the large reservoir of Glenfarg Waterworks at Deuglie. At the little community of Abbot's Deuglie, there are the remains of a stone circle near the highest point of the road, with one upright monolith incorporated in a fence, another recumbent close by, with some old Caledonian pines near by. At Abbot's Deuglie also is a small early 18th century house with crowstepped gable, and lintel with initials A.B. and K.B. dated 1732, now used as the cowhouse of a croft.

Fortingall. Here is one of the most interesting, and at the same time picturesque, villages in all Scotland. It lies almost in the yawning mouth of Glen Lyon, 3 miles north-west of Kenmore, a single attractive street of houses, some of them thatched, a good hotel, and a fine church with most ancient graveyard. To the east stands Glenlyon House, mainly modern with an ancient nucleus, celebrated as the home of Campbell of Glenlyon, who played so dastardly a part in the Massacre of Glencoe. And behind rises the steep, rocky, wooded escarpment on the crest of which perches the site of Dun Geal, a fort of unrecorded age. Or not quite unrecorded, for here, it is alleged, was the birthplace of no less than Pontius Pilate. If this seems scarcely credible, here is the story. The father, a Roman officer, was sent on a mission of peace to Pictish King Metellanus, whose seat was at this Dun Geal. Whether the envoy brought his wife with him—which seems unlikely—or whether the mother of the child was a member of Metellanus's household, we are not told. But here Pilate was allegedly born. A curious 5-foot-high staff, iron-cased in leather with a pair of extended wings at the top, was shown to the 18th century traveller, Pennant, as relic of the visit. Be this as it may, not far away, near Bridge of Lyon, is what is thought is a Roman camp, said to be an outpost of the Emperor Serverus, beyond Tay, whose grass-grown mounds may be traced. This certainly seems a more likely birthplace.

But Fortingall can do even better than this. It claims to have the oldest piece of growing vegetation in all Europe. In the kirkyard is the famous yew tree, accepted by experts as at least 3000 years old. In Pennant's time its circumference was 56 feet—although it is now much reduced from that. Beneath it lie buried the Stewarts of Garth. Also Sir Donald Currie of Garth, the shipowner who in 1900 restored this attractive village. Near by is the Campbell tomb.

The church is handsomely furnished, and contains a plethora of interest. Behind the porch is Adamnan's font. He was Abbot of Iona in 697, and died hereabouts in 704. Inside the building is a 7th century monk's bell, shaped like a large alpine cow-bell. Another bell here preserved is the third and last in Scotland cast by Johannes Sprecht of Rotterdam, in 1765. There are also a number of fragments of Celtic stone carvings, on the chancel window-ledge, and a pewter Communion plate dated 1740; while the chancel itself has a modern screen by the famous Sir Robert Lorimer. Altogether a place of significance—not unsuitably so when we consider that the minister's parish extends to 204,346½ acres, or 319 square miles; of which, however, we can be relieved to hear, 7663½ acres are of water.

To the east, near the church, is a Caledonian stone circle of nine uprights in groups of three; and there are no fewer than 14 circular forts in the area, presumably Pictish. Sir James MacGregor, the famous Dean of Lismore, was also Vicar of Fortigall, and died here in 1551. He compiled the *Book of the Dean of Lismore* in which many Gaelic poems of the 14th, 15th and 16th centuries are collected.

The Bridge of Lyon, less than a mile to the west, is a picturesque hump-backed structure of three arches, plus a small one as safety-valve—needed not infrequently. It has a panel *Archibald Ballantyne his work* 1793.

Fowlis-Wester. There are two Fowlis parishes in Perthshire, Easter, near Dundee, and this one, 5 miles east of Crieff. The parish is large, comprising much of the empty uplands which divide Glen Almond from Strathearn, as well as a sizeable slice of the Earn's plain. But the village is small, situated half a mile north of the main A.85 road from Perth to Crieff, on the rising slopes of the Braes of Fowlis, looking out across Strathearn.

The place has the charm of quiet remoteness. But it was an important enough place once; for not only did the main road formerly run through it but the great castle of the later, Stewart, Earls of Strathearn, now only grass-grown mounds, lay half a mile to the east, at the side of a ravine; and this was the Castleton. Here, too, large cattle sales were held annually; and its inn must have been a busy hostelry. The ancient church of St. Bean, or Beanus, still remains as the parish kirk, however, after seven centuries.

This is a typical long, low, pre-Reformation building, most excellently restored in 1927 as memorial for the First World War, to make a highly attractive place of worship. It dates from the 13th century, replacing a still earlier church. The Pictish Symbol Stone, displayed within, was discovered at the restoration, and may date from St. Bean's time. He was a great-grandson of King Aodh Dubh, or Dark Hugh, of Leinster, one of seven brothers who became missionaries, dying in 720. The stone is a fascinating thing, richly carved, with Celtic cross and much interlacing decoration, depicting Jonah being swallowed by the whale. But most significant, it is unfinished; for sadly, a large portion of the base has broken off during carving, and though the artist has sought for a while to continue the work over the broken area, he has given up—a small tragedy in stone. The church also has a lepers' squint, for sufferers to watch the celebration of Mass from outside. There is a fine lych-gate at the kirkyard entrance, bearing the date 1644, with Latin-inscribed lintel.

In the village centre is the Cross of Fowlis; but this does not really belong here, having been transported from Balnacroisk, at the mouth of the Sma' Glen. It is another fine Celtic cross, 10 feet high, of red sandstone, lavishly carved, with horsemen, animals and decoration. These magnificent cross-slabs indicate a high level of artistic culture amongst our Celtic forefathers whom southern historians are so apt to write off as mere barbarians.

Fowlis-Wester parish extends northwards right to the Almond, over lofty uplands traversed by numerous tracks for walkers. Near the steeply-climbing road to Buchanty, in open moorland to the left about a mile up, is a highly unusual double concentric stone circle, 54 feet in circumference, comprising 40 stones, all now recumbent but one. The views from here are very fine. To the south, where the village road joints A.85, is a standing-stone, cromlech and large cairn.

To the west lies the great estate of Abercairney, once boasting the largest house in Perthshire, a vast neo-Gothic mansion recently demolished in favour of a more convenient modern house. The present laird, 21st of his line, is Major James Stirling-Home-Drum-mond-Moray, and the Moray of Abercairney pedigree is as long as their name. The first here was Sir John Moray of Drumsagard, scion of Bothwell, kinsman of the Patriot Andrew Moray, who married the 7th Earl of Strathearn's daughter in 1320. The estate is richly wooded, and amongst its fine trees are some of the largest in the country. The scanty remains of Inchbrakie Castle, in another ancient estate, lie to the south. And a third property, Cultoquhey, adjoins, a seat of the Maxtones since 1410, now a hotel.

To the east, more modern forestry has taken over in the Keillour and Gorthy area. Another side-road probes northwards here to Glen Almond, by modern Keillour Castle with its splendid and re-nowned gardens, threading the wooded hills. And south of the A.85 was the birthplace of the Hero of Barossa, General Sir Thomas Graham of Balgowan, who lies buried under a monstrosity of a tomb in Methven churchyard. His earthly mansion is now no more.

Gartmore. Two miles south of Aberfoyle, but well up to the west, off the main A.81 road, lies the quite large village of Gart-more, isolated amongst rising foothills of the Ben Lomond range, and facing south towards the Campsie Fells and east over the great levels of the Flanders Moss. It is a very lovely situation, although the village itself could be more lovely; taken in hand, however, Gartmore could be attractive. It consists mainly of a long street climbing from south to north. A number of houses are, these days, being refurbished as 'commuter-homes' for people whose work is in Glasgow—which lies less than twenty-five miles to the south.

The church, in its old graveyard, was built as a chapel-of-ease in 1790—for this was then part of Port of Menteith parish. It was greatly improved in 1872. There is an attractive little private burial-ground for the Cayzer family, lately of Gartmore House, behind. The former Free Church, further up the hill at a widening of the street, never was beautiful; but now, neglected and desolate, it is an eyesore.

Gartmore House, in its large estate to the east, is now an institution, its great and comparatively modern mansion facing out over the Moss. Before the Cayzer baronets, this was for centuries the property of the Cunninghame-Graham family, of which the 19th laird, the famous Don Roberto, writer, politico and fighter for causes, was the most notable. The old castle of Gartmore, though very ruinous, still stands, lower down the hill, near the gardens; and enough survives to show that it has been a pleasing little fortalice of the late 16th century, with circular stair-tower and angle-turrets—the sort of place which still might be saved and built up into a fine home.

The Kelty Water, a major tributary which runs to join the Forth in the Gartrenich Moss 2 miles to the east, flows to the south of Gartmore, in its valley; and where the road crosses this, by an old bridge, is the joint hamlet of Chapelarroch on the north bank and Dalmary on the south. This is over the border into Stirlingshire. Chapelarroch is now only a farm; but here was the site of a church dedicated to the Virgin Mary, formerly belonging to the Priory of Inchmahome. There was the usual graveyard, and ruins were still visible last century; but no traces remain. Here was also an inn, made famous by Rob Roy, who much frequented it. So also did the Duke of Montrose's factor, Graham of Killearn, who used it as collecting-point for his master's rents. Here, in 1716, Rob kidnapped Graham, took his rents, and led the factor prisoner to the islet of Eilean Dubh in Loch Katrine, where he held him, in retribution for his shameful molestation of Rob's wife—though eventually he was released, unharmed. Dalmary, which means the Field of Mary, and no doubt was the manse and glebe of the priest in charge of the chapel, is across the burn. Oddly enough, a mile to the north-west, and nearer Gartmore, is the former croft of Spittal —which indicates that there has been a hospital or religious refuge of some sort here; so apparently this area was once important ecclesiastically, empty as it is today. Seventy yards north-east of the croft are the remains of an ancient quarry for mill-stones.

Gask. There is not one place called Gask, but many. It is not even a parish, but two—Findo-Gask and Trinity-Gask. There is an ancient estate of Gask House, but no village of that name—although the village of Clathy lies in the middle of the area. And there is a ruined castle called Gascon Hall, near Mill of Gask, which some assume to be the origin of the name. But there are in fact many Gasks scattered over the country, some with the prefix *Fin*, meaning white or pale; so that Gask is probably the corruption of the Gaelic word *gasg*, or *gasgan*, meaning a tailing ridge. This

Grandtully Castle

Huntingtower Castle

St. Mary's pre-Reformation Church, Grandtully. Tempera-painted ceiling

Innerpeffray. Ancient Library

Gask area of mid-Strathearn is certainly a low, hog's-back ridge some five miles long, lying between the River Earn and the Cowgask Burn to the north.

This ridge is responsible for a very special feature—the fine series of no fewer than nine Roman Signal Stations, marking the line of the Roman road from the camp at Innerpeffray to the Tay. The road has a breadth of 20 feet, and is metalled, under the turf, with a compact paving of rough stones. The Signal Stations are at intervals of mostly less than a mile, a unique series in Scotland, even though only sites now. The seventh from the west is at Witch Knowe, near Clathy, where sad executions took place in the bad old days. The whole area is now becoming much afforested.

There are two Gask Houses, the old and the new—although the latter dates from 1801. The famous Auld Hoose o' Gask, renowned in song, is near by, and unfortunately has been so enthusiastically but unknowledgeably 'restored' as to be now little more than a fancified folly. Sir William Oliphant received broad lands here, in the broken earldom of Strathearn, from Robert the Bruce, becoming Lord of Gasknes and Aberdalgie. His descendant was created Lord Oliphant, in 1458. The 5th Lord, 'a base and unworthy man', sold all his great estates in 1600, but Gask itself was purchased by his cousin. The succeeding lairds were fervent Jacobites, and Prince Charles Edward breakfasted here on 11th September 1745, leaving a lock of his hair as family heirloom. Here was born the famous Caroline Oliphant, who became Lady Nairne (1766–1878) and wrote *The Land o' the Leal*, *The Laird o' Cockpen* and other songs, including of course *The Auld Hoose*.

A mile to the south-west are the scanty remains of Gascon Hall, in a former orchard at the riverside. Tradition has it that William Wallace here encountered the ghost of Faudon, according to Blind Harry; but this has been a fortalice of much later date, and the original Gascon Hall is thought to have been sited about one and a half miles to the north-east, up on the ridge.

Findo-Gask is a parish but not a village. It has an attractive little whitewashed 18th century church, with graveyard, on the ridge east of Witch Knowe and Clathy, with fine views all around. Clathy hamlet is strangely placed on a small dead-end side-road 'in the middle of nowhere'. Houses here are being taken over and renovated, nevertheless—for it is in a highly scenic area only 7 miles from Perth.

Trinity-Gask—pronounced locally Tarnty—is another parish lacking a village, lying to the west of Findo, on the ridge. The church is at Kirkton, and is a fairly plain structure without special features. There is a story that it received its name on becoming the united parish of three, the others being the pre-Reformation parishes of Kinkell and Easter Gask—the latter having been sited at the spot still called Chapelhill a mile to the north. But this seems an unlikely derivation—especially as there was a renowned well, dedicated to the Holy Trinity, just south of the Manse, famed for its

G

cures and for affording protection against the plague and witch-craft. A curiously-sculptured standing-stone, 5½ feet high, known as the Borestone, no doubt of Celtic workmanship, was removed from here to Moncreiffe in 1884.

Laurence MacDonald, a humble stone-mason of Gask, so excelled in carving that, in 1822, the Oliphants took him to Rome, where he became a famous sculptor under the name of Lorenzo de Gasco.

Lower Glen Almond. The valley of the Almond is formed in two very distinct parts. The upper, reaching from its rise at 2750 feet, only 3 miles south of Loch Tay, for 17 miles eastwards to Fendoch and Buchanty at the foot of what is known as The Sma' Glen, is truly Highland, empty, narrow, amongst high heather mountains; the remaining 13 miles, to its junction with Tay 2 miles above Perth, is gentle and abruptly different, a wide and fertile green vale, cultivated and populous. When people talk about Glen Almond it is usually this to which they refer.

For some four miles up from Tay, the Huntingtower and Almond-bank area could hardly be described as a glen. Then, above Dalcrue Bridge, the gently rolling hills begin to close in, and for 9 miles embosom a smiling green valley of fields, woodland, small villages and estates, between the Highland Line to the north and the high moorland separating it from mid-Strathearn on the south. Roads serve both sides.

The lower part of this vale is called Logiealmond, and is now a parish of its own. It was renowned in the old days as the meeting-point of the sees of Dunblane, Dunkeld and St. Andrews, a place of conference for the three bishops. So the setting up of the famous episcopal boarding-school of Trinity College, Glenalmond here, in 1841, was entirely suitable. This great educational institution, one of the most famous in Scotland, occupies a delightful and extensive site on the rising south bank of the river, 5 miles up, founded not as any seminary for the training of priests but for general education with a religious background—not confined to Episcopalians. Prime Minister Gladstone, whose father was a founder, was one of the governors; the bishops of the Episcopal Church in Scotland being members of the council.

There are no villages or hamlets on this south side, which is more thickly wooded than the north. Four side-roads go off southwards, over the high ground to Strathearn, all productive of excellent views. There are a number of prehistoric monuments on these moorlands. On the north side there is more to inspect. After Lynedoch estate, described under Pitcairngreen, is the ancient property which gives Logiealmond its name—Logie House. This estate, now in the possession of the Earl of Mansfield, grew from an old fortalice set in a dramatic situation above a steep wooded gorge of the river. It has recently been demolished, save for a single circular stair-tower to mark the spot. Far back in time there was a family of Logie of that Ilk, descending from the Thanes of Logie, themselves probably a branch of the dynastic Celtic house of Strathearn. The widow of Sir John Logie, in 1363, married Bruce's son, David II, and so became Queen of Scotland. The Tower of Logie, passing by marriage to the Hays of Erroll, was known as 'a nest of Catholics' at the Reformation period.

North of Logie a passing-bay side-road leads off up into the big hills, to end at Little Glenshee—not to be confused with the better-known glen far to the north-east. This is a steep pass, by which a foot-track and former drove-road crosses over to Strath Braan; and the road thereto makes a pleasant run. Less than four miles up, it crosses a ford, and makes a sharp bend eastwards, leading in another 6 miles to Bankfoot, on the main A.9. The area around the mouth of Little Glenshee used to be known as the Barony of Mullion, or Moulin, an awkwardly detached portion of the parish of Redgorton, and looked on somewhat askance as a dangerously Hielant place.

Back on the Glenalmond B.8063, the hamlet of Chapelhill is reached, where is a hotel, a house or two and an abandoned church in its old graveyard. This has had a chequered career. Originally an ancient place of worship, it fell into ruin soon after the Reformation; then, owing the initiative of local folk, it was restored and reopened in 1834, becoming the church of the new parish of Logiealmond, with seating for 320. Now it is again deserted, the parish church being removed to Harrietfield.

This village should really be Heriotfield. It is attractively placed, facing south high above the river opposite Trinity College. It hides its church behind, to the north, a plain but pleasant building with a notable down-sloping floor to allow an excellent view of the pulpit, and a fine collection of pewter on display. The parish is now combined with Almondbank, and the Manse no longer contains the minister.

A mile beyond, a private road rises steeply for 2 miles, to lead to the heather hills and Logiealmond Lodge, following the rushing Milton Burn which there cascades in waterfalls. Up here were formerly great slate quarries in the hill-face. A great monolith, 12 feet high, known as the Kor Stone, stands isolated on the hillside north-east of Milton.

B.8063 continues for another 2 miles, and then descends steeply to the river at Buchanty Bridge, where it is joined by the south road. Here there is a picturesque den of chasms and pools and a small loch; also a school and house or two. At Buchanty the great Montrose erected his standard prior to the Battle of Tippermuir in 1644. The Sma' Glen can be seen opening right ahead, with the site of the Roman Camp at Fendoch to the left.

Glen Artney. Most people probably have heard vaguely of Glen Artney, thanks to Sir Walter Scott if nothing else, in *The Lady of the Lake* and *The Legend of Montrose*; but surprisingly few, by comparison, ever visit it. In fact, quite knowledgeable folk will confess that they do not know exactly where it is. Yet it is readily accessible from the populous parts of the country, and attractive once you are there—although there are finer glens. It strikes in a south-westerly direction into the Ben Vorlich–Stuc a Chroin group of mountains of South Perthshire, between Loch Earn and Callander, its entry being only 2 miles south of Comrie, and runs fairly straight into the hills for some seven miles. Oddly, its river is the Water of Ruchill —how it got the name of Artney is not clear. The road up, rising quickly from 250 to 600 feet, takes the south side of the glen, but contours high above the wooded valley-foot. There is a private road for some way up the other side, becoming a track; but the few houses are on the south side, save for two. The public road stops near Glenartney Lodge, but a foot-track continues westwards to Callander, another nine or ten miles, crossing the high 1000-foot watershed to the Glen of the Keltie Water. It is also possible to walk to Loch Earn-side, by leaving this footpath just over a mile up, and swinging right, northwards, along the valley of the Allt an Dubh Choirean, over the east shoulder of Ben Vorlich and so down Glen Vorlich to Ardvorlich and the road.

The public road up Glen Artney gives some fine views, especially towards the north-west, with deep side glens coming in from the Mor Bheinn–Halton-Sron na Maoile–Carn Labhruinn massif. The main Vorlich–Stuc a Chroin group are not well seen from here; it is not until a mile or so up the track beyond the road-end that their magnificent, craggy prospect opens out. Here the Water of Ruchill splits into a number of tributaries.

About half-way up the glen, the waterfall called Sput a Chleibh, or Spout of Dalness, lies far below the road. Nearly two miles on, the road dips and, beyond a narrow bridge where the Findhu Glen opens on the south, the remote little church of Glenartney sits high on a mound between the two waters, an inspiring if scarcely convenient situation for a place of worship. It is a fairly modern building, with Drummond heraldic decoration and no graveyard, and a brave place to have a functioning church.

The Forest of Glenartney, as it is still called, is of course a deer-forest—where as we all know, the stag at eve drank his fill; and where the Prince Consort Albert shot his first stag. Queen Victoria's husband was only a guest of the Drummonds; but long before his day this was a royal hunting forest, and a favourite with the Scots kings. The hereditary keepers were the Drummonds of Drummond Ernoch, down near Comrie—the name being the same as Earn, really Eireannach, meaning from Ireland, indicative of the early religious pioneers who came here to missionarise. In the late 16th century the then Drummond of Drummond Ernoch, coming across some deer-poaching MacGregors in his forest, had their ears cut off, as lesson. But MacGregors being as they were, they had their revenge. One day Drummond was ambushed, slain in a lonely corrie and decapitated. The head was then carried in a plaid to Ardvorlich House, where the absent Stewart laird's wife was Drummond's sister. Requested hospitality, she gave the visitors bread and cheese, and left them to it. When she returned, the MacGregors had gone—but her brother's head was on the table, with bread and cheese stuffed into the mouth. The poor woman, pregnant, lost her reason, and fled into the hills, where, eventually, at a loch still called the Lochan of the Woman, she gave birth to the heir of Ardvorlich. The tragedy did not end there, for the child grew up to become the Mad Major Stewart of Ardvorlich, a compulsive killer of MacGregors; not only that—in a mad rage one day he slew his own friend, a fellow-officer in Montrose's army, the Lord Kilpont, heir to the Earl of Airth. An old story, not forgotten on Loch Earn-side.

Glen Devon. This attractive Ochils valley is almost an unexpected foretaste of the Highlands, threaded by the A.823 Dunfermline–Crieff highway. It starts quite abruptly—for the south faces of the Ochils are very abrupt—at the interestingly-named Yetts of Muckhart (meaning Gates of the Swineherd) near where the clear-running Devon makes its spectacular 160 degrees bend to the west, in the Rumbling Bridge area. Only a short distance up the winding road, the B.934 forks off on its lonely but picturesque way to Dunning and Strathearn; while the main road continues twisting in its deep green valley, but high above the river.

Two miles up, road crosses river near the hamlet of Burnfoot, or Tormaukin, and the character of the glen changes, as it opens out into a verdant upland vale. Here are two hotels, one an old inn, the other converted from a sham-castellated mansion—which the uninitiated may tend to mistake for Glendevon Castle. From here a track climbs westwards up the side glen of Quhey, to a hill-bound loch.

For the next 3 miles road and river keep company between grassy pastoral hills and knowes, flanked by the small fields and farm-places of a scattered rural community, with small church, manse, laird's-house and post office and modern caravan-park, under the remote regard of 2004-foot Innerdownie to the west. Once it had a woollen mill and no fewer than five fairs a year. Glendevon House, midway up the glen, across the river, is a smallish classical mansion; but it is presumably on the site of an older house, for its Gallows Knowe is near by. Glendevon Castle, again, stands apart, high on a terrace of the east side of the valley, a tall and whitewashed tower-house mainly of the 17th century, but containing a much older nucleus, built on the Z-plan but now much altered as to roofline. The original castle is said to have belonged to the illustrious William, 8th Earl of Douglas, who was stabbed to death by his king, James II, at Stirling in 1452. It was presumably a hunting-seat. The 9-foot-thick east walling of the main block no doubt dates from this period. It is now a hotel.

Nearly a mile up, a bridge crosses the river to Wester Glensherup, and a track leads on up another little side glen to another loch, like that of Glen Quhey. At Glenhead Farm, the main road swings off to the north, to climb out of the valley, by a small pass at 900 feet, into Glen Eagles. The river, however, curves away west by south, and widens, by damming, to a large reservoir. The Devon does not end therein, nevertheless, but probes on for a further six miles or so into the empty hills—oddly enough, to rise, at 1800 feet, only about another six miles, as the crow flies, from where it eventually enters the Forth, after a winding course of 34 miles, near Alloa.

Glen Eagles. Glen Eagles is best known for its famous hotel and golf-courses—which is rather a pity. For fine as that great establishment is, it has little relevance to the glen—although a splendid prospect of the yawning V-shaped gap in the Ochils may be seen from it. In fact, the hotel is not in Glen Eagles at all but more than a mile north of its foot, in the Tullibardine area.

The valley is oddly-named also—for the river which plunges down it does not provide its name, as is usual; this is the Ruthven Water. Neither does the name refer to eagles, however romantic and suitable the short, steep glen may look for their eyries. It comes from the old Gaelic word *eaglais*, a church, often corrupted to eccles—the Glen of the Church—St. Mungo's Chapel and Well.

After crossing the pass northwards out of Glen Devon, the A.823 plunges down this most attractive steep valley for nearly four miles, to reach the main A.9 Edinburgh--Inverness highway between Blackford and Auchterarder. It is a straight descent, with no side glens, the road contouring high on the flank of Eastbow Hill, with warnings as to falling stones. About half-way down is the old Tollhouse, relic of days when a certain amount of private initiative was involved in developing the road system. Almost directly below, deep in the valley floor, St. Mungo's Well may still be traced, with the old drove-road climbing above.

Farther down is St. Mungo's Chapel, dating from 1149, and restored as a family war memorial by General Sir Aylmer Haldane in 1925. The commodious old whitewashed late 17th century mansion of Gleneagles stands within pleasant wooded policies near by, with the fragmentary remains of the Haldanes' much older castle on a knoll to the south. This renowned and ancient line, still in possession, has produced some notable characters, including the two extraordinary brothers Robert and James Haldane, who in the late 18th century became first distinguished naval officers and then graduated to being vigorous and unconventional Dissenting evangelists and religious authors; also the 1st Earl of Camperdown, Haldane-Duncan; and the Liberal statesman, Lord Haldane of Cloan—Cloanden being a property near by to the north-east.

The road that leads thereto strikes off near the house gates along the hillfoots towards Dunning, a pleasant, winding, rural road serving many scattered farms of the lower and wide Ruthven valley. Here also is Kincardine Castle, one of at least seven places of that name in Scotland, a modern mansion but with the remains of an ancient fortalice of the Grahams near by, from which the Duke of

Montrose, chief of that name, takes the secondary title of Earl of Kincardine. It was a powerful place once, a quadrangular strong-hold, with many associations with the great Marquis of Montrose—which was why it was dismantled by the Marquis of Argyll, in his savage campaign of 1645, to spite his hated Graham enemy.

The enormous Gleneagles Hotel stands in its 700-acre estate to the north, with a very lovely setting of pinewoods, moorland and splendid vistas for its two championship golf-courses and 9-hole course, with other sporting facilities, almost a little town in itself—but a town for those with deep pockets.

Glen Farg and Arngask. Glen Farg has for some time now been a name synonymous with frustration, delay, somewhere to avoid if you are a motorist or traveller; which is a pity, for this was once a place of delight and much interest, and should be still. Queen Victoria, for instance, described it as 'really lovely'. Unfortunately the main A.90 highway, from the Forth Road Bridge to Perth and the North, probes through the glen's winding, falling, wooded course for 4 twisting if beautiful, sylvan miles—and seldom indeed is the visitor thereto able to do more than fume and crawl, watching the lorry immediately in front and more than aware of that immediately on his tail, inhaling diesel fumes and unable to draw aside and admire the hanging woods, tumbling river and romantic prospects of what is in fact a beauty-spot. For long years there has been talk of a by-pass, but . . . !

The Glen of the River Farg is one of the eastmost gaps in the Ochil Hills, and its descent, from the Kinross-shire boundary near the attractive, quiet and unspoiled hamlet of Duncrevie, north-wards to the level plain of the Earn, makes a notable drop of almost five hundred feet. The Farg rises at a little-known but quite large reservoir-loch amongst the Ochils 2 miles west of Glenfarg village, in the Deuglie area, a pleasant setting. Glenfarg village is fairly modern, and used to be known as Damhead. Here is a hotel, garages, shops and the modern parish church, all rather dominated by the so-busy highway. The original settlement and parish kirkton was at Arngask, half a mile to the east. Here, behind Arngask House, is the ruined former church, secluded in woodland, ivy-grown now, and in a kirkyard with ancient tombstones. In this is the belfry of a still earlier church, with its bell dated 1710. Also, beside the roofless mort-house, is a massive red-sandstone effigy of the Virgin and Child. The original kirk was a private chapel of the Balvaird family, whose fine castle stands about two miles to the east, almost on the Fife border, on an isolated site east of the A.912 road. This is one of the most interesting castles in the land, ruinous but fairly well preserved, and highly advanced for a late 15th century structure, with many excellent features—even an ingenious arrange-ment of stone spouts from the roof, enabling wall-closets to be flushed out by rain-water. Balvaird was a Barclay property, which went with an heiress to Sir Andrew Murray, youngest son of Tullibardine, ancestor of the Dukes of Atholl, in the 15th century. Oddly enough a descendant, the Reverend Andrew Murray of Balvaird, minister of Abdie, was created Lord Balvaird by Charles I purely to spite the Kirk, with whom he was unpopular. His title is now merged with that of the Murray Earls of Mansfield, who still own the castle.

Where A.90 and A.912 join, in the lower glen of the Farg, is the Bein Inn, a famed hostelry. From here footpaths go round Binn Hill to Abernethy Glen on the east, and on the west round a smaller eminence to Clochridgestone—a 'duplicate' name, *clach* meaning stone—where there is a standing-stone. This area has also two rocking-stones, one near Blairstruie, on Balmanno Hill, and the other just south of the Bein Inn. The hamlet of Aberargie—which should be Aber-fargie—at the mouth of the glen, looks out over the fertile carse, where Farg joins Earn and Earn joins Tay. Also near the Bein Inn, at the former mill of Pottie, was once a pre-Reformation chapel, now gone.

Glen Garry and Dalnaspidal. The Perthshire Garry threads Atholl all the way from its junction with Tummel at Pitlochry, almost to the county boundary, where the bare mountains draw in around Dalnaspidal and the Pass of Drumochter, on the way to Inverness. But only that part of its course north of Struan and Calvine, where it is joined by Glen Errochty, is known as Glen Garry.

The lower reaches are pleasantly wooded with birch. But quickly the great heather hills take command, and road, river and railway cling together for fragile mutual support against the limitless, brooding wilderness. This country is not so much spectacular as sheerly daunting, the mountains massive and lumpish, rather than shapely and exciting; but huge, the distances vast. Motorists are wise to remember that, after Calvine, there is not another petrol-station for 20 miles.

There are few oases in this upheaved desolation, and these are in the main shooting-lodges—for this is notable deer-stalking and grouse country. Clunes, Dalnamine and Dalnacardoch Lodges, at 2-mile intervals, are close to the road. Dalnacardoch, once a stage-coach hostelry, where Prince Charles Edward passed the night of 29th August 1745, is indeed a road junction of a sort; for here the high and adventurous road comes in, on the south, from Trinafour in Glen Errochty, dropping 500 feet in 2 miles; and here, to the north, a still more adventurous private road and walkers' track strikes up the brawling Edendon Water for many a long mile, past the Lodge 6 miles up, past lonely Loch an Duin, past lonelier Loch Bhradain in Gaick deer-forest, over the watershed to bare Loch an-t-Seilich and so down attractive Glen Tromie to the Spey near Kingussie, 25 tough miles. Not for the tyro.

The A.9 highway reaches a height of 1500 feet at the lofty railway-halt of Dalnaspidal. The Gaelic *spideal* is the same as hospital, and commemorates an ancient hospitium in this unlikely spot—though it is a place for a refuge, if ever there was one. Here a party of Cromwell's troops were defeated by Athollmen. Loch Garry itself can be seen, to the west. It is now linked by tunnel to the larger Loch Ericht, farther north, with the result that much of its water is carried off, to the detriment of the River Garry, which is reduced to a poor thing until the hearty Edendon joins it—this in the interests of hydro-electricity. Just to the north is the county boundary, where the hog-backed Sow of Atholl stares across at the equally louring Boar of Badenoch, on the very hunched shoulders of the spine of Scotland.

Glen Lednock. Glens Lednock and Artney have much in common. Their mouths are only 2 miles apart, with Comrie in between, the former striking north-westwards, the latter south-westwards, at right angles to each other; and both are approximately the same length, with their roads ending abruptly. But there are major differences too, and no visitor would mistake one for the other. The present author, if anything, prefers the Lednock.

It is entered by way of a very deep and winding wooded ravine, directly north of Comrie, though the road takes a bend round Twenty Shilling Wood and hill on the way. A mile up, a very steep path leads up from the road to the lofty monument to a less-than-lofty individual, Henry Dundas, 1st Viscount Melville and Lord Dunira (1742–1811) once 'uncrowned king of Scotland' and one of the most influential Scots politicians, using the word in its less complimentary sense, of all time; who brought the business of patronage to a fine and profitable art, was Secretary for War, Treasurer of the Navy and First Lord of the Admiralty—until being impeached for malversation of funds and breach of duty—and though technically acquitted, ruined in his headlong career. His estate of Dunira lies a couple of miles to the west. Opposite the notice of the monument path, another notice points the way down below the road, by an equally steep track, which eventually leads to viewpoints for the renowned Devil's Cauldron waterfalls, cataracts and chasm—well worth the clamber, especially if the Lednock is in spate.

Beyond these attractions, the road abruptly runs out of the woodland and into a wide, open, hanging valley, continuing at round about the 600-foot contour, under the mass of Ben Chonzie, sometimes called Ben y Hone, to the north (3048 feet). It is a pleasant undramatic glen here, with scattered hill-farms, and is flanked by ever-heightening mountains. Crossing a fine old bridge, we pass the little school, 4½ miles from Comrie. At Invergeldie, where a sizeable side-glen comes in from the north-east, there is a shooting-lodge; and from here onwards the road is private, but only closed at nights to cars. A farther mile up, it swings uphill to the right, climbing steeply now, to lead to a large hydro-electric dam, the road rising about six hundred feet in a mile and passing an unusual apron-type waterfall called Spout Rollo on the way, all white lacework over black rock. The dam, at the 1250-foot contour, has formed a large new loch, about one and a half miles long, flooding the bare valley around the former place of Bovane. From the bottom of the dam road, the track is closed to cars; but a footpath leads north-westwards over the hills to Ardeonaig on Loch Tay-side, about eight strenuous miles, at its highest point reaching 1900 feet. There was local agitation for a road through to Tay as long as a century ago, following the line of this old drove-road. There is also a footpath over the hills to Tay by Invergeldie, this reaching a height of over two thousand feet.

There is nothing particularly exciting about Glen Lednock, except its river, which, rising high on the side of Creag Uigeach (2887 feet)—seen from the south a fine peak—has a fall of 1800 feet in under ten miles, with many cataracts; but it is all attractive.

Glen Lyon. Deservedly one of the most renowned, yet not so frequently visited glens in all the Highlands, Lyon is also one of the longest—at least, for a mountain cul-de-sac as distinct from a great rift valley. It opens from the Appin of Dull, at Fortingall, and probes westwards, roughly parallel with Loch Tay to the south, for 25 miles, winding in wild beauty amongst ever more lonely peaks until, past Loch Lyon, it fades into the high pass, near the Argyll border, which leads over the watershed of Mamlorn to the head of Glen Orchy.

Throughout that long course it varies much in character, as in width and altitude. Indeed its constant variety, between soft beauty and fierce grandeur, is part of its great attraction. At its mouth the jaws are steep and frowning; in fact, so abrupt and narrow is this Pass of Lyon that, from Fortingall, it seems most unlikely that a great valley could open therefrom.

Only a mile up, in the throat of it, is MacGregor's Leap, where, in 1565, the Chief of the landless Gregalach himself made a remarkable leap across the fearsome river chasm when pursued by Campbell bloodhounds. Although Gregor MacGregor thereby saved his life, he was later caught and murdered by the determined Campbells. Their feud was the more bitter in that this glen had been MacGregor land:

> Glen Orchy's proud mountains, Kilchurn and her towers,
> Glen Strae and Glen Lyon no longer are ours
> We're landless, landless, landless, Gregalach . . .!

A couple of twisting miles farther, opposite Chesthill House, once the property of the notorious Captain Campbell, there are a series of spectacular waterfalls, as the Allt Da-ghob hurtles down to meet the Lyon, easily seen from the road. There is a footbridge here. Then the wooded defile opens out somewhat, and vistas are granted of wider loveliness. Soon the ruined castle of Carnbane rises on top of a steep bluff to the right of the road, hidden in trees, but displaying vaults, gunloops and the traces of a cramped courtyard. It is said to have been built by Red Duncan Campbell the Hospitable, in 1564. Somewhere hereabouts was the scene of the sanguinary battle between the Clan MacIvor and the Stewarts of Garth, in the 15th century.

At Invervar there is a hamlet and laird's house, and a narrow side-road crosses to the other side of the river by a bridge from which, at times, leaping salmon may be seen. There are hidden ruins of meal and lint mills, and weavers' cottages, here, relics of the days when this was a populous glen.

There are still quite a number of farms, however, here on both sides of the river; and at the next hamlet, Innerwick, there is Glen-lyon parish church, of 18th century construction but on the site of another of the busy Adamnan's foundations, with his bell still preserved. Here a former drove-road, now a walker's track, comes in over the Larig Chalbhath pass from Dall, on Loch Rannoch-side. Today, however, the hub of the glen is a little farther on, at Bridge of Balgie, with its school and post office, and Milton of Eonan near by, again commemorating Adamnan. Here the road forks, one branch turning off south-westwards to climb steeply (1 in 6) over the shoulder of Ben Lawers to Loch Tay; the other to continue on up the glen, climbing also to avoid the riverside policies of Meggernie Castle, a fine late 16th century fortalice, whitewashed amidst old trees, now the seat of a wealthy southern proprietor. It was built by one *Cailean Gorach*, or Mad Colin Campbell in 1580, who amongst other exploits abducted the Countess of Erroll and held her here. Another sad lady—although we have no certainty that the countess was indeed sad at this rough wooing—is said to haunt Meggernie. She was the wife of a later Menzes laird, who murdered her in a fit of jealousy, and then cut up her body into halves for readier disposal. Perhaps for the best, it is her upper half which is alleged to materialise.

Three miles on, another side road leads 2 miles up, through scattered noble Scots pines, relics of the Caledonian Forest, to a great dam, where the Hydro-Electric Board have united two smaller lochs to form a 4-mile long reservoir, amidst fine views, submerging the hamlet of Lochs in the process. The main road continues, to pass new Loch Cashlie where, at the side of the road are a group of cairns and what seems to be an ancient earth-house, this under the steep cone of Stuchd an Lochainn (3144 feet).

As the head of the glen is neared—or, at least, the road-end, at the foot of Loch Lyon—the surroundings become more bleak and treeless. Yet here is the largest population centre in the long valley, Pubill, a mixed community of Hydro-Electric Board employees and estate shepherds, in modern cottages, under the towering dam which has extended the loch from under two miles to over six long. Beyond rear the giants, Bens Achallader and Heasgarnich (3404 and 3530 feet), and ranging to the south the fierce contours of the Tarmachan group.

Glen Shee and Blacklunans. For long, Glen Shee was looked upon by the generality as a remote and uncomfortable back-door route to the north-east and Deeside, with the Devil's Elbow as its main and daunting feature, and its Cairnwell Pass, at 2199 feet, the highest classified road summit in Great Britain. The sort of place one avoided if possible, unless young and adventurous. For some years now, however, the skiing boom has put Upper Glen Shee on the map; for in its remote high corries and smooth steep slopes the snow lingers longer. And skiers must eat and sleep—so the area has not only become better known but is developing its accommodation potential. There is more, however, to Glen Shee, than its road, A.93, to Deeside, and its skiing—always has been. It is in fact a long and quite pleasant valley in the extreme north-east of Perthshire, on the line of one of General Wade's military roads, from Perth to Fort George, with many traces of ancient habitation, and still with a fair population although containing no real village. It stretches from Bridge of Cally, north of Blairgowrie, for 25 miles to the Aberdeenshire border at the Cairnwell Pass.

The glen may be divided into three sections. From the junction of its Black Water and the River Ardle, at Bridge of Cally, for 6 miles up to Blacklunans, it is a wide, open valley with estates, farms, woodlands and a fertile strip. Two miles up, on a high shelf, is Persie, a former *quod-sacra* parish whose church, built in 1738 as a chapel-of-ease, is now a cart-shed. This was part of the original huge parish of Bendochy, near Coupar Angus where, before this chapel, worshippers had to travel 13 miles to church. Now there is a more modern church at Bridge of Cally, and another near Blacklunans. Pilgrims used to come here from afar to drink the healing waters of a fine chalybeate spring on Persie Hill. Two miles farther north, near the hamlet of Dalrulzion with its hotel, school and caravan-park, is a large group of burial-cairns and hut circles. And near by, where the B.950 branches off westwards for Kirkmichael, the roadside is flanked by a row of massive boulders with all the signs of antiquity. At Blacklunans itself, a mile more, Glen Shee is at its most attractive. Here, for 3 miles, there is a secondary road on the other side of the Black Water. The hamlet lies at the southern end of this, with a standing-stone near by, where another side-road strikes off eastwards over the hills by Drumore House Hotel to Glen Isla in Angus. A similar but B-class road takes a parallel course only 2 miles to the north, for some reason, strange in hills otherwise so roadless as these. At the start of the latter is the pleasing hamlet of Clackavoid, with a small bright church.

The second division of Glen Shee continues for 8 miles northwards, to the Spittal thereof. Now the hills heighten to over two thousand feet, and close in. The large but modern Dalnaglar Castle is prominent across the river, with the Angus boundary just behind it. Glenshee Lodge, farther on, is now a ski centre. From here onwards, indeed, signs of winter sports multiply; but otherwise there are fewer features of interest.

Spittal of Glenshee is a famous name. Here, where the A.93 bends sharply to the right over the river, by a high, old arched bridge, was formerly a hospice for travellers—and much needed, with the Pass ahead. Now there is a hamlet, with guest-houses, a most modern hotel for skiers, with pony-trekking and other facilities, a craft-centre, ski-school and further marks of progress. This is a welcome return to life, after a period of declension; for much went on here once. Queen Victoria used to stop here for refreshment on her way to and from Balmoral; it was a staging centre; and even boasted an annual fair in October. The church of 1831 stands in an old graveyard, on a mound beyond the bridge, with a standing-stone directly behind. Other antiquities lie to the east, some distance from the road—a stone circle, and a tumulus known as the Tomb of Diarmid, alleged to refer to Diarmid O'Duine, contemporary of the Ossianic heroes, whose descendant, Eva O'Duine, married the first of the Campbells, and gave that famous line the Celtic denomination of the Siol Diarmid. At the south end of the bridge, the long driveway opens to the remotely-situated but large Dalmunzie Castle Hotel, a converted modern mansion and shooting-lodge on the southern of the two headwaters of the Black Water—this properly called Glen Lochsie.

In fact the final section of Glen Shee should really be named Glen Beg. Here the A.93 begins to climb in earnest through the ever-steepening mountains, passing the well-known ski chair-lift on the side of Ben Gulabin (2341 feet), and rising from 1100 feet to exactly double that at the Cairnwell Pass, in 6 miles. Near the summit is the notorious Devil's Elbow ascent, now greatly improved and deprived of most of its terrors, yet still giving a long ascent of generally one-in-nine, with one-in-five steeps at the much-ironed-out hairpin bends. This, of course, is one of the first stretches of main road to be snow-blocked in winter, and great activity is required to keep it open. Now, thanks to the winter-sports enthusiasts, it has entered into its own.

Beyond, the road drops down through Glen Clunie to Braemar on Deeside, 9 miles, with the mighty mass of the White Mounth on the east, and the roadless mountain wilderness for 40 miles to Atholl, on the west.

Huntingtower, Ruthvenfield and Almondbank. This area, 3 miles or so west by north of Perth, has a character all its own. Here the Almond winds to join the Tay, and for three miles or so becomes quite industrialised with bleachfields, dyeing and finishing plants, a process requiring much and good water. This was a late 18th and early 19th century development; but despite the concentration of this industry, the area retains a rural aspect, the various mills and their villages being hidden in the bends of the river valley, and the vistas of the surrounding high lands predominate.

The district's impact on the Scots scene was originally far from industrial and peaceful. This was the terrain of the powerful Ruthven family, later Earls of Gowrie, and their Castle of Ruthven

99

still stands, now in the care of the Ministry of Works, and named Huntingtower. The change of name is very significant. James VI was abducted in 1583, aged 16, and brought to Ruthven Castle, where a group of nobles held him captive, and ruled Scotland for a while from here. His tears on this occasion drew from the Master of Glamis the famous words—"better bairns greet than bearded men!" James never forgot or forgave; and in 1600 he had his revenge, at the infamous Gowrie Conspiracy, so-called, when the young son of one of the abductors, the Earl of Gowrie and his brother, were assassinated in the King's presence at Perth. James decreed that the name of Ruthven be proscribed, never to be mentioned again, for places as for people. He gave the Ruthven lands to Murray of Tullibardine, who had aided him in the enterprise, and who called the castle Huntingtower. As such it comes into the well-known song by a later Murray, Duke of Atholl:

Blair in Atholl's mine, Jeannie; Little Dunkeld is mine, Jeannie;
Saint Johnston's Bower and Huntingtower, and all that's mine is thine,
Jeannie.

The name Ruthven came back, of course, eventually; and now there is Ruthvenfield, Ruthven House and so on.

The castle is highly impressive and interesting, looking all of a piece but actually being two large towers of the early 15th and late 16th centuries, five storeys high with parapets. These two towers originally had no other connection than a gangway at parapet level —highly inconvenient, however secure. Later, lower work was built to link them internally. A story tells how a daughter of the Ruthvens once leapt from one parapet to the other to escape discovery in her lover's chamber—he being disapproved of by her parents.

Below the castle, in the haughland, is quite an attractive scattered village, its bleachfields now greens and the pitch of a football club. Through this runs one of the most ancient canals in Scotland, allegedly constructed in the 12th century, to carry water to the King's Mills of Perth, to the various monasteries there, and on occasion to flood the city's moat. It starts at the weir called Low's Wark, at Almondbank. A small stone bridge crosses it at Huntingtower Haugh. There is an old mill here called the Beetling Mill. At the far west end of the Haugh is a large modern mill, beside its early predecessor, still engaged in the bleaching, dyeing and finishing trade. These bleachfields, as they were called, started in 1774. There is a large hotel near by. These places are all screened in old trees.

Almondbank, not far up-river to the north-west, demands quite a lengthy circuit to reach by road. This is quite a large village, with a long main street above the river, with the aforementioned Low's Wark just below. This was important enough to be part of the chartered property of Perth, and is mentioned in many documents. It is not clear who Low was—presumably the very skilful builder. Almondbank is now dominated by the great Royal Navy Stores

Depot, a vast and hush-hush establishment spread out along the valley, much given to notices, guard-dogs, etc. Amongst all this strangely-sited modernity, is an old burial-ground above the road, with no chapel attached. To the north-east of the village, on higher ground, is the site of a rather earlier armed camp, a Caledonian one, now tree-clad, presumably a kind of opposition to the Roman Camp at Bertha—from which the name of Perth is thought to derive—a mile or so to the east, where Almond joins Tay.

Inchture. Just south of the busy A.85 dual-carriageway between Perth and Dundee, 7 miles west of the latter, is the village of Inchture—as its name implies once an island in the flooded Carse of Gowrie. It must have been a very low island, for its eminence is hardly noticeable in the level flats; indeed the church and church-yard are alleged to be built up 6 to 8 feet artificially, presumably to afford suitable burial facilities in the early days. *Tuir*, in Gaelic means a dirge, or lament for the dead, and it may be that the original inch got its name thus; although another claimed deriva-tion is *innis-t-ear*, the island to the east. Today there is a neat red-stone estate-type village, with church, school, hotel and a shop or two, all under an avenue of tall old trees, and rather attractive.

The parish church is distinctly ambitious for so small a com-munity; but the parish itself is fairly large, and now incorporates the former parish of Rossie. The Gothic building dates from 1834, and is unusual in having handsome red ashlar stone at front and sides, but only harling at the rear, an economy the present author has not seen elsewhere in a church. It stands amongst many ancient gravestones, with another Kinnaird vault below the build-ing—additional to that at the old chapel at Rossie.

Most of the antiquities of this parish are in the higher ground of the Rossie area, and dealt with under that name. A battle was allegedly fought near the ruined castle of Moncur, across the main road to the north of the village, in 728, when in a civil war Hungus, or Angus, defeated Nectan and gained the leadership of the Picts.

The Parish covers 5330 acres, of which no fewer than 1200 are described as foreshore or have been reclaimed from the firth. A long dead-straight road of 2 miles runs down over the rich flat cornlands to salt water at Powgavie. Pow or poll is the name given to the sluggish streams or stanks which drain the carse. At Powgavie there was formerly a harbour, once quite important, where there was a hamlet and alehouse, all now gone and only a sea of reeds and rushes remaining. At low tide, the Powgavie Burn winds its way out through the mud-flats and sandbanks of Dog Bank for almost three miles. Some of the farms in these fertile carselands have odd names —such as Maggotland, Mammiesroom, Waterbutts and Unthank. At Grange, 3 miles south-west of Inchture, there is a sizeable com-munity, amongst scattered orchards and broiler-houses. Inchture district is famous for the cultivation of strawberries. All this Carse of Gowrie, of course, claims the title of the Garden of Scotland.

Inchtuthill, Caputh and Spittalfield. Inchtuthill is a famous name for all interested in matters Roman. Here, on the private, finely-timbered estate of Delvine, in the parish of Caputh, a dozen miles north of Perth, was one of the greatest encampments in the country, the only legionary headquarters in Scotland, a place once as important to the Roman power as Chester, Caerleon or Lincoln. The site covers a large area north of the Tay just before the river takes its great bend southwards and the Isla joins it. Unfortunately for the visitor, there is little left to be seen save a low plateau of level, cattle-dotted parkland, with a few green mounds and barely distinguishable embankments; for though much excavation has been done in recent years, all has been filled in again so as not to interfere with agriculture. This is the general policy in Scotland, with Roman remains; but it seems strange to possess such a heritage, and to prefer to keep it as cattle pasture.

This was the base of Agricola's favourite legion, the Twentieth, housing 6000 men; and from here they advanced to the famous and vital Battle of Mons Grampius, wherever it was fought, where they defeated the Caledonians, or Picts, under Calgacus, killing 10,000 according to Tacitus. Here was discovered, at the excavations, the renowned 7-ton hoard of Roman nails, some as long as 16 inches. The camp covered an area some five hundred yards square, with outlying forts and redoubts. It is thought that the Romans took over the town of Tamea, or Tulina, here, of the Pictish tribe of the Vacomagi. It seems absurd that this is not all laid open, and maintained as a national showpiece.

Delvine mansionhouse has been demolished.

Caputh village, the site of the parish church, lies over two miles to the west, where a bridge carries the B.9099 across Tay from Murthly. It is a pleasantly-situated little place, turning its back on the high hills and facing south across the levels of the great river, 5 miles east of Dunkeld. The name is a form of Keppoch, from *ceapach*, a garden. The church, standing on a terrace above the old village, is plain and large, rebuilt in 1865, with an attractive lych-gate dated 1928. Its predecessor stood on rising ground called the Moothill, or Mote-hill, 600 yards to the west, where its ancient burial ground, enlarged, is still the area's cemetery, a pleasant, peaceful spot crowning a little tree-sheltered ridge. There are many old stones, quite a number of the 17th century built in as walling; and a handsome bronze group commemorating a member of the Lyle of Glendelvine family.

The quite large village of Spittalfield lies 1½ miles to the east, and, with its green and old cottages would be quite picturesque were it not rather dominated by the enormous transport-park for heavy vehicles sited strangely here. I can recollect no other remote and rural village far from a major road, so 'enhanced'. Presumably, from the name, there was a hospital or house of refuge here, prior to the Reformation; and here was established the parish school.

Inchmahome Priory, Lake of Menteith

Kenmore across foot of Loch Tay

Celtic Dupplin Cross, Forteviot

Celtic Dupplin Cross, Forteviot

Meigle.
Museum of sculptured Celtic ston

This area of the Stormont—the district east of Dunkeld bounded by Tay, Ericht and Isla—is notable for the number of prehistoric relics, particularly burial-cairns. Cairnmure, or the Great Cairn, the largest of these, rises 1½ miles north of Caputh Church, and is no less than 456 feet in circumference. Another measures 357 feet, with a third somewhat smaller. Near the burial-ground is still another, called the Crosscairn. Such large cairns may well indicate that a great battle was fought here, these being the resting-places of the slain. The top of the conical hill of Craig of Stenton, a mile west of the burial-ground, has evidently been fortified, and is known as Kemp's Hold. And high on the dorsal ridge of the area, between the northern valley of the Lunan, with its string of lochs, and that of Tay, on the farm of East Cult, are two large standing-stones, one 10 feet high, the other 7 feet, with, beside them, a large sloping boulder cut with numerous circular cup-marks. The views from this ridge are magnificent.

Innerpeffray, Madderty and Kinkell. These areas of the great and wide tract of mid-Strathearn lie between Gask and Crieff, the first two on the north side of the Earn, Kinkell on the south. Although they contain no true villages, they have always had their own importance in Scotland's story, their names recurring again and again over the centuries. These are level, fertile lands, between the Ochils and the Highland hills, dotted with farms, woodlands and old estates.

Innerpeffray is a strange place to find down at the end of a mile-long and unmetalled side-road, near the steep banks of the river, a place packed with history and interest, yet not even a hamlet. Here there is a nationally-renowned ancient library, a pre-Reformation chapel of some distinction, an early endowed school and a ruined castle. The chapel was old in 1508, when it rebuilt by the first Lord Drummond, father of James IV's love, Margaret Drummond, as a Collegiate foundation, and long used as the burial-place of that great family, later Earls of Perth. It is a typically long and low, two-apartment building, with stone-slated roof, warm sandstone dressings and moulded doorways. There is a niche high on the east gable, and a leper's squint in the north wall, where the unfortunates could watch the celebration of Mass without entering the church. Also a stone altar, part of a painted ceiling and a priest's loft.

Near by is the handsome whitewashed 18th century building which houses the famous Innerpeffray Library, the second-oldest in Scotland, and open to the public. There are about three thousand volumes shelved in a fine, well-lit room on the upper floor, many of great age and value, one of the most interesting being the great Marquis of Montrose's personal pocket Bible, in French, bearing his autograph. The library was founded in 1691 by David Drummond, 3rd Lord Madderty, Montrose's brother-in-law, who also endowed the school in an adjoining building. Many of the books were added, about sixty years later by Robert Hay Drummond,

Archbishop of Canterbury, who had inherited Innerpeffray and other great estates, and who erected the present library building.

The castle is not often visited, being not visible from the rest, on lower ground at a bend of the river to the east. It is ruinous, but the main features survive, a commodious L-planned house of the early 17th century, built by James Drummond, 1st Lord Madderty, younger brother of the 3rd Lord Drummond, and whose nephews became Earls of Perth and of Melfort, and ruled Scotland between them, for James VII in London. Grazing cattle alone now inherit all this circumstance.

Madderty parish covers nearly five thousand acres in mid-strath, its comparatively modern church having no village nearer than the hamlet of St. Davids, a mile away. But this must have been a highly populous area once, for just to the north-east is the site of the Abbey of Inchaffray, one of the great ancient religious houses of Scotland—now, alas, only a few neglected fangs and fragments of masonry, mostly of fairly late date, with rubbish dumped around. Yet this was the most favoured endowment of many Scottish kings, an Augustinian foundation of great influence and wealth, founded by Gilbert, 3rd Earl of Strathearn in 1200. Its famous Abbot Maurice was Bruce's great supporter, who celebrated the Mass before the Scots army at Bannockburn, and carried the Brecbennoch of Columba throughout the battle. Another Abbot was killed at Flodden. At the Reformation the huge lands were erected into a temporal lordship for the infant James Drummond, aforementioned, who became 1st Lord Madderty. It is shameful that a people so attached as the Scots to their history should abandon so many of their ancient monuments to utter neglect.

Not far to the east is the most attractive small fortified laird's house of Williamstoun, now a farmhouse and in excellent condition. It dates from the mid-17th century, with stair-tower and watch-chamber reached by a tiny turnpike in an angle-turret. It was built for the heir of Oliphant of Gask, who insisted on marrying the minister of Trinity-Gask's young daughter, instead of the 45-year-old sister of the Marquis of Douglas, and so was disinherited of Gask in favour of his younger brother.

Also in Madderty are two Roman camps, flanking Innerpeffray on either side of the river; and two of the nine Signal Stations mentioned under Gask. And there is, not far away, the oddly-named former railway station of Highlandman, 2 miles south-east of Crieff.

Kinkell is now best known, probably, for its bridge over the Earn—for there is not another between Crieff and Dalreoch on the main A.9, a stretch of nearly a dozen miles. But it was a place of some importance once—a parish, indeed, and a notorious one:

> Oh, what a parish, what a terrible parish,
>   Oh, what a parish is that of Kinkell;
> They hae hangit the minister, drowned the precentor,
>   Dang doon the steeple and drucken the bell!

This alludes to the 17th century Reverend Richard Duncan, who was convicted of child-murder and executed at Muthill, 4 miles away, much to the anger of his parishioners, and just before the reprieve they had sought reached Strathearn. The said parishioners thereupon drowned the precentor in the Earn—presumably they considered him the guilty party, though the dead child was found under the minister's fireplace—and sold the church bell, possibly to pay the expenses of the reprieve.

The ruined, ancient pre-Reformation chapel of St. Bean is still there, near the Machany Water's confluence with Earn, in a cottage garden, with its overgrown graveyard around it, another typical two-apartment building, with no particular features. Just across the road is the lumpish and very plain yellow-washed successor, which was formerly a United Presbyterian church. The fine bridge itself, hump-backed, four-arched and picturesque, is half a mile to the north-west.

Kenmore. Lying on green knolls where the broad smooth Tay issues from its great loch, under the long wooded hog's-back of Drummond Hill, the white houses, white hotel and kirk of Kenmore, all tastefully grouped around a wide 'place' amid ancient trees, seem to speak of settled peace and serenity—by no means the normal impression of this challenging, vehement if beautiful land. Charm, a much misused word, is one that might decently be applied here. The village of Kenmore might appear to have been dropped down here as from some altogether different, softer and non-Highland ambience.

Yet Kenmore's history and background conflicts notably with this aura of peace. And always has done. It could hardly be otherwise, with the principal seat of the great and turbulent house of Campbell of Glenorchy, later Earls of Breadalbane, close by. And long before the Campbells came, in the 15th century, the area had been prominent. For, off the north shore of the loch near by is the tiny wooded islet of *Eilean nan Bannoamh*, the Isle of the Female Saints. Here died Queen Sybilla, daughter of Henry I of England and wife of Alexander I of Scotland, in 1122. In memoriam, Alexander founded a nunnery thereon, which became famous. Only once a year its nuns were allowed to emerge from the isle's seclusion, oddly enough to attend one of the six annual fairs which kept Kenmore in a stir. One wonders who got most out of this recurrent liberty? But sanctity did not save the Priory at the Reformation. Campbell fortified it as another of his many castles; it was besieged by Montrose; and later held by General Monk.

With Taymouth Castle so near it would hardly have been thought worth Campbell's while. This enormous blue-stone pile, now government property and standing in its vast policies, after being put to a number of uses, dates only from the early 19th century, succeeding a much less grandiose but authentic 16th century fortalice called the Castle of Balloch. To consider it now is as good as a sermon on the vanity of human ambitions This was the vaunted nerve-centre of one of the greatest feudal empires in the land. From Taymouth, the later Earls of Breadalbane ruled over a single estate of 437,696 acres, as much as the three Lothians put together, a property 100 miles long. Today all is dispersed. Presumably, however grand, successive Earls failed to take after the first of them, Sir John Campbell of Glenorchy (1635–1716), the doubtful Jacobite, described as 'grave as a Spaniard, cunning as a fox, wise as a serpent, and slippery as an eel'. The building is at present used as a co-ed school for the children of Americans in Europe.

It was the 3rd Earl who built the handsome bridge over Tay in 1774, with the equivocal inscription proclaiming the great generosity of King George who subscribed £1000 towards the cost out of the fortified Jacobite estates. It was the view from this bridge which inspired Robert Burns to write his poem, in pencil, on the chimney-piece of the Kenmore Inn, now the Hotel, part of which runs:

The Tay meand'ring sweet in infant pride, the palace rising on its verdant side,
  The lawns wood-fring'd in Nature's native task, the hillocks dropt in Nature's careless haste,
The arches striding o'er the newborn stream, the village glist'ning in the noontide beam——

Some have hailed this as the Bard's best exercise in English heroics. I wonder?

The church on its green hillock is attractive, and dates from 1760 —the work of the same well-doing 3rd Earl, replacing one of 1579. The kirkyard here used to be part of the green and market-place, the previous burial-ground being about a mile away to the north-east, at the pre-Reformation church site of Inchadney.

Much, much older than all this, even than the English princess's death on the islet, is the very fine stone circle at Croftmoraig, on the Aberfeldy road 3 miles to the east, one of the most complete groups of standing-stones.

Kilbryde. Three miles to the north-west of Dunblane, at the eastern end of the Braes of Doune, lies a secluded area, now little populated, around the valley of the Ardoch Water—not to be confused with the other and more famous Ardoch only a few miles to the north-east, the parish in which lies Braco and Greenloaning. This Ardoch runs for about seven miles, to fall into the Teith at Doune. Yet this quiet and remote district had its own claims to fame also. And still it provides an attractive, 'away-from-it-all' atmosphere, amongst the green foothills that rise up to the great heather hills.

There are a number of Kilbrides in Scotland, in Lanarkshire, Ayrshire, Arran and Argyll—but this is the only one that spells its name with a y. It gained its importance from its large castle, a seat first of the Earls of Menteith, and then of the Campbells of Aberuchill, a vigorous race who took an active part in affairs. But the name refers to the cell or chapel of St. Bride, or Bridget, a Celtic missionary—and this religious establishment is still there, after a fashion, in the form of an abandoned little church and neglected ancient graveyard, standing back even from the side road, above the steep bank of the Ardoch, half a mile south of the castle. The church is still sound enough, but deserted, and with broken windows and fallen plaster makes a sad picture, attractive as is the site. It has been used as a burial-place for the Campbell baronets, and it speaks a salutary commentary on past glories and resounding deeds to see their memorials in this state. At least those of lesser folk, out in the open, mossy and overgrown with weeds as they are, seem less rejected.

The castle, farther up the valley in its wooded policies, has not descended to these depths, although the estate is no longer what it was. It stands on a strong site, at a sharp bend in a ravine, and at first glance the building looks no more than a typical large Victorian sham castle in the Scottish-baronial style. But round at the south side, it can be seen that the modern work only encases the old, the south gable being little affected, still tall, with its twin square angle-turrets, steep roofing and early brown stone-work. Though the original castle dated from 1460, this remaining visible portion appears to belong to the early 17th century. Sir Colin Campbell of Aberuchill did not purchase the property until 1669. The Aberuchill Campbells were a branch of Lawers, a line strongly supporting the Reformation and the Revolution settlement. The first was Lord Justice Clerk, who nevertheless was careful to pay Rob Roy his black-mail, to ensure the safety of his flocks. His son, Sir James, was less canny—until Rob came personally one night to Kilbryde Castle door with a large force of men who had already rounded up all the laird's stock in readiness to drive off into the hills. Leaving his guests at the dinner-table, Sir James had to go and pay off the free-booters—and Rob had no difficulty with him thereafter.

The narrow dead-end road which runs attractively up the winding valley of the Ardoch into the rolling Braes of Doune ends eventually at a lonely farm called The Bows, passing on the way a green conical mound on a small ridge, called the Judge's Cairn. Whether this judge refers to the aforementioned Lord Justice Clerk is not clear.

Killiecrankie, Tenandry and Strathgarry. Killiecrankie is one of the famous names of Scotland, renowned both for its history and its scenery. The Pass of Killiecrankie lies 3 miles north of Pitlochry, and for a mile threads the deep, steep, thickly-wooded gorge of the Garry, between a spur of Ben Vrackie (2757 feet) and Tenandry Hill, with the village at the north end. Through this narrow winding defile, above the rushing river, run the A.9 highway and the railway to Inverness.

About a mile beyond the Pass, to the north, was fought in 1689 the famous battle, between the forces of William of Orange, newly brought to the throne, and the unseated and exiled James VII and

II. General Mackay, a veteran of the foreign wars, led the government forces, and Graham of Claverhouse, Viscount Dundee, the Jacobites. It is rather strange how popular a hero he has become in Scottish minds—for he was scarcely popular at the time, his stern hand at the putting down of the Covenanters, during the preceding 'Killing Times', making his name execrated by many. However, his looks and the well-known song between them, seem to have metamorphosed him. 'Bonnie Dundee' won this battle, but fell in the moment of victory, a stone marking the spot. His dying words are famed. "How goes the day?" he gasped, of a man named Johnson, who had aided him down from his saddle. "Well for King James," the other answered. "But I am sorry for your lordship." The dying Dundee said, "If it is well for him, it matters the less for me." He did not speak again. Two thousand of the government troops were killed or captured, for a loss of 900 Highlanders. Nevertheless, with Dundee's death, the victory was more or less fruitless, and that Jacobite campaign soon ended.

The Pass, once a dangerous trap for travellers, and the key to Atholl, is now a popular venue for visitors, and the National Trust for Scotland, owners of the property, have an attractive centre here. Towards the north end is the famed Soldier's Leap, where one of Mackay's fleeing men managed to jump the foaming cataract between two fearsome rocks, and so escape the pursuing enemy.

Spanning the river to the south is Bridge of Garry, recently replaced by a modern structure. This carries the B.8019 road to Tummel and Rannoch. Just over the bridge, a small and very steeply-climbing side-road branches off to the right, to ascend high above the Pass on the west side, passing the remotely but beautifully sited church and manse of Tenandry. Although an ancient parish, the present church was built only in 1836, with seating for 430— an extraordinary provision for a place of worship with no centre of population for miles around. The graveyard is most attractively carved out of the steep birchwoods.

This high back-road drops as steeply beyond, to rejoin the A.9 by another bridge, at Killiecrankie village, passing a lofty-sited dun on the way. But a branch-road continues on up the south side of the Garry for nearly four miles, coming to a dead-end opposite Blair Atholl, with which it communicates only by a footbridge. On the way, this riverside road serves the scattered farms and mansion of Strathgarry, and the large and inevitably unsightly quarry near Glackmore. Two fords are marked on the map as crossing the wide and rushing river; but it would be a bold motorist who attempted them.

Killin and Glen Lochay. The name Killin is said to be a corruption of *Cil-Fhinn*, or Fingal's Burial-place, and a stone is alleged to mark the site. Certainly the area is rich in Fingalian lore—even though this is apt to be overlaid by the somewhat more recent activities of the MacNabs and Campbells, heroes* of a different calibre. It is a place altogether steeped in history, as in fine scenery

—although the lower portion of the little town is itself rather less than scenic.

Anyone will tell you that Killin lies at the head of Loch Tay. Indeed, it used to have a special branch railway-line to its little steamboat port on the loch. Yet, unlike Kenmore at the other end, no feeling of the loch permeates Killin; indeed, it cannot be seen from the town. Nevertheless, the sight and sound of water dominates all—but running water. For Killin lies on the peninsula between the rushing River Dochart and the calmer Lochay, which join up just before the loch; and the former at least makes an enormous and picturesque impact on the scene. The Falls of Dochart in their majestic, headlong descent at the head of the town are too well known to require description here, but deservedly so. From the old bridge with its five unequal arches, the scene is unforgettable.

Just below the bridge, on a long, narrow wooded island in the cascading river, Inch Buie, the Yellow Island, is the burial-ground of the MacNab chiefs. This formidable and warlike clan, although descended from the hereditary abbots of the Culdee Abbey of St. Fillan, in Glen Dochart, was never very large but made up for their lack of numbers in other ways, their chiefs in especial tending to be characters in a major way. Typical was the remark of one of them, when other lords and chieftains were squabbling as to who was to sit at the head of some mutual table, while he contented himself with quite a lowly seat, announcing that wherever MacNab sat was the head of that table! The 13th chief lost the clan lands, and emigrated to Canada; but in recent times the late chief re-purchased their seat of Kinnel House, here, and lived again by the Dochart. There is a good stone circle of six uprights in the parkland close to the house. Achmore House, near by, is noted for its famous Black Hamburg vine, said to be half as large again as that at Hampton Court. It still produces 600 bunches a year.

Just across Bridge of Dochart is the old mill, with wheel and lade, now a tweed and tartan showroom; a small tweed factory was long a local industry. The parish church, down at the other end of the town, near the cattle market, is a plain, substantial whitewashed edifice, bearing the inscription *Thos. Clark the builder of this church 1744.* Another inscription is said to be on the bell, cracked but rewelded: *Sir Coline Campbel of Glenurchy Knygth Barronet causid cast yis Bel 1632 R.H.*

Sir Colin was the son of the notorious Black Duncan of the Cowl, who built the 16th century Finlarig Castle, the shattered ruins of which stand amidst trees and thick undergrowth near the side-road which crosses the bridge at the north-east end of the town on the way to the former steamer port. It was a notable place, where many dark deeds were done, with two vaults remaining, many gunloops and shot-holes. There is a good heraldic panel above the door, and near by a gruesome heading-pit, with block and sunken cavity for the head, one of the few surviving examples. This was but one of seven castles Duncan built.

Half a mile north Glen Lochay branches off to the north-west, a highly attractive valley, particularly in its lower reaches, richly wooded, flanked by high and shapely mountains, and threaded by a fine river, 17 miles in length. The Falls of Lochay, about two miles up are very worth visiting, a series of six cataracts in two groups, in a deep rocky gorge—even the turbine-house of the hydro-electric scheme below them detracts but little from the scene. The glen itself runs deep into the high fastnesses of the ancient Forest of Mamlorn, where once Bruce roamed, a fugitive after the defeat at Dalrigh in Strathfillan. In the mid-glen, near the farmhouse of Duncroisk, are sundry ancient stones with cup-and-ring markings; but also others with inscribed crosses within circles, probably early-Christian.

Kilmadock and Lanrick. Between Doune and Callander lies a stretch of pleasant rural country about the wide, open valley of the Teith, flanked by high moorland to the south and the Braes of Doune foothills of the Grampians to the north. In the 7 miles there is no village, but a few small hamlets and scattered farms; also two large estates—the Earl of Moray's Doune Lodge, north of the road, and Lanrick Castle to the south, farther west. All this is comprised in the old ecclesiastical parish of Kilmadock, the church for which was removed to Doune in 1744. It is threaded by the A.84.

One and a half miles west of Doune are the hamlets of Buchany and Burn of Cambus, running together; the fine coronet-decorated gates of Doune Lodge, with the mansion sitting genially on a green terrace behind, to the north; and a very awkwardly-opening side-road on the south leading down to the Kirkton, and old ruined church of Kilmadock. These hamlets are all connected with the estate, home farm, factor's office and so on. The mansion itself, which used to be called Cambuswallace, where the Edmonstone family of Newton Doune, hereditary captains of Doune Castle for the Moray Stewarts, were seated, is a charming whitewashed place, now the home of the Earl of Moray's heir, the Lord Doune. Charles Edward was here in 1745. The last of the Edmonstone line died in 1852, when their feudal superiors took over. The home farm, near the road at Burn of Cambus, is conspicuous for its steeple.

The old church is in a sad state of neglect, picturesque though it is on a mound near the river, with the old manse near by converted into estate houses. St. Madock was one of the early Celtic missionaries. Only a broken gable and decayed vault remain, amongst weed-grown tombstones. Most of the tightly-packed stones refer to Doune folk, for this was formerly parish graveyard for the town. Here, too, is the burial-enclosure of the Edmonstones, no better cared-for than the rest, including one, a major-general, last survivor of Lucknow. One interesting monument, within railings, commemorates makers of the renowned Doune pistols, 18th century Cadells and Campbells—the latter offshoots of the Campbells of Barbreck.

A further mile along the road, lies Lanrick estate, mostly across the river and so reachable from the B.8032 'back-road', Deanston to Torrie; but a private suspension bridge carries the driveway over from the main A.84. The castle has a core of old work of the Haldanes of Gleneagles, but is to all intents a modern castellated edifice, built by one of the great tea moguls, William Jardine, of the well-known Jardine, Matheson Company, around 1840. Prior to that it had been the seat of General Sir Evan Murray MacGregor of MacGregor (1785–1841), 19th chief, and Governor of Dominica and the Windwards. He sold Lanrick in 1830, and built Edinchip at Balquhidder, now the seat of the 23rd chief.

The pleasant little riverside hamlet of Drumvaich lies a mile farther, still attractive despite recent road-widening.

North of all this rise the Braes of Doune, and amongst the heather hills behind, stretching to Glen Artney, Uamh Mhor (pronounced Weem Vore) is the most prominent. Oddly enough, Uamh Mhor is only a slightly lower shoulder of Uamh Beag (2181 feet). Probably the reason for this reversal of adjectives is that the cave, to which the word Uamh refers, is larger than any on Beag. Actually it is not a true cavern, but a great hollow under mighty stones, in legend the home of a giant, and later the refuge of caterans and robbers—whom Scott declares "have only been extirpated within these 40 or 50 years". It produces notable echoes. Scott brings it into *The Lady of the Lake*. Near by is a hidden little rift-valley known as Rob Roy's Cattle Fank, a self-explanatory title. A large spring near the Garvald Burn, to the south-east, spouts out of the solid rock. And here, in the lap of the hills, is half-mile-long Loch Maghaig, very deep, out of which flows eastwards the Ardoch Burn, to join Teith at Doune. A rough track leads from Burn of Cambus to the loch, and eventually to the oddly-named hill-farm of Calziebohalzie.

The lower Braes of Doune is an area of green rolling, whin-and-broom-dotted knowes and small farms, served by a winding side-road by Drumloist to Dalvorlich, near Callander. At its start are large gravel-pit workings, a common feature in the Teith valley, indicative of glacial moraine-forming.

The district to the south of the Teith is more bare, moorland rising to the ridge between this valley and the Forth. It has few features, beyond the twin lochs of Daldorn and the large planted forest of Torrie. B.8032 threading it, eventually joins the A.81 at Torrie, which comes over from Port of Menteith to Callander, passing the lonely Loch Rusky on the way.

Kilspindie, Pitroddie and Glendoick. These are a parish, a hamlet and an estate, with another hamlet, in the north-central area of the Carse of Gowrie, about eight miles east of Perth. Kilspindie is one of those most attractive small communities tucked into the Sidlaw dens, or ravines, which open out on to the Carse, similar to Rait and Kinnaird. It consists only of a few houses, a small parish church and large manse, a farm with the walled garden and doocote of an ancient castle now no more, all highly picturesque. The church is built on a strong position which the castle might have envied, on a knoll above the junction of two streams, with the sound of falling water always present, its ancient graveyard entered by a lych-gate. Many old worked stones are built into the walling, obviously from the defunct castle, and there is a sundial on the west wall dated 1666. Amongst the old gravestones is the massive tomb of General Robert Stuart of Rait, a local laird and renowned commander, who distinguished himself in the Middle East campaigns and died 1820. Over the door is a Persian inscription translated "SERVANT OF THE KING EMPEROR, HONOURABLE MAN OF THE SWORD, WARRIOR, DEVOTED LION, GENERAL ROBERT STUART, PILLAR OF THE STATE, YEAR 1212 (1801 A.D.)". It was a period of superlatives.

The castle of Kilspindie is mentioned in Blind Harry's narrative as providing a refuge for the young William Wallace and his mother —he was brought up in the Dundee area. Today no traces of this building remain, the mellow walled garden and doocote belonging to a much later period. Also later are two carved stones built into a manse outhouse near by, one, much worn, displaying what appears to be the Douglas heart quartered with either Stewart or Lindsay. It has been suggested that this castle belonged to the Douglas Earls of Angus; but this appears to be a confusion with the Kil-spindie Castle at Aberlady in East Lothian; the only families recorded as owning this Kilspindie before 1718 were Crawfords and Lindsays. The castle was pulled down in 1740.

There is another Wallace link in the neighbourhood, from the hero's later life—Wallace's Cave, at Pitroddie quarry, blocked up in the 19th century. Presumably he hid therein during his fugitive days. Pitroddie is a glen, a farm and a hamlet lying south-west of Kilspindie. The glen is steep and picturesque, with a road winding down it, its den famed for the agates found therein. Above the high ground of the glen rises Pole Hill (944 feet), on the summit of which is a tumulus, and, some fifty feet lower, the remains of an ancient circular fort. Not far east of these, and reached by a narrow climbing side-road which passes Kilspindie itself, is the remote farm and ruined castle of Evelick. Though greatly neglected, most of the stonework is entire to the wallhead, and shows it to have been quite a fine place of the early 16th century, with a notable profusion of shot-holes, L-planned and with a circular stair-tower. The Lindsays of Evelick were quite a powerful lot, and were granted a baronetcy in 1666. The second son of this first baronet was most brutally murdered by his own stepbrother, while at play. The last of the Lindsays was drowned in 1799. After Evelick, the road winds on over the high moorland northwards, with fine views over Strath-more.

In the lower ground of the Carse, south-west of Kilspindie and Pitroddie, is Glendoick. The tall white mansion house is very fine, and was built by the somewhat notorious Lord President Robert

Craigie (1685–1760). It is a splendid example of the period, with many interesting features. Part of an earlier house extends to the rear, which was the property of the Murrays, Sir Thomas Murray of Glendoick being Lord Clerk Register in the late 16th century. There is a local tradition that Prince Charles spent a night here after Culloden; but this is disproved by his known itinerary. Probably the mistake arose from the fact that a house near by was the property of the Lord George Murray, his Lieutenant-General. The hamlet of Glendoick is a mile away, on the main Carse road. But much nearer was a larger village, now only a farm, called Clien. This was on the line of the old road, which clung to the higher flanks of the hillfoots before the Carse was drained—hence so many little communities along these slopes. It is said that Clien "had a reeking lum for every house in the parish of Semmiedores" (St. Madoes, near by)—which indicated a large village indeed to have vanished without trace.

Kinclaven. Probably not one in a hundred of even knowledgeable Scots will be able to tell you where Kinclaven is; even many Perthshire folk know it not. Yet it is a distinct entity, not remotely placed, and has had much importance in the past. It is a parish without any real village; an ancient castle, an unusual church, a definite area. Ten miles north of Perth, the Tay takes a huge sweep from north-east to due west, and in the process encloses an area shaped like a truncated cone, with 4-mile base and sides, that base the road from Stanley to Murthly across the former Cairnleith Moss and Muir of Thorn. This is Kinclaven parish—though its significant features are concentrated at the extreme eastern tip, where the river makes its sharpest bend. This, in fact, is the reason for the name—*Caen*, a headland; *Kil*, a church; and *Abhainn*, a river. Moreover, just opposite this great bend, the Tay's great tributary, the Isla, comes in from the east. Obviously this would be a strategically significant spot. The Romans found it so, as witness their great camp at Inchtuthill, their fort at Castlehill and their signal-station at Black Hill, all just across the Tay. There are now two bridges here, across Tay and Isla, set close together; but these are comparatively modern, and Kinclaven Ferry was long important, indeed vital. Hence, in medieval times, the need to control it with a castle.

Kinclaven Castle has claims to fame. It stands on a steep wooded ridge above the apex of the bend, and for so ancient a strength is remarkably intact, its great wall of enceinte perhaps a hundred feet square and twenty feet high—this despite Fordun's assertion that it was wholly destroyed in the Edward Baliol wars of 1336. Within, no building remains—indeed we read that it was planted as an orchard at one time, like a walled-garden. The massive curtain-walls reveal its early rude strength. The odd postern-gate to the south is interesting. Blind Harry records that Wallace took the castle in 1297; and a plaque declares this. It was a royal stronghold, said to have been built by Malcolm Canmore, and therefore one of the earliest stone castles. Several charters of Scots kings were signed from Kinclaven. The Duke of Atholl is still nominally its Keeper.

An interesting sight may sometimes be seen from here. In times of spate, the two rivers tend to come down in different colours, the Isla thick and 'drumly', the Tay clear and peat-stained; and they flow on together thus distinct for a considerable distance.

The parish church is surely one of the most charmingly set, yet inconveniently placed, in all Perthshire—which is saying something. Not only is there no village anywhere near, but it is placed well away from the road, hidden out of sight. It is a handsome building, of 1848, well cared-for, all its windows stained-glass, standing in an old kirkyard approached by a fine war memorial lych-gate. The bell is old, in a rather fancy belfry. The original church seems to have stood immediately to the south; for here, now part of an embankment, is a formerly internal memorial heraldic stone of much interest. It refers to a somewhat scoundrelly Bishop of Brechin, of the Tulchan-bishops period, one Alexander Campbell, notorious for alienating most of the see's lands to his chief, the Earl of Argyll—no doubt much sticking to his own fingers. He was himself Laird of Kercock near by—these lands and farms, with that of Bishopshall, still remaining. The weathered inscription is recorded in bronze below:

✠ *Heir lyis Alexr Cabel Bischop of Breichin Laird of Cargo and quha haid onlie ta docters the elder Mareit on Sir Ione Hybeltoune of Letrick; ye younger on ye Laird of Veime quha deit ye 1 of Feb 1608 & of his age 65.*

There is an arch showing five shields, mainly Campbell. Also a good clansman's gesture, intimating that the bronze plaque was placed there by Archibald Campbell Campbell, Lord Blythswood, 1896.

Noteworthy here is the fact that, brought up in the manse when his father was parish minister, was the Reverend John Glass, founder of the Glassite sect.

There is no true village of Kinclaven; but a hamlet, with large farm and mansion-house near by, stands astride the road from Stanley a mile south-west of the bridge. Above it rises the wooded Court-hill, with a cairn, where the King's representatives dispensed justice. A more ancient cairn, doubtless a burial-mound, now grown with Scots pines, stands at the roadside half a mile farther south. Still farther is the amusingly-named farm of Innernytie. The salmon fishings of this area, particularly those of the estate of Ballathie, are renowned.

Kinfauns and Glencarse. Kinfauns is a parish, a castle, a forest and a notable name—but not a village, although the hamlet of Glencarse lies within the parish. The name is said to derive from *ceann-fàn*, the head of the slope—which could apply to places innumerable in Scotland! Certainly neither the castle, the kirkton

nor the parish itself could be said to stand at the head of this particular slope, which is the steep, lofty and craggy side of Kinnoull
Hill, about three miles east of Perth. The two former lie on shelves
of the hillside, and the small parish covers partly the extreme
western end of the Sidlaws, and partly the beginnings of the Carse
of Gowrie.

Kinfauns is undoubtedly best known for its castle. It stands
impressively on its wooded terrace above gardens and orchards,
readily seen from the main A.85 road to Dundee, a great Gothic
pile erected in 1822 by the eminent architect Sir Robert Smirke,
for the Lord Gray of the period. It is now a holiday home connected
with the co-operative movement. There was an ancient fortalice on
the site, now gone. The lands were given by Robert the Bruce to a
picturesque character who supported him, a French pirate named
Thomas de Longueville, of Chartres, known as The Red Rover.
It is said that he founded the Charteris family; but this seems unlikely, as we read that Edward I of England, in 1298, forfeited the
lands of certain Scots lairds who opposed his invasion, including
those of Andrew Charteris. Be that as it may, Sir Thomas's great
two-handed sword, which he wielded in Bruce's cause, was long kept at
Kinfauns Castle. Several of his descendants were Provosts of Perth;
and one, Sir Patrick Charteris of Kinfauns, features in Scott's
Fair Maid. The property passed through various hands, and in
1721, by marriage of the then Blair heiress, came to the 12th Lord
Gray—which line had long been settled at the other end of the
Carse, at Castle Huntly.

About a mile east of the castle, with the wooded, tower-crowned
Binn Hill rising steeply between, is the parish church and the school,
in a secluded position on another shelf. The church itself is rather
gaunt, dating from 1870; but there is an old graveyard, with watch-
house, and the remains of the former church now the burial-crypt
of the Charteris and Gray families, with vault beneath, sadly
neglected. The Blairs of nearby Balthayock were buried outside—as
their reputation made suitable! Indeed, to the north, is quite an
avenue of lairdly tombs.

Below the main road, in the carseland immediately to the south,
is the old estate of Seggieden, its Georgian mansion now superseded
by a small modern house. The Drummond-Hay family have been
here for many centuries. Once the Hays dominated the Carse from
many castles, stemming from their chiefs, the Earls of Erroll.

An attractive side-road climbs northwards past the church, forking
variously amongst the green hills. One branch, after passing the
delightful thatched-roof mansion of Westwood, swings westwards
again, much higher, to contour the hillside above the castle, with
splendid views, turning presently into a little pass between Kinnoul
and Kinfauns Hills, where what was called Deuchny Wood, now
Kinfauns Forest, closes in. Another branch climbs north-eastwards,
and soon passes the gates of Balthdyock House and Castle. This is a
very ancient property, the modern mansion of which recently was

used as a boarding-school. But near by, on a strong site above a steep ravine, stands the massive square keep of the Blairs of Balthayock, now also sadly neglected but not yet a ruin. There have been changes in the floor-levels, and the roof is now flat, instead of gabled, within the parapet; but the immensely thick walls, honeycombed with mural chambers, remain unaltered. A heraldic panel is dated 1578, but the castle is obviously much older. The Blairs of Balthayock claimed chiefship of the name, and were one of the most turbulent and lawless families in the land—which is saying something. A chronicle of their feudings and ongoings would fill volumes.

The third and main section of the aforementioned side-road goes down the quite dramatic Glen Carse, something of a pass between Glencarse Hill and Pans Hill, straight, deep and picturesque—though unfortunately an unsightly quarry has been opened to spoil the picture. The Georgian mansion of Glencarse House sits in the eastern mouth of the valley. The hamlet of Glencarse, however, lies down on the main road, almost a mile to the south, with its hotel, rather out-of-place black-and-white 'Tudor' episcopal church, and abandoned railway station.

Kinnaird. There are many Kinnairds in Scotland, the name meaning merely the head of the height. But there is only one actual parish and village of the name. It is one of those picturesque little communities which nestle in the south-facing folds of the Carse Braes, overlooking the plain of Tay and Gowrie, standing about two miles west of Inchture. Here there is a quite delightful little village, with parish church and manse, all overlooked and dominated by a tall castle. The parish rises from the 50-foot level in the carselands almost to the 1000-foot contour at Blacklaw; so there is much of climbing, green hillsides, hanging woods and splendid vistas. There was formerly another village at Pitmiddle, much higher on the Braes, to the north-east about a mile; but this, like a number of other Gowrie villages has dwindled into obscurity with the draining of the level plain, and the roads in consequence tending to abandon the heights. There is still a large wood of that name.

Kinnaird village itself sits on broken hillside terraces beside the ravine of its own burn, facing south amongst its orchards, with no village street or scheme of lay-out, but no less attractive therefor. Some of the cottages still retain their thatched roofs. The church dates only from 1815, and is a plain but pleasing building of red stone, with a watch-house; presumably it was necessary to counter the activities of body-snatchers even in this peaceful and arcadian spot. The Threipland of Fingask burial-place flanks the church door.

Kinnaird Castle, not to be confused with the much larger seat of that name in Angus, is much more in evidence here than is usual, not hidden away in any large wooded estate but soaring impressively on an open green knoll above the village, still occupied and in good order. It is an interesting and dramatic place, a tall, red-stone keep of the 15th century with earlier nucleus, thick-walled, with a small projecting tower or buttress at one corner, which is not a stair-tower, as it seems, and highly unusual, its summit forming a watch-chamber at high parapet level. Another unusual feature is the two-storeyed 17th century addition to the east—for this is not actually attached to the keep. It contains an old kitchen with an enormous arched fireplace 13 feet wide by 6 deep, with an outside service window, evidently for viands to be pushed through for the castle's family. Hot dishes cannot have been a speciality at Kinnaird.

It is claimed that one Randolph Rufus obtained, from William the Lyon, these lands in 1170; and his descendants took their name therefrom. One, Sir Richard Kinnaird of that Ilk, married his son Reginald to the heiress of Sir John Kirkcaldy of Inchture, and so gained these neighbouring carselands, in the time of Robert III. Just when the Kinnairds moved to live at Moncur Castle, nearer Inchture—now itself a ruin and abandoned by them for Rossie Priory in the vicinity—is not clear. But Sir Patrick Threipland, 1st Baronet of Fingask, bought Kinnaird in the 17th century. Just beforehand, in 1617, James VI on a rare return visit to Scotland, spent some days hunting from here. Later the castle became ruinous, but happily was restored towards the close of the last century.

Kinnoull. This is the name of a parish, a hill, a public park and a 17th century earldom which once spoke loud in Scotland, and though still extant, is now reduced to some thirty acres of the hilltop. Only thrusting height, and the fact that the Tay runs between, has prevented the Fair City of Perth from swallowing up Kinnoull as it has done other villages on its periphery.

The hill, so well known as a splendid landmark overlooking Perth and Tay, is in fact the final flourish of the Sidlaw range, only 729 feet high but presenting a strikingly precipitous face to the south for almost two miles. To west and north it is gentler and wooded, and on the east a deep cleft separates it from the Binn Hill of Kinfauns. On the dizzy edge of both hills are set sham castles, or follies, said to have been built by an Earl of Kinnoull who had been impressed by the castles of the Rhine, a river which the Tay here resembles. Kinnoull Hill, thanks largely to the generosity of Lord Dewar, of the Perth whisky family, is now a magnificent public park for the town, with a nature trail, woodlands paths, seats and picnic-places. The summit, with its direction-indicators, offers breathtaking views over the city, the winding Tay, the Carse of Gowrie, Strathearn and the serried ridges of the Highland Line, infinitely worth the climb. A winding carriage-road, built by a Duke of Montague, so it is said, led to the top in the estate days, and can still be traced—but not used by cars. On the face of the cliff is a cave called the Dragon Hole, claimed to have sheltered the elusive Wallace. Beltane festivals used to be held here prior to the Reformation. And in the Windy Gowl, a steep narrow gap between summits, a famous echo can be raised. Fine agates have been found here—and there is talk even of diamonds.

At the wooded western skirts of the hill is what is now the Perth suburb of Bridgend—once a village occupied by boatmen for the ferries when there was, in fact, no bridge. Here was the ancient castle and church of Kinnoull, called in old charters indeed a burgh of barony, with a burgh's privileges. The castle lay a quarter-mile from the church, but no traces remain. A new Gothic-style parish church was built here, by the well-known architect Burn, in 1826, with 1000 sittings. The old church of St. Constantine—an unusual dedication—lies disused nearer the river, and is famed for a fine memorial to George Hay of Megginch, Viscount Dupplin and 1st Earl of Kinnoull, so created in 1633. He was Chancellor of Scotland and a robust character, who did not hesitate to put his king right. It is recorded that when the episcopally-minded Charles I ordered that Archbishop Spottiswoode of St. Andrews should have precedence at the Scottish coronation, Kinnoull "would not suffer him to have place of him, doe quhat he could, all the dayes of his liffetime". Charles, on this occasion, was unusually philosophical, for he declared ". . . letts go to bussiness. I will not meddle furder with that olde cankered gootishe man, at quhose hands there is nothing to be gained bot soure wordes." The King won, of course, for Kinnoull died next year—and Spottiswoode was made Chancellor *and* Primate.

Up the pleasant hillside from Bridgend the villas spread, with some good modern housing—but not sufficient to spoil the prospect. Here is the large modern Roman Catholic Monastery of St. Mary, of the Congregation of the Holy Redeemer, for the training of novices for the priesthood, interesting continuity, in that Perth was once fuller of monasteries than almost anywhere else in Scotland. And here was established in 1827 the well-known James Murray's Royal Asylum for Lunatics, built also by Burn, at vast cost, by the inheritor of a huge East India fortune. Earlier, in 1767, a famous nursery was established in the same area, by the brothers Dickson from Hassendeanburn in Teviotdale, an enterprising family that branched out in other directions also. Their project here prospered exceedingly, growing to cover 60 acres and to employ as many as 80 people.

To the south of Bridgend, where the Dundee road begins to bend round the corner of Kinnoull Hill, is the former village of Barnhill, more properly Baronhill, still with a few old and picturesque houses. Amongst the large modern villas is one which has a special interest, Branklyn, in that it has a most notable garden, specialising in Alpine plants, open to the public and now under the auspices of the National Trust for Scotland, described as "the finest 2 acres of private garden in the country".

Tucked away into the north-east face of Kinnoull Hill over a mile away, is the picturesque and hidden little hamlet of Corsiehill, oddly remote to be so near Perth. Thereafter a very attractive backroad winds its way through the pass-like gap below Deuchny

Muthill. Celtic church saddle-roofed tower, and pre-Reformation ruins

New Scone. Greystanes modern housing enshrining Stone Circle

Perth. 15th century St. John's Kirk

Wood, contouring round the hillside high above Kinfauns Castle
and on between the Deuchny and Binn Hills, eventually to lead to
either Balthayock, Glen Carse or Kinfauns Kirk and the main A.85
Dundee road again—a pleasant run with splendid vistas.

Kirkmichael and Strathardle. By no means everyone knowledgeable about Scotland could tell you where Strathardle was, or
Kirkmichael either; but they are becoming better known because
of the boom in skiing and their near proximity to the ski-slopes of
Glen Shee, their accommodation possibilities recommending them
to visitors in an area where population is scanty. Strathardle is a
long, fair and wide valley probing into the Grampians north-west
of the Blairgowrie district, the A.924 running up it eventually to
Pitlochry and passing Kirkmichael roughly half-way. The River
Ardle joins the Black Water, coming down Glen Shee, at Bridge of
Cally. Forking left here, the road climbs gently up the pleasant
strath 7 miles to Kirkmichael, and on another 12 to Pitlochry, over
the hills.

Less than two miles up from Bridge of Cally is Monks Cally,
reminder of the time when this area was an apanage of the great
Abbey of Coupar Angus. At Steps of Cally farm—where there
would once be stepping-stones across the Ardle—is a small graveyard
by the waterside, all that is left of the religious establishment here,
with no sign of a chapel. The burial-ground has been sifted free of
stones. Across the river is the large forest of Blackcraig; and Blackcraig Castle, a mile on, over its own bridge, is so notably effective a
reproduction of an old Scots fortalice as to almost deceive the
practised eye, partly because of the weathering of the soft sandstone.
The hamlet of Ballintium comes next, with its mansion now a hotel;
and the very small Episcopal Church of St. Michael isolated on a
bank. A mile farther, at the Balnabroich road-end, in a wood on a
knoll, are two standing-stones, with another in a field to the north.

Just before Kirkmichael is reached, the B.950 strikes off over high
ground to the east to join the A.93 in Glen Shee again. At the road-
end is a tall Celtic-type cross erected to one James Small, a local
magistrate, who died in 1900, by 350 of his friends who loved and
trusted him—as the inscription touchingly declares—fair testimony.
Set remotely in the hills off this B.950, at the end of a long drive, are
two fortalices, strangely close to each other—Ashintully and
Whitefield Castles, less than a mile apart. The former is still occupied as a mansion, the latter very ruinous. Ashintully is a smallish
late 16th century building on the L-plan, somewhat altered and of
unusual appearance, with an open bartizan or parapet at eaves-
level above the door in the angle, for protection. There are also a
number of gunloops and shot-holes and a panel dated 1583, inscribed *THE LORD DEFEND THIS HOUS*—so obviously defence
was a major preoccupation. Not unsuitably, it seems—for in 1587
Ashintully was besieged by a group of high-born brigands, and the
laird, Andro Spalding, maltreated—for which the offenders were

I

eventually put to the horn by the Privy Council. Despite, or perhaps because of, its remote situation, there were other similar attacks on the Spaldings' house. No doubt that is why Whitefield Castle, also a Spalding place, was built so near at hand. The area cannot have been quite so lonely once, however, for we read that the laird here had the right to hold two annual fairs and a weekly market.

Just before the Ashintully road-end on this B.950, above Dunidea farm, is An Dun, an early fortification on a hilltop. There is now a large limestone quarry working near by. Near the junction with A.93, at Dalrulzeon, on the south side of the road, is a row of massive boulders set as a kind of dyke, quite long. This whole area is rich in the remains of antiquity.

Back on A.924, sequestered Kirkmichael village is not particularly beautiful, despite attractive surroundings. It lies on both sides of the Ardle, linked by a bridge, and has a small and very plain, yellow-washed parish church and cramped graveyard by the riverside. Signs of the skiing boom show in the Edelweiss Restaurant, a horn-carver's establishment and the Highland Home Industries centre. The village is not large, although its parish is, covering nearly fifty-eight thousand acres, larger than the counties of Clackmannan or Kinross.

Strathardle continues for another 4 miles, to the junction of Glens Fernate and Brerachan, at Straloch. This area is notable for its curiously-built early lime-kilns, looking almost like earth-houses to the uninitiated; one is at the roadside at Balvarran House drive. A mile on is the hamlet of Enochdu, with, at the lodge-gates of Dirna-dean House, an unusual narrow stone shaft at the head of a long burial-mound, locally known as a giant's grave, but reputed to be the resting-place of a Pictish chief named *Ard-fhuil*, meaning of high and noble blood, who was killed here fighting the Danes, and gave his name to the Strath. There are two more normal standing-stones at the roadside near by. Indeed, with the concentric stone circles, and large burial cairns, in the hills 3 miles south-east of Kirkmichael, and the 3-ton rocking-stone near by, this is very much a place to be visited by those interested in the remote past.

Straloch itself, where the road swings widely to the west, is another tiny hamlet, the last before the abiding heather, green cultivation in the face of the ever-heighting hills. Here is a fairly modern little church, formerly under royal bounty, its interior bright with a sky-blue ceiling. There is a little loch in the mouth of Glen Fernate, to give the place its name, and a long, long private road that goes on up that wild, remote glen into the heart of Atholl. The A.924 climbs instead up Glen Brerachan, on its own lonely moorland way to Pitlochry, 9 miles, touching 1260 feet in the process.

Ben Lawers. This mountain deserves especial treatment here, not only because it is the highest in Perthshire, or anywhere south of the Nevis–Cairngorm line, but because it is notable for many

other features, not the least its great botanical interest. It rises
3984 feet, on the north side of Loch Tay, and is readily accessible
(for a great mountain) from the road which climbs northwards
steeply half-way along the loch-side. About two miles up, at 1400
feet, is a large car-park and Information Centre of the National
Trust for Scotland, which owns 8000 acres here. As well as facilities,
there is an elaborate finger-post showing climbing times for a great
number of the surrounding peaks. Two or three miles climb from
here, on Beinn Ghlas, is the ski hut of the Scottish Ski Club, this
area providing good opportunities for that energetic sport. From
the top of Ben Lawers the view, on a clear day, is quite superb, with
both the Atlantic and the North Sea visible, and a tremendous
prospect of the Central Highlands.

The district is geologically interesting, and the Alpine plants are
of particular note, some of them rare. And on the lower slopes, the
Trust has laid out a Nature Trail, where much of wild life may be
glimpsed. Altogether a most worthwhile area to visit.

The road, narrow but now well-metalled, climbs on past the car-
park and up to the summit of a high pass at about 1800 feet, skirting
on the way the dam-extended Lochan na Lairige. A modern cairn
marks the summit of the pass. Thereafter the road descends, by
many tight bends and steep hills (1 in 6) another 5 miles, to Glen
Lyon at Bridge of Balgie, no road for buses but perfectly fit for cars
if driven with care. Half a mile south of the Lyon there is a most
attractive waterfall and rapids in a little gorge of the *Allt Bail a
Mhuillinn*, literally the Milton Burn—Milton of Eonan, or St.
Adamnan, lying at the foot, in a most picturesque setting.

Lecropt and Keir. Lecropt is not a name which most people,
probably, will find familiar—even though thousands pass by and
through it. An unusual name, too—being a corruption of *leth-
croch*, Gaelic for The Half Hill. It is, in fact, a small parish, lying
between the confluences of Teith and Allan with Forth, on the very
southern edge of Perthshire; and there is no village, only an isolated
parish church and a section of the Carse of Forth called the Carse of
Lecropt—in which, in the 2nd century and thereabouts, stood the
Damnonii capital of Alauna, this town of the ancient Caledonians
acting as guardian for the lands north of the Forth as Stirling was to
do later. Numerous of the old Caledonian forts and standing-stones
dot the higher ground of what is now the Keir estate. The half-hill
to which the name refers is a long 300-foot-high bank which runs
through the parish above the rich carseland.

The church stands on the crest of this escarpment just half a mile
west of Bridge of Allan, on the A.9—and just where the new Stirling
by-pass of the motorway comes in across the levels, from the south.
It is a comparatively modern Gothic edifice, and unremarkable.
Near by were the Court and Gallows Hills of the barony of Keir.

The policies of this important estate lie immediately to the west.
The mansionhouse is very large, a composite structure of many

periods, with an ancient nucleus. Its approach from the north is highly unusual, the driveway winding through deep tunnels in the hillside and terraces, to emerge practically in the back court. The property was acquired from Leslie of that Ilk in 1448 by Lucas de Strevelyn, or Stirling, and the Stirling family still remain the lairds. There is a tradition that one of the Stirlings of Keir it was who slew James III after the Battle of Sauchieburn—though this deed is usually ascribed to the then Lord Gray. Sir William Stirling-Maxwell succeeded, through the female line, in 1865, to the baronetcy of Maxwell of Pollock. He was an author of some note, and greatly enlarged the house.

On the Keir estate less than a mile to the west of the mansion, in pleasant rising parkland on the 'half-hill', is the ruined castle of Arnhall. Not a great deal survives, but enough to reveal it as having been a fine place.

Oddly enough this small and never populous parish used to have a number of mills for the manufacture of coarse paper.

The Lochs Ard to Arklet Road. West of Aberfoyle, partly in Perthshire, partly in Stirlingshire, runs one of the most delightful stretches of road in mid-Scotland—and considering how accessible it is, how close relatively to the great centres of population, remarkably little appreciated. Reasons probably are that it is a dead-end road, requiring a return by the same route; and that, for long, the final 4 miles was virtually impassable, and therefore discouraging—though this no longer applies. The B.829, based on an ancient drove-road for the Highland cattle-traders and MacGregor caterans, runs for some fifteen miles west by north, through the mountains, by Lochs Ard, Chon and Arklet, to Inversnaid on the east side of Loch Lomond; and two-thirds of the way, sends off a half-mile spur to the west end of Loch Katrine at Stronachlacher—thus threading some of the finest scenery in the South Highlands. It is a perfectly good road now, though narrow, winding and not to be rushed over. But who would wish to rush over this, in less than an emergency?

Leaving Aberfoyle and its western 'suburb' of the Milton, it follows the course of the Avondhu, or Black Water, the northern of the two sources of the River Forth, passing several most attractively-placed houses in the hilly woodlands. Quickly it reaches Loch Ard, the 'lower loch', or narrow eastern reach, of which is really only a widening of the Avondhu. Then the loch widens out into a delightful sheet of water, 2½ miles long, forest-girt, isle-dotted at the western end, with first medium-wooded hills and then high mountains rising behind, culminating in Ben Lomond itself (3192 feet). The scanty ruins of a small fortalice are sited at the far side, called Duke Murdoch's Castle, and reputedly built by that unfortunate Regent of Scotland, whom James I executed for treason, at Stirling, in 1425. He had the earldom of Menteith, with its main castle at Doune; so this must have been only a hunting-house.

The road, keeping close to the north shore, amongst the woodlands of birch and oak, passes the former shooting-lodges of Alts-
keith and Forest Hills, now hotels, and the Youth Hostel at Ledard.
Here a steep little side-glen comes in on the north, with a hurtling
burn, which produces a waterfall in two sections. Walter Scott has
described this in *Rob Roy*. Indeed all this area has been much
utilised by Sir Walter, and is rich in Rob Roy lore.

A private side-road swings southwards round the head of the
loch, and takes 7 afforested miles to return to Kirkton of Aberfoyle,
via Duchray. The main road continues by the Water of Chon for 2
miles, latterly very switch-backed and ever growing in beauty,
passing the hump-backed bridge and little former ale-house
amusingly known as the Tea-pot, also with Rob Roy links. Then to
Loch Chon—the Lake of the Dog. This is narrower than Loch Ard
and about two miles long, also wood-girt, with three small islets
which once formed a heronry. The mountains now close in. The
Loch Katrine Aqueduct, carrying its water to thirsty Glasgow,
skirts the western shore; and while this was being constructed about
a century ago a temporary village was erected near the head of the
loch, called Sebastopol.

Beyond, the road rises over a little pass, suddenly to emerge upon
a tremendous and vastly different scene. Ahead is another loch,
quite changed in character, wilder, bare of trees, shouldered by
lofty heather hills, and, dominating the far end, the impressive
jagged peaks of the 'Arrochar Alps', Bens Vane, Ime, Narnain,
Vorlich and so on. These all seem much closer than in fact they are;
and what is scarcely acceptable to most who look, at first, is that
they are at the *far* side of Loch Lomond; and that that great loch
lies hidden in a trough 400 feet lower than the end of this Loch
Arklet, though the two lochs are little more than a mile apart. In
almost any weather, the abrupt change and scale of the vista is
breathtaking.

Less than two miles from the head of the pass, a T-junction is
reached. The right fork turns off to the east and in a short distance
is at the western shore of Loch Katrine, at Stronachlachar, where
this public road stops, a private Glasgow Waterworks road going on
to the north and Glen Gyle. Loch Katrine, of course, is much larger
than any of the other lochs hitherto described, being 8 miles long
and a mile wide, curling rather in the shape of an S. Its beauties
and fame are well known, and best dealt with under The Trossachs,
the normal access. But it may be mentioned that this Stirlingshire
approach gives a very different aspect, much more open and less
wooded, with the mountains lying farther back. Because this is
Glasgow's main water supply, no public roads encircle the loch,
unfortunately—although a steamer plies in summer from foot to
head, at Stronachlacher. This is a little 'institutional' community of
Glasgow Corporation, in a most attractive setting. The private road
and walking-track goes on another 3 miles to Glengyle. This remote
and romantic glen and former laird's house was the seat of a power-

ful branch of the Clan Alpine, or Gregor, known as the Clan Dougal Keir, and here was born, in 1671, Rob Roy MacGregor, second son of the chieftain, Colonel Donald MacGregor of Glengyle. Rob, though he came to captain the clan in the earlier Jacobite risings, never was chieftain, this being his brother and his nephew's place; but the whole area resounds with his deeds and fame, and hardly an item of the splendid landscape does not echo some stirring story—as Walter Scott made known to so many in his *Lady of the Lake*, *Rob Roy* and so on. A mile across from Stronachlachar, for instance, lies Portanellan, where Glengyle had another house and where, in a little walled graveyard of the Dougal Keir chieftains, Rob's father was buried. Rob found this house a frequent refuge. And out on the loch from it, lies the little islet of Eilean Dubh, or Black Isle, where in 1716 the freebooter held the kidnapped factor of the Montrose estates, Graham of Killearn, who had so shamefully molested Rob's wife. This is all magnificent country for walkers.

Back to the T-junction, the left fork runs along Loch Arklet-side for 4 miles, to Inversnaid on Loch Lomond. This road is now as good as the rest; but for long it was practically impassable, and deliberately, so, by policy of Glasgow Corporation, to discourage visitors, in the interests of water purity. However, a few years ago, the present author, with one or two others, engaged in a lively campaign to change all this; and after much pressure and some hot words, Glasgow capitulated, and thereafter handsomely renewed the road, and handed it over to Stirlingshire County Council to maintain for public access. This was done at least as much in the interests of the little community at Inversnaid as for the travelling public. So now the motorist may proceed along this delightful stretch—so long as he does not contaminate the water!

Half-way along, he will pass the farm of Corryarklet, once a township of 20 houses, important to the MacGregors, and a holding of kinsmen of the Glengyle lairds. Here, to her uncle's house, Rob Roy's wife fled, after the attack on her at Inversnaid. Just across the loch is still to be discerned the lonely house of Corryheichen, tenanted then by a brother of Corryarklet. These two were also brothers of MacGregor of Comar, a still more remote hill property lying up on the flanks of Ben Lomond, to the south, still a hill-farm. And it was Mary MacGregor of Comar a second-cousin, whom Rob married, in 1693. The Buchanan parish register notes the fact, and adds in the margin "Married at Coreklet". It is amusing to note that the lady's name was Mary, or Marie, not Helen, as Scott says in his novel—and which posterity accepts as for gospel.

Below the dam at the west end of Arklet, the road dips rapidly into softer country, to where the green glen of the Snaid Burn comes in from the north, and where the government fort known as the Garrison of Inversnaid, scene of dramatic happenings, was sited. Rob Roy was himself laird of Inversnaid, of course. But this area deserves separate attention.

Lochearnhead, Glen Ogle and St. Fillans. Like so many others in Perthshire, Loch Earn is long, narrow and beautiful, lying at the head of Strathearn, in an east–west valley, with a village at each end and roads skirting both north and south shores, the latter being the more interesting if less fast. The loch is 7 miles long, and once a small steamer used to ply; now yachts and motor-boats for water-skiing sail instead. The southern hills are the higher, Ben Vorlich and Stuc a Chroin (3224 and 3189 feet) rearing amongst a welter of summits to form a great isolated group at the head of the Forest of Glenartney. Earn got its name from Eire, or Ireland, because of the early Irish Celtic missionaries' and colonists' especial influence here, just after the Roman tide ebbed.

St. Fillans, at the foot of the loch, called after one of these missionaries, is an attractive village set amidst trees by the waterside, with many hotels and a modern church. A mile to the south-east, is the golf-course and at the foot of the conical hill of Dundurn, is the ruined original church in an old graveyard. One of the tombstones reminds us of that harsh law of 1603 which proscribed the very name of MacGregor, so that none might legally bear it—even Rob Roy having to sign himself Robert Campbell. This stone, though nominally a Drummond tomb, has the crossed pine tree and sword bearing the royal crown, carved on the back—the proud MacGregor arms. On the summit of the hillock at the back, is the site of a large dun, or Pictish fort, called both Dun Faolain (or Fillan) and Dundurn. This Fillan appears to be other than the saint of Strathfillan and Glen Dochart. However, since there are alleged to have been no fewer than 16 saints of this name, some confusion is natural. This one is thought to have been a leper. He had a miraculous well near by, long a place of pilgrimage for various sufferers—presumably not from leprosy—and more especially for barren women. Also a natural stone seat on the hilltop.

In the loch, near the village, is the small wooded Neishes' Isle, in whose ruined castle the chief of the Neishes was slain by the twelve sons of MacNab, after their epic crossing of the mountains from Tayside with the boat necessary to get them out to the islet. The MacNabs thereafter added insult to injury by adopting as crest MacNeish's head, which they had carried home to their grim sire. The name Neish is a corruption of Naois, the lover of Deirdre, one of the aforementioned Irish heroes—or so say the Neishes.

Of the ancient lairdships dotting the south shore of the loch, the two most interesting are those at the foot of Glens Vorlich and Ample. Ardvorlich is the seat of a renowned branch of the Stewarts, hailing from Balquhidder and Glen Buckie, whose progenitor, marrying a daughter of the Drummond keeper of the royal forest of Glen Artney, gained these lands in the 16th century. There was a grim sequel to this marriage. Some marauding MacGregors, having at Balquhidder sworn to 'liquidate' Drummond, duly ambushed and slew him. Then they took his head to Ardvorlich, where the sister was married to the Stewart, and were feeding the head bread and cheese when the lady herself came in. She rushed off, crazed, and her baby was born up in the hills by a small loch still called the Lochan of the Woman. This child became the celebrated Mad Major James Stewart, one of Montrose's captains, who, apart from slaying any and every MacGregor he could find, ended by dirking to death his own greatest friend and fellow-officer the Lord Kilpont, heir of the Graham Earl of Airth and Menteith, in 1640. The present laird is the 14th *Mac Mhic Bhaltair*. A precious relic is the Clach Dearg, a crystal, supposedly brought back from a Crusade, allegedly with healing properties. Down near the road is a stone inscribed: "Near this spot were interred the bodies of 7 MacDonalds of Glencoe, killed when attempting to harry Ardvorlich Anno Domini 1620."

Glen Ample, to the west, is a longer, wider valley, with a notable waterfall and a track over to Ardchullarie on Loch Lubnaig. At its foot is the fine, whitewashed castle of Edinample, prominently seen from across the loch, a tall, Z-shaped fortalice of the late 16th century with an older nucleus, picturesque with round towers and turrets and an alarming bottle-dungeon. Originally a MacGregor stronghold, it was one of the many filched from them by the up-and-coming Campbells, and rebuilt.

Near the head of the loch is the site of St. Blane's Chapel. Blane was another of those determined Celtic missionaries from Ireland, after whom Dunblane also is named. Today there is a St. Blane's craft-centre and tea-garden near by. The modern church of Lochearnhead, whitewashed, by the side of the main A.84 road is also in this vicinity, attractive amongst the woodlands.

The loch's north-side road, A.85, Crieff to Crianlarich, has less steep gradients and is wider, with fine views of Ben Vorlich and some hydro-electric developments. Towards the west end, Glen Beich opens to the north, its river falling in some fine cascades. In the mouth of the glen, a little back from the road, are the scanty remains of Dalveich Castle, in a small field.

Lochearnhead, at the junction of the A.84 and A.85, pleasingly sited on the green slopes above the loch, looking eastwards, is a most attractive scattered village, a nest of hotels, its houses stretching along both roads. It has long been famed as a tourist centre, and is now also renowned for water-skiing and yachting, thanks to the initiative of the Lochearnhead Hotel proprietor. Edinchip, the seat of Sir Gregor MacGregor of MacGregor, 23rd chief of the Children of the Mist, lies a mile to the south-west. The small, high-hanging valley of Glen Kendrum climbs behind the village, to a high craggy pass. Lochearnhead makes a convenient centre for visiting much of the West Perthshire Highlands.

To the north, A.85 strikes off up steep and narrow Glen Ogle, a stern and dramatic defile which in 3 miles climbs 620 feet from the loch to the high pass of the Larig Cheile, carrying the main route to the north-west over into Glen Dochart. The name is said to derive from *eagal*, meaning the glen of dread, and certainly it can look sufficiently daunting in bad weather, with scores of foaming burns crashing down the dark rock sides, amongst the wilderness of fallen boulders. Queen Victoria named it the Khyber Pass of Scotland. The old General Wade road traversed it by many hazards; but the modern highway makes light of it, long as the climb is, on the east side, the former railway-line making a spectacular ascent on the west. The view from the summit, especially forward, as the prospect opens out, is inspiring after the constrictions of the pass.

Loch Tay. This famous sheet of water has a character all its own. It has a placid, calm, undemanding look about it, very different from, say, the striking loveliness of Rannoch of the winds, or of the gentler, green-flanked Tummel, or even of fair, wooded Loch Earn. Which is strange, for though the mountains that surround it are rounded rather than jagged and fierce, some of them are very high, Ben Lawers, mid-way along the north shore, at 3984 feet, being the highest in Perthshire, indeed the highest, after Nevis and the Cairngorm giants, in all Scotland. Moreover, the hills throng fairly closely.

The loch is 14 miles long and averages something under a mile in width. With Killin at its head and Kenmore at its foot, it spans the very centre of Scotland. Two roads flank it, to north and south. For the visitor the latter is the more picturesque and interesting, the former, A.827, the faster. Both sides of the loch are grievously depopulated, compared with not so very long ago, let alone in the heyday of the clans; but the southern flank is less noticeably so. It is said that early last century the north side of Tay had a population of 1500; whereas today the former parish of Lawers, to which most of it belongs, can produce barely a hundred. Yet in 1872 it was recorded that this same parish had reared 1 Member of Parliament, 1 professor, 9 ministers, 11 teachers and 7 doctors.

The north road, keeping for the most part to the higher ground, is less scenic, less preoccupied with the ins and outs of the loch-shore. From Kenmore, after threading the woods of Drummond Hill, it passes the hamlet of Fearnan, more properly Stronfearnan, where a side-road strikes northwards for Fortingall and Glen Lyon. Five miles on is Lawers, where the remains of the parish church can be seen down near the loch-side. The Campbells of Lawers were an important branch of that great clan, who eventually climbed the brae to become Earls of Loudoun, in Ayrshire. Midway between here and Bridge of Lochay, and the mouth of that fine glen, the narrow, steeply-climbing but improved road turns off over the shoulder of Ben Lawers for Bridge of Balgie, Glen Lyon.

The south shore road is much more congenial and 'loch-conscious', serving many old estates and hamlets. The first, Acharn, is pictur-esque by its burnside, with the old water-mill turned into a craft-centre. Higher up the burn are a series of notable waterfalls, with a grotto near by, remarked upon by the indefatigable Dorothy Wordsworth.

By Ardtalnaig, 5 miles on, where the old drove-road comes in from upper Glen Almond, we come to Ardeonaig, named after Eonan, or St. Adamnan, who presumably had a cell here. Here also was based a ferry across the loch, with its inn now a small hotel. It was not the public ferry, however, which the twelve stout sons of The MacNab used, one Yuletide night in the early 16th century, when they rowed across the loch from their father's house, disembarked here, and raising their boat on their shoulders, commenced the appalling climb right up and over the watershed and down to Loch Earn by Glen Beich, 10 grim miles and a 1600-foot ascent, in order to row it out to the MacNeish islet in that loch and there slay the chief thereof, to avenge an ancient wrong. A sardonic touch is added to this fierce tale by the fact that the returning brothers actually carried their boat up again, right to the high watershed, along with MacNeish's head, before wearily abandoning it. Remains of the craft were still to be discerned up there on the mountain until late last century.

On the little promontory at Ardeonaig are the scanty remains of the ancient castle of Mains.

Logierait. *Lag an rath*, the hollow of the castle, is a small village but a large parish (61 square miles) set in the mouth of Strathtay—the section of the Tay valley which swings westwards, below Pitlochry, and where it is joined by Tummel. The Rivers Tay and Tummel here form a very pronounced peninsula, with a prow or bluff; and here was an ancient castle of Robert III—which gives the place its name. There are still vestiges of masonry crowning the bluff, and the hollow of a ditch to guard it. But now a great Celtic-type cross rears on the summit, a memorial to the 6th Duke of Atholl, and a most impressive monument, though much neglected. Logierait was the seat of an Atholl court of regality, and its courthouse and a renowned hall, 70 feet long with galleries at both ends—now, alas, gone. Rob Roy escaped from it in 1717; and Prince Charles Edward housed 600 prisoners here after Prestonpans—a long way to bring them.

The hamlet is on low ground near the Tay, where there was a ferry formerly. The hotel here, an inn where Wordsworth stayed in 1803, handles the fishing rights for stretches of the river. The parish church near by is large, yellow-washed and not particularly attractive, built in 1806. Here is a small Celtic cross-slab, defaced, but showing part of a horse and rider, with a version of the Pictish serpent motif. There are three cage-type iron mort-safes, one for a child; also many old gravestones. A rather gaunt large building, to the west, houses an old folks' home. And to the east, a bridge carries the A.827 over Tummel to join the A.9 at the former Ballinluig Junction. Logierait was once a large and important village, with its own annual cattle fair, and no fewer than six distilleries in the parish. The famous Adam Fergusson, historian, was a son of the manse here.

To the north, a narrow climbing road leads to Pitlochry by west side of Tummel, 5 miles. Two and a half miles up is the farm of Killichangie, where once there was a small chapel. At the foot of a steep grassy bank here is a very plain cross-slab stone, with unusually high top to the cross, and a smaller stone beside it. It is sometimes called the Priest's Stone, and has probably been removed from the chapel near by. Two miles farther is the Dunfallandy House Hotel and farm, where there is one of the most renowned Pictish cross-slabs in the country. The Dunfallandy Stone stands on a knoll behind the farm, beside the private burial-ground of the Fergussons of Dunfallandy, under yew trees, and is now in the care of the Ministry of Works. On one side is a large Celtic cross in magnificent workmanship; and on the other various spirited symbols, including a mounted traveller in robes, with hammer, anvil and tongs, thought to indicate a priestly iron-worker. There are claims that this was brought here from Killiecrankie, but this is almost certainly a mistake; there was a chapel at Dunfolenthi in 1115, as one at Kilchemi, or Killichangie, which may have caused the confusion. Near by, to the south, in a corner of the field, is the Bloody Stone, a plain large boulder alleged to commemorate a massacre.

At the other side of Logierait, a succession of old estates stretch westwards into Strathtay, those of Ballechin and Pitnacree also having hamlets of these names. The former's mansion has been demolished. It was anciently a Stewart place, its lairds Chamberlains of Atholl. The son of one, reputedly a clergyman, fought at Killiecrankie with such sustained vigour that the basket-hilt of his broadsword had to be cut away to free his swollen hand. Pitnacree was a Menzies property. Formerly it had its own cattle market held each spring—so there must have been more than a hamlet once.

In the empty hills to the north are many small lochs, and one quite large—Derculich.

Longforgan and Kingoodie. Longforgan is long indeed, over a mile long, a straggling but quite attractive village stretching along a ridge above the eastern end of the Carse of Gowrie, turning its back on the busy A.85 dual-carriageway, some five miles west of Dundee. It grew up as a dependency of the great Castle Huntly, seat of the Lords Gray; and these being a turbulent lot, it no doubt saw considerable excitements. Today, Castle Huntly is a Borstal institution. Longforgan, after Errol the largest village in the Carse, was advanced to the status of the Lordship of Lyon in 1672, and became a burgh of barony, with many privileges, including the holding of fairs and markets. The Forgan Fair became a notable event. But the village fell away from such heights. The parish of Longforgan contains also the villages of Kingoodie, on the coast to the east, and Mylnefield inland, nearer Dundee.

The parish church stands towards the west end of the long winding street, in an old kirkyard with venerable monuments. It was built as a replacement in 1795, a pleasing building with a small spire and clock. Outside, at the tower-foot, lies a detached circular stone inscribed: *Founded in the year 1690 and finished at the charges of Patrick, Earl of Strathmore and Kinghorn, Viscount Lyon. The bells were given by the Session and the clock by* . . . (indecipherable). Elsewhere, it is recorded that the clock in the steeple was reconstructed in 1878 by a self-taught carpenter.

Like Errol farther east, the village tends to spill over down the south-facing bank of the ridge, giving pleasant views over carse and estuary. This ridge, which commences at the coast at Kingoodie, runs north-westwards away from the firth for about three miles, to end rather abruptly at what is called the Snabs of Drimmie, north of Castle Huntly. 2687 of the parish's 11,247 acres are foreshore, accounted for by the great tidal flats of the Dog Bank, down into which the Huntly Burn winds its way.

Castle Huntly has always dominated Longforgan, as it does all the east end of the Carse. Seen from the west it is one of the most impressively-sited fortalices in the land, crowning a steep rocky bluff above the levels, part of the Snab ridge-end, out of which it seems to grow naturally, soaring for a further seven storeys to the dizzy parapet-walk and garret storey 116 feet above the plain. Unfortunately, in the 'gothic-crazy' early 19th century, some 'improver' added small sham turrets at the parapet angles and an English-style crenellated round caphouse, quite out of proportion, much spoiling the roofline appearance. But nothing can wholly ruin the massive and lofty aspect, thrusting above its gardens and orchards. The other, northern and eastern aspects are not impressive, for, owing to the rise in the ground level, these are two storeys lower, and modern extensions have been added. The castle dates from 1452, when the first Lord Gray received a licence to build. Its 10-foot-thick walls of Kingoodie sandstone are honeycombed with mural closets and passages, the pit or prison, dug deep into the solid rock foundations, being a fearsome place. The castle remained with the Grays until 1614, and volumes have been written about the activities of that spirited line, the famous Master of Gray, handsomest and wickedest man in Europe of his day, being particularly notorious, during the reign of James VI. His son sold Castle Huntly to the 11th Lord Glamis, who became 1st Earl of Strathmore and Kinghorne—hence the 17th century Lordship of Lyon, the family name. It is a strange turn of fate that it should now house delinquent youth. A cottage in the village bears a plaque commemorating the spot where the hero Wallace rested, as a mere schoolboy, in his flight after slaying the arrogant son of the English governor of Dundee, Selby by name—perhaps the first blow struck in the Wars of Independence.

Kingoodie is an interesting place. Here were famous stone quarries, from a very early date. The old Tower of Dundee is said to have been built of Kingoodie stone, in the 12th century. Likewise Falkland Palace and some of Stirling Castle. It is of a superb quality and takes a fine polish. At one time fifty-three families were employed here, with a harbour and three vessels for the export of the stone. There was also a salmon-fishery community. The quarries were worked until comparatively recently; but now only the great flooded ponds remain. A most attractive scheme of council housing has recently been completed here, fronting the firth and harbour, over a wide green and backed by rising woodland, a credit to the authorities concerned.

Inland, the village of Mylnefield grew up near the house of the Mylne family, long famed as King's Master Masons for Scotland, who owned the Kingoodie quarries. This village now tends to run into what has become the Dundee suburb of Invergowrie, itself an ancient place of character, largely in Angus.

Luncarty. Luncarty is an abiding proof that the Scots have long memories. For this village's only noteworthy impact on the scene took place in 990—which by any standards is a while ago. Yet the remote Battle of Luncarty is still argued about—especially if Hays are present. According to many of that great clan, this is where the Hays really got their heads above ground. More sober genealogists say otherwise.

In 990, Kenneth III of the fairly newly-united Scotland assailed invading Danes here, 4 miles north of Perth, to raise their siege of Perth—according to Boece. Things were allegedly looking grim for the Scots, when the peasant-ancestor of the Hays, ploughing near by with his two sons, seized the ox-yoke of his team and rushed across Tay, presumably with more than his sons, to assail the Danes' right wing—an unexpected assault which cheered the King's faltering forces and in the end saved the day. Gratefully, Kenneth promised old Hay, or Haya, whatever lands his falcon might over-fly, from Kinnoull Hill. The canny bird flew east, and covered a lot of ground. Various hawk-stanes are pointed out in the Carse of Gowrie to this day, as where the creature alighted, miles apart. Possibly the enterprising Hay had more than one fowl on the job. At any rate, the Hays became, one way or another, the principal proprietors in the Carse, and in due course Earls of Erroll. More-over, they show a hawk in flight clutching a coronet, as crest, and the clan's badge is an ox-yoke. Nevertheless, the heralds and genealogists claim that the name is derived from La Haye, on the Cotentin peninsula of Normandy, and that the first Hay, a Norman, appeared in Scotland only in 1160. This discrepancy, of course, might only indicate the snobbism, at one time rampant, of preferring to acknowledge Norman blood to 'native'.

The site of the battlefield is still pointed out between the A.9 highway and the Tay, just south of the Redgorton road-end. The farm here is still called Denmarkfield, with a monolith boulder erected near the riverside known as the King's Stone. Near by is another farm named Battleby. A permanent tinkers' encampment is planned for here by the county authorities, arousing fierce local resentment in an area defined as of landscape value—so that con-flict is not all in the distant past. A pleasant riverside walk from

Perth passes the site, and on half a mile to the former Hatton Ferry. This ferry has recently been discontinued, although a boat is still there, for salmon fishers, and a bell for summoning the ferryman from his house at Waulkmill on the other shore.

The village of Luncarty lies a mile north of Denmarkfield, mainly a modern place and a strange mixture of the humdrum and the attractive. Here was established, in the late 18th century, the most extensive bleachfield in Scotland, covering 130 acres. There is still a large works, though now cloth-bleaching is done indoors. Even in 1837, 2,000,000 yards of cloth, mainly damask, were processed here annually, employing as many as 130 people. One group of the workers' houses is very pleasing.

Luncarty was once a parish, indeed seat of an independent rectory, suppressed at the Reformation. The old burial-ground, with modern cemetery adjoining, is still a prominent object from the main road, crowning a hillock. There is no sign of the church, but an arched-roofed crypt-cum-watch-house, dated 1832, stands at the corner.

Half a mile on, where the road takes an awkward bend beneath the railway bridge, and the Ordie Burn comes in from Strathord, is the former shuttle-mill, now deserted, and hamlet, a spot once picturesque. A canal carries the waters of the Ordie, and the Shochie which joins it near by, to the mill at Luncarty.

Meigle and Ardler. Meigle is a large village at the Perthshire end of Strathmore, on the verge of Angus; and quite a busy road junction on the A.94 and A.927, lying in the level plain of the Isla about five miles north-east of Coupar Angus. It is also a parish, containing the village of Ardler, or Washington, to the south-west.

Meigle, a pleasant place, has three claims to fame, one less substantial than the others. It is alleged to be the burial-place of King Arthur's unfaithful Queen Guinevere—who is said to have been imprisoned in the Pictish fort on Barry Hill at Alyth, 5 miles to the north. Boece was claiming this as early as the 15th century. The village's other outstanding features are the magnificent collection of sculptured Pictish symbol stones and cross-slabs, housed in a little museum, quite the finest in the land; and the remarkable pre-Reformation font in the parish church. Another more recent claim to fame is the quite frequent presence of royalty here, since Lord and Lady Elphinstone, cousins of the Queen, came to live at nearby Drumkilbo House—a former seat of the Nairne family, with fine gardens.

The village spreads itself around a rather complicated series of road junctions. The parish church, dedicated to St. Peter, is a very ancient foundation, and stands, between the main roads, in a kirk-yard of much interest. The building was gutted by fire in 1869 and rebuilt, and now makes a bright place of worship. Its pride, of course, is the ancient font—although it was once cast away, in Reforming zeal, as rubbish; and having been dug up in due course, was used later as a mere ornament in the manse garden. Now it stands in the church vestibule, of octagonal design with carved representations of the Passion and Eastertide scenes on its eight panels. The kirkyard has many interesting gravestones, other prominent folk than Queen Guinevere having been interred here, including two Bishops of Dunkeld—who used to reside here occasionally—and Sir Henry Campbell-Bannerman, one-time Prime Minister. Indeed Meigle was once a burial-place of the Knights Templar. There is a handsome heraldic double memorial, dated 1661, built into the church wall.

But Meigle's true glory is the little museum in the former parochial school, housing the Pictish stones, maintained by the Ministry of Works. Here has been assembled a quite wonderful collection of Dark Age, approximately 6th to 10th century, Celtic stones and cross-slabs, some very local, others brought from a distance. Nobody at all interested in the story of their country should miss these, with the excellent booklet provided; nothing could more dramatically give the lie to the old canard that the Picts were a race of mere savage barbarians who painted their bodies and ran more or less naked. Something of their civilisation can be gathered from even a cursory glance at these remarkable and elaborate stone-carvings, their clothing, weapons, sports and pastimes, decorative ability and beliefs. Even though many of the 14 Pictish symbols here so excellently delineated remain a mystery, there is enough not only to fascinate but to raise the Picts out of the scornful disesteem, so long and generally their lot, to being ancestors we should be proud of. Here are the raw materials of a study which in almost any other country than Britain would have been the pride of university and scholarly research.

On the northern outskirts of the village lies 18th century Meigle House, now a hotel. Here, at the roadside, is an extraordinary stableyard, large and so notably well-built in antique ecclesiastical style, in soft red sandstone, arcading, vaulting, stone-slates and slit-windows, as almost to deceive the viewer into believing that it is an ancient grange of nearby Coupar Angus Abbey. Indeed, locals do revere it as ancient; but it is only an 18th century folly. The Kinloch of Kinloch family bought this property from the Earl of Strathmore in the 19th century, so presumably this was a Bowes-Lyon extravagance. Kinloch House itself, a mile to the west, is also now a hotel, its roadside hamlet having a chapel and mausoleum. A mile in the other direction, north-eastwards, is the very old bridge, of two arches, over the Dean Burn, at Cardean ruined mansion, glimpsed from the more modern bridge. Just over the Angus border, near by, are the sites of two Roman forts, accounting for the name, Caer-dean.

Belmont Castle, in its large estate south of Meigle, is now a Church of Scotland Eventide Home. The original castle was known as Kirkhill, a seat of the Bishops of Dunkeld, and was a small, plain, square tower rising three storeys to a parapet and walk. It is still discernible, incorporated in all the spread of modern building. After the Reformation it became another property of the Nairne family, later passing to the notorious 'Bloody Mackenzie of Rosehaugh', of the Killing Times. Campbell-Bannerman was a still later laird. In the grounds is a tumulus called Belliduff, purporting to be where MacDuff slew MacBeth—although in fact this happened at Lumphannan. There is also a large boulder called the MacBeth Stone—Dunsinane, of course, being only 9 miles away.

The village of Ardler, also called Washington, lies 2 miles southwest of Meigle, on Teuchat Muir, quite a pleasant place amongst fields. It is more than a hamlet, with a church built in 1883 as a chapel-of-ease, and a former railway station: but no other remarkable features—save that the gazetteers treat Ardler and Washington as separate villages, whereas they are one and the same.

Meikleour, Cargill and Burrelton. Where Isla joins Tay, some ten miles north of Perth, was inevitably an important situation, geographically as well as historically, from earliest times, both rivers being too large to ford, or bridge satisfactorily until modern developments. The Romans found this area significant, and have left many traces hereabouts. The early Scots kings had their strong castle at Kinclaven, on the west side of Tay here, described elsewhere. And the Lords Drummond, chiefs of one of the great houses of Scotland, and later Earls of Perth, had their seat at Stobhall near by on the east side.

Meikleour, just north of the double crossing, is nowadays probably most famed for its splendid and spectacular beech hedge, which flanks the A.93 for 580 yards on the edge of the policies of Meikleour House. This extraordinary sight, claimed as one of the arboreal wonders of the world, was planted in 1746, and rises now to an average of 85 feet. The problems of trimming such a hedge may be left to the imagination. Meikleour House (pronounced M'Clure) was a Nairne possession, and still belongs to the Marquis of Landsdowne—who is also Lord Nairne, the lands and title having been transmitted in the female line. The mansion is a large chateau-like building dating mainly from 1869. An earthwork called the Craw Law lies just at the north end of the beech hedge. There is another in the haugh of Isla less than two miles to the east, indicative that this area was also considered important to the pre-Roman peoples.

Meikleour village, near by to the north at a rather complicated road junction, is an attractive place, very much under the wing of the estate. It has an unusual Mercat Cross dated 1618, with four St. Andrew's Crosses on the plinth and a not very tall shaft surmounted by a cross. There used to be large markets and fairs here, three times a year. Close by, in a park, is the Tron, a rusticated stone column with a hole for a weigh-beam, for the weighing of grain and wool. A pair of iron jougs now hang therefrom. Strangely enough, there is no church, Meikleour being part of the parish of

Perth.   Georgian houses of Marshall Place, facing the South Inch, with
St. Leonards-in-the-Fields Church

Perth.   Bell's Sports Centre, North Inch

Pitlochry. Hydro-electric dam at Loch Faskally, with Fish-Ladder in
foreground. Ben-y-Vrackie in background

Caputh, whose church is 5 miles to the west. Nearer is Cargill Church, across the rivers to the east.

A mile north-east of Meikleour, on the Coupar Angus road, near the farm of Littleour, is the extraordinary grass-grown rampart and ditches of the Cleaven Dyke, now planted with young trees. This appears to be a Roman boundary, marking the limits of their defended area at the head of Strathmore. It still stretches for 2070 yards, mainly on the west side of the road; but originally it would reach the Isla on the east, and at the other end finished at a former channel of the Tay. Its great width, of over a hundred and fifty feet, is explained by the original woodland through which it was driven as a defensive cleared belt for the great and strategic Camp at Inchtuthill to the west. The Signal Station at Black Hill, a mile to the south, was no doubt complementary. Skene would place here Agricola's famous Battle of Mons Grampius—but this seems very questionable.

Cargill is a parish now, its villages Burrelton, Woodside and Wolf-hill, though there is a small, scattered hamlet near the church. This is delightfully situated on the east bank of Tay in peaceful and rural seclusion a mile south of the confluence with Isla. It is a large plain building of 1831, bright internally, with galleries on three sides. The old kirkyard is detached, nearer the river, with, in the centre, all that remains of the original church, now used as burial-place for the Wright family. Below the west wall, externally, is a large and ancient flat stone, in two pieces, depicting Adam and Eve, and the Ram caught in the Thicket. Near Cargill Mains farm, to the north, is a wooded mound called Castle Hill, above the river, another Roman establishment, with fosse and traces of an aqueduct. This is directly opposite Kinclaven Castle.

Over two miles to the south of Cargill is the romantic castle of Stobhall, once again the seat of the Drummond chiefs, Earls of Perth. A highly interesting place, it is set on a lofty tongue of ridge above the Tay, unusual in that it contains not one but four buildings within its courtyard, none large, and unconnected, placed at odd levels and angles dictated by the nature of the site. The result is striking. A picturesque arched pend through the gatehouse range, now the main living quarters, admits to the courtyard. In the centre is the tall, L-shaped chapel block, with an angle-turret, and formerly the banqueting-hall, with a fine tempora-painted ceiling. Next is a two-storeyed domestic block, containing laundry, brewhouse and bakehouse. And farther east, kitchen and storehouse premises. None of these can represent the original castle, for the Drummonds were settled here from the 14th century. A great-granddaughter of the first, Annabella Drummond, was the Queen of Robert III, and much loved. The family moved its main seat to the new Drummond Castle near Crieff in 1487, when Stobhall became a dower-house.

South of Stobhall the Tay is crossed by a basaltic dyke, which forms the picturesque cataracts known as the Linn of Campsie, featured in Scott's *Fair Maid of Perth*. Overlooking this from a high rock are traces of a former daughter monastery of the Abbey of Coupar Angus, seemingly set here so that its inmates might supply the abbey with large supplies of fuel from the great Campsie Wood. The road by which this timber was hauled to Coupar, 7 miles away, is still marked on the maps as the Abbey Road, through Strelitz Wood, near Burrelton.

This village of Burrelton, on the main A.94 Perth–Coupar–Forfar road, with Woodside adjoining to the north, is fairly modern and quite large. It is not unattractive, especially the Woodside part, sequestered in trees off the road to the west. Fairs were held here annually, in July.

Menteith. This really should deal with a vast area of land, perhaps more than 200 square miles; and the name should properly be *Mon*teith, the mounth or watershed of the River Teith. Or, indeed, should refer to the even greater area of the once important earldom of Menteith, one of the great, ancient divisions of the land. But since, today, by Menteith is generally meant only the district around the Lake of Menteith and the village of Port of Menteith; and since the rest of the district is dealt with under Doune, Callander, Aberfoyle, the Trossachs and so on—it will serve to confine this present description to the modern Menteith. Nevertheless, probably some indication of the ancient importance of the whole should be included, since it bears on the significance of the Lake and its islands.

With Strathearn to the north, Menteith made up the early subkingdom of Fortrenn, whose capital was at Forteviot, on the Earn. It was important long before the first Celtic earl thereof, Gilbert, appears about 1160. Excepting Balquhidder parish, which always belonged to Strathearn, it comprised all the lands west of the Ochils whose waters drained into the Forth, with the vale of the Teith itself central. The Teith has two main tributaries which, strangely enough, rise within three-quarters of a mile of each other, east of the head of Loch Lomond, and then diverge to the extent of being 10 miles apart, before joining again just west of Callander. The northern arm is the longer, 26 miles, starting as the Lochlarig River, widening into Lochs Doine and Voil, in Balquhidder, becoming the Balvaig in Strathyre, then widening into Loch Lubnaig, and finally flowing out through the Pass of Leny. The southern arm flows down Glen Gyle into Loch Katrine, out beyond into Loch Achray and then into Loch Vennachar, from which it emerges as the Eas Gobhain, The Water of the Smith, to meet the Leny and become the Teith, 21 miles. Thus the Teith connects some of the most romantic and beautiful lochs in the Southern Highlands, and Menteith included an enormous area of exciting country, including the Trossachs. The river joins the Forth, eventually, only 2 miles from Stirling. In fact, it is odd indeed that the Teith is not accepted as the greater river, since it is here broader, longer and brings down the greater volume of water. Just why the Forth's twisting course through the Flanders Moss from Ben Lomond is accepted as the parent stream is one of the mysteries of topography. Perhaps a campaign should be initiated to rename the estuary the Firth of Teith!

In history, too, the Teith, or at least Monteith, has not had a fair deal—in more than misspelling its name. Its Celtic earls failed in two heiresses, sisters, one of whom married Walter Comyn, a son of the Earl of Buchan, and the other Walter Stewart, third son of the 3rd High Steward of Scotland, in the mid-13th century. Comyn dying without heir, Walter Stewart became Earl of Menteith in his wife's right, and their Stewart successors held the earldom until another heiress carried it to Robert Stewart, Duke of Albany, brother of Robert III, who built Doune Castle as its new messuage-place. His son Duke Murdoch was beheaded for treason, and the earldom forfeited to the Crown, in 1425. Two years later it was granted to Malise Graham, in place of the earldom of Strathearn, which the King desired. The Graham earls held Menteith until 1633, when, in one of the meanest pieces of royal chicanery, Charles I deprived William, 8th, of the earldom for no better reason apparently than that he had boasted that his descent was more truly royal than was the King's—which was true, if impolitic. He was fobbed off with a new and empty earldom of Airth. And that, to all intents, was the end of Menteith as an important separate entity in Scotland.

We are therefore concerned here with the Lake of Menteith and the Port thereof. There has been much nonsense written about the former, to the effect that it is Scotland's only lake, as distinct from loch, and seeking for significance in this. In fact, there is none. Until the middle of last century it was called the Loch of Menteith, just like any other sheet of water in Scotland. Then some topographer, map-maker or gazetteer, in the sorry 'North British' period when anglification was the thing, seems to have put it down as Lake—and for some reason it stuck, here, though not elsewhere. The early maps all show it as loch, as does the Gazetteer of 1842.

It lies on the northern edge of the great Flanders Moss, 3 miles east of Aberfoyle; yet strangely, it is not a widening of the River Forth which largely creates the Moss, lying in fact 2 miles north of the river, and only 55 feet above sea-level. No major stream forms it, and only the sluggish, canal-like Goodie Water flows out, to the east. It is quite a large loch, embosomed in ancient trees, a mile and a half long by a mile wide, with a long wooded peninsula jutting in from the south. It is fairly shallow, with three islands—and it is these which give the lake its importance, apart from the very pleasing prospects. They are called Inchmahome, Inch Talla and Dog Isle. On the first is the ruined Priory thereof, now in the care of the Ministry of Works, who take visitors out by boat from a pier near the Port of Menteith Hotel, at a charge of 2s., from 10 a.m. to 7 p.m. in summer and 10 to 4 in winter. Inch Talla, which means the Isle of the Hall, was the site of the Earls of Menteith's castle, before Doune was built to supersede. And the Dog Isle was where the hounds were kennelled—the horses, for convenience, being stabled on the 'mainland' to the west.

Inchmahome Priory is deservedly famous, not only for its beauty and setting but for the fact that Mary Queen of Scots was brought here, for safety, in 1547, when Henry VIII was invading Scotland to try to force a marriage with his son on the infant Queen, so that he might win the country thus, having failed by war and intrigue. She was only five years old at the time; and perhaps this figure accounts for the mistaken statement so often made that she spent five years on Inchmahome—whereas it was only five months, before she was sent off to France for greater security, with consequences we all know. Her Bower—though it is really a little sunk garden—is still pointed out. A less well-known fact is that Robert the Bruce three times visited here. Books have been written about Inchmahome and its Priory, the grandeur combined with elegance of its architecture, its gardens, orchards and ancient sepulchres—a lovely place. It is said to have been founded by King Edgar, a son of Malcolm Canmore, at the beginning of the 12th century; but more certainly Walter Comyn, in 1238, obtained authority from Pope Gregory IX to erect an Augustinian priory on the island of 'Inchmaquhomok'. At the Reformation it was bestowed on the Lord Erskine—whose descendants lived at Cardross, 2 miles to the south. There is no need to describe the Priory here; but special mention may perhaps be made of the particularly fine and moving medieval tomb, and double recumbent effigy, of Walter, 1st Stewart Earl of Menteith and his heiress-Countess Mary. He died in 1294, his wife five years earlier; and the monument is a loving and lovely thing, unique in Scotland, showing them lying side by side and hand in hand, she with an arm around his neck, he in the armour of the period, with his heraldic shield on his back. Weather-worn as it is, the effigy, when fresh sculptured and painted in splendid colours, must have been as fine as it is touching. The graves of other notable Scottish families share this quiet island refuge. To mention two, there are those of that unfortunate Lord Kilpont, heir of the Graham Earl of Airth and Menteith, who was murdered in Montrose's camp by his own friend and fellow-officer, Mad James Stewart of Ardvorlich—as referred to under Loch Earn; and of Don Roberto, the famous R. B. Cunninghame Graham of Gartmore and Ardoch.

There are the ruins of the earls' castle, as well as gardens and ancient trees, on Inch Talla; and a delightful secluded demesne it must have made in war-torn days. But inconvenient for amongst the most important nobles in the land; so that it was not to be wondered at that when Duke Robert of Albany, Regent of Scotland, married the heiress, he built Doune as a more accessible castle.

Port of Menteith lies at the north-east extremity of the loch, and is an attractive little hamlet, facing south over water and moss, under the long ridge of the Highland Line and Menteith Hills. It was, naturally, once a great deal larger and more important, when it was the capital of Menteith; in fact, it was made a burgh of barony by James III in 1467, a status out of which in due course Doune nudged it. There is no hint of such glories now; only a tiny but delightful resort. The parish church stands at the waterside, next to the quite large hotel; and its parish is also a large one, of 23,600 acres—admittedly mainly empty. The present church was built on an ancient site only in 1878, in Gothic style, and is still surrounded by its old graveyard. The doorway facing west appears to be part of the ancient building. Queen Victoria was much impressed by the beauty of Menteith in 1869. The loch is notable for its large pike; also for an early way of fishing therefor, wherein a baited hook was attached to the leg of a goose, which was then turned loose to swim around and do the fishing—the pike usually tiring before the geese did. It would be interesting to know when this was last practised.

The surrounding district is full of interest, with forestry ever increasing. Cardross, already mentioned, is a fine old mansion of 16th and 18th century date, developed from a tall, five-storeyed tower-house, with circular stair-tower and angle-turrets. There is excellent Memel-pine panelling within; and the house stands in spreading parkland. The Erskines of Mar, having obtained the Inchmahome Priory lands at the Reformation carve-up, became secular Commendator-priors, and retained this property until comparatively modern times. Another ancient family are the Grahams of Rednock, still in possession of their estate a mile to the east—although the old castle thereof, standing on a mound to the west of the A.81 road over the mounth to Callander, is now fragmentary. A mile farther up the same road, amidst high moorland, is the small Loch Rusky, under the escarpment of Ben Gulipen, notable for freezing over in winter. On an islet here was reputedly the castle of the notorious False Menteith—Sir John Stewart, uncle and tutor of the young Earl, who, as Sheriff of Dumbarton, was responsible for receiving the captured hero Wallace, in 1305, and handing him over to the occupying English—an act for which his name has been execrated in Scotland ever since. Bruce however forgave him, recognising, perhaps, that since he had accepted the office of Sheriff under the occupation, he could hardly do otherwise.

Another loch with a story is that of Macanrie, which lies remote from any road, half a mile south-west of Lake of Menteith, in the moss. Here legend has it that some unspecified king's son was saved from drowning by a girl, while hunting. Less uncertain is the battle fought in 1489, wherein the young King James IV obtained his first victory, and distinguished himself, against the Earl of Lennox, an augury for his reign. This took place in the marshes to the west, in the Tullimoss vicinity.

It is perhaps worth mentioning that, from the main A.873 road approaching Port of Menteith from Thornhill, in the pleasant Ruskie hamlet area, some of the best prospects of the far-flung Flanders Moss, and some appreciation of its extent, may be obtained.

Methven and Tibbermore. The large village of Methven, almost a town, lies 6 miles north-west of Perth, near the end of the wedge of rising ground which lies between the Earn and the Almond, and overlooking the wide and marshy vale of the Pow Water. It is not a beautiful place, rather dull as to aspect, although its history is far from dull. Lying on the A.85 highway from Perth to Crieff, it is a great hub of roads.

There is nothing so ancient as its story would indicate here. Even Methven Castle is only a mid-17th century building; and the detached aisle of the plain 18th century church dates only from the 16th century. Yet long before that Methven was important, in Church and State—as the name Culdeesland, to the south-east implies, and with the Battles of Methven and Tippermuir fought near by. The former took place in June 1306, soon after Bruce's coronation, when he was attacked by the English Earl of Pembroke and hostile Scots—including Sir Roger Moubray of Methven—and grievously defeated. The Moubrays were a powerful Scoto-Norman family, always a thorn in Bruce's flesh. When he regained power he bestowed the lands on his daughter Marjory's husband, Walter the High Steward.

Methven Castle is a handsome mid-17th century fortalice, splendidly situated on the long low ridge a mile east of the village. Older work is incorporated, but as it stands it was built mainly by Ludovick, 2nd Duke of Lennox, a distant cousin and favourite of James VI. It comprises a tall, five-storeyed block with ogee-roofed round towers at the angles, and later work to the east. James IV settled Methven on his wife, Margaret Tudor, sister of Henry VIII, who, widowed after Flodden, married the weakling, Henry Stewart, of the Ochiltree family, whom she got made Lord Methven. She, the Queen-Dowager, died here in 1540.

The church stands in the higher, south part of the village. It was founded as a collegiate establishment in 1433, but of this nothing remains. The detached aisle was built, it is thought, by Margaret Tudor, the crowned Lion of Scotland featuring thereon. The north gable has a fine tracery window, now built up, with St. Andrew's Cross above. Near by is the enormous and quite overpoweringly ugly tomb of General Sir Thomas Graham, Lord Lynedoch, known as the Hero of Barossa, who was born at Balgowan House 3 miles to the west.

Methven Moss lies to the south, a rather dreary expanse, which looks as though it could be reclaimed by drainage. A little to the east of it is Tibbermore, a hamlet and parish, with church and manse. The name derives from *Tobar-mhor*, a great well, and there was a Lady Well behind the church, which was destroyed in the mid-19th century when the land was drained. To the east again, at Tullilum, was once a Carmelite priory and chapel, attached to the bishopric of Dunkeld. The last Prior thereof, Alexander Young, embraced the reformed faith and became the first Protestant minister of Tibbermore. A mile to the south-east was fought, in

1644, the Battle of Tibbermore, more usually called Tippermuir, between Montrose and the Covenanters, in which the former, though much outnumbered, won a resounding victory, the Covenant forces, numbering 6000, losing 2000 dead and 2000 captured.

Moncreiffe, Rhynd and Elcho. Moncreiffe is one of those ancient names which have meant much in Scotland over long, successive centuries. It derives from the Gaelic *monadh craoibhe*, the Hill of the Sacred Bough; but the lengthy hog's-back of wooded upland dominating the peninsula between Tay and Earn for 3 miles south-east of Perth, is also sometimes called Moredun Hill—although, properly, this refers only to one of the summits, at 750 feet. The dun is a Pictish royal fort, called Dun Monadh, its circular fosse 50 feet in diameter. It was here that the Roman legionaries paused on their first advance northwards, to gaze at the Tay's windings and the site of Perth, crying "Behold the Tiber, behold the Field of Mars!" Certainly the vista from this summit is quite superlative, in every direction, standing isolated between the Ochils and the Highlands, with wide Strathearn to the west and the Tay estuary opening to the east, backed by the Sidlaw Hills. Pennant called it 'The Glory of Scotland'.

On both flanks of this long hill are items of interest. To the south lie the mansions of Moncreiffe House and Easter Moncreiffe both still in the possession of the Moncreiffe family, which has been settled here from beyond recorded time, but which probably stemmed from the Celtic royal house whose dun crowned their hill. The first surviving charter by a recorded progenitor concerns Sir Matthew de Moncreiffe in 1248. Sir John Moncreiffe of that Ilk sheltered Wallace in a cave of the hill. The present laird is Sir Iain Moncreiffe of that Ilk, 11th baronet. He succeeded his cousin, the 23rd Laird, who died when the late 17th century Moncreiffe House was burned down in 1957. A new mansion, incorporating Sir William Bruce's fine doorway from the early house, was built for the laird's sister, Elizabeth Moncreiffe, 24th of Moncreiffe; while Sir Iain, well-known writer and genealogist, Albany Herald, lives at Easter Moncreiffe a mile along the hill. Within the richly-wooded estate are the scanty remains of the old fortalice of Moredun Hall; also the ancient pre-Reformation chapel of Moncreiffe, used since 1357 as a family burial-place. There is also a stone circle midway along the 600-yard-long beech avenue.

The road which encircles Moncreiffe Hill east-abouts gives access to a smaller one which probes into the flat carselands of the peninsula towards its point at Easter Rhynd, where Earn meets the suddenly-widening Tay. Here, beside the large farm-toun, is another ancient pre-Reformation chapel, highly remote as to situation but its graveyard not neglected. Amongst others are the tombs of the Moncreiffs of Kinmonth—this branch, which occupied the most easterly part of the hill, having chosen to drop the *e* from its name.

The hamlet of Rhynd itself lies on higher ground more than two miles to the north-west, attractively sited, with a more modern parish church embosomed in trees. This parish, strangely, was a dependency of the monastery of St. Adrian on the Isle of May, in the mouth of the Forth; and a stone built into the east gable commemorates one of the early Priors. A mile down the winding road northwards, nearly to the banks of Tay, leads to the splendid 16th century castle of Elcho, one of the finest in the land, long a seat of the Earls of Wemyss, to whose heir it gave title—and now excellently cared for by the Ministry of Works. It is a large, four-storeyed building, with no fewer than four towers projecting from the main block, and heavily defended by splayed gunloops. The Wemyss family's first charter here is dated 1468. Sir John Wemyss of that Ilk was created first Earl of Wemyss in 1633, at the Coronation of Charles I at Holyroodhouse. David, Lord Elcho, eldest son of the 5th Earl, was Prince Charles Edward's Master of Horse, and after Culloden was forfeited, the earldom being obtained by his younger brother who adopted his wife's name of Charteris. A Perth mob marched here in 1773 when, during a great grain famine, the local farmer was using the castle to hoard grain.

The farm of Grange of Elcho—the word grange meaning a religious establishment's farmery—a mile to the west, is notable in that here, in the 13th century, Lindsay of Glenesk, in Angus, founded a Cistercian nunnery. And here, in 1346, the Earl of Ross assassinated Ranald of the Isles. It is interesting that an amateur group of archaeologists from Perth are presently excavating the site of this ancient foundation, in a field above the oddly-named Sleepless Inch island of the Tay.

Monzie and Gilmerton. Monzie—pronounced Mon-ee—is a tiny hamlet, a far-flung parish of 33 square miles, and a large estate, lying in a secluded vale behind the Knock of Crieff; and Gilmerton a village in the parish, on the main Perth–Crieff road. Monzie is highly interesting, for many reasons. A sheltered, hidden, fertile hollow, it has been a favoured place of habitation from earliest times. Many are the relics of antiquity. There are two stone circles, and the site of weems or subterranean dwellings, in the park of Monzie Castle; an Iron Age fort called Knockdarrach; and a standing-stone west of Mains of Callander. Another so-called Druid's Stone, with carvings, now lost, stood near the church; and there was an ancient chapel and burial-ground at Tom an Bowie, down the glen.

Monzie Castle in its large park, is a huge, castellated pile of the early 19th century. But at its rear is the small and attractive early 17th century castle from which it grew, a simple L-planned fortalice dated 1634, with probably an older nucleus, with thick walling, heraldry, shot-holes, panelling and other typical features. It was given by Sir Duncan Campbell 7th of Glenorchy, the famous Black Duncan of the Castles, to his fifth son. For the last century the owners have been the Maitland-Macgill-Crichton family; and the present young laird is gallantly tackling a great modernisation and improvement of the 5000-acre estate. A small factory for the manufacture of Scandinavian-type furniture has been established; and modern farming methods are being vigorously pursued. Most unusual is the private electric-power station, run by the waters of the Shaggie Burn, supplying current not only to the estate but selling it to the national grid. The computer here succeeds one of the first installed in Scotland.

The best of the stone circles, marked on the Ordnance Map as a *cairn* circle, lies close to the East Lodge and driveway, and consists of twelve smallish stones in a tight circle, with outside it a large recumbent boulder with many cup-marks. Nothing now remains of the weems or earth-dwellings; but a sword and stone axe were found in one, near Cuilt Farm. The Iron Age camp, of earthworks and ramparts at Knockdarrach, are on rising hilly ground, oak-covered—*darach* means oak—north-west of church and hamlet, and here spearheads have been uncovered. Near the castle are three tall and ancient larch trees, relics of those brought from the Tyrol in 1738, of the same batch as the better-known Dunkeld larches. These have thriven even better—to the chagrin of successive Dukes of Atholl.

The parish church dates only from 1830 and is rather plain; but it stands, attractively-sited, on a tree-girt mound in the kirkyard of its ancient predecessor, with the former's iron jougs still hanging on the porch. There are two 17th century Campbell of Monzie heraldic tombstones; and an interesting 'multiple memorial' entitled *Graves of our ain folks. The Mackenzies of the Cuilt, Monzie, from period beyond record.* In the hamlet is a disused and ancient single-arch bridge, very narrow, alongside the more modern one. It is recounted of the earlier post-Reformation church, that there was a local custom of playing football on Sunday mornings, on the green of Monzie, before the service, with even the minister joining in—a refreshing slant on repressive Calvinist times. A St. Lawrence's Fair used to be held here each August 22nd; and there are plans to revive this.

The fertile, sheltered Vale of Monzie is surrounded by shouldering hills, and watered by three boisterous streams, the Shaggie, the Keltie and the Barvick, each with their cascades and waterfalls. The hydro-electric schemes, public and private, have made the falls less notable, however. Where the Barvick joins the Shaggie, to the south-west of the vale, lies the hamlet of Hosh, where, hidden amongst the trees, is the Glen Turret Distillery, founded in 1775. The odd name of Hosh appears to be only a corruption of haughs. From Hosh, Glen Turret strikes off north-westwards, a private road leading up it to the large reservoir of Loch Turret 4 miles up, with Falls of Turret after a mile or so, again reduced by the waterworks. The glen used to be famous for its falcons. It is also claimed that here were the last two wolves in Scotland killed—but this claim has been made for elsewhere.

The village of Gilmerton lies at the other end of the parish, 2 miles east of Crieff. It is a comparatively modern place, with no history; but it is pleasantly situated where the A.822 strikes off northwards, for the Sma' Glen, from the Crieff–Perth highway. It has both traditional and very modern housing, and a trim appearance, despite its 19th century church standing abandoned and neglected. Near by is the ancient estate of Cultoquhey, long the home of the Maxtone family and now a hotel. In its grounds are earthworks alleged to be Roman but more probably Pictish, like those at Knockdarrach.

Monzievaird and Strowan. Between Crieff and Comrie, in upper Strathearn, lie the parishes, united in 1662, of Monzievaird and Strowan, a very pleasing area of fertile carseland with the wooded hills coming ever closer, and every prospect fair. Basically, Monzievaird lies north of the River Earn, and Strowan south. Despite its proximity to Monzie on the east, Monzievaird's name seems to have no connection, and is thought to mean the Hill of the Bards, anciently Moivard; whereas Monzie is from *moighidh* meaning a level tract. Strowan is derived from St. Ronan or Rowan, its tutelary saint. A great battle was fought on this Plain of the Bards in 1001, in the Latin, *Campus Bardorum*, when Malcolm son of Kenneth II defeated and slew the usurper of the throne of Alban, one Gryme or Girgh Mackinat MacDuff, who had reigned for eight years—the slain king then being taken to Iona to be buried amongst his legitimate predecessors. The victor became Malcolm II, whose grandson was the famous King Duncan, of *MacBeth*.

Monzievaird's most important feature is the great Ochtertyre estate, with its attractive, wood-girt loch, lying just over a mile west of Crieff. The mansion house, readily seen from the main road, though half a mile away, stands high on a terrace of the forested hillside above the loch, a substantial Georgian house in a glorious position. It is the seat of the ancient family of Murray, the first of whom, Patrick, third son of the 6th Baron of Tullibardine, died here in 1476. Their previous house was down at a peninsula of the lochside, named Castle Cluggy, the ruins of which remain. Although a great antiquity is claimed for this strength, it having been a Comyn stronghold in the 13th and 14th centuries, and was known as 'an ancient fortalice' in 1467, nevertheless the present remains do not seem quite so old as that. Here, it is also claimed, in 1306 the Red Comyn besieged Malise, Earl of Strathearn—but the same Red Comyn was slain by Bruce at Dumfries that year, in February—so this seems improbable. Sir William Murray, 1st Baronet of Ochtertyre, was still inhabiting this castle in 1650. Robert Burns visited the later mansion on the hill in 1787, and was impressed enough by the daughter of the house to write a song in her honour.

Monzievaird Loch is more than half a mile long, and can be seen from the road. It has a crannog, or artificial island, towards its head. To the west is the burial-place of large numbers of victims of the plague, of a 17th century visitation. And not far from its other end, on the main drive to the House, is the site of the original St. Serf's parish church of Monzievaird, in its ancient graveyard. It is now a mausoleum, built 1809, for the Murray family—which is apt enough. For here, in 1511, was enacted a famous and terrible tragedy, when the Master of Drummond, with Campbell allies, besieged in the church a large number of Murrays, and presently set it on fire, burning all within. King James IV imposed stern justice on the main perpetrators, beheading the Master, although he was his friend, Lord Drummond's heir, and brother of his beloved Margaret Drummond.

Sadly, the next parish church of Monzievaird—united now with Strowan—is also gone, demolished and leaving only a gable, with the dates 1808–1964, a war memorial, and another and less old graveyard. This lies north of the main road, near the Strowan road-end, and below the house of Quoig—where, it is said, the Murrays first settled when they came to Monzievaird.

To the west of Quoig lie the estates of Clathick, Ballaig and Lawers. Near the first is a reputed Roman burial-ground, full of large stone slabs, where in 1783 was found a bronze vessel like a coffee-pot. Lawers, with a large Italianate mansion, was formerly called Fordie, and became the seat of the Campbells of Lawers, later Earls of Loudoun, from Loch Tay-side, who changed the name—so that there are now two Lawers in Perthshire. In its grounds is another ruined chapel turned into a mausoleum.

On the other side of the river is Strowan. This was once an important place, when there were Thanes of Strowan. Earlier still it held the religious establishment of one of the Celtic saints, Ronan or Rowan, bishop and confessor, about A.D. 730. The site of his church still remains, in the grounds of Strowan House, surrounded by an overgrown graveyard; but the ruins of the building thereon are of much later date, probably immediately post-Reformation. A 17th century heraldic stone has been built into one wall, with Murray device. These Celtic saints always had their bell, and St. Rowan was no exception. As in other cases, it was placed in the custodianship of a hereditary Dewar, called the Ballindewar, who had a croft of 3 acres at Strowan, amongst whose duties was to ring the bell under his gown when mass was said. For many generations the Dewars remained, and their croft can still be traced; but one of the Graham-Stirling lairds of Strowan bought the croft and the bell with it—lacking its tongue. Where this bell is now, is not known. The Graham-Stirlings are gone, and the early 19th century mansion demolished, with, in its place, a most delightful garden and a smaller modern house for the present laird.

Two other interesting features are near by. On a wooded mound to the west is what is called the Market Cross of Strowan. But this is not that sort of cross. It is an ancient ecclesiastical cross of unusual design, its arms on the Maltese pattern, with the sacred initials I.N.R.L.; probably removed from the nearby Celtic church, and made use of by the later barons of Strowan whose rights would include the holding of fairs or markets. It is interesting that the Cross of Crieff, another Celtic ecclesiastical cross, is said to have come from here. The other feature is the fine, lofty but narrow bridge of 1760, which used to carry the road but is now disused, spanning the Earn just below the House. It is interesting in that its foundations rest on reed matting, after the Dutch fashion.

To the east, rears the wooded hill of Tom a Chasteal, on which once stood the earliest castle of the Celtic Earls of Strathearn, a magnificent site. The only traces now are of the roundabout road which corkscrews to the top, some of the stone revetments for which still remain. The last relics of this castle were cleared when the 82-foot-high obelisk to Sir David Baird, the hero of Seringapatam, was erected here.

To the west of Strowan lie two farms, below a long ridge of wooded hill, with ancient and significant names—Lennoch and Drummond Earnoch. These were both Drummond estates once. Lennoch and Concraig were the lands of the Crowner and Forester of Strathearn, and the first Lord Drummond bought them from his cousin, and at Concraig built what is now Drummond Castle. The Lennoch Drummonds in due course became Drummonds of Megginch, in Carse of Gowrie, where they still flourish. Drummond Earnoch—or Erinach—was the property of the Deputy-Keeper of the royal forest of Glenartney, when in 1589 John Drummond thereof cut off the ears of certain poaching MacGregors—for which rash act he was waylaid, his head cut off, and presented to his sister, the Lady of Ardvorlich. The place allegedly got the Erinach name because its laird, in the 1511 burning, befriended one of the Murrays at Monzievaird Church, enabling him to escape. So incensed were his fellow Drummonds at this, that they hounded him out of the country, and he went to Ireland to live. He eventually came home, and his property has been so named since.

Muckhart and Rumbling Bridge. This parish of Perthshire seems as though it should belong to either Clackmannanshire or Kinross-shire, separated from the rest of its great county by the Ochil Hills, at the southern end of Glen Devon, and facing the plain of Forth. It used to be known as Muckhartshire. It is not large, containing only about six square miles; but it has interesting features and is rurally attractive against its close backcloth of the green hills, Seamab Hill, a conical peak of 1442 feet, presiding.

Basically the parish covers the area where the River Devon, released from its steep constrictions, makes its dramatic swing from east to west—although the village of Crook of Devon, at the apex of the bend, is in Kinross-shire. From there, the Devon changes character excitingly, and carves for itself a most notable deep and narrow chasm in the limestone rock, often so steep a fissure that the bottom may not be seen from the top. The best-known stretch of the Falls of Devon is at Rumbling Bridge, where the river drives through an awesome abyss 120 feet below the bridge. Yet so narrow is it, and so tree-clad the crests, that few indeed on the busy A.823 road that crosses it realise what they are missing. The present bridge of 1816 has been built exactly above the old one of 1713, which is a very narrow and parapet-less single arch—a place which formerly must have given many a traveller a queasy stomach. The river is the Perthshire border. On the north side, in the grounds of the large Rumbling Bridge Hotel, is a riverside walk with many viewpoints of the spectacular falls and cauldrons, not always now very safe. The name refers to the noise made by boulders trapped in pot-holes of the cascades. One, 400 yards upstream of the bridge, and called the Devil's Mill, is particularly noisy.

To the east, a pleasant side road of less than two miles leads to Crook of Devon, reaching that village by a hump-backed old bridge, and passing on the way the Georgian mansion of Naemoor, now Lendrick Muir School, in a wooded estate. On the other side of the A.823, an equally attractive road leads, by the golf-course, the little parish school and Leys of Muckhart farm, westwards to the A.91 highway, Stirling to Perth via Milnathort and Glenfarg. At the road-end is Cowden Castle, 2 miles east of Dollar. The mansion of this large estate is now demolished, and was anyway of no great antiquity; but there remains on the site an arched courtyard gateway with roll moulding and deep bar-holes, indicative of an earlier fortified building. Also a little corner-tower, romanticised but dated 1707. To the north, in the foothills at the farm of Castleton, is a standing-stone. This Castleton refers not to Cowden but to the ancient house of Bruce's friend, Bishop William Lamberton of St. Andrews, who built a seat here in 1320, now completely gone.

The village of Muckhart parish is called Pool of Muckhart, although it is nowhere near the river. It is quite a picturesque place. On a mound to the north, below the hill, stands the parish church, a plain building of the early 19th century but incorporating 17th century and later work. It is bright and pleasing within. There are some old gravestones in the kirkyard. The village was burned by Montrose's Highland troops in 1644, at the same time as Castle Campbell, at Dollar, was sacked, the seat of his enemy Argyll. It is interesting that, in 1490, the superior of the parish, the then Archbishop of St. Andrews, to get the then Earl of Argyll to side with him against his rival Archbishop of Glasgow, feud him the whole Lordship of Muckhartshire for £101 Scots—which is why Castle Campbell got that name.

At the south-west end of the parish is Muckhart Mill, remote and attractive in its deep dean, now a guest-house and restored, but with its old mill-wheel and granaries still there and looking most picturesque. Near by is Vicar's Bridge, a modern replacement of the bridge where Thomas Forret, Vicar of Dollar, one of the first martyrs of the Reformation, met his end.

Murthly. Murthly is off the beaten track—even though on the main railway-line—despite its situation close to the south bank of great Tay, the main highways passing it by at some distance. It lies in the vast bend of the river, 4 miles north of Stanley and 7 east of Dunkeld, in countryside that is very attractive, and still Lowland —though the Highlands, commencing at Birnam, loom near.

There are two Murthlys, the great estate, castle and farms, to the west; and the fairly modern village, huge hospital and railway station, 2 miles to the east. Murthly Castle is a most ancient property, said to have been a hunting seat of the Scots kings. It came to the Stewarts of Grandtully (in Strathtay) in 1615. They descend from the 4th High Steward by a younger son, Sir John of Bonkyl, from whom also derived the houses of Atholl, Lennox, Darnley and D'Aubigny. Through the female line, the lairds are now Steuart-Fotheringham. The castle is large and fine, forming three sides of a square, clustering round a tall, originally free-standing, tower of early date, the upper storeys of which were altered in the late 16th century when angle-turrets were added. Extensions were made at various times in the 17th century and later. In the 1830s Sir William Drummond Stewart decided to outdo the Duke of Atholl by building a huge new mansion, to designs of Gillespie Graham, all the main apartments being just that little bit larger than the Duke's. Perhaps fortunately, this Tudor-type palace was never finished; and not so long ago the walls were demolished. The estate is very large and most splendid, with magnificent ancient trees, fine gardens, avenues, pools and so on. Just north of the castle is a large and imposing private church, enlarged in 1846, in the Roman Catholic interest, from a pre-Reformation chapel of St. Anthony the Eremite. There is a standing-stone near by. A handsome Celtic, or Pictish symbol-stone was removed from Murthly to the museum at Meigle.

The wooded northern flanks of the former Muir of Thorn lie between castle and village. At the latter there is a plain little modern church, not of parish status for this is in the parish of Little Dunkeld. The main-line railway has a level-crossing over the village street—no convenience. The great hospital which rather dominates the place, was erected, in some sixty acres, as Perth Lunatic Asylum in 1864, and has been much enlarged since. Fortunately the trees have been retained, which helps. Half a mile north, nearer the bridge across Tay to Caputh, is the hamlet of Gellyburn, mainly modern now, but a place with old roots; for the ancient quarries here were famous, producing a light ash-coloured fine sandstone, of which was built Dunkeld Cathedral.

In the other direction, southwards, the quite large school is pleasantly if scarcely conveniently situated about a mile up the road to Stanley, in an enclave of the Muir of Thorn woodlands. This area was more populous once, of course—as witness the site of the Kirk o' the Muir, a mile farther to the east and far from any road.

Muthill. Like Dunning, which it somewhat resembles, Muthill is one of those unspoiled Strathearn villages, clustering round an ancient church, which still very much convey the atmosphere of an old Scots burgh, sturdy and independent. It lies 3 miles south of Crieff, on the A.822 road from Gleneagles, on rising ground above the Earn, and again like Dunning and others, was burned by the retreating Jacobite Earl of Mar, after Sheriffmuir, in 1715.

It was quite an important place in Roman times; and although the Road itself by-passes the village a mile to the south-east, from Ardoch to the Tay, there are no fewer than four forts or camps near by. One is at Strageath, a mile to the south-east; another two farther east, across the Earn in the Innerpeffray vicinity, where starts the notable line of Signal Stations along the Gask ridge; and 4 miles southwards is Kaims Castle on the Muir of Orchill, described as a fortlet.

A mile south-east of the village is the large wooded estate of Culdees, a name which emphasises the links with the ancient Celtic Church, which was so strong in this area, as the many chapels of Strathearn dedicated to Celtic saints indicate. The splendid red-stone tower of the ruined Celtic church of Muthill dominates the village, 70 feet high, and saddle-roofed. It is similar to that of Dunning, but kept in better order, in the care of the Ministry of Works. It was built in the 12th century, and we read that in 1170 Michael, Culdee and parson of Mothill, witnessed a charter of Simon, Bishop of Dunblane. The pre-Reformation church whose ruins we now see was added in 1430 by Michael Ochiltree, Dean of Dunblane—the Vicars of Muthill were usually Deans of the diocese. It is interesting to note that the same Ochiltree, when he became Bishop himself, built the notable Bishop's Bridge over the Machany Water, well known to travellers on the A.822. In the chancel of the old church is the recumbent effigy of Ada, daughter of Henry, Seneschal of Strathearn, and her husband Sir Maurice Drummond, first Knight of Concraig, who died in 1362—the forerunner of the great Drummond family in this area. Concraig is actually the name of a notable greenstone trap-dike, easily seen from the main road.

Drummond Castle stands about two miles to the north-west, in its great estate. Its nucleus is an impressive and lofty 15th century keep, erected on a rock high above magnificent gardens, the Scottish seat of the Drummond-Willoughby Earls of Ancaster, who descend in the female line from the early Drummonds. The ancient castle stands quite distinct from the later house, and is maintained as an armoury and museum. It was badly damaged by Cromwell; and again by its own chatelaine, the Countess of Perth in 1715, so that it could not again be used by the Hanoverians.

There are many other items of interest in the parish of Muthill—pronunciation should provide no difficulties if it is remembered that the name derives from the Moot-hill, or hill of meeting. The low-lying and fertile eastern section is in marked contrast to the western heights, the latter reaching their climax in Ben Clach (1748 feet) to the south, and the isolated and conspicuous pine-clad Torlum Hill (1291 feet) to the north. On the high ground, almost at Glen Artney, is Blairinroar (*Blar-an-roinn*, the Battle of Division), where there was a chapel and two holy wells, dedicated to St. Patrick—that at Straid asserted to be excellent for the whooping-cough. Some have claimed this to be the site of the famed battle of Mons Grampius—but this seems unlikely. There was another chapel and well of St. Patrick at Struthill, south of Muthill, recommended for the relief of lunacy! And still another at Strageath, to the north, where, just across the Earn, the farm of Dalpatrick still remains. St. Patrick, patron of Ireland, came to Scotland as a fugitive at the age of 22, in the mid-5th century, and was so busy hereabouts that the inhabitants of Muthill used to observe his day as a public holiday. Not far from Struthill, on the Machany Water, is Mill of Steps, where, in the mid-18th century was born to the blacksmith, Gloag, a daughter of great beauty, who, emigrating to America, was captured by corsairs, sold as a slave to the Emperor of Morocco, and who so captivated that dusky monarch that she became Empress.

Perth. This famous place, formerly called St. John's-toun of Perth, traces its history farther back than do most Scottish communities—which is saying something. The Roman fort of Bertha was sited about two miles northwards, where Almond joins Tay, and it is assumed that hence came the name. Obviously Perth, the first bridgeable point up the Tay, would be of vital importance from earliest times, especially as the area around is rich and fertile. Not quite so important strategically as Stirling, Perth was more secure, more richly endowed, a greater trading centre. Here, then, inevitably grew up a vital community. Though the city's earliest charter, sometimes thrown doubt upon, is dated 1210, in 1127 David I refers to the burgh of Perth in a charter of Dunfermline Abbey. The town's antiquity therefore cannot be challenged.

Nor can the beauty of the site. Here the western end of the Sidlaws range comes to an abrupt halt at the precipitous Kinnoull Hill, just across the Tay. To the south-east the long ridge of Moncreiffe Hill hems it in; while to the south-west the high ground of Craigend, Kirkton Hill and the Burgh Muir embosom the town. But to the north all is open, fair and entrancing, to the ultimate enclosing Highland mountains, with Tay, one of the longest and finest rivers in all Britain, winding through the rich plain. Flanking the Tay, and mightily enhancing the town, lie the North and South Inches, great green parks, edged with trees. It is not accurate to call Perth a Highland town; but it is an ideal gateway to the Highlands. As far as situation, surroundings and many prospects are concerned, it is well deserving of its proud title of the Fair City.

> Behold the Tiber! the vain Roman cried,
> Viewing the ample Tay from Baiglie's side.
> But where's the Scot that would the vaunt repay,
> And hail the puny Tiber for the Tay!

So wrote Sir Walter Scott; and few, looking down on Perth from any of its surrounding heights, would disagree.

Strathbraan. The Hermitage and Falls of Braan

Tullibardine.
Pre-Reformation Chapel
of the Holy Trinity

The Pass of Tummel, Pitlochry

Yet the town itself is not beautiful—not to be compared with Stirling, for instance, however much more *convenient* a municipality. The reasons are twofold. First is that undulation of site is necessary to provide beauty and prospect; and Perth is built on a flat. Second, great as was the city's architectural heritage from the past, practically all of it has been swept away and replaced by, in the main, the utilitarian and the humdrum. This is perhaps less than fair, for there are many fine modern or semi-modern buildings; but compared with what has been lost and destroyed, these scarcely count.

Because of its safe and rich position, and its proximity to Scone, the first capital of the united Scotland of Kenneth MacAlpine—the Abbey of which became Scotland's Westminster—Perth came to contain the most important concentration of religious establishments in the kingdom. It is not quite true to say, as is often done, that it was once itself the capital of Scotland, because James I chose to make it his favourite place of residence. By such standards Turnberry, Dunfermline, Cardross, Linlithgow and Falkland all might be called one-time capitals. Stirling was the true capital, the principal palace and fortress and permanent seat of government, until Edinburgh superseded it. But it is very strange that Perth did not become the ecclesiastical metropolis; that St. Andrews should have gained this eminence instead. For St. Andrews was isolated, inconvenient and at first had nothing like so many monasteries, priories, nunneries and so on, nor of course the proximity to Scone. It had its traditional connection with St. Andrew and his relics, of course, the patron saint; but this seems insufficient, especially when Perth was in the centre of greatest influence of the old Celtic Church. Perhaps this was part of the trouble, as far as the Romish polity was concerned. Here is no place to go into this problem; but it is strange indeed that Perth in fact was not even the seat of a bishop. Yet here, under the eye of Scone the great religious houses proliferated, the monastic institutions of the Black Friars, the Grey Friars, the White Friars, the Carthusians and so on, in splendid, sometimes princely establishments, with nunneries, hospices, chapels and churches to match. Alas, all are gone—although there is still a modern Roman Catholic monastery across the river on the side of Kinnoull Hill. Happily, the great St. John's Kirk of Perth, and the episcopal cathedral of St. Ninian, carry on after a fashion the ecclesiastical tradition—though the latter is the seat of the See of Dunkeld, not of Perth.

The title of Fair City, therefore, is slightly suspect, in the second word's implication, as of the first—since a city is usually indicative either of a very large community or the seat of its own cathedral. The population here is only 41,000. Yet, by any standards, this is a major Scots town, quite apart from being the capital of one of the really great counties, a place of resounding fame, notable character and very real interest, even charm. Its attractions are innumerable. Although it was a walled town in the Middle Ages—indeed, besieged and captured, in person, by Robert the Bruce—only a 50-foot section of the old walling remains, down a narrow lane off George Street. There are some foundations of the Speygate Tower opposite the Greyfriars Burial-ground in Canal Street.

Any description of Perth should almost certainly begin at St. John's Kirk, since this is not only the oldest extant building but the reason for the place's medieval name of St. John's-toun. It stands in the centre of the town, all the streets seeming to enshrine it. Dedicated to John the Baptist, there was a church on the site as early as 1126, when its revenues were granted to the new Abbey of Dunfermline. In this church was interred the heart of the good Alexander III, who fell over the cliff at Kinghorn in 1286—though the rest of the body was buried at Dunfermline. But nothing of this early building survives. What we now see is basically a 15th century church, which had fallen into ruin and was restored, divided into three parish churches for the town; and then renovated and made one again, as a memorial to the dead of the First World War, by the famous architect Sir Robert Lorimer. It is a cruciform building with a tall and graceful central battlemented tower, with clock and chimes, a short leaded spire rising above, and a smaller and truncated porch-tower, with gables, to the north. Internally it measures 190 by 60 feet, and consists of a nave of five bays, with aisles, north and south transepts, the former shortened and now containing the War Memorial Shrine, and to the east an aisled choir also of five bays. The central porch of the Halkerston Tower has a superb groined vault. The crossing, under the main tower, is also very fine, carried on four great piers, with a vault which displays a painted carving of the *Agnus Dei*, the emblem of Perth. Although less full of treasures than, say, Dunblane Cathedral or the Holy Rude at Stirling, there is a great deal to be seen in this splendid church. Here, in 1336, Edward III is alleged to have stabbed to death his brother the Earl of Cornwall. Admittedly the Earl died at Perth; but by then Edward was back in England. It is thought that he died of a fever. The church suffered terrible destruction by the Reforming mob in 1559, John Knox having preached his famous incendiary sermon herein, and, like many another orator, lit a fire too big to be controlled. Here in Perth, indeed, began that shameful storm of devastation which was to cost Scotland the best of her ecclesiastical heritage of architecture. Here, in the next century, 800 Covenanting prisoners were cooped; and later, the Covenanting Colonel Strachan, who defeated Montrose at Carbisdale, was "excommunicat and delivered to the deivell". Cromwell used part of the building as a court-house. When divided into three parish churches, the three ministers took it in turn to officiate in each part—less than convenient. Over £50,000 was subscribed for the 1923 restoration to a single and magnificent church, the first Lord Forteviot, of the Dewar of Perth whisky family, being notably generous. A Trust, under the Society of the Friends of Saint John's Kirk of Perth, maintains the building.

This great church is really the heart and centre of Perth. There was a castle once, to the north, but it was never as important as the church. Around St. John's the streets are laid out in notably regular and systematic fashion unusual in an ancient town in Scotland. The main two, running east and west, are South Street and High, or North, Street. St. John's Square lies between the two; and here, west of the church and the City Hall, is an attractive new development, a traffic-free shopping precinct centred round a replica of the old Mercat Cross—the latter erected in 1913 in memory of King Edward VII.

With items of interest and sites of former splendour scattered widespread over a great network of streets and lanes, it is difficult to follow any pattern of delineation. Of truly ancient building, practically nothing remains. The Fair Maid's House in North Port, celebrated in Scott's novel, is so 'antiqued' as to be quaint rather than authentic, and now an attractive craft and curio shop. Hal o' the Wynd's House, similarly famous, in Mill Wynd, has more authenticity, and a good gablet, but it is very neglected and with no other noteworthy features surviving. More interesting are the Perth, or King's, Mills nearby, a group of water-mills still with their lades running beneath, fed from the distant Almond, these being transferred to the town by charter of Robert III. All are now stores, and the surroundings less than worthy. Another building which could look very attractive, and an asset to the town, if it was white-washed and made the most of, is King James VI's Hospital, at the corner of King Street and County Place. This is a tall, rather dingy, five-storeyed tenement on the E-plan, dating substantially from 1750 but having a core of 16th century work, possibly earlier—for here was the ancient Charterhouse, the Carthusian Monastery, which, taken over at the Reformation, the Regent Moray rather than his nephew James VI turned into a hospital. It is now occupied as flats, but has potential.

The Dominican or Blackfriars Monastery stood in Blackfriars Street, near the Fair Maid's House, and is completely gone. This was a princely place, and used by James I as his favourite residence. Here, indeed, he was assassinated by Sir Robert Graham and other conspirators in 1437, when Catherine Douglas, the famous Barlass, sought to bar the door in his aid with her arm. Near by is the 18th century town house of General the Lord John Murray. And across the road is another 18th century building, now housing an antique shop, on the site of the former Castle of Perth, destroyed by a flood in 1210. This would be a timber castle, plastered with clay to make it fireproof—but not floodproof! In this northern area also is the rather fine modern St. Ninian's Episcopal Cathedral, a large building at the corner of Atholl Street, dating from 1850.

Although there are few buildings of real antiquity, the ancient streets and lanes remain, with their original names, such as Kirkgate, Fleshers' Vennel, Cutlog Vennel, Horners' Lane, Ropemakers' Close, Cow Vennel, Meal Vennel and Skinnergate. The last, although extremely narrow, was once the only access into the walled town from the north. The Greyfriars or Franciscan Monastery stood to the south of the town, off Canal Street, and here the old burial-ground still remains an open space. In the vicinity several martyrs were burned for heresy in the pre-Reformation struggles, in 1544, Cardinal Davie Beaton watching. The Tay runs near by, to the east, and Tay Street is an attractive boulevard —although the main road traffic artery—with fine prospects across the river. Here once stood the palatial Gowrie House, its site now marked only by one more plaque, on the walling of the old County Buildings. This was the town house of the Lords Ruthven, Earls of Gowrie, of Ruthven Castle, now Huntingtower, on the Almond; and here in 1600 took place the notorious murder, in the King's presence and at his urging, of the young Earl of Gowrie, Provost of Perth, and his brother, a deed, known as the Gowrie Conspiracy, which has intrigued posterity ever since—and not to Jamie the Saxt's credit. Near by, in Tay Street, at Number 44, are the original offices of that great modern financial corporation, the General Accident Insurance Corporation, founded here in 1885, and still having its headquarters in the town, round the corner in High Street—surely a notable example of resisting the pressures of 'Londonisation', in which the founding Norie-Miller family are to be congratulated. On the General Accident's present site once stood what was called the Castle o' the Green, at the corner of Watergate, where golfers of the past kept their clubs and did what golfers always do when they are not actually on the ball. The course, King James the Sixth's Golf Course, still so named, is on Moncreiffe Island in the Tay, only a few hundred yards away, reachable by a footbridge combined with the rail bridge.

Two other bridges cross the river from Tay Street, to the Bridgend suburb of Kinnoull parish and the north and east. The oldest and highest, to the north, is Perth Bridge proper, built by Smeaton in 1772. There was a timber bridge here, allegedly thrown across by Agricola's Romans. Whatever its origins, it was swept away in the same flood that destroyed the Castle in 1210. But replaced, for another is on record as being repaired in 1329. Floods in 1573, 1582 and 1589 all caused more trouble, until it was finally swept away in 1621—a great loss which the folk of Perth blamed on divine wrath over the last General Assembly held here. Thereafter all crossing had to be by ferry for 150 years, until the Smeaton bridge was erected at a cost of £26,631, with nine arches and length of 840 feet. Since widened, it carries a great weight of traffic. The view from this bridge is delightful, with, north and south the Inches and the distant hills, and eastwards the riverside gardens of Bridgend. Here the visitor may watch the anglers at their patient casting. Tay is, of course, one of the most famous salmon rivers in the world.

There are, needless to say, many modern buildings of worth and many items of interest. The handsome church of St. Leonards-in-the-Fields, for instance, with its lantern tower, dates from 1835, and faces out across the South Inch, being sometimes mistaken for St. John's. The old County Buildings, by the architect Smirke, date from 1819 and have an elegant portico of twelve fluted pillars in the Grecian style. The Art Gallery and Museum, at the junction of George Street and Charlotte Street, is deservedly renowned as one of the finest in the land for a town of this size, with collections of pictures and sculpture, modern as well as ancient, furniture, china, silver, costume, medals and so on. Here, for instance, is the original Celtic St. Fillan's Bell, rather like a large cow-bell, from Struan, with its own Gaelic name of *Am Buidhean,* one of the five Culdee bells of Perthshire, purchased in 1939. Perth Repertory Theatre in the High Street is notable in Scotland, as it should be; and so is the Salutation Hotel, on another level, in South Street, one of the best-known hotels in the land, with Prince Charles Edward connections.

Because of the Inches, Perth's latter-day extension has been spread at some distance, leaving the old town pleasantly islanded within its green moats. Inch, of course, means island, and once these were just that, when Tay was less disciplined than today. Even now there are three islands, in addition to that of Moncreiffe, in the river here. The North Inch is the larger park, measuring 98 acres. It has always been used for sporting events, from earliest days; now cricket, rugby and other games are played. And here, recently has been built by the Gannochy Trust, at a cost of £230,000, the remarkable, circular and most modern Bell's Sports Centre, with its great 200-foot translucent dome, with under-cover facilities for almost all kinds of sport and physical exercise. There used to be a racecourse here, as indeed there was also on the South Inch. The famous Battle of the Clans, a trial by combat held in 1396 before Robert III, between teams of 30 each of Clan Chattan and the Comyns, took place here, when the smith Henry Gow, or Hal o' the Wynd, distinguished himself; all the Comyns were slain, and only 11 Shaws of Clan Chattan survived, all wounded. The South Inch is smaller, of 72 acres, and was notable for archery practice and displays, stones marking the 500 fathoms of an arrow's correct flight. Here also witch-burnings took place. Nowadays fairs still offer their entertainment, and there are boating and paddling pools for the youngsters. It is claimed that these Inches were given to Perth by John Mercer of Aldie, who was Provost at the time, and a Scots ambassador, in the 14th century, in exchange for a family-burial vault under St. John's Kirk. However exclusive an interment-place, this seems a poor exchange. Yet this jingle appears to indicate the reverse:

> *Folk say the Mercers tried the toun to cheat,*
> *When for twa inches they did win six feet!*

A large and strong citadel was built by Cromwell's army, in 1652, on the South Inch—tearing down a great many fine old buildings for the stones—one of the four designed to overawe Scotland. All traces of it have now vanished, in their turn.

Before leaving the old town within its Inches, some indication of its renown as a trading, business and shopping centre should be given. Perth has always been one of the rich towns of Scotland. As far back as 1217 the Abbot of Cirencester is quoted in Camden's *Britannia,* as saying:

> *Great Tay, through Perth, through towns, through country flies,*
> *Perth the whole kingdom with her wealth supplies.*

The town's trade was not only with the rest of the kingdom, but with the Low Countries and the Hanseatic states, her port a busy one. Reference to the port follows. Perthshire has always been one of the great cattle-raising areas of Britain, and excelled in the products thereof. Her cattle-market is one of the largest and most renowned in the country, its annual pedigree cattle sales world-famous. Despite its great spread—it was planned to house 1500 cattle and 15,000 sheep—it is still situated within the old town, in the Market Street–Caledonian Road area. Naturally, the subsidiaries of livestock production have also been of great importance, tanning, leatherwork, harness and especially glove-making. Also shoemaking—South Street used to be called Shoegate. Pre-eminent was the Incorporation of Glovers, amongst Perth's rich guilds. Skinnergate was inhabited mainly by glovers; and it will be re-collected that the Fair Maid's father was Simon Glover. At one time linen was the staple export, with 1500 looms working. Today, whisky blending and bottling, dyeing and glass manufacture—Perth glass paper-weights are particularly sought-after—are the most prominent, with agricultural industries. Dewar's and Bell's great Scotch whisky establishments are here. The shopping facilities are renowned, certain of the shops having a nation-wide fame. George Street is a most attractive shopping street of great character, with St. John Street likewise.

The port has been mentioned—and to many this may seem an unlikely feature, so far up Tay. Sand and gravel banks have always been a problem; but there is still a harbour for sea-going ships, situated now down Shore Road, to the east of the South Inch, though formerly it was higher up, at the foot of High Street. It is now rather an unlovely area—dockland is seldom beautiful—despite the fine sylvan prospects unusual in a port. Two coasting steamers were unloading silica sand and fertiliser on the author's recent visit.

There is still much of interest to see beyond the old town area. The great barracks flanking the North Inch, former headquarters of the Black Watch, have now been demolished, so far leaving only an open space; but a link with the famous regiment remains in the Regimental Museum at Balhousie Castle, actually on the west fringe of the Inch itself. Part of the grounds are made into a small memorial garden, with superb modern wrought-iron gates, to the late Earl Wavell, Field Marshal, Colonel of the Regiment, Freeman of Perth and Viceroy of India, erected in 1966. Balhousie Castle itself, once the seat of the Drummold-Hay Earls of Kinnoull, is disappointing; for though a late 16th century fortalice, it has been wholly encased in modern stonework so that no authentic features survive externally, although internally its vaulted basements, turnpike stairs and original apartments remain, though modernised. Close by, in the Inch Park, is the aforementioned modernistic Bell's Sports Centre, in startling contrast. And on the other side, at the end of Hay Street, is a most attractive block of modern flats, white and skilfully designed, with old silver birches retained to enhance the setting, recent recipient of a Scottish Civic Trust award.

In these northern outskirts was the old combined Perth Academy and Grammar School, united in 1807, the latter alleged to date from the 12th century, the former, more credibly, from 1760. The Grammar School with an illustrious history claimed the Admirable Crichton as a former pupil; he spent much of his boyhood at Clunie Castle near Dunkeld. The Academy is now housed in large modern premises on high ground west of the town, on the outskirts of the old Burgh Muir which covered a great deal of land towards Tibbermore —land now increasingly given over to modern housing, public and private, hospitals and other institutions. A huge new comprehensive school is going up, on the same ridge farther south, overlooking the old village, now suburban, of Craigie. Near by, below the A.9 approach to the town is a place of which Perth should make more—the fine, late 16th century castle of Pittheavlis. This is a delightful example of the tall fortalice on the L-plan, harled and colour-washed, with stair-tower, angle-turrets, massive chimneystack and gunloops. It is still occupied, although its surroundings are neglected. The fact that Pittheavlis seems to have escaped any recorded historical involvement is certainly no reason for ignoring it. The castle was an Oliphant possession. Farther out along this so-called Glasgow Road, which is in fact the A.9 from Stirling, is the estate of Cleeve, from which the Norie-Miller family of General Accident Insurance took its title of baronetcy, the mansion now divided into flats and with a caravan-park in the grounds.

Perth Prison has more than local significance. It stands, sombre and very self-contained, where the A.90 begins to cross the South Inch from the south-east, after passing the old village suburbs of Craigend and Friarton. It covers 18 acres and was erected in 1812 as a depot for 7000 French prisoners of the Napoleonic Wars, with housing for 300 soldiers to guard them, at a cost of £130,000. It was soon turned into a general civil prison, however, remodelled in 1841 and added to frequently thereafter. As prisons go, it is quite famous.

Although the suburbs of Bridgend—where Ruskin spent his boyhood—and Barnhill, across Tay, are in the parish of Kinnoull and dealt with separately, brief mention here should be made of the attractive situation of this area, under steeply-rising and wooded Kinnoull Hill. The Hill itself (729 feet), is, thanks to the generosity of Lord Dewar, a splendid public park for the city, one of the finest imaginable, surely. The views from the summit are magnificent.

Perth has been called the Gateway to the Highlands. This is true, of course. But it also makes an ideal centre for exploring a vast area of most attractive, interesting and exciting country which is not Highland at all and which tends to receive less than its due measure of praise—and of visitors. Southern Perthshire is a treasure-house of quite enormous riches, and Perth its worthy capital.

We cannot leave Perth without mention of its unique contribution to a luxury trade—the largest fresh-water pearl industry in Europe. Not that this makes it very large; one pearl-fisher, by name Abernethy, and one jeweller's shop, by name Cairncross. But the product is sufficiently splendid to grace even royal throats and tiaras.

Pitcairngreen, Redgorton and Moneydie. These are the names of a village and two rural parishes in the Lower Almond area, some four miles north-west of Perth. Pitcairngreen is really Pitcairn-on-the-Green, and is an attractive place amongst raspberry fields, spread around a large, tree-dotted green, with an old hotel, a quietly rural community half a mile north of the Almond, once moving a lady poet to prophesy that it would one day rival Manchester! This was because it grew up during the bleachfield and cloth-weaving expansion; but fortunately for its appearance, its industrial activities were carried out at some distance, at Pitcairnfield and Cromwell-park bleachfields to south and west, near the necessary river. The occasional modern house does still go up—but it appears that the muse, on this occasion, exaggerated. There are a number of ancient cairns in the neighbourhood—whence no doubt the name—one quite close to the village on the east, in woodland near the house of Cairnton. These are thought to represent burial-mounds of the native victims of some battle between the Caledonians and the Romans, both of whom had camps in the area, the former to the south, the Romans to the east at Bertha, where Almond joins Tay. A more modern and modest cairn stands on the village green, to commemorate the planting of trees by the local children in celebration of Queen Elizabeth's coronation in 1953.

A small loch lies to the east of the aforementioned Cairnton, in the woods.

A mile farther north-east, at Pitmurthly farm, stands the parish church of Redgorton, in an isolated position inconvenient for all. It is a plain T-shaped building, built in 1690 and renewed 1766 and 1841, within a graveyard with some old stones, one at least of the 17th century. The hamlet of Redgorton is modern, and lies to the north half a mile, a pleasant place with quite a large school and fine playing-fields. Not far away to the east, across the main A.9 highway, is the site of the Battle of Luncarty, at Denmarkfield farm, with the King's Stone monolith—dealt with under Luncarty.

Moneydie, pronounced mon-aidie, is another rural parish with an isolated church, the two kirks lying only a mile and a half apart, both indicating a total disregard for centres of population. Money-die church has the former school beside it; and still retains its old pair of iron jougs hanging near the door, an iron collar for holding fast unfortunate transgressors of kirk discipline. It is a building of 1813, slightly ornate without but dully plain within, quite unconcerned with appearances. There is a fine and large manse adjoining. Near by was once the castle of Kinvaid, allegedly built by Bishop Brown of Dunkeld, in the 15th century, for the protection of the parishioners—highly doubtful; he was laird of this property. Later, this was the home of Bessie Bell, mentioned hereafter. Now there is only an old farmhouse. Alexander Myln, who wrote the *Lives of the Bishops of Dunkeld*, and died in 1542, was Prebendary of Moneydie.

In this parish, 2 miles to the south-west, lies the large wooded estate of Lynedoch, formerly Lednock, one-time Graham property, which gained fame when its owner, General Thomas Graham of Balgowan, one of the heroes of the Peninsular War, specifically of Barossa, was created a peer in 1814 with the title of Lord Lynedoch. His mansion is now demolished, and the R.N. Stores Depot at Almondbank has taken over some of the grounds. Here, at the riverside some way west of the former mansion, is the railed-in grave of the aforementioned Bessie Bell and her friend, Mary Gray, daughter of the Laird of Lednock, celebrated in a formerly popular song. The story goes that, in 1645, when the plague struck the district, these two maidens betook themselves to a riverside bower here, to avoid the consequences, and lived in romantic isolation. Unfortunately not quite isolated enough, however—for they were visited by a young man from plague-stricken Perth, admirer of one, or both, and as a consequence caught the infection from him after all, and died. There seems to be a moral here.

Pitlochry and Moulin. Pitlochry is, of course, one of the foremost and famous holiday resorts and touring centres in all Scotland; and deservedly. Set in northern Perthshire, near where the Tummel and Garry valleys join that of Tay, it inevitably is a road centre for a vast area. When the area is so scenically splendid as is Atholl, Strathtummel, Strathtay and Strathardle, with historic places abounding, as at nearby Killiecrankie and Dunkeld, the renown is as inevitable. What is strange is that Pitlochry's fame is of such comparatively recent origin. *The Statistical Account* of 1839 goes on at great lengths about the village and parish of Moulin—in which Pitlochry village was situated—but has only a few words to say about Pitlochry itself, a village which had only newly obtained an inn, and in which a bank had been opened, enterprisingly three years earlier. The population then was 291. Even in 1871 it was only 510—so the development in a century has been phenomenal. Even so, however, the resident population is only 2400. It was General Wade's anti-Jacobite military road which made Pitlochry possible; for before that there was no road north of Dunkeld. The pacification of the Highlands was not all debit.

Pitlochry is likely to grow a great deal more—if it can find space; for the hills shoulder close here, and the great new Loch Faskally, however beautiful, inevitably takes up a lot of the precious low ground. But a multi-million-pound hotel-conference centre and recreational complex is planned, with even an indoor swimming-pool; also other projects and enterprises, as envisaged in the Tay–Tummel Valley Report of the Scottish Tourist Board, in forestry, saw-milling, hill and water sports, even deer-farming.

Basically Pitlochry is only one street flanking the busy A.9 high-way on a shelf above loch and river; though there is climbing development of housing and hotels to north and east. Probably the first impression of the visitor here is the large number of hotels, from the vast Atholl Palace, dominating all, the Hydropathic, and Fisher's well-known establishment in the main street, to 36 other and lesser places and no fewer than 50 bed-and-breakfast houses. The tweed and Highland-goods shops are famous, and every need of the visitor catered for. Most celebrated is the Pitlochry Festival Theatre, a most gallant project founded by the late John Stewart in 1951, renowned as Scotland's tented Theatre in the Hills. It has maintained the highest standards of drama, ballet, concert and recital here, in the mountains, over the years, despite enormous difficulties. It is now past the tented stage, seats 500, holds also art exhibitions, has a Festival Society, a supporters' scheme, mailing lists, a licensed restaurant, cocktail bar, sun lounge and garden café. That such a venture has succeeded in a place of 2000 people far from any city, proclaims the great vision, courage and initiative of all concerned. May it go from strength to strength. Scotland is short on theatres.

Almost as great an attraction is the great hydro-electric complex here, the power station, exhibition hall, fish-ladder, dam and spill-way, down at the recently-created Loch Faskally. This great and highly-attractive sheet of water amongst the wooded hills has con-founded all who saw it as a desecration of the splendid countryside a few years ago. It is now a major asset, scenically as well as for the power it produces, as fine a loch as any in the Central Highlands. Its dam is 478 feet long and 54 feet high, and its Salmon Observa-tion Chamber in the 900 foot Fish Pass is an ever-popular magnet for visitors. The large, airy, silent demonstration hall of the power-house is an education in the harnessing of water-power from these empty mountain tracts. It draws its water from a catchment area of 710 square miles, and its 15,000 kilowatt generators produce 55,000,000 units per year. The eight power stations of the entire Tummel Valley scheme have a capacity of 245,000 kilowatts and produce 650,000,000 units. The Hydro-Electric Board's local head-quarters are in the large red-stone Scottish-baronial mansion of Fonab, west across the loch.

There are other industries represented at Pitlochry, besides catering for visitors and producing electricity. Forestry has been mentioned—for this is a richly wooded area. There is Bell's Blair

Atholl Distillery, just as the town is entered from the south. There is a tweed mill. And so on. A large caravan-park is sited pleasingly across the Port na Craig bridge to the south-east, where there is an attractive hamlet—this on the way to Dunfallandy House Hotel and the famous Pictish symbol-stone.

Pitlochry arose as a sort of suburb of Moulin, the old village. Now the situation is reversed. But Moulin manages successfully to retain its distinct character and identity. It lies on a higher shelf, which was known as the Howe of Moulin, fertile enough to be called the Garden of Atholl; and when Pitlochry had only 291 persons, had 321! It is still a picturesque place, with cottages and a winding street with lanes, even though the A.924 climbs through it on the way to Kirkmichael, Strathardle and Glenshee; and there are fine open views to south and west, with shapely Ben y Vrackie, the Speckled Mountain dominating all to the north. Here is the parish church; an attractive hotel; and the ruins of an ancient castle. This, known as Casteal Dubh, or Black Castle, was built by Sir John Campbell, in 1326. He was son of Bruce's friend and brother-in-law, Sir Neil Campbell of Lochow, and was created Earl of Atholl by Bruce's son. The castle was inhabited until 1512, the year of the great plague. Only a few fragments of walling remain out in a field to the east. The church itself is modern, being rebuilt in 1875, after a fire. But there have been many predecessors, a stone from one, dated 1613, being built in over the door. Indeed it is claimed to be the oldest church site in Atholl, allegedly founded by St. Columba himself in 490. St. Colm's Fair used to be held here each February; and Columba's dove emblem is incorporated in the modern Burgh of Pitlochry's arms. The church interior is plain, with a large semi-circular gallery. A bell from Rotterdam, dated 1749, is displayed at the front, a later bell now being used. There are many old stones in the graveyard, one slab showing a medieval long-handled sword, and another the Maltese Cross of a crusading knight. There is the stump of an ancient ash tree, to which the iron jougs were attached when this was the site of the Barony Court of Moulin. The old estates of Balnakeilly and Baledmund adjoin, Stewart and Fergusson properties. There is a standing-stone just north of the village; and a stone circle lies to the west, near the golf-course.

Pitlochry is renowned as a centre for touring the Central Highlands; and within easy reach are such as the Killiecrankie battlefield and the Soldier's Leap; Blair Castle and Blair Atholl; the lochs Tummel, Rannoch and Tay; the mountains of Ben y Vrackie, Ben y Ghloe, Ben Lawers and Schiehallion, to climb; Dunkeld Cathedral and Birnam Wood; Glenshee for skiing; and so on. All these and more are dealt with separately. Within moderate walking distance are the Dunfallandy Stone, the Linn of Tummel and Pass of Killiecrankie Nature Trails, the Black Spout waterfall on the Edradour Burn. Near this last is the former Edradour House, now the Archie Briggs' National Children's Home and Memorial Chapel, excellently commemorating a Scots contractor with a love for children. There is also the Edradour Distillery farther down the burn. Once there were seven distilleries in Moulin parish.

There is much more to see and hear about than can be indicated here. There is an Information Centre at 20 Atholl Road (Tel. Pitlochry 215) which admirably supplies all that needs to be known about attractions, events, accommodation and so on. The little Burgh of Pitlochry is on to a good thing—and knows it.

Rait, Fingask and Megginch. Rait is a picturesque relic of the past, the largest of the attractive little weaving villages tucked into the south face of the Sidlaws above the Carse of Gowrie. Lying between Kilspindie and Kinnaird, at the foot of the steep Glen of Rait, it is the sort of place artists love to paint, consisting of two lanes —it would not do to call them streets—one on either side of a brawling burn, with little bridges across, many cottages, not a few still thatched, clucking poultry and an air of timeless peace. There are not many Raits left to us, especially within about ten miles of a great city like Dundee. Formerly this was a parish of its own; but it was combined with Kilspindie and its old church abandoned. Needless to say, it has not been entirely overlooked by people with an eye for a quiet and pleasing environment, and some of its houses have been taken over and modernised, a process which is likely to continue. But the original character remains.

Behind the village, the glen-road climbs under Beal or Bale Hill, passing the house of Ladywell, which presumably indicated a holy well dedicated to Our Lady, although no traces of any shrine remain. Bale Hill itself, however, is said to have a haunted air. Higher, the road emerges on to the upland plateau of Dalreich Muir, which is here dotted with the ancient dark Scots pines that speak of the old Caledonian Forest, lending character to an area of small hill-farms. Below Rait, at the cross-roads, is a featureless mound, the site of an ancient earthwork.

The Stuart lairds of Rait, buried in the somewhat florid mausoleum in Kilspindie kirkyard, lived at Annat, to the west of the village; though this mansion is now abandoned, members of the family still occupy modern houses near by. On the other, eastern, side, in its own deep glen, or den, is the renowned estate of Fingask Castle, a most delightful house and property, with a romantic history. The castle stands on a lofty, south-facing terrace, with splendid views, amongst climbing woodland and above a fine ravine. It has suffered many vicissitudes, historically and architecturally; but today, happily, it is restored approximately to its former excellence—although unfortunately it has lost its stair-tower—and, moreover, it has recently returned to the possession of the Murray-Threipland family which lost it for a while. The Threiplands, from Kilbucho in Peebles-shire, bought Fingask from the Bruces in the 17th century. Sir Patrick Threipland was Provost of Perth in 1665, and knighted in 1674 for diligence in suppressing conventicles—which would not endear him to his Drummond neighbours at Megginch. His son Sir David was one of the first to join the Earl of Mar in 1715. The Old Chevalier twice stayed at Fingask in 1716, the castle being thereafter occupied by dragoons and forfeited. Lady Threipland managed to lease it back, but it was again forfeited after the failure of the '45 Rising, when the elder son fell at Prestonpans, but his brother, Sir Stewart, after innumerable adventures with Prince Charles, escaped to France disguised as a bookseller's assistant. He eventually returned to Edinburgh as a physician, and prospered sufficiently to buy back Fingask for £12,207 in 1783. The baronetcy was restored to his son, Sir Patrick, in 1826. It is good that there are Threiplands again at Fingask; also that the Jacobite portraits are back.

Down in the wooded den below the castle is St. Peter's Well. And not far away, on the farm of Flawcraig, was the Bishop's Well, referring to a Bishop of Dunkeld. Here, too, were discovered iron rings set into the rock, for tying craft to in the days before the Carse was drained.

A couple of miles to the south, in the middle of the Carse, is another fascinating and ancient estate, Megginch, with its castle and chapel. The name is thought to derive from *maol-innis*, the bare or bald island—but this is certainly not a description to apply today, the property being notable for its magnificent woodlands. The Drummond family have been settled here since the 17th century, when John Drummond, 8th feudal baron of Lennoch, Hereditary Seneschal of Strathearn bought it from Sir George Hay, the Hays, a branch of the Erroll chiefly house, having been in possession from very early times. Happily, the Drummonds are still at Megginch.

The castle, approached from the busy main A.85 road midway between Perth and Dundee, stands amongst ancient woodlands, many of the trees being renowned for their great age, girth and height. Some of the yews, for instance, are over a thousand years old and 80 feet high. Especially interesting is the avenue of great old holly trees leading to the chapel. The castle itself is a composite structure, highly attractive in mellow red sandstone; indeed, mellowness is the operative word at Megginch. Just how ancient is the original nucleus is impossible to say; but there was a great reconstruction in 1575, and much of the north front, now the back of the house, with its stair-tower, watch-chamber and angle-turrets, belongs to this period. The present front dates from later, with an early 19th century reconstruction. Internally there are many fine features, the large number of mural chambers, stairways and secret passages being particularly interesting. These, it is presumed, were built in for security purposes, the Hays being noted Catholics after the Reformation, and the Drummonds being as pronounced Presbyterians during the repressive later 17th century; so that both had to dodge and hide frequently from the prevailing extremists in religion. A secret brick-vaulted passage, leading south below the main driveway, was recently uncovered during an emergency, when a fire-engine part-fell therein.

To the north is a most delightful stableyard, large, cobbled, whitewashed, and with a central arcaded doocote of unusual style. This adjoins double walled-gardens, lined with the mellow old bricks from Megginch's own former brickwork at Shipbrigs. The chapel lies to the west, beyond picturesque formal gardens and clipped topiary. It is a small place of great peace, used not only as a family burial-vault but still as a private place of worship. It was a pre-Reformation church, burned by John Knox in one of his dire 'cleansing' progresses.

Rannoch. The area surrounding Loch Rannoch merits its fame —even though it is not on the Road to the Isles, as the popular song would have us believe. It is one of the most scenic and rewarding parts of the Central Highlands, and vigorously so—and, considering its sometimes wild and always unspoilt beauty, very accessible, Kinloch Rannoch being only 50 miles from Perth, small mileage as the Highlands go.

Kinloch Rannoch belies its name, strangely—for kinloch means head of the loch, while this pleasant village, with its three quite large hotels, is at the foot, under the towering bluff of Craig Var, and with its own waterfall plunging close by. It makes an excellent centre for exploring, whatever its name.

The loch itself extends westwards for 10 miles, averaging about a mile in width, and is famous both for its fishing and the frequent roughness of its waters. Like so many others, there is a road along both sides. Again, as seems to be usual hereabouts, that to the north, B.846, is the main and faster route; while that to the south is the more picturesque—although the north road has the advantage of providing splendid views of that most shapely mountain, Schiehallion (3547 feet), which presides over the whole area. Unlike Tay and Tummel, neither road ever moves far from the waterside, either in distance or height, and innumerable are the entrancing vistas.

The south shore is most famed for the presence, over some five miles, of the Black Wood of Rannoch, the largest surviving remnant of the ancient Caledonian Forest south of Rothiemurchus. It is a lovely and exciting place, of splendid red-trunked, dark-foliaged natural Scots pine, at all stages of growth—for although in the care of the Forestry Commission it is still in natural regeneration. Rising out of undulating slopes of heather and bracken, the wood offers magnificent walking. The forest is now a place of peace—but many were the dark deeds perpetrated in these fastnesses.

Here, at the east end of the wood, is surely the most romantically-placed boys' boarding-school in Britain—Rannoch School, Dall, in a great whitewashed former mansion of the Robertsons, in the Scottish baronial style. Near by is the old estate saw-mill, with its water-wheel intact, and its mill-lade, led from a tumultuous shouting brown burn, adapted to supply the school's swimming-pool.

At the other end of the Black Wood, in a large clearing, is the hamlet of Camghouran, a lovely spot. Isolated down near the loch-side is the ancient burial-ground of St. Michaels, with old tomb-stones of the Camerons hereof. One stone is known as the *Clach nan Ceann*, the Stone of the Heads, recalling a grim story in which a jealous Mackintosh dashed the heads of his former lover's little sons against this rock.

At the west end of the loch is Braes of Rannoch parish church, on its knoll; and near by is Bridge of Gaur, over the rushing River Gaur, broad indeed considering it is only 3 miles long, and pouring down from the Moor of Rannoch. A mansion here is still named The Barracks after the military post set up to quell the Jacobite clans. The B.846 is rejoined, and it continues on westwards in fine style, suddenly to end in 6 miles, in the middle of nowhere, at Rannoch Station, where the West Highland line makes a great curve round this east side of the vast empty wilderness of the Moor of Rannoch. It is a strange end to a notable road, a station, a hotel and a couple of houses—that and stupendous views in every direction. There are plans to continue the road on across the moor, to Kingshouse, on A.82, at a cost of £1 million—but so far these are not authorised.

The north flank of Rannoch is known as *An Slios Min*, The Side of Gentle Slopes, and here are cornfields and birch-woods to counter the wildness of the opposite shore. Innumerable streams come in from the north, the largest of which, the Ericht, flowing out of its long loch, has a power station at its foot. Out in Loch Rannoch near by is an ancient crannog, or artificial island, crowned now by a particularly artificial-looking 'castle'. Farms, hamlets and shoot-ing-lodges dot this lochside with the delectable views.

East of Kinloch Rannoch is a stretch of flats and water-meadows, turned into a new loch by the Hydro-Electric Board, and named Dunalastair Reservoir. This was the name of the surrounding estate, formerly the seat of the Struan Robertsons, Chiefs of Clan Donnachaidh, or Duncan, descended from the Celtic Mormaers of Atholl. Much of excitement has occurred here. The Robertsons of Struan were always amongst the most loyal to the Stewarts of all the clans. Allegedly, here was fought one of Bruce's battles with the inimical MacDougalls of Lorne.

About three miles south-east of Kinloch Rannoch, at Lassin-tullich, on the attractive road that climbs over the shoulder of Schiehallion to join the B.846 to Aberfeldy, is the tiny St. Blane's Chapel and burial-ground, on top of a steep knoll. The roofless building measures only 25 by 12 feet. About five miles farther, the road rises to 1228 feet, above the lonely Loch Kinardochy, with splendid views up Strath Tummel.

St. Madoes, Pitfour and Inchyra. At the west end of the Carse of Gowrie is the tiny parish of St. Madoes, somewhat overshadowed by the growing village of Pitfour/Cairnie. It lies to the south of the busy, main Perth–Dundee road, quite close—indeed, almost seeming to be an extension of the hamlet of Glencarse; so that there is a major confusion of names here. For the church and part of the little community is indeed St. Madoes—pronounced locally Semmidores—but that part of the village which has grown up to the south, within the parkland of Pitfour Castle, is called Pitfour; while the new private housing which has developed to the west is called Cairnie. There is a caravan-park here. St. Madoch was a missionary bishop of the early Celtic Church, thought to hale from France.

The parish extends to only 1417 acres, and the church is small and plain, inside as out, with three lofts or galleries, and stands amongst old gravestones. Outside the building, but under cover now, is a handsome ancient Celtic cross-slab, 7 feet high and 3 broad, very fine. The manse, standing apart a little way to the east, is attractive in its walled garden. Alexander Lindsay, Bishop of Dunkeld, became minister here in 1591 and remained so throughout his reign as bishop till his death in 1639—one of those who took the Reformation philosophically.

The village is mainly modern, and not especially notable. But preserved amongst the modern council housing to the south is a stone circle, now of only three stones, formerly in the park of the castle. It is a great area for such standing-stones. The Hawk Stane stands in the front garden of a cottage by the roadside, at the hamlet of Chapelhill, half a mile to the east on the B.958 road to Errol. This stone is alleged to be that on which the famous Hay hawk alighted when, after the Battle of Luncarty in 990, Kenneth III told the peasant-ancestor of the great family of Hay, who had saved the day for him against the Danes, that he should have all the lands covered by a single falcon's flight. There are other alleged resting-places of this useful fowl—one as far east as Longforgan—but perhaps the Hays were good at more than fighting, and arranged a relay of hawks. Anyway, thereafter they blossomed out as principal proprietors of the Carse. A third stone, and larger, called the Grey Stone, stands in a field to the south of the same road a mile farther on, near Clashbennie, where there was a famed sandstone quarry of old. The name is obviously derived from the monolith, *clach* meaning stone. This part of the somewhat bare carseland is dotted with hamlets—Chapelhill, Cottown, Leetown. There was a large brickworks here, employing as many as 60 people in the 1880s; relics remain. The area still supports tile-manufacturing, the clay being suitable.

Pitfour Castle lies just south-east of the village. Although the present mansion dates mainly from 1829 when the famous architect Burn built it for the Stewart-Richardson laird, there is a medieval nucleus, as well as additions by the Hays in 1784. The Stewart-Richardsons, now gone, were a Lothian family, the baronetcy being of Pencaitland. A good doocote remains.

A long straight side road leads down past the Cairnie housing, from Pitfour to the Tay, more than a mile away. Here is Cairnie Ferry, where a boat plied across the estuary to Carpow until as recently as the 1930s. Now there is a seasonally-occupied station

The Trossachs. Looking north-westwards across Loch Katrine from Ben Venue

Tummel Bridge, built by General Wade

Airth, Mercat Cross

of the Tay Salmon Fisheries Company, with bothies and storehouses, all very modern; even a little narrow-gauge railway line for bogeys to run along the riverside through the reed-sea, to carry nets and fish-boxes. Some idea of the value of these fisheries is indicated by the fact that even in 1840, on one estate, the rental thereof was £3366, with 104 men employed with nets and cobles. It is interesting to note, here, how the present high-water mark has earlier levels 3, 9 and 14 feet above it.

A mile westwards along the shore is another former fishing-station, Inchyra, still a hamlet, though with a somewhat decayed look. The former pier and harbour, at the mouth of an incoming creek, is long abandoned, though less than a century ago it admitted quite large vessels and ran another ferry across to Rhynd. One traditional salmon-coble remains. The mansion house of Inchyra lies a mile inland, on the north side of the main road, a handsome Grecian edifice is wooded grounds.

St. Martins, Dunsinane and Guildtown. There is a great area north-east of Perth which is relatively little known by the general public, that part of Gowrie lying between the western Sidlaws and the Highland hills which become the Braes of Angus— really the extreme western end of the great vale of Strathmore. This area of Perthshire is no small corner, comprising about fifty square miles, bounded by the Tay on the west, and traversed by the Isla, the Ericht and their tributaries. It should be better known, for it is an attractive, unspoiled, rural countryside, green and fertile and full of interest, being amongst the longest settled in the land. Everybody, for instance, has heard of Dunsinane; but how many have actually been there? This terrain, contained within the rectangle Scone–Blairgowrie–Alyth–Coupar Angus, is well worth visiting and not just passing through. St. Martins parish, just north of that of Scone, forms the south-western corner of it, east of Tay. Its names on the Ordnance Map should act as a magnet —MacBeth's Law, Witches Stone, Druids Seat and so on: for this is an area steeped in the romantic past, its proximity to the ancient Pictish and early Scottish capital of Scone ensuring that. A Roman road led north-east through the parish towards the crossing of Isla. St. Martins itself is a charming small hamlet at the gates of a large wooded estate, with a parish church of 1842 set on a height above a stream, and reached by a hump-backed old bridge. It once belonged to Holyrood Abbey. The large Georgian mansion to the east was formerly called Kirklands, and was built by William MacDonald of Ranachan (1732–1814) the founder of the Royal Highland and Agricultural Society. There are some splendid trees here, including a row of enormous Wellingtonias.

About a mile to the north-east, reached by a dirt road past the church, is a most significant monument—the Witches Stone of MacBeth. This lies in the swampy corner of heath and scrub woodland, as one might expect, about 400 yards west of the said

M

dirt road, beside a cattle-pond, and not easily discovered. But it is worth searching for, an extraordinary anvil-shaped stone. Here it was that MacBeth traditionally consulted the famous witches on the heath, and as a consequence shifted his residence from nearby Cairnbeddie—*Caer-beth*, the Castle of Beth—to Dunsinane Hill. Just at the side of the same road, a quarter-mile nearer the church, is a stone circle. Cairnbeddie, now a farm, lies nearly a mile to the south-west, with only a green mound here to mark the site of MacBeth's Castle; but the ancient well still functions. The modern estate of Dunsinnan lies to the north, at the end of the dirt road; but Macbeth's 'high Dunsinane Hill' is 3 miles to the north-east, lofty on the flank of Black Hill (1182 feet), with its camp. Somewhere below was the famous battlefield, where Birnam Wood came marching to Dunsinane, and vengeance. The ancient fort, large and oval, with rampart and fosses, lies at 1012 feet. It was excavated in 1857, when an underground chamber was discovered, with a fine Celtic silver finger-ring. The estate was long a property of the Nairne family, the last of whom was the judge, Lord Dunsinnan. The mansion dates from 1830.

The eminence of MacBeth's Law lies 2 miles to the north, in the grounds of Lawton House.

The village of Guildtown lies on the A.93 2 miles north-west of St. Martins, Druid's Seat Wood near by containing a stone circle. It is quite a pleasing place, open and fairly large, though without much character. A mile and a half to the west, down a farm track, lies the ruined former parish church of Cambusmichael. The parishes were united about 1700. The church is interesting, obviously pre-Reformation, long and narrow, with a belfry, and ill-lit with slit windows. There are other castle-like features, for it stands in a strong position above the junction of a steep ravine and Tay; and its arched doorway is defended by a draw-bar socket. Internally there are aumbries; and a number of old gravestones remain in the deserted yard.

The detached small village of Wolfhill lies between Guildtown and Dunsinnan, with standing-stones near the farm of Loanhead.

Scone. Scone, a name which means so much in Scotland's history, is definitely a dual-personality place. Indeed there are two different Scones, Old and New—and they are far enough apart to be entirely distinct, more than a mile of open and wooded country separating them. There is also a large parish of the name. Today, New Scone, lying so near to Perth, on the north, has inevitably become something of a dormitory suburb for the Fair City, and is growing. Nevertheless it retains its own individuality.

To complicate things further, Old Scone is not *oldest* Scone! The original community grew up round the great abbey, Scotland's Westminster as it has been called, which enshrined the famous Stone of Destiny and was the coronation-place of the kings. The site of this, with the renowned Moot-hill (sometimes mistakenly called the Boot-hill) is now deep within the policies of the Earl of Mansfield's great estate of Scone Palace, which flanks the Tay to the east 2 miles north of Perth. In due course, when the Reformation had done its worst to ecclesiastical monuments, and the Scots kings had departed for London, it became inconvenient for the Murrays, Lords Stormont and later Earls of Mansfield, to have a village under their windows. So it was removed half a mile to the east, on what is now the A.93 road to Blairgowrie; and the few cottages still there are called Old Scone. Whereas New Scone, almost a town indeed, and dating in the main from the 19th century, lies more than a mile still farther east, over the hill.

Since Scone and the story of Scotland are almost synonymous, it is quite impossible here even to hint at all the storied background. It seems to have been important as occupying a central position between the Picts of north and south; and here, in 710, at the Moot-hill, King Nectan of the Picts publicly announced his adherence to the Romish date for celebrating Easter, contrary to the tenets of the Columban missionaries—a matter much exercising Christendom at that period. The Moot-hill, or Hill of Meeting, in consequence was triumphantly named Caisteal Credi, the Castle of Belief, by the Catholic party; but it is amusing to note that it had become the Hill of Credulity by 906, with the increasing ascendancy of the Celtic Church and Culdees, consequent on the triumph of Kenneth MacAlpine and the Scots of Dalriada over the Picts. In 838 Kenneth had brought the Stone of Destiny here from Dunstaffnage in Argyll (Dalriada), and so Scone thereafter became the most sacred place in the newly united kingdom of Scotland, remaining so for many centuries. In 1114 a great new Augustinian abbey replaced the Celtic monastery, in the new rise of Catholicism, and here the Scots kings were crowned, right up to Charles II—although by his time the reforming mob from Perth—who seem to have been particularly virulent—had demolished the abbey and all the shrines. These great Church lands were bestowed by James VI on David Murray, of the house of Tullibardine—who had aided the King in the murky Gowrie Conspiracy business, and who became Baron Scone in 1605 and Viscount Stormont in 1621. He began building a palace on the abbey site, using the abbey stones; but the palatial mansion, as it now stands, is of later date, erected in 1803–8 in an anglified castellated style—indeed by a London architect, William Atkinson. It is full of treasures, and a magnificent house—but possibly its present noble occupants would have preferred the more modest, authentic and convenient Scots castle. A church was erected, at the same time as the post-Reformation castle, on the top of the Moot-hill, just north of the palace, to replace the abbey-church sacked by the mob in 1559; and this was used as a private burial-ground for the Murrays, with stone effigies.

It is rather strange that Scotland's most precious and sacred place should be within a private estate.

New Scone is a more attractive community than it may appear

from the main A.94 Coupar Angus road which climbs through it. Extending, on rising ground, on both sides, it has grown up where the pleasant wooded Den of Scone comes down to the low ground— this now being the Coshenbank Park, with modern housing flanking it. The parish church dates from 1804, standing back from the road in a sloping graveyard, plain but well-cared-for. Amongst the memorials is a large and unsightly one to a notable man—David Douglas, celebrated botanist and traveller. He was born here in 1798, son of a mason, and killed by falling into a pit dug to trap wild bulls in the Sandwich Islands, in 1834. Although only 35, he had already attained great fame; and though he is best known today for his work with pine and fir trees, he introduced to this country no fewer than 53 species of woodland and 145 of herbaceous plants.

Although none of it is ancient, the older part of the village runs up the hill to the west and north at an angle to the main road, pleasing in simple cottage architecture. At the foot, at a joining of ways, is the old Mercat Cross, 13 feet tall on its plinth, removed here from the palace grounds. On the higher ground, on the way to Old Scone, is some very good modern housing, particularly that called Greystanes. Here the heather and birch trees have been allowed to remain amongst the houses; and in one delightful square of white-washed building is an ancient stone circle of seven stones, with three others separate, dating from 800 to 500 B.C.—an object-lesson in conservation and good taste.

At the other, eastern, side of New Scone, is a single standing-stone in a field opposite the attractive park of the ancient estate of Murrays-hall. The mansion here is fairly modern, as is that of Bonhard near by, where, however, the old dovecote still stands. To the north of New Scone is Scone Aerodrome, the airfield for Perth, with more stone circles near, to the south. This is on the A.94 road. On the Old Scone, A.93 highway, a couple of miles to the north, is another monument of antiquity, a large burial cairn, now tree-grown, easily seen from the road, near Scones Lethendy Farm. So New Scone's newness is only relative.

Sheriffmuir. For everyone who has heard of Sheriffmuir, probably only a very tiny percentage have actually visited it; which is a pity, for unlike many battlefield areas, this is an attractive place in its own right, and well worth experiencing quite apart from the historical associations. Moreover, it is readily accessible. Why comparatively few come here, it is hard to say. Possibly because the busy A.9 to Perth passes near by to the west, and travellers, glancing up towards the Ochils foothills, think that they have really seen all there is to see. A great mistake.

Sheriffmuir is large, an area of roughly fifteen square miles, lying north and east of Dunblane, south of Greenloaning. In the main it consists of a wide slanting shelf dropping gradually from the hills to the Allan Water, with its major portion around the 800 to 900-

foot contour. A perfectly good road runs across it from south to north, approximately parallel with the A.9 but a couple of miles to the east and 500 feet higher. And from here remarkably fine views are to be had over the Forth, Allan and Earn valleys, some highly unusual prospects, such as those south-east to Stirling and Abbey Craig. The little hidden loch on the Wharry Burn, below Lynns, gleams pleasingly amongst woodland.

Perhaps the most dramatic approach to Sheriffmuir is from Bridge of Allan, up the wooded den of the Allan Water first, then striking off along the highly interesting little hanging valley of Drumdruills, lined with old orchards for almost a mile, and thence into the impressive Kippenrait Glen, a deep, steep ravine heavily clad with birch and ash. Thus far the road has followed the Stirlingshire–Perthshire boundary. Then, crossing the rushing Wharry Burn, it climbs sharply westwards to the farm of Pisgah, a mile south-east of Dunblane. At this cross-roads the north-going road begins its ascent to the open moorland of Sheriffmuir, and the contrast from the narrow wooded dens to the wide empty grasslands, is striking.

Two miles up, at the roadside, is the tall Clan MacRae cairn, raised by that clan society 200 years after the battle. This is sometimes assumed to be the site of the famous engagement of November 13th, 1715; but of course the battle took place over a very wide area between here and the Allan Water down in the valley. This, the cairn's plaque tells us, was where the MacRae companies from Kintail and Lochalsh, comprising part of the left wing of the Jacobite army, fell almost to a man. The Rising's leader, 'Bobbing John', Earl of Mar, had his own central stance about half a mile to the north, on high, open ground, marked by a boulder with iron railing, now called the Gathering Stone; and here, to the disgust of many of his lieutenants, including Rob Roy MacGregor, he waited inactive for most of that fatal day. He held the benefit of the ground, the larger force (8400 to 3500) and his troops the better morale. But he squandered all in feeble hesitancy. It has been said that only a fool could have lost Sheriffmuir—and a visit to this lofty moorland tends to confirm that harsh verdict.

Half a mile on, at a road junction, is the lonely whitewashed inn of Sheriffmuir, surely one of the most isolated places to set an hotel in all Central Scotland, with hardly another house in sight; yet a most attractive situation too, if quiet, fine prospects and good walking, is sought. Not far away to the east, on the open moor near a deep burn-channel, is Wallace's Stone, a monolith that has been part of a stone circle, of significance long before Wallace's day. There are other relics on this upland. One is easily seen from the A.9, a tall, single standing-stone, known as the White Stone, and giving its name to the adjoining farm. And another marked on different Ordnance maps as The Roundel or The Mote, half a mile south of Greenloaning, is a mound ringed with trees, presumably the site of a motte-and-bailey timber castle.

The Sma' Glen and Upper Glen Almond. Surely few valleys change so abruptly and dramatically in character in mid-length as does Glen Almond. The lower glen, from its joining with Tay opposite Scone to some thirteen miles westwards at Buchanty, is a gentle pastoral vale, well-wooded and dotted with fine estates. Then, at Dallick, it suddenly swings northwards, and all alters. Steep hills of rock and heather close in, the floor narrows to mere hundreds of yards and the river becomes a mountain torrent. For nearly three miles this quite fierce and rocky defile pierces 2000-foot summits, and is famed as the Sma' Glen, a noted gateway to the Highlands, small only as regards its length and narrowness. There is room only for the river and the road, the A.822 Crieff to Aberfeldy, based on the line of one of General Wade's military roads for the pacification of the Jacobite Highlands. Traces of this may still be seen.

Apart from the sheer drama of the place, there are one or two features of note. Towering impressively on the east side is the craggy bluff of Dun Mor, 1527 feet, with a vitrified hill-fort perched dizzily on its summit—for this was inevitably always a strategic gap in the mountain rampart. At the south end, on a green hog's-back above the incoming Fendoch Burn, are the remains of a Roman camp, from which considerable relics have been gathered. A comprehensive account of the excavations here is given in Volume 73 of the *Proceedings of the Society of Antiquaries of Scotland.* A mile or more up the glen, and near the roadside, is a long green barrow, known as The Giant's Grave, of uncertain significance. And farther up still, near a bend in the road, is Ossian's Stone. This, alleged to be the grave of the famed Gaelic bard and hero, is of doubtful authenticity; for there are other 'Ossian's Graves'. And it is not now a grave at all, for originally it stood higher, on the line of Wade's road, and his soldiers removed it to its present site. But under its former position they found a stone chamber, with bones and metal fragments—and so strong was the local tradition that Highlanders assembled from far and near and carried away the bones, with bagpipes playing and other funeral rites, to deposit them in a safe and hidden spot in the upper glen, to the west. Wordsworth, visiting here, wrote a poem commencing:

> *In this still place, remote from men,*
> *Sleeps Ossian, in the narrow Glen:*

The Sma' Glen proper ends soon after this, at the narrow right-angled Bridge of Newton, where the road begins to climb sharply up to the watershed and Amulree. Upper Glen Almond itself swings due westwards again and, widening considerably, continues to penetrate the lonely mountains for another dozen miles or so. A gate here opens on to a rough unmetalled road which follows the river, serving the half-dozen hill-farms of the upper valley. This must be one of the least-known and quite unspoiled stretches of attractive and accessible mountain territory near to the settled Lowlands. It ends under Ben Chonzie, 3048 feet, where the infant river makes a sharp bend to the south, and a foot-track leads northwards below the long Shee of Ardtalnaig, to Loch Tay-side.

Along this road, apart from natural beauty, are sundry items to look for. High on the towering southern flank are three intriguingly-named locations, close together—the Eagle's Rock, the Kirk of the Grove and the Thieves' Cave. Even the most energetic of Celtic saints would hardly have skied a church up there, and the name refers to a natural formation of great rocks piled like a building. The Thieves' Cave served as a hide-out for a famous sheep-stealer named Alastair Ban, probably a MacGregor, who was eventually captured here in the act of roasting his ill-gotten mutton, and duly hanged at Perth. Farther along the road, a mile east of Auchnafree, is a long cairn, 60 paces long, a neolithic or Later Stone Age burial-place, with, directly opposite, near the waterside, the single remaining upright of a stone circle.

Stanley. Here is a large village, almost a small town, with an English name, in the centre of Perthshire, 7 miles north of Perth. It was so called in honour of the Lady Amelia Stanley, daughter of an Earl of Derby, who married the Murray Marquis of Atholl. It was through her that, eventually, the English barony of Strange and the former sovereignty of the Isle of Man came to the Atholl family— and recently passed to the Drummonds of Megginch, in Gowrie. Lady Amelia's fourth son, the Lord William Murray, married the only child of the 1st Lord Nairne, and by special remainder succeeded as 2nd Lord Nairne. Not only did he succeed to his father-in-law's title and estates but to his politics; for he became a fervent Jacobite, no doubt not altogether to the distress of his Atholl relatives, for it was always a precaution to have somebody on the other side in case your side lost. In this case, the Atholls won, and garnered-in the Nairne estates in due course.

A new community was established at Stanley, 2 miles north-east of the main road at Luncarty, in 1785, by a firm called Dempster & Company, cotton-spinners. This venture had only fluctuating success at first; but in 1823 it was taken over by a new company, which went from strength to strength, eventually employing over 1200 persons in its mills, driven by water-power led from the Tay through a tunnel 800 feet in length. To house the workpeople, the firm built the quite attractive little town of Stanley, taking a paternal interest in the community, an early example of enlightened industrialism—whatever modern Trade Unions would say about it. They built a magnificent church with an 85-foot-high tower, seating for 1150, an excellent interior and much good woodwork, now the parish kirk. They also built and maintained a large school, a hall and other amenities. Perhaps they could afford to, for at this period working hours for a six-day week began at 5.30 a.m. and ended at 7 p.m.—although, admittedly, the children got off with attending the mill from only 9.45 a.m. till 3 p.m., to enable them to attend the school thereafter! Such was the Industrial Revolution.

The great mills still work, pleasantly sited in the wooded haughland of Tay. The village, on a shelf above, is well laid-out, neat, with a green, and little aspect of industrial growth.

Stanley House, of ancient origins though with an earlier name, lies farther along the same riverside woodlands, in a delightful position—but it has long been ruinous. Some of the trees around it are magnificent. It was a seat of the Nairnes, and Lady Nairne's Tea-house stood on the hillside above it—though whether this was the famous Lady Nairne, formerly Caroline Oliphant of Gask, who wrote the *Laird o' Cockpen* and *The Land o' the Leal*, is not clear. The Tay here is wide and tranquil, flowing through a sylvan scene of hanging woods and fine estates, its fishing fabulous. Half a mile farther, along a delightful riverside walk, the Tay takes a very sharp bend back on itself to form a narrow peninsula; and here stands another ruin, in a commanding position, the old castle of Inchbervie. It has been a strong place, with only a large round flanking-tower surviving to any height, vaulted and equipped with four wide-splayed gunloops; but there are foundations of further building, a courtyard and traces of a moat. It has been described as a round fortalice; but this is a mistake. That the circular tower was only the flanking-tower of a greater building is obvious from the fact that it contains no fireplaces. A well still opens in the former courtyard. Although there are the usual claims that this strength sheltered William Wallace, nothing of the present work indicates a date earlier than probably the early 16th century. The property is said to have belonged originally to the Abbey of Dunfermline, and presumably came to the Nairnes at the Reformation.

Stanley lies in pleasant rural country, partly in Auchtergaven parish, partly in Redgorton.

Strathbraan and Trochrie. The River Braan rises in Loch Freuchie, in Glen Quaich above Amulree, and runs for 12 miles to join the Tay near Inver, at Birnam. Despite its name, meaning the river of drizzling rain, it is a fine stream, traversing a pleasant wide valley, with, for almost three miles at its foot, a series of cascades in rocky chasms, known as the Falls of Braan. Along this riverside winds a most attractive forest walk, now in the care of the National Trust for Scotland, reached from a car-park a short distance northwest of the village of Inver where there is a large and old-established estate saw-mill which was exporting railway sleepers to England in the early part of last century. Half a mile up the woodland track is the renowned Hermitage, a classical stone summer-house built by a Duke of Atholl on a rocky bluff above waterfall and chasm, open-ended and most dramatic. It is also called Ossian's Hall. Burns was here in 1787; and Wordsworth visited and wrote about it, with his sister, in 1803. There is a narrow arched bridge below, beside a great cedar of Lebanon 100 feet high, and a track over, so that a circuit can be made to the Strathbraan road again. Some way farther up, on the north side of the river, is Ossian's Cave, so called. Here is a nature trail established by the Trust.

At the head of the long cascade area of the Braan is the Rumbling Bridge, carrying a narrow loop-road over to the north side again. The rumbles duly perform in the chasm below. A mile along this winding road is the ruined former parish church of Lagganallachy, the valley of burying, in its ancient graveyard. There are many old tombs, and certain very early incised stones leaning against the walling. More modern memorials commemorate certain artists buried here. The name of Gow remains—Neil Gow, the famous violinist, being a native of Inver. Farther on is the farm of Ballinloan, where there is a monolith called *Clach a Mhoid*, or the Vows Stone, where baronial courts used to be held, with authority to 'hang and drown'.

The barons with these grim powers lived at Trochrie Castle, a fragment of circular stair-tower and foundations of which still stand at the pleasant hamlet of that name 4 miles up the Strathbraan road from Birnam. It was a hold of the powerful but ill-fated Ruthven of Gowrie family. Near by are cottages, a former mill, a farmhouse containing the post office—unusual combination—an abandoned church and a one-time manse. A little farther, where the road crosses the river, is the quite spectacularly-sited Drumour Lodge, looking like a French château high above the Braan, built by the Stewarts of Murthly. Standing-stones rise on the hillside of Airlich, above Meikle Findowie farm, near by.

Two miles farther, a former drove road strikes off southwards, to climb to over a thousand feet and through the pass of Little Glen Shee, to Strathord and the Luncarty area.

Strathtay and Grandtully. While in theory all the upper valley of the Tay is entitled to be called Strath Tay, there is in fact a fairly small area, oddly enough only on one side of the river between Logierait and Aberfeldy, which is usually accorded this name. There is now a village community using this name, although this is not an ancient usage, just across the river from Grandtully. The district is a sylvan and gently attractive one, and notable for the fact that its settlement is on two levels, the river-haugh and parts near-to, and on a higher, wide shelf to the north, dotted with farms and looking very picturesque against the background of heather hills. There are a large number of estates along this stretch of Tay, some of them ancient, such as Ballechin, Pitnacree, Pitcastle, Derculich—which has its own quite large loch, high amongst the braes to the north—and Edradynate.

Opposite on the south bank are the villages of Balnagard, Grandtully and Little Ballinluig—not to be confused with the better-known Ballinluig Station on the main A.9 highway 5 miles to the east—all attractively situated. At Ballinluig is situated the house that was the famous Daniel Stewart's first Free School. Grandtully is especially interesting, with both a splendid castle and a unique ancient church.

Grandtully Castle lies, quite easily seen from the road, to the west, in a fine wooded estate, a tall and shapely tower-house of the later 16th century, but with a much older nucleus and later additions. It is a seat of the Steuart-Fothringham family, the Stewarts having been here since the late 14th century, descending from Alexander 4th High Steward of Scotland. In 1626 Sir William Stewart, Sheriff of Perth, made various alterations, especially to the picturesque turreted roof-line. Occupying a strategic position, Grandtully was much in demand as a headquarters for commanders, Montrose, General Mackay, Argyll, Mar (of the '15) and Prince Charles Edward all using it. An officer of Mackay's is said to have been shot dead in one of the angle-turrets, the blood allegedly permanently staining the floor. More recently, the famous Admiral Earl Beatty was tenant here; and another shooting-tenant, the Maharajah Duleep Singh, distinguished himself one August Twelfth by personally shooting no fewer than 220 brace of grouse in the one day.

The former ancient church of St. Mary is less well known than it deserves to be. Set rather remotely on higher ground half a mile south-west of the castle, it has a wonderfully scenic position with glorious views. No longer used as a place of worship, it is now in the care of the Ministry of Works. Like Weem and others, it is divided into two separate portions. It was endowed by Sir Alexander Stewart of Grandtully in 1533, and restored in 1636. Its main southern section is most unusual in having a barrel-vaulted roof, lined with timber, which is brilliantly painted in tempera, with renaissance decoration, heraldic panels and portraits of the evangelists and other Biblical subjects. It commemorates Sir William Stewart who died 1646, and his wife Dame Agnes Moncreiff. Included in the heraldry are the arms of 'the Duik of Lennox and the Earle of Athiol', both Stewarts. This part is now very ill-lit with one small window—though artificial light is provided; but other windows in the west wall have been built up. The door into the northern portion has had a lintel inscribed s.w.s. d.a.m. 1636.

A stone circle and a standing-stone are to be found down near the main road.

Strathyre and Loch Lubnaig. Strathyre is one of those names which confuse. Straths are broad valleys, with what follows in the name normally referring to the river thereof. But Strathyre is a village, not a valley; and the river that flows past is the Balvaig. However, be that as it may, it is an attractive place—especially once one gets off the very busy main road, A.84, which threads it, to stand back a bit. It lies a mile north of the head of Loch Lubnaig, and 5 miles south of Lochearnhead.

Strathyre, not a large community, has two functions today—to cater for the visitor, and as a forestry centre. Set in highly scenic country, it has always attracted the tourist. It long had two inns, when many a larger place had none. Here Wordsworth stayed in 1803, and his *Highland Lass* was conceived. The song *Bonnie Strathyre* is well known. Here was born, in 1716, Dugald Buchanan, Gaelic scholar, poet and evangelist; there is a monument to him in the main street. This is an excellent area for touring much of the Southern Highlands, and a large proportion of the houses offer accommodation—and it should be noted that not all of Strathyre is on the so-busy main road. Across the old bridge to the west is another and more leisurely 'suburb', of both old and modern housing, with a forestry group. Also amongst the trees is a delightfully-sited new school.

Trees indeed strike the prevailing note in Strathyre. It has always been a wooded area, but the Forestry Commission established a great Strathyre Forest here in the 1930s; and now this wide valley is clothed with trees right to the hilltop skylines, reaching 1800 feet. Some indication of the forest's extent can be gained by the fact that 80,000 trees were blown down in the hurricane of 1968—but 8,000,000 survived. Fine walks of varying lengths can be taken in this forest, all most admirably planned and described by the Commission in leaflet and map available at the Forest Centre and tree-nursery. This is a feature, a log-cabin designed as demonstration-room and museum, with photographs, plans and exhibits of forestry, topography, and natural and local history, some of the items compiled and presented by the McLaren High School pupils at Callander. Just opposite is a convenient picnic site. Pony-trekking and fishing are also available at Strathyre.

Two miles to the north, on the main road, is Kingshouse, now a hotel, at the Balquhidder road-end. Like other Kingshouses in Scotland, this was originally a barracks and staging-post for troops in the Jacobite times. An alternative route to Balquhidder can be still more scenically taken, crossing the aforementioned bridge at Strathyre and circling north-westwards through the woods, around the base of Beinn an-t-Sithean, the Hill of the Fairies. After 4 miles, this comes out at the foot of Glen Buckie, passing Stroneslaney where, in the 13th century a bloody battle was fought between the McLarens and the Buchanans.

To the south lies the 5-mile-long Loch Lubnaig, one of the few north–south-lying lochs in this part of the country. It has the remains of a crannog, or artificial island refuge, near its head. It is of course well-known to travellers from Edinburgh and the east to the north-west Highlands—and, despite its beauty, is apt to be cursed as a great source of delay, because of its narrow and winding lochside highway. A pity, for it is a place which should be lingered at, not rushed over. The western side is the one the traveller sees, across the water; for there is no public road up the other shore, and the eastern slopes are too steep above the road to be seen. And a pleasing backcloth the far side makes, with the series of fine peaks from Ben Ledi northwards, clothed high in forest, with streams pouring down in waterfalls. Half-way down, on the east, is the old mansion of Ardchullarie, whitewashed and of the early 18th century, where the famous Abyssinian traveller, Bruce of Kinnaird, retired and died, a saddened man, his discoveries of the source of the Nile, and all the strange things seen there, ridiculed by society. A foot-track crosses from here, by Glen Ample, to Earn, about eight miles.

Across the loch, near the foot, is the isolated but easily seen farm rejoicing in the name of Stank, with the wooded Stank Glen rising steeply behind it, embosoming a large waterfall at the 750-foot contour. This is the most rewarding way to climb Ben Ledi and Ben Vane. It can be reached by a bridge across the Leny.

Where Loch Lubnaig pours out into that brief but fast river, at the roadside, is the old burial-ground of St. Bride, and the site of its pre-Reformation chapel, now sadly neglected. A few gravestones survive, with the church-foundations lost amongst the weeds, and a fragment of an ancient incised cross built into the dyke. It has been a lovely site for a place of worship. A mile below, in the Pass of Leny, are the Falls thereof, so popular with visitors. Actually, for a connoisseur of waterfalls, these are disappointing, being more a series of large rapids than true falls; but they are scenically fine and are much photographed. Another mile, and the road runs out into the broad vale of the Teith, at Kilmahog near Callander, and so out of the Highlands proper.

Struan, Bruar and Glen Errochty. Two fine but very different streams join the brawling Perthshire Garry near the modern hamlet of Calvine in Atholl—the Bruar and the Errochty. The area is called Struan, and it is from here that the chiefs of Clan Donnachaidh, the Struan Robertsons, take their title, although their main seat and clan area latterly centred on Dunalastair in Rannoch.

The Bruar Water has an extraordinarily straight course, coming tumbling down directly southwards out of Glen Bruar in the heights of Atholl, dropping from 1800 to 500 feet in a few miles, and creating the spectacular Falls of Bruar near the foot, visited by Burns and Wordsworth and readily accessible from the A.9 highway. At the roadside there has recently been opened a most excellent Clan Donnachaidh Museum, with resident curator—a model for other clan societies. Pictures, books, documents and items of interest, are here tastefully displayed. There is a hotel close by. The little community of Bruar itself, long failing, is now much revived. The chiefs of the clan stem from one, *Donnachadh Reamhair*, or Stout Duncan, who fought for Bruce. His great-grandson was named Robert, and it is from him that the descendants took their surname.

There is a pleasantly situated village of Struan, although most travellers on the busy main road probably mistake modern Calvine therefor. It lies across the Garry, here spanned in unusual fashion by both rail and road bridges, the one partly beneath the other. From the latter, watching the salmon leap the cataracts is a popular diversion. A little farther is the hotel, formerly an inn, and opposite, a little road leads half a mile down to the riverside, sequestered village, over another hump-backed bridge, a charming place. The church here is not itself very old, though ancient of site, its graveyard the burial-place of the Robertson lairds, its paths laid with old tombstones. It is recounted that, at the funeral of the famous Struan Robertson of the '15 and the '45, 2000 men gathered in his honour and clansmen carried the body for 18 miles, from Carie on the south shore of Loch Tay. Amongst the many interesting stones here is one very massive and ancient, with crosses incised on both sides. In this church was formerly kept one of the five Culdee bells of Perthshire, known as the St. Fillan's-Struan Bell, but having its own Gaelic name of *Am Buidhean*, now in Perth Museum.

Struan is not on the Garry itself but on the Errochty which here joins it. This flows out of a quietly lovely glen, which threads the hills for 6 miles, partnered by the B.847 road, passing the Georgian mansion of Auchleeks, former Robertson seat, until, at the hamlet of Trinafour, the highway swings away southwards to climb up over the 1000-foot contour for Rannoch. This valley makes a pleasant sanctuary, Trinafour lying deep in a quiet hub of the hills. From it another adventurous road, stemming from General Wade like so many others, ascends steeply to the north, making for Dalnacardoch, on the A.9, near the Inverness-shire border—a road rewarding in great prospects. Due west of Trinafour is now a modern loch of the hydro-electric scheme.

B.847, in its southwards climb over the watershed, is also a pleasing route. It sends off a branch, a mile up, by a side valley, to Tummel Bridge. Near the summit of the main road, with splendid vistas to south and west, is a ruined cottage, with a broken stone intimating that the road was made and the cottage built, allegedly as a toll-house, by Colonel Alastair MacDonald in 1876—Highland business acumen at a late date.

Thornhill, Norrieston and Coldoch. These are places rimming the north or Perthshire side of the great Flanders Moss area, between Blair Drummond and Port of Menteith. The village is quite a large one, half a mile long, and is called Thornhill, lying along a slight ridge above the level carseland. Norrieston is the name of the parish, and now only applies to the church at the east end of Thornhill main street, and to a farm to the south. The name comes from one Gabriel Norrie, who endowed the original church in 1670, and who presumably owned the farm. Coldoch is an estate and section of the vast Moss, with an especially interesting ancient monument in the form of a broch.

Thornhill is picturesquely situated, with fine prospects, in an isolated position 5 miles west of Doune and 6 east of Port of Menteith. But it is not a particularly attractive place, and with a rather decayed look; although there is some modern housing. The main road, A.873, takes a sharp and unexpected right-hand turn partway along the elongated street, and immediately the traveller is out of the village and into green foothill country again. From here, a climbing moorland road, B.822, strikes off northwards and rises over the mounth of Menteith, and through the large Torrie Forest, to Callander, 6 miles away. There are splendid views. In the other direction, southwards, the same numbered road strikes down across the Flanders Moss for Kippen, crossing the Goodie Burn, which flows out of the Lake of Menteith and once here formed its own loch. Here Montrose scored a victory over Argyll. The road goes on, to cross the Forth by a bridge near the famous Fords of Frew, where Rob Roy made his celebrated escape from the Duke of Montrose, descendant of the Marquis above; and where, earlier, Rob had had a successful brush with the dragoons after the Hership of Kippen. This entire territory is redolent of the famous free-booter's activities.

Three miles south-east of Thornhill is The Coldoch, a mansion with an early nucleus. In 1513, a year before his death at Flodden, James IV granted his favoured tailor, Robert Spittal, of Stirling—the same who built the Hospital at Stirling, and the Doune and Bannockburn bridges—the right to build a fortalice here. It later came into Graham hands. It is a pleasant place, near where Goodie joins the coiling Forth, facing south across the wide levels. On the crest of a bank, with a track to it from a side-road near Ashentree Farm, are the substantial remains of a broch, one of those circular beehive-shaped fortified refuges which are fairly common in the North of Scotland but rare indeed so far south—though there is another in the Tor Wood, near Larbert, about twelve miles to the south-east. These were strong places, the circular wall measuring between seventeen and nineteen feet in thickness, though it now rises only to five or six feet in height. There are four little mural chambers off, at basement level, and the 2-feet-wide entry passage has been secured by a draw-bar, the slot for which is 7 feet deep. A mural stair has risen to the south-east, but only seven steps remain. These brochs probably date from the 1st and 2nd centuries A.D., when the Roman power was weakening, and may have been built by rovers from the north seeking new lands to conquer.

A mile or so to the north is the late 17th century mansion of Gartincaber, with older nucleus. The farms of Spittalton and Upper Spittalton near by may be further links with King James's tailor.

The Trossachs and Brig o' Turk. To be accurate, the Trossachs refers only to the short and narrow wooded pass of less than a mile, between the head of Loch Achray and the foot of Loch Katrine; but it has long been customary so to term all the area of the valley which contains these two, and also Loch Vennachar to the east.

What is generally known as the Trossachs road, A.821, branches off the A.84 at Kilmahog a mile west of Callander, where the River Leny joins the Eas Gobhain to form the Teith. This Eas Gobhain, the Water of the Smith, though quite a major river in width has only a 2-mile course, issuing from Loch Vennachar, the Trossachs road following the north bank of both. At once there are items of interest. First, on the left, the ancient burial-ground of the Buchanans at Little Leny, with its pre-Reformation chapel site, described under Callander. Then, east by south, the site of a Roman fort, to be traced in the haughland of Bochastle Farm, in the mile-long, low-lying peninsula between the two rivers. Soaring above this, to the north, is Bochastle Hill, a spur of Ben Ledi. This has three crests, the central one, 300 feet high, being crowned by a Pictish dun, known variously as Dunmore, Tarandoun Fort or the Dun of Bochastle. It was a very strong place, with three circles of ditches and ramparts, a gateway and a central well now filled in, staring down at the Roman camp below. Poised on the crest of the eastmost hillock is a great erratic boulder long known as Samson's Putting Stone, a natural feature. High above rears mighty Ben Ledi, said to derive from *Dia*, the Mountain of God, an impressive isolated peak of 2873 feet, one of the most prominent summits of the Highland Line, recognisable from afar. It is not a difficult climb, the usual route being from Coilantogle Farm, a mile farther along the Trossachs road, following a well-defined ridge to the summit. The views therefrom are magnificent, from Ben Nevis to Tinto in Lanarkshire, from Arran to the Cairngorms. Lead used to be mined on Ledi once.

In the col a mile to the north is the small Lochan nan Corp, where one winter long ago a funeral party on its very lofty way to St. Bride's burial-ground at Loch Lubnaig-side far below, fell through the skin of ice in a macabre tragedy.

Below Coilantogle Farm there used to be a famous ford on the Eas Gobhain, which Scott called "Clan Alpine's outmost guard", in the *Lady of the Lake*, meaning that all to the west was the MacGregors' jealously guarded territory. Unfortunately the Glasgow Waterworks schemes have changed all this. East of the former ford is Gartchonzie Bridge carrying the pleasant A.892 'back-road' from Callander. The bridge is old, narrow and arched, and has been used for filming scenes in the *Dr. Finlay's Casebook* TV series.

Loch Vennachar is a fine sheet of water 4 miles long, pretty without being spectacular. The road follows the north shore; but a dead-end road via Gartchonzie Bridge runs for 2 miles along the south shore, offering excellent picnic sites, before stopping at East Lodge to become a private route leading 3 more miles to Inver-trossachs, a mansion in which Queen Victoria stayed for some weeks in 1869. There is an ancient earthwork near it; and the oddly-named but delightfully-wooded Loch Drunkie lies behind, only quarter of a mile from Vennacher but 200 feet higher. The north road is without special features. At the west end of the loch is Lendrick Lodge, once a shooting-lodge of the Earl of Moray, now a popular Youth Hostel. Nearer the waterside is Lendrick Mead— not to be confused with Lanrick on the other side of Callender—the traditional mustering-place of the MacGregors of Clan Alpine.

A mile farther is the delightful scattered village of Brig o' Turk, lying within the steep jaws of Glen Finglas. The houses, at different levels, probe some way into the wooded glen. Half a mile up, past the little school, is an ancient graveyard—one of the few actually with heather growing therein. Here are many ancient Stewart stones, and some MacGregors; and a notable modern one, recumbent and coffin-shaped, with a wrought-iron shepherd's crook thereon, to one Donald Campbell 'beloved of all who knew him'— not perhaps the normal Campbell epitaph. It is related that when the plague came to Perthshire in 1500, the Brig o' Turk folk burned juniper—which grows here abundantly—three times a day, and kept the sickness at bay. The road up Glen Finglas becomes private to the Lower Clyde Waterworks after a mile, for the glen has now been flooded and contains a large reservoir-loch some five miles long, and fortunately, very beautiful. Walkers of course may use it, and a delightful route it makes, for this is a most attractive glen. The dam and flooding has inevitably changed much, but has added a new dimension. Formerly, in a recess under a waterfall here, Scott relates, a hunted outlaw dwelt secure, food being lowered by a woman from the precipice above in a basket. He also makes this the scene of the hermit monk Brian's oracular remarks on the fate of Roderick Dhu. Glen Finglas used to be a favourite hunting-ground of the Scots kings, and was peopled by Stewarts under the Earls of Moray. It splits into three higher up, the river of the lower part being called the Turk, from *tuirc* meaning wild boar. The Finglas itself comes in from the west, after a 5-mile course from the flanks of Creagan Sgiath (2269 feet); while on the opposite side, Glen Casaig forks off to the right, a hanging valley 3 miles long between Ben Ledi and Ben Vane (2685 feet). The central valley, Glen nan Meann, has a foot-track leading from the farm of Duart for 8 miles to Glen Buckie in Balquhidder, wet at its highest parts.

Just beyond the Glen Finglas road-end, on the left, is the former old inn of Brig o' Turk, now a pleasantly renewed guest-house, and so still catering for travellers. Here was the home of the famous Muckle Kate Ferguson, alleged to have been the fattest woman in the kingdom, weighing 24 stones, whom even Queen Victoria came to see.

Half a mile beyond, Loch Achray opens out, a small but scenically attractive loch, praised not only by Scott but by Wordsworth and Coleridge—although Dorothy Wordsworth's memories of it, at least, are scarcely to be trusted, for she makes it 4 miles long when it is not half that. Yachts and even speed-boats now furrow its waters—but its wooded fairness remains. Half-way along its north shore, on a green peninsula, is the delightful little parish church of the Trossachs, in its fairly modern graveyard. It was built in 1849 as a chapel-of-ease from Callander parish, and a pleasanter spot for kirk and God's-acre would be hard to find. Just beyond it is Blair House, a former mansion, now a Church of Scotland Eventide Home—and used in the TV series as the Tannochbrae Cottage Hospital.

Field of Bannockburn. The Bruce Statue, Pilkington Jackson's masterpiece

Cambuskenneth Abbey, Stirling

The huge Trossachs Hotel comes next, a famous establishment, built in 1852, with its château-like towers, one of the great hotels of Scotland, catering for a large variety of pursuits and set amongst woodlands. The more modest but still large Loch Achray Hotel stands whitewashed at the head of the loch. Behind it a comparatively little-used track leads by the Pass of Achray to the north-eastern flanks of Ben Venue, via the Bealach nam Bo, the Pass of the Cattle, so much used by Rob Roy and the MacGregors for the droving back to Glengyle, at the head of Loch Katrine, of their cattle herds lifted from Lowland estates. They came this way, since the parallel Pass of the Trossachs half a mile to the north, could be so readily held against them; presumably this Achray Pass was always less known. It makes a pleasant walk, at any rate, rising through wooded jaws, now all part of the Queen Elizabeth Forest Park, to above the head of Katrine. The second part of this route, the Bealach nam Bo, is much higher, rising to over the 1000-foot contour; and below it is a great amphitheatre, with caves, called Coire na' Uruisgean—which on maps and elsewhere has been translated the Corrie of the Goblins, but would be better called of the Satyrs. This is the favourite route to climb the double peaked Ben Venue (2386 feet), so beloved of photographers of the Trossachs.

The true Trossachs Pass divides the Venue shoulder from the spectacular and steep peak of Ben A'an to the north, only 1520 feet high and a spur of the featureless Meall Gainmheich, but the most exciting hill of this region, with a lot of clean bare rock. The road that threads the Trossachs Pass, though usually busy with traffic, is less than a mile long, coming to an abrupt halt at the great car-park at the foot of Loch Katrine. Admittedly tar-macadam goes on a lot farther—but only for those with passes issued by Glasgow Corporation Water Department. The car-park is for those who take the steamer which plies on the loch—a strange facility to find on a water kept so otherwise inviolate as this. It all makes of Loch Katrine a frustrating and paradoxical place, so easily reached from the Lowlands, one of the finest of Scotland's lochs, so beautiful and rich in history and romance—yet its shores *terra incognita* at the dictate of Glasgow councillors, allegedly in the interests of the purity of the water, who nevertheless ply a steamer on it, and profitably. Other water authorities have public roads along their reservoir shores. In these days of the appreciation and official encouragement of improved access to the countryside, here is an obvious target for, say, the new Countryside Commission.

Much could be, and has been, written about Loch Katrine—so there is no need to expand on it here. This is, of course, the lake of Scott's *Lady* thereof; indeed Scott has almost been credited with the discovery of it! But for centuries it had been the MacGregors' own inland sea, every inch of its lovely shores, its wooded promontories and islets, rich in stories of that warlike and exciting clan, the Children of the Mist. Glen Gyle, Rob's own birthplace, and the seat of a senior sept of the clan, lies 9 miles away at the head of the loch; with Stronachlacher, which can be reached by road from Aberfoyle, two-thirds of the way. Ellen's Isle, near the east end everyone knows of, but Eilean Dubh, near the other end, has the more exciting story, where Rob Roy imprisoned Graham of Killearn for the savaging of his wife. Interesting is the name of the loch—for it has been called variously Katrine, Ketterine, Catherine and of the Caterans.

The A.821 branches off southwards round the head of Loch Achray, to climb over low hills some five miles to Aberfoyle, the route being known as the Duke's Road, the reference being to a Duke of Montrose who owned the land. This is a scenic and popular highway, with glimpses of Loch Drunkie and fine views both going and coming. There are large slate quarries in the rather gloomy higher stretches—but this is outwith the Trossachs proper. The round-trip of Callander–the Trossachs–Aberfoyle–Port of Menteith–Loch Ruskie–Callander, is probably one of the most popular runs in the Southern Highlands.

Tullibardine and Strathallan. Tullibardine was a very significant name in Scotland for long—although probably most Scots could not tell you today where it is. The Murrays of Tullibardine, descending from the great de Moravia line, gained this territory in southern Perthshire by marrying the heiress of the Earls of Strathearn around 1320, in Bruce's time, and for centuries they cut a very wide swathe in the land, becoming Earls thereof in 1606, a title now merged in the Stewart-Murray dukedom of Atholl. Nothing is left of their Tullibardine Castle save its site; nor is there any real village of the name. But there are still many features of the area well worth visiting.

Although originally much larger, the district of Tullibardine proper spreads over that part of mid-Strathearn and Strathallan between the Earn and the Ochils foothills, north of Blackford, Glen Eagles and Auchterarder. The name itself is preserved in Tullibardine Chapel, Wood, Mill, Cottage, East and West Mains thereof, and disused railway station; much of this being now part of the large estate of Strathallan Castle.

The pre-Reformation Chapel of the Holy Trinity is a fine redstone building in the Second Pointed and cruciform tradition, no longer in use save as burial-place of the Drummond Earls of Perth, but restored and in the good care of the Ministry of Works. It was founded as a collegiate church in 1446 by Sir David Murray, Bailiff of Strathearn, for a provost and four prebendaries; and is one of the few collegiate establishments unaltered since foundation. Suppressed at the Reformation, it was nevertheless still used for worship until 1745. The transept window is handsomely traceried, some of the original roof timbering remains, and there is a built-up shot-hole in the tower. The site of the former great castle is amongst woodland, to the north, behind the farm of East Mains.

The extensive Moor of Tullibardine, now usually termed Wood thereof, lies to the west, on slightly higher ground, and merges with the Moor of Orchill which is crossed by the Roman Road from Ardoch, with the sites of a Marching Camp and a Signal Station. Part of Gleneagles golf-course encroaches on Tullibardine Moor, which forms the divide between Strathallan and Strathearn proper. The growing modern village of Muirton at its eastern end, at the cross-roads near Gleneagles Hotel, has splendid views to north and south. An ancient earthwork lies about a mile to the south.

The hamlet of Tullibardine Mill lies 2 miles to the north, amidst old woodland, on the edge of the Strathallan estate. This is a very large property, formerly belonging to the Drummonds, Viscounts Strathallan, a title now merged in the Earldom of Perth. The 1st Viscount was the Cavalier commander Sir William, 4th Lord Madderty, who had previously been Governor of Smolensk, in the Russian wars, like his colleague and friend, General Tam Dalyell of the Binns; he is alleged to have introduced the torture of thumb-screws into Scotland. The 4th Viscount was mortally wounded at Culloden, and is said to have received the last sacrament in whisky and oatmeal, bread and wine not being available. The present castle is comparatively modern, but with a core of old work.

A mile to the west is the lesser mansion of Machany, to which the Lords of Strathallan retired when forfeiture for Jacobite activities and other troubles brought them low. The 7th Viscount, living here, had the misfortune to lose his arm in a tenant's threshing-mill; but philosophically he recovered the limb and had it interred in its own little coffin at Tullibardine Chapel, to await the larger container with the rest of him, in due course.

The Machany Water, with its Falls of Ness at Culdees, runs near by. This district should indeed be named Strathmachany rather than Strathallan, for the Allan Water rises in the Ochils south of Blackford and does not touch this area.

Tummel. It is strange indeed how different can be two great lochs, lying almost end to end, in the same strath amongst the same mountains. Lochs Tummel and Rannoch are apt to be referred to in the same breath, but they are far from twins, in character and atmosphere. Tummel is gentler, greener, less dramatic, yet entirely and beautifully Highland. That it is smaller is nothing to the point.

The size of Loch Tummel is indeed hard to assess. What was originally only a 3-mile 'bulge' in the River Tummel has been greatly increased by the developments of the Tummel–Garry hydro-electric scheme, and at its very narrow, lower end it is hard to say where loch ends and river recommences. But from the dam there to the other narrows at its head is about seven miles. The width varies greatly, from a few hundred yards to three-quarters of a mile.

Like Rannoch, Tummel has a road on each side, the northern, B.8019, much the faster, and more scenic in that it rises higher and gives wider prospects, especially of Schiehallion to the south-west. The renowned Queen's View, 2 miles up from the dam, which Victoria made famous in 1866, tops a pine-crowned bluff high above the water. But the southern road has many pleasing vistas also, and is quieter. At its eastern end, where it threads the deep, swiftly-dropping wooded gorge of the lower River Tummel, it becomes quite impressive. Much here has been affected by the hydro-electric developments, and the famed waterfalls down-graded. But to compensate there is the highly picturesque new Loch Faskally, and the two sets of salmon-ladders to aid the fish up past the dams, both magnets for visitors. A nature trail through 2 miles of riverside forest has been opened at Linn of Tummel by the National Trust for Scotland.

There are few haunts of man on the southern shore of the loch, but at its west end is the hamlet of Foss, where there is an attractive church within an ancient graveyard, burial-place of various old Stewart and Menzies families. The older ruined kirk is tiny, and its holy-water stoup, or small font, is built into the wall of its successor.

Tummel Bridge, above the head of the loch, is a community of old and new. The ancient bridge, built by Wade in 1730, now has a less hump-backed successor alongside, to carry the road from Aberfeldy. Near by is a great power station, one of the earliest, and less well designed to fit into the landscape than later models; its radiating pylons and power-lines, do however tend to get absorbed by the lovely birch trees. Across the river, as well as some modern housing, are two caravan-parks, one especially attractive as to site. Amongst those who have stayed at the inn here are Mendelssohn and Swinburne.

The north loch-road is dotted with the sites of duns, forts and a cairn circle. Rather more recent is a tiny graveyard in a sloping field between road and loch, only about 21 feet square, amongst the tight pack of its fallen memorials a little iron cross labelled merely 'Kirsty'. At the east end are two fine hostels, both former mansion houses, one Strathtummel S.Y.H.A., and the other Bonskeid House, of the Y.M.C.A. Fortunate are the young people who find these.

In this vicinity opens the attractive, fertile, cul-de-sac valley of Glen Fincastle, with a little church under a high-set dun, called Caisteal Dubh, at its mouth. Fincastle House, a 17th century seat of a branch of the Stewarts, with Forty-Five links and relics, is shelved high to the north on the 1000-foot contour. At the head of the glen, footpaths lead off in various directions, not least to the standing-stones group of Clachan Aoraidh in the Allean Forest.

STIRLINGSHIRE

This county is the very heart of Scotland, historically speaking. It lies in the slender waist of the land; indeed, it almost reaches salt water on the west as it does on the east, coming to within four miles of the Clyde at Bowling. Thus it straddles the country at its narrowest point, and so inevitably was of vital strategic importance when national conflict was involved—as indeed was the case for most of Scotland's history. It is medium-sized as Scots counties go, covering 288,842 acres, or 451 square miles; which makes it only twentieth in size out of 33, but fifth in population, after the great cities. This despite the fact that its central portion consists of the empty Lennox Hills area; its north-western section is the wild, mountainous east side of Loch Lomond; and the great Flanders Moss region of the upper Forth plain is almost unpopulated. So that probably two-thirds of the land area is almost empty—which indicates a high concentration of population in the rest.

Stirlingshire, then, is a country of contrasts. It is part Highland, part Lowland. It has mountains of over 3000 feet, yet much of the central area is the lowest and flattest land in Scotland, the carselands of Stirling and Forth. Its extreme south-eastern portion is the industrial boom area of the country, with Grangemouth and Falkirk ever growing, ever burgeoning into new and exciting forms of production; yet its centre, only a few miles therefrom, is probably more lonely and deserted than ever it was before, despite the planting of myriads of trees and the flooding of its valleys for reservoirs; and the north-west, Rob Roy's country, is just heather, rock and bog, beautiful but for ever empty. Stirling itself, the famous county town, is sited at the extreme north-eastern corner; but a score of miles to the south-west, places like Strathblane, Killearn and Campsie, look towards Glasgow, and seem to have little connection with the rest. That these areas were ever included in Stirlingshire seems strange, for the country is essentially the basin of the Forth, and these have no discernible relation thereto, their affinities rather with the Clyde. No doubt it all stems from the interests of great lords, at the period when such boundaries and divisions were being finalised.

It is strange that the two industrial developments, which have so greatly transformed the face of the county, should have taken place within two or three miles of each other, yet for totally different reasons. These are the establishment of the mighty Carron Iron-works at Falkirk, in the second half of the 18th century; and the growth of the oil and petro-chemical industry at Grangemouth since the Second World War. Both have been revolutionary, and of tremendous impact. The first developed here almost by accident, for William Cadell was an East Lothian man, and intended his dream of great iron-foundries for the new age to materialise near his own estate of Cockenzie, in that county, 10 miles east of Edinburgh. Only the short-sighted, penny-wise attitude of the Tranent and Prestonpans coal-owners in refusing to sell him great quantities of coal at a low rate, sent him to the Stirlingshire coalfield, just developing, where the famous Abyssinian traveller, Bruce of Kinnaird, co-operated, selling him cheaply unlimited supplies of fuel for the furnaces. So here, to Carronshore, the ironstone was brought from all over Scotland, and here rose the huge works with their forest of smoking chimneys, which were to spread and proliferate until Falkirk area became the light-castings centre of all Britain, with Grangemouth growing up, to replace tidal Carronshore, for importing the ore and exporting the products.

The oil development took place at Grangemouth because here was a port, deep in the heart of industrialised Scotland, where deep-sea tankers could reach, and where there was available large areas of level empty carseland for the erection of the huge and space-consuming complex of refineries, cracking-plants, storage-tanks, cooling-towers and all the sprawling nightmare of futuristic installations. And here was the narrowest part of Scotland, where a pipeline could most economically be brought across from the west coast, to carry the flood of oil from the deep-water terminal at Finnart on Loch Long.

Stirlingshire has other great industries than these, of course, although the coal on which so much was founded is, as elsewhere, being worked less and less—leaving, unfortunately its unsightly detritus to scar the landscape. Distilling, brick-making and fireclay, timber, tar-making, and of course agriculture, are all important; but it is iron-founding and petro-chemicals that dominate.

Undoubtedly this county has seen more bloodshed than any other in Scotland, even the Border ones, its history more war-torn. This because of sheer geography. Here was the cockpit between the Highlands and the Lowlands, seldom at peace. More important, here was the narrow way which all armies must tread that sought to conquer Scotland. For Scotland beyond Forth and Clyde, the major part of the land area, could only be reached, by land, by crossing Stirling Bridge. East of that famed bridge the Forth was too wide to cross save by boat; and west stretched the broad, 15-mile, quaking barrier of the Flanders Moss, right to the stern mountains of the Ben Lomond range, with its loch beyond and then more mountains, impassable for armies. So here invaders must be held, and hereabouts more great battles were fought than anywhere else —Stirling Brig itself, Bannockburn, Sauchieburn, Sheriffmuir, Falkirk twice, Kilsyth and so on. Few were the Kings of Scots who did not fight at least one battle in Stirlingshire.

The scenery of the county is as contrasting as the rest. Almost everywhere the distant views, the background, is quite superb. Yet the foregrounds tend to be scarred and spoiled by the commercial exploitation of man; and tame on account of the flat and extensive carselands, reminiscent of the Dutch polders. This contrast itself, of course, can be inspiriting, challenging. No one who has not seen, for instance, from the Roman Wall area of Polmont, the long, sun-bathed, shadow-slashed barrier of the green Ochils over and beyond the contorted, flaming, smoking monstrosities of Grangemouth, can say they really know modern Scotland. Who will not feel a lift of the heart at the sight, coming over the brow of the hill on A.9 south of Bannockburn village, of the spread plain before him, disfigured as it is, threaded by the coiling Forth, and out of it all rising abruptly the proud castle-crowned rock of Stirling, with its grey climbing town, all against the background of wooded Abbey Craig, the thrusting Wallace Monument and the shapely peak of Dumyat? Who, in these islands, can point to a finer or more signi-ficant prospect than the long, long, purple-brown, snow-streaked rampart of the Highland Line, seen across the wide flats of the Flanders Moss, from Kippen or anywhere on the Gargunnock and Fintry Hills, stern, serene, magnificent?

The Highland part of Stirlingshire reaches much farther north by west than is sometimes realised; for the county boundary, here, is at Inverarnan in Glen Falloch, only some six miles south of Crian-larich; on a level with, for instance, Strathyre, Muthill and the Tay, on the east, and the Ross of Mull and Iona on the west. So that this section contains the eastern half of Loch Lomond, Loch Arklet and even a corner of Loch Katrine, areas which many people probably would think of as in Perthshire. When one considers that Stirlingshire also reaches to within a mile or so of Linlithgow town, and elsewhere overlooks the road between Armadale and Airdrie, some idea will be gained of the diversity of this county—and the problems of its local authority. But then, this was always the way; for it was for long the debatable land, not only between Highlands and Lowlands, but between the Angles, the Picts and the Britons of Strathclyde—as well as the Roman frontier.

Abbey Craig, Wallace Monument and Causewayhead. The great Wallace Monument, thrusting dramatically up on top of Abbey Craig, across the Forth flats from Stirling Castle, is one of the famed landmarks of Scotland—and deservedly so. The conception of putting a monument to the patriot here, overlooking the site of his greatest victory of Stirling Bridge, was an inspired one, the site magnificent and apt, the proportions tremendous in every respect. If the vast tower itself is a little over-ornate, this does not greatly detract from its impact.

Abbey Craig is a long hog's-back of rocky wooded hill, rising some 360 feet above the carse, directly behind the former village of Causewayhead, now a northern suburb of Stirling. It takes its name, of course, from the Abbey of Cambuskenneth which lies below, in a meander of the Forth. This steep and impressive ridge has obvious tactical value, dominating as it does the first crossing of the Forth, in the very strategic waist of Scotland. This was recog-nised long before the Wars of Independence, as is proved by the siting here of an ancient Caledonian vitrified fort, crowning the summit—indeed, the great monument is built within the perimeter of the fort's turf-covered embankment, which may still be traced. Eleven bronze spears are said to have been found here, in 1784.

The approach to this position demands a stiff and steady climb, from the foothills road to Logie, A.997, the modern Sword Hotel and the car-park lying at the foot. On the way up are passed the practice butts of the Stirling Archery Club. The climb is infinitely worthwhile—for, apart from the monument itself, the views from here are superb, in all directions. Particularly interesting is the clear impression given of the intricate windings of the Forth, spread below, which is said to take 14 miles to cover 4—as well can be believed. Also interesting, from the other, northern side, is the excellent panoramic vista of the new University of Stirling's lay-out in the wooded Airthrey Castle grounds. There is a picnic site on the clifftop, some two hundred yards to the south, an exhilarating spot amongst the pines and whins—but hardly one in which to allow children to roam free! It is notable, too, that from here five battlefields can be seen—Stirling Bridge, Bannockburn, Sauchieburn, Sheriffmuir and Logie, where in 843 Kenneth MacAlpine defeated the Picts, paving the way for the unity of Scotland.

The Monument, of somewhat mixed architectural derivation, takes the form of a lofty and massive parapeted Scots keep, distinctly elongated, on top of which is set a lantern-spire crown of ecclesiastical type, as at St. Giles, Edinburgh, with much corbelling, crenellation, gunloops, pinnacles and so on, all done in quite splendid masonry, 220 feet high. A tall bronze statue of Wallace stands at one corner, looking out towards Stirling. Architectural correctness apart, it is a tremendous and inspiring monument. It was built in 1861–69, at a cost of £16,000, as a national memorial. Two hundred and forty-six steps lead up a twisting turnpike stair to the dizzy parapet and its breath-taking views. The interior contains the famed two-handed sword of the patriot, 5 feet 4 inches long, renowned in later days as being 'abstracted' for a while by Miss Wendy Wood, as a nationalist gesture. There are suits of armour, busts of heroes and national figures, documents and other displays.

Causewayhead lay, as its name indicates, at the northern end of the long causeway across the marshy levels of the carse from Stirling Bridge, and here it was that the great battle was fought in 1297, when Wallace defeated the proud English might of Edward I, in one of the epic struggles of all time. New housing, ever spreading, has swamped the little village now, and it is probably best known to travellers as a large and rather complicated traffic roundabout. There is a pleasant park under the Abbey Craig, and from here is reached conveniently the Abbey of Cambuskenneth.

Airthrey Castle was a Haldane property, passing to the Abercrombys of Menstrie. Mineral wells here gave rise to the spa of Bridge of Allan. The University is dealt with under Stirling.

Airth. Airth was once a place of considerable importance, a port, indeed a royal dockyard—unlikely as this seems today—a burgh, the seat of an earldom and an ecclesiastical centre of some note. As ships grew larger, industry developed elsewhere, and the tidelands of Forth were reclaimed, so Airth declined. Now it is growing again somewhat, in residential fashion; but it is safe to prophesy that never again will it boast a harbour.

The medieval burgh was the old town of High Airth, set on top of the brae above the spreading carselands, 6 miles north-east of Falkirk. Here also were, and still are, the castle and original church. Founded in the reign of William the Lion, Airth was made a burgh of barony and free port in 1597. As the port developed and drainage of the marshland below improved, it was found more convenient to have the town down on the low ground. So Lower Airth began to supersede the older burgh. The Mercat Cross dates from 1696, but it may have been re-erected. However, the Tolbooth, Fleshmarket and a number of what are today the old houses down there, were under construction in 1723. It took longer for Holy Church to come down the hill; but the people below—as distinct from the laird up above—finally won in 1820, when the North Church was built and the old kirk on its rock above the Pow Burn was abandoned, after having been a place of worship from at least 1128, when it was granted to Holyrood Abbey by David I. The site of the early burgh, like the kirk itself, then became included in the castle policies.

The Forth seems a long way from Airth today; but much land has been reclaimed from the sea—300 acres as early as 1792, by the erecting of 'a strong dike of sods'. Moreover, the harbour was not actually on the estuary, but some way up the tidal channel of a stream, the access to which was regulated by a basin and sluice. All this dried out and disappeared, thanks to improved land-drainage, and only a grassy mound represents a one-time quay, some two hundred yards from the village. That the Forth itself has receded eastwards is indicated by the fact that the skeleton of a whale was found even in 1817, a quarter-mile from the then shore.

The 18th century burgh—though it has long lost that status—is attractive, and more travellers should pause instead of driving past on the A.905 to Stirling. For though the road may seem to go through Airth, in fact only the more modern part of the village has grown up flanking it. The old burgh strikes off at an angle north-westwards with Shore Road reaching eastwards and remains largely unspoiled. Here are some excellent, traditional Scots houses; and in the days when it was a cobbled High Street, leading up to its widening around the Mercat Cross, it would rival the well-known Culross not so far across the Forth. Amongst the most characterful of the buildings is the Herring House, indicative of the one-time fishing activities here, with its handsome moulded doorway. There is some fine modern housing in character.

Up the hill, Airth Castle is visible from afar off on the southern approach, occupying a strong position above the ravine of the Pow Burn. It is a large and composite building, rather spoiled on the north by the addition of a tasteless sham-Gothic frontage; but finely authentic to the south, where it extends eastwards from a formerly free-standing square tower of the 15th century, called Wallace's Tower—although it dates from later than his period. There *was* a castle here then, however, for Blind Harry tells how the Patriot sacked it, when held by 100 Englishmen, to release his uncle, the priest of Dunipace. The second son of Bruce of Clackmannan married the heiress of Airth of that Ilk in the early 15th century, presumably building this tower. The castle was burned in 1488 by James III, before the fatal Battle of Sauchieburn, its laird having joined the nobles opposed to the King. His son, James IV, a year later sent compensation of £100 "for byggen his Place that was byrnt". The castle is still occupied and maintained in good condition.

Near by is the old abandoned church in its graveyard, once a fine place, oblong, with a 12th century nucleus in Transitional style, but mainly reconstructed in the mid-17th century. Three aisles project, of different dates—the Airth Aisle, built about 1450 by Alexander Bruce of Stenhouse; the Elphinstone, erected by the 4th Lord Elphinstone in 1593; and the Bruce, by Sir James Bruce of Powfoulis—a property near by, now a hotel—in 1614. There are a number of interesting gravestones; and three mort-safes, in the form of massive iron coffins dated 1831, 1832 and 1837—no doubt coming conveniently from nearby Carron Ironworks.

In the lower ground are the more modern South Church of 1809 renovated early this century; and the more ambitious North Church in Perpendicular style, with Gothic tracery.

In 1633 Airth was involved in a very unpleasing piece of royal chicanery, which makes one wonder about Charles the Martyr. The King, resenting an alleged remark that William Graham, 18th Earl of Menteith, was more illustriously descended than himself, took the ancient great earldom—and its revenues—from him and made him merely Earl of Airth instead. The title became extinct with the second holder, in 1693.

The great estate of Dunmore lies to the north. In 1686 Charles Murray, second son of the first Marquis of Atholl, was created Earl of Dunmore. There are a number of Dunmores in Scotland—it merely means the great castle or fort—and which one the Earl took his title from is not clear; for this one did not get that name until 1784. Its mansion is large, but not particularly remarkable. But in the grounds still rises the Tower of Elphinstone, a much altered fragment of a larger building, probably of the late 15th century. This was the seat of the Lords Elphinstone, the father of the first lord, 'the King's familiar shieldbearer', having gained the lands by marriage with the heiress of Airthbeg, as it was called, before 1340, and changed the name. The 11th Lord sold to the Earl of Dunmore in 1784, who renamed it again. Also in Dunmore grounds is the famed and curious stone Pineapple, a large garden ornament.

A mile south of Airth, at the former little haven of Higginsneuk, the main Glasgow–Fife road, A.876, strikes eastwards to cross the quickly narrowing Forth by the great Kincardine Bridge. This, built in 1936, as a poor substitute for the later and mighty Forth Road Bridge opened at Queensferry in 1964, does save a major detour by Stirling for west–east traffic.

Arnprior and Garden. A string of quite attractive villages dot the two sides of the great Flanders Moss area of the Forth valley. Arnprior is a small one, but pleasing. It lies less than three miles west of Kippen, on the A.811 Stirling–Dumbarton road, where a side-road comes in over the high moors from Fintry on the south, and another goes off northwards to Port of Menteith. Strangely, although on the wrong side of Forth, Arnprior used to be in Perthshire.

The hamlet itself, with its school, mill, smithy and cottages, does not call for special description. There was a castle here once, of which no trace remains. Arnprior farmhouse, close to the road, has been a small mansion of the late 18th century, well-planned, little-altered and with some architectural pretensions. The Buchanans of Arnprior were quite a prominent family, in a small way. One of the lairds was a 'founder-member' of Rob Roy's elaborate system of insurance against their cattle being stolen, by paying the MacGregor protection money. Indeed the next laird, Robert, had a daughter married to Hamilton of Bardowie, whose sister Mary wed Gregor MacGregor of Glengyle, Rob's chieftain and nephew. At the inn at Arnprior, too, Rob Roy and Henry Cunningham of Boquhan, an estate 4 miles to the east, met and quarrelled, whereat the bold and dandified Boquhan not only boxed the famous freebooter's ears but actually bested him in the duel which inevitably followed—though admittedly Rob was three-parts drunk. However, the hero was a good loser, and returned to shake Cunningham's hand, and spend the rest of the night drinking with him. They remained the best of friends thereafter.

A mile west of Arnprior is Garden, a very ancient estate, on which formerly was an old castle, now demolished. It stood in the midst of an artificial lake, and even had a small cannon to guard its draw-bridge. The present mansion, visible from the road, was built in 1749 and 1830, to replace it, and is an impressive edifice of its periods, yellow-washed and standing high amidst old trees. The Stirlings of Garden are an old and well-known family, a branch of that of Keir, across the Forth, Sir John, first of Garden, receiving it from his father in 1613. The Jacobite laird, of the early 18th century, was another of Rob Roy's clients; but he unfortunately, after years of protection, decided that he had spent enough, and stopped payment. Rob could not allow this, and repairing to Garden Castle, found the laird from home, and decided to await his return. When the laird came back, it was to find his own draw-bridge raised against him; and after some long-range bargaining, the payment was duly renewed. Before the Stirlings, at Garden, were the Foresters, a family which long held, and took their name from, the hereditary keepership of the royal forest of the Tor Wood.

On the B.8034 road across a slightly raised division of the great Moss, between Parks of Garden and Cardross House, a fine stone bridge of three arches, 200 feet long, crosses the Forth and into Perthshire. On the east side is a panel declaring that it was erected in 1774, with a subvention of £250 from the King, out of the confiscated Jacobite estates, with the Latin injunction that travellers should be grateful for this royal benefaction!

Baldernock, Bardowie and Torrance. Baldernock is the most south-westerly of all Stirlingshire parishes, a relatively small one, lying only 7 miles north of Glasgow G.P.O., in the pleasant moor-and-foothill country rising to the Campsie Fells, between Milngavie and Lennoxtown. Bardowie is a developing residential area a mile to the south. And Torrance, not to be confused with the parish of that name in Lanarkshire, is a large village to the east of the parish, only 2 miles from Kirkintilloch.

There is no village, or even hamlet, of Baldernock; only the parish church agreeably set on high ground, at a road junction, with its old manse near by, its graveyard and war memorial; all looking out over the wide prospect of reservoir-dotted and populous low country to the south. The church, small and fairly plain but not unattrac-tive, dates from 1795, replacing an earlier structure, and is unusual in having its belfry midway along the south front, surmounting a sort of gablet; and there are two outside stairs to galleries at opposing ends. The interior, with its coved ceiling, is designed to centre on the pulpit, which stands raised above the Communion-table—indication of the emphasis on the Word, when this was built. An octagonal watch-house, with fireplace, precaution against body-snatchers, stands amidst the old tombstones.

Bardowie is perhaps best known for its loch, half a mile by a quarter, a favourite recreation-place for the Bearsden–Milngavie area, with boating and other facilities. But because of its castle, on the north shore of the loch, it has featured in history quite prominently. Now, the district is a favoured one for housing, so close to the great centres of population, yet with much pleasant amenity and open country around. The castle, still a private house, is of early 16th century construction with later additions. The quite massive keep has had an early and elaborate reconstruction, to roof-in its parapets and walks in unusual fashion, to provide an upper hall with fine open timber roof, the former wall-walks still forming narrow flanking corridors. Bardowie was a seat of the once-powerful Galbraiths; but, in the 14th century, heiresses carried the property to the Hamiltons of Cadzow, ancestors of the Dukes of Hamilton. A branch built the present castle, and kept cropping up in history, being a turbulent lot, much addicted to feuding. John Hamilton was killed near by in a fight with Logans of Balvie in 1526. His successor, Alan, died fighting Campbells; another laird was involved in 1591 in a serious affray with Graham of Dougalston close by. And so on. The last and 16th of the line, Robert left only a sister, who married Buchanan of Leny. In 1707 Mary Hamilton of Bardowie married the gallant Gregor Black-Knee MacGregor of Glengyle, Rob Roy's nephew; and her brother, John of Bardowie, though not a Jacobite, aided Rob financially when he suffered loss for his share of the Rising of 1715. The estate of Dougalston, a mile to the west, has a smaller loch notable for rare water-plants.

Just north of Baldernock church is the farm of Blochairn, interesting for the number of prehistoric chambered cairns, or burial mounds, in its vicinity, in which urns, bones and a bronze dagger have been found. An ancient battle is supposed to have been fought here. At North Blochairn, on still higher ground, is a more spectacular item, known as The Auld Wife's Lift. This was long thought to be a cromlech, of the Stonehenge variety, but is now known to be a natural phenomenon. It is sited out on the open moor 400 yards north of the farm, and consists of an enormous boulder raised on top of two others, highly impressive and presumably the work of glaciation. Near by are several small shallow quarries out of which millstones have been worked.

There is much moorland in this area, Craigmaddie, Craigend and Blairskaith Muirs—though much of the latter has been engulfed in the great Lennox planted forest. It is a district of small pastoral farms and twisting side-roads, oddly remote-seeming to be so near Glasgow. On the way to Torrance is Barraston Farm, which used to be an old inn; and a mile south-east is Balgrochan, now just a 'suburb' of Torrance, but where once there was a 17th century mansion, hamlet and mill. The old Craw Road over the hills to Fintry started near here, and traces may still be discovered. Torrance itself is not a prepossessing place, despite its good situation. There used to be a railway station, on the former Kelvin Valley line, when the tide of industrial development was strong and ruthless. Stirling county boundary follows the sluggish Kelvin, at Torrance's back-door.

Balfron and Edinbellie. Balfron sits in the mouth of the Endrick valley, backed by the Campsie Fells and the Fintry Hills. It is a large and growing village, its comparatively convenient access to Glasgow, 19 miles away, making it a favoured residential area in attractive country. The village itself is not old, taking its rise from a cotton-spinning venture of 1789, started by Robert Dunmore of Ballindalloch, a local estate. But the parish is ancient, and the present church, although built only in 1832, is on the site of an old one, for there are early gravestones in the kirkyard, including one from pre-Reformation times, incised with the likeness of a sword. The village climbs a hill on the north bank of the Endrick, some two miles north-east of Killearn. This is the later part, and many of the 18th century cottages remain, though modernised. There is also much present-day housing, some of it imaginative and characterful. The older hamlet, called the Clachan, centres round the church, at the top of the brae, and is more attractive. Two of the larger houses here, Orchardfield and the Old Manse, are good examples of 18th century building. There is a handsome new school to the east. At the junction of two side-roads from the upper and lower village, at the commencement of the moorland route to Kippen, is a low motte, now overgrown with conifers.

Balfron's name is alleged to derive from *baile-bhroin*, the town of mourning, referring to the legend that in faraway times many of the place's children were killed by wolves. Rather more recent is the tradition that the murderers of Archbishop Sharpe, in 1679, first drew rein here after the fatal work at Magus Muir, near St. Andrews —an epic ride indeed, if true, since the places are nearly seventy miles apart.

Edinbellie is now only a farm, lying 2 miles to the east; but it was a more important place, and estate, once. It belonged to the family of Napier of Merchiston, and it is thought that the famous John, inventor of logarithms, was born here, in 1550. Certainly his father was Sir Alexander Napier of Edinbellie. And here, in exactly two centuries, Rob Roy's rather disreputable sons abducted forcibly Jean Key, a deed for which Robin Og was hanged in Edinburgh in 1753. There was a church here also, the first Secession church in this area, and then known as the Holm Associate Church; and its first minister, the Rev. John Cleland, was ordained in it in 1742. It is now used by the farm as a cart-shed.

To the north, between Balfron and the Carse of Forth area, lie the high wastes of Ballindalloch, Buchlyvie and Kippen Muirs, lying between the 500- to 600-foot contours. The road past Edinbellie joins the B.822, Fintry–Kippen, 3 miles farther east, under the steep escarpment of Stronend (1677 feet). Here is the area of Balgair, once a larger community than Balfron, with a public house and shops all disappeared. On Balgair Muir was formerly the site of a large annual cattle fair. There are the foundation traces of old farms here, near the present Croftalpine farmhouse; and nearly a mile to the south, nearer the river, is the ruined shell of the Old Place of Balgair, formerly a classical-style laird's house of 1721, belonging to the Galbraiths.

Balmaha and Rowardennan. Here is one of the most delightful stretches of country within easy reach of Glasgow, flanking lower Loch Lomond on the east. The road, B.837, which runs west from Drymen for a dozen miles and then stops at Rowardennan, is highly attractive. There have long been complaints that this is not continued right up the east side of the loch, permitting a circuit of this famous place, and providing an alternative route to the much over-laden A.82, Glasgow–Argyll highway, on the west side. This is an entirely valid demand, and one the present author has long advocated; but at least, in the present situation, the dead-end road helps to keep this Balmaha–Rowardennan area much less crowded and exploited than it might be otherwise. And considering its natural beauties, this is highly desirable.

It is all part of Buchanan parish. Balmaha village lies some four miles west of Drymen, under the steep wooded slopes of Canic Hill, at the head of a deep little bay, with the tree-girt islands of Inchcailleach, Clarinch and Torrinch just opposite. It is a picturesque little community of scattered houses, old and new—one, the Old Manse, renowned as the home of the late Lord Bannerman of Kildonan, that famous and lovable Scot. Balmaha is not yet spoiled, although it has become a great boating and yachting centre, something of a 'marina'. There is a pier, where the steamer calls in summer. Formerly there was, indeed, a small chemical works here, which used the local Scots pines to produce what were called 'pyroligneous acids and dye-stuffs'. There is a heather and heath nursery. Immediately beyond the hamlet, the road turns sharply to climb steeply up through the little Pass of Balmaha, quite an impressive gap in the shoulder of Canic Hill—and a good place for Rob Roy and the MacGregors to close, for strategic or commercial reasons. Many were the stirring incidents that this pass has seen. It was through here that Gregor Black-Knee MacGregor of Glengyle drove, or was driven by, the White Bull of Gallangad, on that famous occasion.

Beyond the pass, the road winds and twists along the loch shore in delightful fashion another seven miles or so to Rowardennan, by little bays, over knolls, amongst woodlands of birch and pine, with splendid views of the ever-heightening mountains across the loch, and the scattered islands between. Of these, Inchcailleach is the most important, rising to 278 feet, wooded thickly, and having the ruins of the ancient parish church of Buchanan, with its burial-ground, where are the remains of St. Kentigerna, the Celtic missionary who founded a nunnery here and died in 733; also the graves of many notables, including chiefs of MacGregor. Just south of Inchcailleach—which means the island of old women or cowled women (nuns)—is Clarinch, a smaller islet, which was the Buchanan rallying-place (it being easier to muster by boat in this country) and which provided the clan slogan, of *Clar Innis*! There are at least a dozen more islands, but this will be dealt with under Loch Lomond.

Along the Rowardennan road there are a number of caravan-parks; but because of the hilly, forested nature of the area, they do not obtrude unduly. Here the road enters the great Queen Elizabeth Forest Park, which covers a vast area of the Ben Lomond range foothills. There are one or two old bridges on this road, which was only finished in 1792, after thirty years of building.

At Strathcashel Point, opposite the island of Inchlonaig, hidden from the road by woodland, is the site of a cashel of the early Celtic Church, a religious community, the remaining roughly circular walling enclosing an area 93 by 80 feet, with an oblong building's foundations within, probably the chapel. Also, 150 yards offshore, is one of a number of loch crannogs, artificial islets of stone and timber, Dark Age defensive features.

Two miles farther, past Sallachy School, at the high wooded peninsula of Ross Point, is a University of Glasgow Field Station, a group of cedar buildings and glass-houses, picturesquely sited where the small Lochan Dubh lies under the hill, at a higher level than Loch Lomond. Here zoological study, particularly of animalcules from the loch-floor, and plankton, is carried on. Sometimes powans are caught, the famed specialised fish of Loch Lomond, thought to have been trapped here untold ages ago when the loch ceased to be an arm of the sea. Though sometimes called freshwater herring, they are in fact vendace, a fish more like the salmon family, though with white flesh. They are also to be found in the Castle Loch at Lochmaben, and in Loch Eck, and nowhere else. One specimen, of about two pounds, is shown here in preserving-fluid.

Another two miles and the road ends. Rowardennan is a most attractive spot, scarcely a hamlet, but with a hotel, lodge, youth hostel, large car-park and steamer-pier. Most car-parks lack beauty; but this one is a gem, amongst fine old Scots pines, on a rocky promontory with fine vistas. There was formerly a ferry connecting Rowardennan with Inverbeg across the loch. And on this line, in the old clan days, the cattle herds were swum across from west to east, to save the long circuit of the loch-foot, on their way to the Lowland trysts. Here is the popular starting-point for the ascent of Ben Lomond, which rears itself about four miles to the north.

Although the road stops here, a track of sorts continues northwards, now by the loch-shore, now high above, by Ardess, Ptarmigan Lodge and eventually Rowchoish and Cailness, to Inversnaid, another 8 exceedingly difficult miles, recommended for hardened walkers only. This was Rob Roy's Craigrostan lairdship, its then more numerous houses and crofts mainly approachable by boat. It is strange, but not unpleasing, to have such inaccessible wilderness on the bonnie banks of Loch Lomond, and less than thirty miles from Glasgow G.P.O.

Bannockburn. For a place of such resounding fame, Bannockburn must often be a sore disappointment to the eager visitor. And not only disappointing but confusing. For the actual site of the great battle is neither at the village nor up at the Borestone, where the ambitious National Trust for Scotland rotunda and information centre, splendid equestrian statue and monument of Robert the Bruce by Pilkington Jackson, and Stirling Guildry's Memorial Cairn, all are situated; it is in fact more than a mile away to the north, down in the level carselands of the Forth, due east of St. Ninians. The reason for this will be explained.

The Bannock Burn rises, at 1250 feet, on Touchadam Muir in the

Falkirk. Modern Muncipal Buildings

Grangemouth. Port, oil terminal and industrial complex

Strathblane. Rural scene in the Lennox Hills only 9 miles from the
centre of Glasgow

Inversnaid. Garrison Farm and remains of military fort built to restrain
Rob Roy MacGregor

Dundaff Hills, and flows eastwards for over a dozen miles, to reach the Forth 2 miles east of Stirling. The large village, almost a town, which takes its name from the burn, is not ancient, and lies athwart the Bannock 2 miles inland from the Forth, on rising ground above the carse; and through it now runs the main A.9 Edinburgh–Perth highway. There was no village here at the time of the battle, although there was the Milton of Bannock near by; and the community did not really start to grow until the beginning of the 19th century, when the Industrial Revolution period brought industry in the shape of woollen mills, the spinning, weaving and dyeing of tweeds, tartans, carpets and so on, followed by the opening up of pits all around in the Stirlingshire coalfield. That kind of development is not calculated to enhance the appearance of any place, and Bannockburn grew with little of the character which its name might conjure up. There have been improvements of late, however, and it is to be hoped that these will continue. Until recently, on the other hand, the village had a fairly distinct identity, and a population of over three thousand; but now it is tending to coalesce with St. Ninians to the north, itself fast becoming a suburb of Stirling.

The National Trust's and other memorials to the famous battle are concentrated some distance to the west of the village, on the higher ground—indeed, at the far side of the A.80, the Glasgow–Stirling road, which joins the A.9 at St. Ninians. Here is the Borestone, reputed to be the spot where Bruce set up his standard the evening before the battle—and fragments of the stone itself, with its socket-hole (the bored stone), are now displayed in the Trust's auditorium. This was the stone which had such an effect on Robert Burns that he was moved to compose the stirring song which is now almost Scotland's national anthem, and which we rather inadequately call *Scots Wha Hae*—based on Bruce's address to his troops before the engagement. The quite magnificent equestrian statue of the hero-king was unveiled by the Queen in June 1964. The Rotunda is perhaps not quite so successful. But the simple cairn of the Stirling Guildry near by is dignified with its moving quotation from the famous Declaration of Arbroath of six years later though it is a pity it misquotes that resounding document in one word.

Bannockburn was one of the great decisive battles, when a small army of war-hardened veterans, with the help of a mass of the ordinary Scots folk fighting for their lives and homes, and led by one of the great war-leaders of history, utterly defeated the vastly greater invading martial host of England, considered to be unbeatable in Christendom. The encounter developed over two days, June 23rd and 24th, 1314—which is responsible for the frequent confusion as to sites. For the first day's skirmishing and waiting, including Bruce's own famed personal encounter with Sir Humphrey de Bohun, took place largely on this higher ground; while the true major battle of the second day was fought out down in the carselands and marshy flats to the east, between the St. Ninians escarpment and the Forth. Here, denied better camping-ground, King Edward II's huge array passed the night of June 23rd; and here, as the mists of early morning dispersed, Bruce, deserting his strong position on the heights, came down to surprise his enemies and force them to fight in appalling ground for heavy cavalry, trapped against the Forth and the Bannock and Pelstream Burns. Here the great English advantage in numbers, mounted knights and bowmen was nullified by the swampy ground and the impossibility of bringing any large proportion of the total force to bear on the enemy. Yet there could be no way out save through the Scots line—or by swimming the Forth. All day the battle raged, but long before the bloody end it was obvious that the Scots had won. King Edward made his own escape, with some of his great nobles, deserting the rest, and allegedly not pausing in his flight until he reached Dunbar, to take boat to Berwick. The victory was not just a battle won, but represented the turning-point in the thirty-year-long Wars of Independence. Thereafter, although it was another fifteen years before a peace treaty was finally signed, there was no longer doubt that Scotland would be free and independent, and that the Bruce was her undisputed monarch. Here, then, in the Carse of Stirling, almost under the walls of her rockgirt fortress, was a watershed in Scotland's story.

But this is not Bannockburn's only claim to fame. The Battle of Sauchieburn, also, was fought only a couple of miles to the west, in June 1488, when James III, Bruce's sixth generation weakly descendant, was defeated by his insurgent nobles, and died, in flight, at the Milton of Bannock—see Sauchieburn. Moreover, at Bannockburn House, a handsome and commodious mansion of the late 17th century, which lies in a green hollow of the rising ground approximately midway between the two battlefields, Prince Charles Edward, a still later descendant, spent a night on his southern march in 1745; and again made it his headquarters for some time in January 1746, on his return northwards, at the time of the victorious Battle of Falkirk—though Culloden was looming ahead. While lodging here, tradition has it that an assailant sought to assassinate the Prince, and the mark of the missing bullet is still pointed out in one of the rooms.

Near by a section of the Roman Road is to be traced, in the Snabhead vicinity.

Bonnybridge. Despite its name, this is no beauty-spot. The Bonny Water rises near Cumbernauld, in Dunbartonshire, and flows eastwards 7 miles through industrialised country to reach the Carron at Dunipace. Two miles west of that, and the same distance south of Denny, it was bridged, and here has grown up a wide-scattered complex of clanging foundries, brick-works and the like, guaranteed to ruin the appearance of any area. Yet this has been an attractive district, as evidenced by the stretch of broken, wooded, hilly ground which lies to the south of the Bonny and the Forth and Clyde Canal which here follows roughly the same course, along the side of the B.816 road to Castlecary.

It is a pity that Bonnybridge is so uninspiring a place to the visitor—unless he be an industrialist—for here are to be found some of the finest Roman remains in Scotland. The great Rough Castle fort on the Antonine Wall lies on the higher ground, not very readily approached either, 1½ miles to the south-east. Here, in open country with far-reaching views, bracken-covered yet though surrounded with the detritus of industry, is a magnificent stretch of the Wall, the Military Way, and, within ramparts, the extensive complex of fort, annexe, barracks, bath-house and their related buildings, with evocative names like the Frigidarium, Caldarium, Tepidarium, the Praefurnium and the Sudatorium. All this, covering a large area, was carefully excavated and investigated by a team of archaeologists under Sir George MacDonald and Mr. A. O. Curle, from 1931 onwards—an account of which may be read in the *Proceedings of the Society of Antiquaries of Scotland* for 1932/33. Unfortunately for the casual visitor, the earth and spoil has been all filled in again, over the remains, so that now the area has reverted to only green banks and mounds—which, however significant to the expert, fails to interpret the treasures beneath to the tyro. This is the general procedure with such sites—which seems a pity; although without adequate wardening and protection, undoubtedly vandalism would take its sad toll. But surely any country fortunate enough to possess such antiquities and ancient monuments to its past, should accept the responsibility and privilege of looking after them and keeping them safe and available for inspection? Especially in an area where natural beauty has been so blatantly sacrificed for commercial profit.

Here the archaeologists found an inscribed tablet set up by the 6th Cohort of the Nervii, who, it declares, erected the Principium (or Headquarters building) *in honour of the Emperor Caesar Titus Aelius Hadrianus Antonius Pius, Father of his country.*

There are other sections of the Wall and Military Way in the vicinity.

Bonnybridge area has more to offer than this to those interested in the past. Just to the west, on either side of the aforementioned B.816 road, lies the former great barony of Seabegs, and now represented by a Seabegs Terrace of undistinguished modern houses to the south, and the farmstead of Seanores on a sort of island in the boggy vale of the Bonny Water, to the north. Hereabouts are several mottes and earthen mounds which in the Middle Ages served as courts of justice and meeting sites.

There are a number of colliery and other industrial villages round about Bonnybridge, such as Bankier—where there is a distillery—Dennyloanhead, Longcroft, Haggs, Banknock and High Bonnybridge. But however fair these places may have been once, man has done his worst with them—though recent council housing seeks to improve. Yet, all around, the vistas are fair.

Bridge of Allan. Bridge of Allan lays no claim to great antiquity. Indeed it is alleged to have grown up round an inn, near the old bridge over the Allan Water, which joins the Forth a mile to the south. In 1827 Chalmers describes it as "a confusion of straw-roofed cottages and many trees, possessed of a bridge and a mill, together with kailyards, beeskeps, colleys, callants and old inns". It has come a long way since then—and in fact became a burgh in 1870. But unlike most newly-arisen burghs, it has not developed as an unsightly industrial town. For it was not industry which caused Bridge of Allan to grow, but the discovery and exploitation of mineral wells in the Airthrey estate to the east; so that the village became a spa and fashionable watering-place. Long before that, we are told that the local inhabitants used to drink the water which flowed from the old 17th century copper-mine working here—still to be traced in Minewood, on the Hill of Airthrey—recognising that it had medicinal qualities. When the mine failed, the Airthrey laird turned to the water—and found it more profitable than the copper. He offered to lease the wells to nearby Stirling, and on the town council's refusal, built a well-house himself. So the spa was born. By 1891 the population had risen to 3200, around which figure it remains. There were then 140 private boarding-houses.

So, although there are no ancient buildings—apart from an old water-mill, and the small Georgian house of East Lodge—there are no ugly industrial premises and detritus either, to mar the scene. Not that Bridge of Allan is a particularly beautiful place; but it has its undoubted attractions, and gives a clean, spacious and tidy impression, strung out along the A.9, with parks, gardens, trees and large houses and hotels. But it is not as a watering-place that it prides itself today—although the spa activities and buildings still remain as part of the large Allan Water Hotel; it is as a tourist and holiday centre in its own right, excellently placed, under the shelter of the Ochils, with easy access both to the Southern Highlands and to a large area of Central Scotland, with Stirling only 3 miles to the south, and Perth, Callander, Aberfoyle, Dunfermline and Linlithgow all within 25 miles. Near at hand is Dunblane and its cathedral, the site of the Battle of Sheriffmuir, and that of the age-old capital of the Damnonii, Alauna, down in the carse where Allan and Forth meet. Also there is available golf, tennis, bowling, fishing in the Allan and in lochs, a boat club at Stirling, and walks in the woodland behind the town. This is a conference-place, with many hotels and a meeting-centre in the Museum Hall. And here on the first Saturday of August are held the Strathallan Games, one of the major athletic events of Scotland.

Although lacking in old buildings and history, there are monuments to antiquity here. A quarter-mile south-east of Sunnylaws farm, up on the golf-course, is the so-called Fairy Knowe, a round cairn 60 feet in diameter, with a flat top. Excavated in 1868, a stone burial cist was discovered at the centre, containing human remains—possibly one of the great ones from ancient Alauna. Also in the cairn was found a beaker and spear- and arrow-heads. Further prehistoric monuments remain in Airthrey Castle grounds, in the shape of two standing-stones, one, broken, a half-mile to the west of the castle; and the other, nearly six feet high, a quarter-mile to the east. Still another lies recumbent up on the Pendreich Muir, near the 900-foot contour, on the way to Sheriffmuir.

Today the new University of Stirling burgeons and grows in the Airthrey grounds, and so is in effect very much part of Bridge of Allan, and must inevitably have a great impact on the little town. Its attractive lay-out, amongst the parklands, woods and hillocks, and the interesting and adventurous architecture, as well as its unconventional academic ambitions and development, ensure that it will remain a mecca of interest for a long time to come.

Buchlyvie. This is one of those rather pleasant villages which flank the south rim of the Flanders Moss, facing across to the Highland Line, with the Gargunnock and Fintry Hills rising to the south. It consists of a long climbing street, now part of the A.811, Stirling–Dumbarton road, with an almost hidden turning off to the north, to form a second street, which carries the B.835 away across the mosses to Aberfoyle. Although only a small place, with some three hundred of population, the village has boasted three churches—the Established, United Free and United Presbyterian. Though the last, at the top of the street, is now a community hall. The parish church dates only from 1876; but the North Church, on the Aberfoyle road, was built in 1751, by the Seceders who had previously formed part of the Balfron, or Holm, congregation, 5 miles away across the moors. It is a plain building, but pleasing, long, low and whitewashed. The village architecture is a mixture from the late 18th century to the present day; but the Red Lion Inn probably has a 17th century nucleus. On the farm of Mains of Buchlyvie, a few hundred yards south of the main A.811 road, is a long grassy mound, seemingly natural, but in which a stone cist was found, containing human bones.

Less than two miles along the Aberfoyle road is the very attractive late 18th century whitewashed farmhouse of Gartinstarry, now modernised to make a charming residence. It was a former Buchanan possession. Half a mile further, within the estate of Auchentroig, now a Roman Catholic institution, is Old Auchentroig, a small but delightful and interesting laird's house of 1702, used only as a store but in good condition still. It is a very modest but sturdy and authentic structure, containing only four rooms, with crowstepped gables and steep roof, its walled garden adjoining. There is a handsome moulded doorway, with original iron-studded door, complete with early fittings and lock; also a draw-bar with deep mural socket. Above is an inscribed lintel, bearing the initials M.S., L.M. and B.G., and the date 1702. Also a heraldic panel. The heraldry and initials refer to John MacLachlan and his two wives. The MacLachlans were lairds of Auchentroig for six centuries. Rob Roy is reputed to have captured this house by burning down the door.

About a mile and a half farther north-west, out on the edge of the Flanders Moss, and near the side of the A.81, Glasgow–Aberfoyle road, is what the Ordnance Map calls the Peel of Gartfarran. It is in fact an earthwork, a homestead motte, and one of the finest of its kind in Scotland, almost square in plan, about fifty yards each way, with a 9-foot-deep ditch surrounding it. No traces of building remain, but there are signs of a causeway thereinto. A Thomas son of Malcolm, of Gartfarran, is recorded in 1296; and fragments of 13th and 14th century pottery have been found here.

Cambusbarron and Torbrex. These two villages, now almost run together and both all but swallowed up by Stirling, lie to the south-west of the town, at the foot of the Touch Hills. Indeed they might be described as the first of that interesting series of small communities which string the Lennox foothills to the north, along the edge of the great Forth mosses, and end at Buchlyvie. Cambusbarron, a mile and a half from the centre of Stirling, was much the larger, and was a place of some standing, sometimes described as a town, on the old military and drove-road to Dumbarton, with its own commonty—relics of which are still called the Free Green— industry, especially woollen spinning and weaving, and a population, in the 1870s, of 1200.

Unlike Torbrex it still possesses an air of independence, the intervening King's Park golf-course of Stirling aiding. It lies on the side of the wooded Gillies Hill, with a long main street and subsidiaries, three prongs forking at the east end, towards Stirling, and the large Hayford Mills down in the vale. The oldest remaining houses are of the late 18th and early 19th century, some of them weavers' cottages. The old church, now in a bad state of repair, has had an odd history, having apparently been a carpet-weaving factory once, before being converted into a place of worship, and then degenerating again into a store. There was a mansion house here once, one of its 17th century gate-piers remaining; also a 15th century chapel, which pertained to Cambuskenneth Abbey. Its well was reputed to be medicinal. There was also a St. Thomas's Well, at the farm of that name, now submerged in a pond. The village has a small modern park and paddling-pool.

Torbrex lies half a mile to the east, and is now almost completely lost in modern housing, although, rather amusingly, a little twisting lane still links the old cottages that remain, some of the 18th century. Most of these were thatched, but re-roofed this century. How long they will survive is doubtful, in the circumstances. The Wordies of Torbrex were an old family, based here from the 17th century.

To the south of Torbrex rises the property of Polmaise, on the slopes of Gillies Hill—where Bruce's non-military followers were stationed at Bannockburn. This is not to be confused with Lower

Polmaise, or Stewarthall, down in the carse near Fallin. A fine Roman fibula was found here. A Cunningham family were lairds of Polmaise in the 16th century, when an heiress carried the property to the Murrays of Touchadam, who long remained in possession.

Cambuskenneth Abbey. This famous place lies within a loop of the winding Forth, across the river from Stirling town. Its site used to be within Clackmannanshire, and the tradition is that it got its name from a conflict between King Kenneth MacAlpine and the Picts—the Field of Kenneth, the Battle of Logie in fact. The Abbey was founded by David I, that 'sair sanct to the Crown'—meaning that he gave overmuch of Crown land and treasure to the Church—in 1147, for a colony of Augustinian monks from Arras, in France, and dedicated to the Virgin Mary. It was sometimes called the Monastery of Stirling. Situated here, at the very heart of Scotland, it inevitably was a highly important establishment, especially as its rich Forth carselands were so notably fertile—whence the saying that "A crook o' the Forth is worth an Earldom in the North". Many of its abbots rose to high position in the state; Abbot Henry was High Treasurer of Scotland in 1493; Abbot Patrick Pantler (1470–1519) was secretary to James IV; Abbot Alexander Miln was a great scholar, ambassador and became first President of the Court of Session; and the last, Abbot David Pantler was Secretary of State and ambassador.

There is not a great deal left of the former imposing establishment, although the restored square Bell-tower is a noted landmark. But this stood separate from the main body of the Abbey. The rest is now presented mainly by foundations; even these are not all of early date but reconstructions. There are remains of a large, 13th century cruciform church, 180 by 37 feet, with nave, north and south transepts, presbytery and sacristy; a large central cloister; a chapter-house to the east; and a refectory to the south. The west door to the nave is almost complete, and very fine. In 1864 a large slab of coarse blue marble was found before the high altar, and beneath it coffined remains which were believed to be those of James III and his wife Queen Margaret of Denmark, both buried at Cambuskenneth. Queen Victoria caused a memorial stone to be erected.

The most interesting building, of course, is the Bell-tower, a highly unusual structure which appears to have been erected after the completion of the rest, at the end of the 13th century. It is in First Pointed style, and contains now three storeys beneath a platform roof surrounded by a crenellated parapet and walk, at a height of 64 feet. But formerly the roof was saddlebacked and steep, and would contain the usual garret. A turnpike stair rises in a polygonal turret at the north-east angle, and ends in a gabled caphouse. The entrance is quite handsome, and has been partially renewed. The basement is rib-vaulted, and contains sundry relics, including fragments of the aforementioned blue marble from the royal tomb, thought to have been brought from Tournai. The upper floors are lit by fine single- and double-pointed windows.

The history of Cambuskenneth is almost that of Scotland. Edward I of England was here in 1303. The Abbey featured prominently in the events connected with the Battle of Bannockburn. Here Bruce held a parliament in 1326, the first at which representatives of the burghs were minuted as appearing. Here was married Christian Bruce, the King's sister, and Andrew Moray of Bothwell, son of the patriot who died at Stirling Bridge. Other parliaments sat here also. The Abbey was pillaged during the wars of David II's reign, and rewarded with the revenues of the Vicarage of Clackmannan, in consequence. In 1559 the reforming mob sacked the place. Cambuskenneth was then turned into a secular lordship for the Earl of Mar, who became Regent. In 1709 it was purchased by Stirling town, for the benefit of Cowane's Hospital.

Today, Cambuskenneth makes a peaceful enclave, islanded, in the coils of the river, from the busy town.

Campsie and Lennoxtown. Campsie is a well-known name in Scotland, largely because of the Campsie Fells, that attractive range in the long procession of the Lennox Hills, so prominent to the north of Glasgow. But Campsie itself is an interesting and large parish, which once was even larger, when it extended for 11 miles, from Craigmaddie, near Milngavie, to Garrel Glen, near Kilsyth. It is still a somewhat disjointed and scattered community, with the Clachan of Campsie and the Milton thereof almost four miles apart, and Lennoxtown in between. But it is an entity, nevertheless. Lennoxtown, which might well have been named Newton of Campsie, is the largest centre of population, as well as the most central point; but the Clachan, at the mouth of Campsie Glen, is the ancient nucleus, and should be dealt with first.

The Clachan is still what it always was, and sounds—a small village huddled within a cleft of the steeply-rising hills, picturesque and little-spoiled. There has been a community here for untold ages, for, just to the east of the scattered houses, ancient cultivation-terraces may still be discerned. Later, amongst these banks and linchets, arose the now-vanished fortalice of Balcorrah, from which the Lennox family moved to the new tower of Woodhead a mile to the south. The parish church also was removed to Lennoxtown, in 1828 but the scanty remains of the old kirk, dedicated to St. Machan, remain within a locked graveyard. There was a church noted here in 1216. A watch-house still guards the gate from body-snatchers; and within the enclosure, amongst the many moss-grown tombs, is the lofty, domed, 18th century burial-vault of the Kincaid-Lennox family. Here also, although now indistinguishable, is the grave of William Boick, or Boyack, a Glasgow Covenanter who was martyred in 1683; also that of the parish minister of 1648, the Rev. John Collins, murdered by the Bontine laird of Balglass on his way from a presbytery meeting. Near by was St. Machan's Well, not now to be traced.

Campsie Glen, reached by a path from the Clachan, is a deep wooded ravine famed for its series of waterfalls and rocky pools. Actually there are two glens, one swinging away north-eastwards, properly called Kirkton Glen, the other going north-westwards and named Fin Glen, the latter being the longer and rising high on the 1000-foot contour on Craigbarnet Muir. Sometimes the Clachan itself is miscalled Campsie Glen.

At the junction of the little Clachan road and the main A.891, within an estate, stands the late 17th century whitewashed laird's house of Ballencleroch, with extensive additions, now the Campsie Glen Hotel. The old mansion, still clearly discernible, with its stair-tower, steep roofs and crowstepped gables, dates from 1665, and was the seat of a branch of the MacFarlane clan from then until 1921. Just to the west is the little hamlet of Haughhead, pleasantly grouped round its old farmery.

Lennoxtown, founded at the end of the 18th century, lies 1½ miles to the south-east, on the banks of the Glazert Water, and is indeed a town, with over three thousand inhabitants, but not a burgh. Although its position is fine, under the hill, it is not an especially attractive place; and the spreading pit-bings near by do not help. Coal, bleachfields, print-works and other industries were the reason for its development, and such seldom aided amenity whatever else they did. Lennoxtown seems to have been a great place for religion, for no fewer than five churches enhance the centre of the little town, including a highly modern evangelical building. Most prominent, set high on a knoll overlooking all, is the large Gothic parish church removed here from the Clachan, known as the High Church of Campsie. It was designed by the well-known Glasgow architect David Hamilton in 1828, with sittings for 1550, and has a tall bell-and-clock tower with projecting buttresses. The view from the church-hill is widespread, and the hills rise steeply behind.

From the centre of the town the justly renowned Craw Road heads off northwards, to climb rapidly slantwise up the face of the Fells, to a point high above Campsie Glen, passing the golf-course on the way, and then to swing off north-eastwards across the hills to Fintry, crossing the oddly-named Nineteen-times Burn and the source of the east-running River Carron, the last near the former Campsiemuir Tollhouse, a lonely late 18th century building now used as a store for a modern cottage. The stone slab inscribed with the toll-charges is built-in. This was a drove-road over the hills from early times, much used by Rob Roy and his MacGregors—who in fact extorted much protection-money from the Campsie lairds and farmers—but was later utilised to carry coal from the pits of the south to the new industries that sprang up in the Endrick valley. The coal-cart horses must have had a stiff climb. In the throat of the pass, above Campsie Glen, is a large car-park and excellent viewpoint; and some way farther up, on the right, is

Jamie Wright's Well—which the coal-horses would no doubt much appreciate. Oddly enough, the inscription declares that it was erected by friends of the poet, James M. Slimmon, in 1900, with a lengthy quotation of his verse—though Jamie Wright's name is at the top. Was James Slimmon a wright, then?

To the east of Lennoxtown, within the former great estate of Lennox Castle, is the large mental hospital of that name. The southern part of the estate, spreading over into the moorlands of Craigend and Blairskaith Muirs, is now planted up as a huge forest. Lennox Castle itself is comparatively modern, built 1837–41, in place of the old tower of Woodhead close by. It is an enormous and grandiloquent red-stone pile in allegedly Norman style, designed by David Hamilton. It was erected by John Kincaid-Lennox, who succeeded to Woodhead in 1833, and who claimed the ancient earldom of Lennox, building this vast mansion to be in keeping with his anticipated new dignity as earl—which did not materialise. It is now used as a nurses' home for the institution. Old Woodhead stands in ivy-clad ruin just across the driveway, at the steep lip of the escarpment above the Glazert, and was a typical L-shaped tower-house, built about 1572, the vaulted basements, first-floor hall and part of the stair-tower still remaining. It replaced the still earlier tower of Balcorrah, near the Clachan, when John Lennox, 6th thereof, descended from Duncan, 8th Earl of Lennox, moved across the valley. His heiress-descendant Celia Lennox married John Kincaid of that Ilk, and it was their son, above, who sought to regain the old earldom. The Kincaid-Lennox family, needless to say, made an enormous impact on this area.

Milton of Campsie lies another 1½ miles to the east, with, half-way, the ancient estate of Glorat snug amongst the foothill braes to the north. The Stirlings of Glorat are one of the oldest families in Stirlingshire, stemming from William, second son of Sir John Strivelyn, 3rd of Craigbernard, who was granted Glorat in 1508, by Matthew, Earl of Lennox. Craigbernard, or Craigbarnet as it is now called, is another estate roughly the same distance at the other side of the Clachan, the mansion now demolished; and these Stirlings descended from the still more ancient Cadder line, chiefs of the name, the first of whom is recorded in 1147. Glorat House, still containing an early nucleus. with its wooded estate and fine walled gardens, remains the home of the Stirlings. High above the mansion is the site of the motte-and-bailey Maiden Castle, its history lost in the mists. And still farther up the hillside to the west. is the early Iron Age fort of Meikle Reive, an elaborate system of circular defensive embankments, with a modern cairn.

Milton village has a pleasant position astride the Glazert Water, but is otherwise undistinguished, having also developed industrially at an early date, with print-works of the 18th and 19th centuries. To the south is the estate of Kincaid, its mansion of the late 17th to the early 19th centuries now a hotel. This was the seat of the

208

family of Kincaid of that Ilk, one of whom married the heiress Celia Lennox of Woodhead, and assumed the name of Kincaid-Lennox. South of Kincaid is the hamlet of Birdston, centring round a rather fine small laird's house of the mid-18th century, now a farm. A number of old coins of the Stewart period were found near by, thought to have been hidden when the inhabitants fled before the troops of the victorious Montrose after the Battle of Kilsyth. Here was born the Campsie poet, William Muir.

Near the hamlet of Burnfoot, where the Milton, A.891, road joins the Kilsyth–Kirkintilloch, A.803, south of Antermony Loch, is a somewhat neglected roadside memorial to two local Covenanters, John Wharry and James Smith, who were hanged in chains at Glasgow, in 1683, after having their right hands cut off, and buried here; all in the name of Christianity. Antermony House, formerly Achterminnie, near the loch, is now demolished; it was the birthplace of John Bell, traveller and physician, linked with the Stirlings of Craigbernard, who went to the Russian court at St. Petersburg, and from there made several most dramatic journeys, to Persia, Afghanistan and Tibet. He even went to China, via Siberia. In his book *Travels from St. Petersburg* (1763), he comments on this "after a tedious journey of exactly 16 months".

The Carron Valley. This is a surprising and comparatively little-known feature of the Central Scotland landscape—and a very useful as well as picturesque one for the great industrial areas of Falkirk and Grangemouth, providing a convenient source of plentiful water for the industrialists, as well as a delightful 'lung' for those citizens wise enough to avail themselves of it. And all so near-at-hand as to be phenomenal, in the circumstances.

The clustered hill ranges which make up the centre of Stirlingshire, stretching almost from Forth to Clyde, and sometimes called the Lennox Hills, are divided into north and south sections by two great valleys, which join at their lonely hearts—the Carron and the Endrick. Although the actual sources of the two rivers are about five miles apart, they formerly flowed to within a mile of each other, before the Carron swung eastwards towards the Forth, and the Endrick westwards to Loch Lomond and the Clyde. However, the Stirlingshire and Falkirk Water Board, in due course, perceived the potentialities of the long and wide upper Carron valley, and built a great dam, so that a huge reservoir was created. The head of this vast sheet of water, 4 miles long, lapped back until it was indeed *west* of the west-flowing Endrick's course, and only some hundreds of yards therefrom—a strange situation in hydrology.

So the bottom of the Carron valley was flooded, for the benefit of the eastern lowlands. And the new loch makes a most pleasing feature, embosomed in green hills and with planted forest growing up on all the surrounding braes. But, before we say that, for once, man has actually improved the scenery in Stirlingshire, let us consider what was here before. For this was no ordinary valley. It was

in fact a famous place, an enormous and fertile meadow, the largest
of its kind in Scotland—even though it was called the Carron Bog.
But a bog of a special sort; in fact, a water-meadow of vast extent,
comprising no less than 500 acres. A report of 1842 describes it
thus:

". . . this remarkable meadow, besides its utility in producing hay
and affording pasturage, imparts great loveliness and beauty to the
landscape which surrounds it. In the months of July and August,
it is thickly and cheerfully dotted over with hay-ricks and very
numerous parties of hay-makers; and during winter, the greater
part of it being naturally flooded by the Carron, and the rest brought
industriously under water to fertilise it for the ensuing crop, it
assumes the appearance of a large and beautiful lake."

So man has destroyed something here also, in the cause of industry
—and today certainly no numerous parties of people, hay-makers
or otherwise, are to be seen in the Carron valley.

All the valley is not flooded, of course. There are about five
miles more of it, to the east, before the river issues from its hills at
Carron Glen, just west of Denny and Dunipace. This comparatively
empty tract is threaded by the B.818 road to Fintry, and flanked
by the summits of the Dundaff and Kilsyth Hills.

The road rises to 730 feet at the dam, from 150 at Denny, passing
with extraordinary abruptness from the industrial scene into an
upland country of a few small hill-farms, empty braes and burgeoning forests. But we can see the signs of the population that was here
once. There are even cultivation terraces to be discerned, about
three miles up, at the junction of the Buckie Burn and the Carron,
dating from a very early period. And this was, of course, one of the
main drove-roads for cattle coming from the west to the Falkirk
trysts.

Two miles farther up is Carron Bridge, where the old inn is still a
hotel, and the hill-road from Kilsyth to Stirling comes in from the
south, to cross the B.818. A little farther is the riverside hamlet of
Muirlands, where the Earl's Burn descends from the smaller and
remote reservoirs in the hills to the north. Here there is a school,
a telephone-kiosk and even a community centre with ambitions
to expand, tiny but lively metropolis of this now lonely hill area—
yet less than half a dozen miles, as the crow flies, from both Denny
and Kilsyth, and only 10 from the centre of Falkirk.

Soon thereafter rises the great dam, and the face of the valley
changes, as it opens out to the wide upland basin of the wooded
hills, now sheeted in shining water. A mile farther, at the roadside,
is an ancient graveyard, the site of the one-time Kirk o' Muir,
indication of the days when this was a comparatively populous area.
It was a 15th century chapel, dedicated to the Virgin. Later it
had the distinction of being one of the first churches in Scotland
where the sacrament of the Lord's Supper was dispensed by the

Reformers. Now no trace of the building remains; but the old gravestones within their protective wall, persist, the earliest dated 1695.

Two miles more along the lochside and a significant further indication of man's residence remains. For here, crowning a natural mound some two hundred yards back from the road, is the site of the patriot Sir John the Graham's castle, the same who died at Wallace's side at Falkirk in 1298, and is buried in Falkirk parish kirkyard. He was head of the powerful Graham of Dundaff family, progenitors of the great Montrose line—Dundaff Hill lies 4 miles to the east—and he could field a large body of men from these now empty hills. His castle is highly interesting. It commands the watershed between Carron and Endrick, east and west; and consists of a notably square motte on top of a tall grassy mound, the motte itself surrounded by a deep, 18-foot-wide ditch, which could be crossed only by a drawbridge. Close by, to the east, are a few fangs of masonry, which probably represent a later extension of the castle. The site is well worth a visit, for apart from the antiquarian interest, the position is highly attractive, in an enclave of the forest and looking out over the loch from a height, with far-flung vistas.

Castlecary. Modern road developments, motorways and the like, may be great aids to travel and speedy transport; but they have left Castlecary extremely difficult to find and reach. For the busy and renewed Glasgow–Stirling highway, after leaving the spreading New Town of Cumbernauld, has driven ruthlessly on through the valley of the Walton and Red Burns, with extremely limited turnings-off; and Castlecary, though close to all this rushing progress, is left islanded. This is ironical, for it was as a most strategic road centre on vital routes of communication, that Castlecary developed in the first place. For here, 7 miles west of Falkirk, was one of the principal stations on the Antonine Wall and Roman Military Road; here was a railway station on the Edinburgh–Glasgow North British route, and the Caledonian Gartsherrie line; and here came not only a main road but the Forth and Clyde Canal. Transport could hardly have been more concerned with Castlecary—but now it shuns it.

The castle which gives it its name, of course, was concerned in all this—for such places were frequently placed to command strategic routes and communications. The castle is still there, sited above the Red Burn, a substantial square keep of the late 15th or early 16th century, with a lower addition dating from 1679. The tower is five storeys high, with a projecting crenellated parapet and gabled and crowstepped roof, and still in good repair. It was a seat of the Baillie family, who descend from the great house of Baliol, and thought to have been the birthplace of Alexander Baillie the famous antiquary. The castle was burned by a party of Highlanders during the Jacobite Rising of 1715. It passed later to the acquisitive family of Dundas, to be Earls and Marquises of Zetland.

The Roman Road had here an auxiliary fort, showing now only as some green mounds near the railway-line. Many of the Antonine forts had turf walls, but this was of stone, there being suitable out-cropping rock in the vicinity. In excavations, many Roman remains were found, coins, weapons, urns and so on. Also was found an altar, inscribed: *To the god Mercury, soldiers of the Sixth Legion, the Victorious, Faithful and Loyal citizens of Italy and Noricum [Austria], dedicated this shrine and image; and have performed their vows willingly, gladly and deservedly.* It is thought by some that this was the place Ptolemy called Coria Damniorum, and which Nennius called Caer Ceri—which sounds conveniently like Castlecary.

Denny and Dunipace. Nobody will claim that the Burgh of Denny and Dunipace is a scenic and architectural gem; but there is here more of interest than meets the eye, in one of those East Stirlingshire industrial townships that cluster round Falkirk. It is rather attractively sited on the Carron just below where the river emerges from its hill fastnesses, and, though Denny gives little appearance of a hill-town, only a couple of miles off summits rise to over a thousand feet and heathlands stretch in their scores of square miles. It is probably because the old drove-roads merged here, on their way from the cattle-strewn uplands to Falkirk's trysts, that Denny became established. Two of these drove-roads are still to be traced, south of the Carron; one by Tarduff Hill and Carron Bridge, the other by Castlerankine and The Doups.

If Denny itself was never a very important place, Dunipace made up for it. But not the present part of the burgh, so-called, which was in fact the Milton of Dunipace. The old *Kirkton* of Dunipace was on the other side of Denny altogether, 2 miles to the east, half-way to Larbert, where now there is only a mill, the site of the demolished mansion, and a disused and abandoned churchyard. These, and the famous 'Hills of Dunipace', spectacular green mounds by the side of the A.876 road, long assumed to be artificial but now asserted to be natural kames or eskers, glacial deposits moulded by the elements. Behind these strange knolls lies the ancient kirkyard, its church now gone—though its mort-house, or watch-house, to counter the activi-ties of the body-snatchers, remains. Amongst bushes and long grass lie many tombstones, some as old as the 1650s. But this site claims more than domestic interest, for here Wallace is said to have met Bruce the day after the grim Battle of Falkirk, and convinced him of his duty to Scotland—to which, admittedly, the future hero-king had not been consistently attached hitherto. If true, this little lost graveyard marks a turning-place in Scottish history.

Their mutual enemy, Edward I, certainly was here in October 1301, when he signed a warrant to treat with the King of France over the Scots alliance. Much later, in 1746, after the second Battle of Falkirk, the Laird of Dunipace, Primrose by name, was beheaded and his lands forfeited for showing Prince Charlie's Highlanders the way across a ford of Carron. Lady Primrose attempted thereafter to buy back the property, but the Edinburgh lawyer she patronised, Spottiswoode by name, looked after his own interests better than his client's, and in due course managed to obtain the estate for himself. His and his descendants' tombstone is still to be seen in the kirkyard.

Denny itself was part of Falkirk parish until 1601, and the Rector of Falkirk had a Vicar here. At the Reformation, as so often happened, the shrewd incumbent, by name Vicar Oswald, managed to hang on to the valuable church-lands—as did his descendants, until the last of the Oswalds in the 1820s. Temple Denny near by, as its name suggests, was a seat of the Knights Templar. It lies at the foot of the peculiar conical hill known as Myot, thought to be a corruption of the Pictish tribal MAEATAE, and on the top of which an ancient fort was sited.

Drymen and Buchanan. These are two very large parishes, of some 30,000 and 48,000 acres respectively, at the very western edge of Stirlingshire; yet between them today probably mustering a population of not much more than two thousand. Here, quite abruptly, commence the Highlands, the heather, the clan country. Yet Glasgow is only 18 miles away. This is the quite narrow watershed between Forth and Clyde, and the heart of the Graham country.

Drymen is the easternmost of the two, and its only real village lies at the very south-west corner of it; whereas Buchanan's hamlet, church and castle lie in the south-*east* corner of that huge parish. So that the two name-centres are only a mile or so apart; whereas their extremities lie 20 miles away.

Drymen village is pleasantly sited on rising foothills overlooking the windings of the Endrick Water as it nears the foot of Loch Lomond. It is quite small, though growing—but may well have been larger once, for here were held fairs for cattle, sheep and horses, also hiring fairs. In the clan days this would be an important outlet. But, as may be clear from the above, Drymen though 'capital' of its own parish, is rather dominated by the name of Buchanan, with the great and popular Buchanan Castle golf-course to the west, the well-known venue, the Buchanan Arms Hotel in the village itself and the Buchanan estate in one way or another providing much of the local employment.

The place clusters round a sloping green, with a row of houses on the west dating from about 1800, and a modernised 18th century inn at the north-east corner. The church, for 1771, is rather fussy, picked out now in black-and-white. It was, as usual, built on the site of an earlier edifice, which on sundry occasions served Rob Roy as a convenient collecting place for his 'mail' from the elaborate protection-racket. There are a number of old gravestones, one as early as 1618. Drymen features much in the Rob Roy saga. Here a force of unenthusiastic Glasgow volunteers were marched in 1713, with a price of £1000 on Rob's head—but when it came to the bit, preferred to run rather than collect the reward. An unkind ballad is sung of the event. Then we read that after the defeat of Sheriff-muir in 1716, Rob marched here with 100 MacGregors on his way home to Inversnaid, but only "Proclaimed the Pretender and tore the guager's books". Drymen was where the great Drummond family hailed from—the one name a corruption of the other; or, at least, both corruptions of the Gaelic *druim*, a ridge. They seem to have been closely related to the Celtic Earls of Lennox, holding the hereditary office of Law-Thane, or Crowner, of Lennox.

Due north of the village is a road the visitor might, but should not, miss. Older maps show it as petering out into a mere track fairly soon on its 7-mile way to Gartmore, across the moors, forest and hill; but it is in fact now a good passing-bay road all the way, on the line of an ancient drove-road which many a MacGregor herd must have taken. It gives most splendid views, south-westwards over Loch Lomond and the low lands, and north-eastwards along the Highland Line. Oddly enough much of this heather waste and lofty tableland rejoices in the name of the Muir Park. There is a loch, now a reservoir, at the roadside about half-way, and much attractive forest on the road thereto. Out on the open moors to the east, exactly on the 500-foot contour, is the lonely mid-18th century laird's house of Craigievairn, a Buchanan place.

South-east of Drymen, across the Endrick, rises another and different type of moorland area, 400 feet lower, and really the northern skirts of the Kilpatrick Hills. This is Cameron Muir, and dotted with small grazing farms. There have been settlements here for long, for there are traces of ancient enclosures and cultiva-tion, as well as a chambered cairn about one mile east-south-east of Wester Cameron farm, where in 1830 were found two stone coffins and human bones. Only a flat projecting boulder now shows. Another old drove-road crossed to Finnich Toll.

Buchanan estate was once enormous, over 100,000 acres; though much reduced, it is still extensive and a ducal domain, although the large 19th century castle is abandoned and roofless, and the rather lumpish remains of its predecessor, largely destroyed by fire in 1850, serves the golf club. This was built on the site of the original old House of Buchanan, seat of the chiefs of that Ilk, which they lost to the Grahams in 1682, when the 3rd Marquis and 1st Duke, Rob Roy's enemy, bought up the lands of the bankrupt Laird of Buchanan. The Montrose family are still here; and though the present Duke lives in Rhodesia, his son, the Marquis of Graham, resides at Auchmar, a modern house in a pleasant glen 2 miles to the north-west. The Buchanan community is a scattered one, ranging all the way from Drymen to Balmaha, and comprising Buchanan Smithy and hamlet, the larger Milton hamlet and school, nearly 2 miles on, and beyond that the kirk and manse, with Auchmar House a half-mile behind. All have something of a terraced setting, amidst woodland, above the Endrick levels, with prospects over the foot of Loch Lomond. The church is most

Loch Lomond. From head of loch looking south to Ben Lomond
and Inversnaid

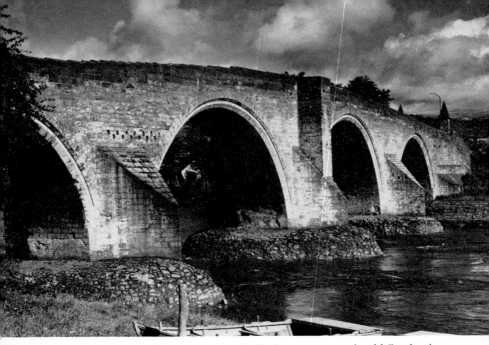

Stirling Bridge. The most strategically important spot in old Scotland

Stirling University, still in the process of construction. Abbey Craig and
Wallace Monument in background

pleasing, inside and out, set on a knoll and with an old graveyard around. Here are buried the later Dukes of Montrose—their predecessors being interred at old St. Kattans Church, Aberuthven, near the Graham castle of Kincardine. This present parish church was built about 1764 to succeed an earlier 17th century chapel which lay near Buchanan Castle, its site now lost in woodland. This in turn had succeeded the original parish kirk, which was on the island of Inchcailleach in Loch Lomond, of all places, 200 yards out from Balmaha—inconvenient place of worship as this must have been. Here a community of nuns once existed—hence the name, meaning island of the old or cowled women. The ruins of this still remain, with a very ancient graveyard containing some highly interesting stones, including one thought to mark the grave of St. Kentigerna herself, the founding Irish missionary saint who died in 733.

Falkirk. Falkirk could be described in a marked variety of ways. One of the boom towns of Scotland. A smoky, sprawling, unlovely place of factories, foundries and furnaces. A large burgh, the largest in Stirlingshire, of great antiquity but undistinguished appearance, that has gobbled up too many villages equally ancient. A hive of industry, initiative and modernisation, and a new city-in-the-making. A Roman military station and a traffic centre through the ages. One of the great historical epicentres of the kingdom. And one of the most attractively-sited towns in the land. All would be true—even though the last assertion might raise some eyebrows.

It is so, nevertheless, however unapparent it is apt to be from the lower approaches to the town, from either Edinburgh, Glasgow or the North. But go higher, go some hundreds of feet higher, even only to Falkirk High Station and its railway-line, and something of the splendour of the site, even yet, cannot be hidden. Here, where the narrowing Forth estuary makes a sudden bend northwards, and a great horseshoe of enclosing green escarpments to south and west enfolds the spreading plain, the winding River Carron finds its devious way to the sea; to the east the wooded ridge of Callendar, site of Wallace's battle, protects; to the north is a prospect of quite surpassing fairness—the heights and remnants of the great Tor Wood, once vying with Ettrick Forest as the most important in the Lowlands; then the rolling ridge-and-valley system to Bannockburn, with the noble grey citadel of Stirling Castle on its rock rearing like a leviathan beyond; and thereafter the almost theatrical backcloth of the Ochil Hills soaring abruptly from the carse in an unbroken wall a thousand feet high, with behind and beyond, to all infinity, the blue giants of the Highland Line, in endless proud array. Falkirk has it all—and not all the belching chimneys of the iron-works, the sprawling housing-schemes, the crouching coal-bings, the contorted fantasies and spouting flares of the refineries and cracking-plants, can do more than emphasise the magnificence of it all.

The pity that the town itself is less inspiring—for its story should

P

make it a magnet for visitors. Here the routes from south, east and west converge; from the Border by A.73, via Motherwell and Airdrie; from Edinburgh by A.9; from Glasgow by A.80. Stirling, and the gateway to the North is only 10 miles ahead. These routes are just the modern counterparts of age-old highways. Here even the Romans laid their road, alongside Antonine's Wall—indeed here it was given its good Scots name of Graham's Dyke. For on the site of the present impressive but stolid parish kirk was the ancient church, and when in 1811 the one was being demolished to build the other, a white marble slab was unearthed inscribed, in faulty Latin, FVNERATVS . HIC . DEZN . ROB . GRAHAM . ILLE . EVERSVS . VALL . SEVERVS . A.C. D.15 . FERGVSIVS 11 . R . SCO. This professes to commemorate the Thane Robert Graham, who first broke through the Roman Wall in this neighbourhood, in the reign of Fergus II (5th–6th century)—so seeming to solve the mystery of how the rampart got its local name, however accurate the tradition. The great Graham family had its headquarters at Dundaff, near Fintry— but whether as early as this is highly doubtful. A later member, Sir John de Graham, was one of the few nobles who truly supported Wallace. He fell heroically at the Battle of Falkirk and lies in the kirkyard here.

> Here lyes Sir Jhonn the Greme baith wight and wise,
> Ane of the chief rescuit Scotland thrise,
> An better knight not to the world was lent,
> Nor was gude Greme of trueth and hardiment. Anno 1298.

Also near by is a stone to the memory of Sir John Stewart of Bonkyl, brother of Bruce's friend the High Steward, who fell in the same bloody battle.

Oddly enough, the Romans, the Gaels and the Anglo-Saxons all accepted the same description for the church here, calling it the Church of the Mixed People—presumably a reference to the mixed Highland–Lowland population. The Latin name was *Varia Capella*; the Celtic, *Eaglais-breac*, or Ecclesbreck, meaning speckled; the Anglo-Saxon *fah-circe*, or Faw-kirk, variously coloured.

Unfortunately, there are now no buildings in the town of any architectural merit erected before the last quarter of the 18th century. Yet it was formerly a walled town. An item in the Court Book of 1647 reads: "It is statute and ordanit that ilk quarter of the toune of falkirk come forthe dey aboute for building of ane dyk about the said burgh for keipeing forthe of streingeris sua that nane mey enter bot at the ports thairof Viz. the eist and west portis kirkwynd pantaskenes wynde and kow wynde." This latter was the route by which the burgesses' cattle were daily led out to pasture on the common lands of South Muir. Cow Wynd and Kirk Wynd still remain as street names.

The Town Steeple is prominent, erected only in 1813 to replace an earlier tolbooth, narrowing the High Street in the old familiar mid-row style. Of classical rather than traditional architecture, it rears 140 feet high, with a tiny, narrow lane at its side nicely named Wooers' Street, and an old well at its foot.

Falkirk was a great place for wells, holy and otherwise. Some are still to be traced. There was Cross Well, as above; the Minister's Well, in the old Glebe; Marion's Well, named after one of the Callendar family who turned nun; Christ's Well, and others. The last speaks loud of the bigotry and intoleration of the post-Reformation period. It had long been reckoned to have curative properties, like many another. But by 1628 this was anathema. So the Kirk Session ordained: ". . . if any person be found superstitiously and idolatrously, after this, to have passed in pilgrimage to Christ's Well, on Sundays of May, to seek their health, they shall repent in *sacco* and linen three several Sabbaths and pay twenty lib., *toties quoties*, for ilk fault." And if the shameless health-seekers could not pay, they were to be clapped in jail and fed on bread and water for eight days. That would teach them Christian behaviour!

There is even a Pretender's Well, but this is at some distance, up at the side of the old drove-road that led towards Bonnybridge, a mossy basin in woodland. It harks back, of course, to the second Battle of Falkirk, fought up here on the high ground of South Bantaskine, amidst gale and sleet, on January 17th, 1746, three months before fatal Culloden—but which the Jacobites won nevertheless, even after weary weeks of retreat from Derby. The area of the battlefield is partly built up now, but part remains within the policies of Bantaskine House, which still remain even though the mansion is demolished, only the walled garden and the rather attractive 18th century doocote surviving, but precariously. Prince Charles Edward spend the night before the battle here. A little to the west stands a monument, erected in 1927, commemorating the battle. From it a little path leads down by a burnside to where a great many of the victims were buried. A local tradition sheds a significant light on conditions and attitudes, rather at odds with the accepted romantic pattern. This large pit was dug to receive not only the dead but the dying, apparently. For as the Highlanders were dragging thereto one of their number, a MacDonald from Skye, they got him as far as the edge when he made protest, pleading for a little longer of this life, ill as it was. "Och, just gang in wi' quiet," he was advised by his companions, "for the Prince may be angry."

Falkirk is today seeking to make up for its lack of inspiring architecture, and the new town hall and municipal buildings are a vast pile of glass and concrete, islanded amidst green lawns and gardens, airy, spacious and spectacular after their own fashion—certainly a sufficient contrast to the cramped grey huddle of so much around them. The nearby Dollar Park, the Arnotdale mansion and grounds gifted by a native of the burgh who made his fortune in America, makes an extensive and attractive lung for the town. On the other, eastern side, the great estate of Callendar Park, seat for so long of the

Livingstones, Earls of Callendar and Linlithgow who for centuries dominated Falkirk, now provides a major asset for the burgh. Although the great house stands empty and threatened, its undulating parklands, though still intact, indeed cattle-dotted, are now at least partly the demesne of the people. For here, amongst well-kept lawns and ancient trees, well-spaced, rise the multi-storey high flats, over a dozen soaring monsters to look down on the cawing rooks and the verdant pastures. They may not please all, but given the need, they are magnificently sited and their views quite superb. And still farther to the east, in the Park, is one of the most attractively-placed Colleges of Education that could be imagined, a pleasant complex of red cedar and glass in mellow woodland behind a stretch of Antonine's Wall. None can deny that Falkirk has here seized its opportunity with both hands. It makes an extraordinary contrast to the nearby narrow crowded streets and traffic nightmare.

The Livingstones gained Callendar in the 14th century by marrying the heiress of the de Callentyrs, and retained the estate until James, 5th Earl of Linlithgow and 4th Earl of Callendar was forfeited for his share in the Jacobite Rising of 1715. The notorious York Buildings Company took the entire property, including most of the burgh of Falkirk. But the 'bairns' as the Falkirk folk have been known for centuries, refused to pay their rents to absentee Londoners, and in the end it was found more profitable to lease back the estates to the Countess of Kilmarnock, the Livingstones' heiress, and her husband. However, he also was a Jacobite, and in Charles Edward's Rising of 1745 he was captured and beheaded. Incidentally, it was with his widow, the Countess, that General Hawley was dining, at Callendar, when the Prince's Highlanders attacked the Hanoverians on that January 17th, routing them and seriously embarrassing the General. Lady Kilmarnock, no doubt, permitted herself a smile. The York Buildings Company in due course failed—after making ill-gotten fortunes for many in high places—and William Forbes, a London merchant descended from the Forbeses of Colquhany in Aberdeenshire, a coppersmith who had amassed an enormous fortune from copper-bottoming the keels of the entire British Navy as well as the East India Company's fleet, bought Callendar for £85,000, not much more than half the value of the timber growing on it. This was in 1783. The Forbes family are still the owners of the estate. Mary Queen of Scots stayed here when attending the christening of a child of the Earl of Linlithgow. Cromwell captured it, when it was a castellated house. General Monk made it his headquarters when he ruled Scotland for his master. Charles Edward slept here on his way south to Derby.

Falkirk was famous for more than battles. The noted Falkirk Trysts were the largest cattle sales in all the United Kingdom—so that the present traffic chaos can be no new development. The trysts were originally held on Redding Ridge, to the south-east of the town; then as numbers increased they were moved to the vicinity of Rough Castle, the former Roman fort near Bonnybridge; and finally to Stenhousemuir. The vastness of these sales is scarcely to be comprehended in today's conditions. As many as 60,000 head of cattle and 100,000 of sheep are said to have changed hands in a single day. The buyers were mainly large English dealers. One, by name McTurk—he does not sound over-Anglicised—whose credit was good with the Highland sellers, is reported to have bought as many as 70 score of cattle without so much as dismounting from his pony. In contemplating these extraordinary numbers, it must be remembered that the beasts were the product of the Highland glens in the days when those glens were teeming with folk. The entire clan economy was built on cattle, and since winter feed was scarce, astronomical numbers had to be disposed of each autumn, not only to Falkirk but to other trysts such as Crieff and Aberdeen. It is salutary to consider how many millions of beasts that vast empty area could rear today, with improved methods of aerial seeding, liming and fodder-dropping (as the Canadian Government does for its caribou herds of the North-West) and means of transport and marketing. But it would require government, and enthusiastic government, participation. Perhaps, one day . . .

At any rate, Falkirk at tryst time must have been an inspiriting, not to say a hectic, place, with thousands of Highland drovers in town with money to burn, not to mention the south-country dealers and all the hangers-on. The dogs alone must have been a major problem, to say nothing of rampaging cattle.

It was not cattle, however, any more than battles and history, on which Falkirk's modern prosperity was based, but heavy industry. And that not so modern either. It all started not long after Prince Charlie's visits indeed, with the setting up of the famous Carron Company in 1759. I have indicated that Falkirk swallowed up many villages. Carron was the first of them. Yet it so almost was not. It is strange to think that only a short-sighted meanness on the part of Tranent coal-owners made the Carron Company, and so made Falkirk the iron-founding and light-castings centre of Scotland. It might so easily have been the Cockenzie Company, and East Lothian the industrial boom area. For William Cadell, Laird of Cockenzie, it was who conceived the idea of developing this industry, and with the aid of Dr. John Roebuck, a Birmingham medico with a taste for industrial chemistry, perfected the method of smelting iron by using coke from pit coal. There was plenty of coal being mined near Cockenzie, and a source of ironstone locally, at Jovey's Neuk near Gullane, and elsewhere; also a good harbour for the import of ore from Sweden and export of iron goods. But the Tranent coal-owners would not reduce their prices to Cadell to an economic rate for the process. A fellow-laird, however, James Bruce of Kinnaird, the renowned Abyssinian traveller and man of vision, owned the coalfield 30 miles farther up the Forth, near Falkirk. He gave Cadell the coal at the price he wanted, thereby making both their fortunes. And his kinsman, Bruce of Stenhouse, provided the land and necessary water, reasonably near the port of

Grangemouth. Moreover, Falkirk was an excellent road centre for all Scotland. So Carron it was, and the iron was cast. The blast furnaces rose and the proliferating chimney-stacks.

After some early financial difficulties, when Joseph Stainton stepped in to the rescue, the company prospered mightily. The Napoleonic Wars were a great help, with demands for guns and other munitions. The famous light cannon at Waterloo, known as carronades, were manufactured here; and Major Henry Shrapnel experimented at Carron on the type of shell bearing his name. But it was baths and stoves, grates and pipes, and the hetero-geneous ironware of the burgeoning Industrial Revolution period that really made a household word of Carron. And not only Carron, for other foundries and ironworks began to spring up on all sides. Falkirk had stepped with vast strides into the new age, amid the smoke and glare of its furnaces. Not all approved, of course, and with reason. Even Robert Burns has this to say when, making a trip to see the great works, he was refused admission by the gate-porter;

> We cam na here to view your warks
> In hopes to be mair wise,
> But only, lest we gang to hell,
> It may be nae surprise.

> But when we tirl'd at your door,
> Your porter dought na hear us;
> Sae may when we to hell's yett come,
> Your billy Satan sairve us!

The Carron Company still marches on, employing its thousands, and supplying the insatiable demand for cast-iron goods for modern housing, a great firm with a great reputation. Unfortunately, considering its own traditions and comparative antiquity, it saw fit fairly recently to demolish the fine early 17th century castellated mansion of Stenhouse, which had more or less fathered it, after owning it for years and letting it fall into disrepair—surely a grave lapse of both taste and vision. A housing scheme now covers the site, of which this fortalice could have made a splendid centre-piece. Perhaps this was poetic justice, as far as the Bruces were concerned, for Sir Michael of Stenhouse in 1743 demolished the famous Arthur's O'on which stood close by. This most remarkable monument of antiquity he pulled down to provide masonry to repair the dam-head of the ironworks reservoir. A beehive-shaped structure of well-cut, unmortared stones, 22 feet high and 28 feet in diameter, having a perfect dome with an aperture at the apex, it was probably a Roman chapel in which ensigns were kept, and its name a Celtic corruption—although other origins have been ascribed. Its destruction, even in 1743, produced loud protest.

It is not every industrial company which has its own burial

ground. Carron has, in the old parish kirkyard of Larbert about two miles to the west, another of the Falkirk area villages. Here are buried, under memorials of varying magnificence, William Cadell and others of his family; Joseph Stainton; and a number of early managers of the company called Dawson, a clear indication of the role played by this industrial empire. There are less splendid but perhaps even more notable graves here. James Bruce of Kinnaird himself, the great 18th century traveller, discoverer of the source of the Blue Nile, who after braving the dangers of unexplored Africa, died here in 1794 by falling down his own stairs at Kinnaird. His memorial is an extraordinary iron monument, rusting and flaking amongst thick weeds—could it have been the Carron Company which cast this tinny obelisk for him? Also here is buried his predecessor in the lairdship by six generations, the Reverend Robert Bruce of Kinnaird (1559–1631), laird and pastor in one, and a noted reforming divine, whom James VI declared to be worth half a kingdom—but whom he later imprisoned and banished, nevertheless. Another ancient heraldic tombstone, dated 1645, commemorates various members of the noble Elphinstone family, linked with that of the Earls of Linlithgow.

Larbert, although attractively sited on the steep banks of the River Carron, is hardly a beautiful place. It has but one fine building remaining, the Old Manse, dating from 1635, and delightfully restored. Larbert was a place for mills, by the riverside—even a snuff-mill—one surviving intact on the Camelon road, and traces of others elsewhere. Near by are the sites of a Roman camp and a Roman fort, now separated by a railway embankment, the former in fields, the latter now in a golf-course. These two establishments are unusual in that they are situated about a mile and a half *north* of the Antonine Wall on a detached spur-road.

Between Larbert and Carron lies Stenhousemuir, originally called Sheeplees, another township lacking in obvious charm, although its modern shopping centre and new housing is a great improvement on what preceded it. This was the scene of the famous cattle trysts, and a north-going avenue from the main street is still called Tryst Road. The vast sale-ground area is now another golf-course, and therefore fortunately still open land. Reports that the sale-yard covered 50 acres, enormous as that is, make one wonder whether it could have been adequate, in view of the numbers of cattle. The estate of Kinnaird lies in trees a mile or so to the north-east, and though the Bruces are gone, one of their heraldic panels remains in the east wall of the very fine walled garden, dated 1602. Larbert House, to the west, is now part of a vast institution for the mentally handicapped.

Midway between the centre of Falkirk and Larbert, lies Camelon of the lovely name but less lovely aspect, with its iron foundries and tar-distillery. Once it was a Roman station, and then a Pictish city apparently of some importance. In 839, however, Kenneth MacAlpine destroyed it utterly, wiping out man, woman and child, in his process of 'uniting' the Picts and Scots to form the basis of the Scotland we know. The story is told that here was kept the secret of brewing the famous heather-ale, the excellence of which was renowned in the ancient world. Amongst other things, King Kenneth wanted this secret. Only two of all Camelon's inhabitants were spared—a father and son, guardians of the cherished recipe. The father declared that they should kill his son, so that he did not look upon his sire's shame; and when the deed was done, assured the balked monarch that no amount of torture and prolonged dying would wring the secret out of *him*. And so the Pictish heather-ale died with him. A stretch of the Antonine Wall to the south of Camelon is the finest remaining sector, its ditch and rampart grass-grown but clear for all to see. A delightful complex of modern housing has recently been erected at the Falkirk end of the main street—hopeful augury.

Other villages engulfed by modern Falkirk include Grahamston, Bainsford, Carronshore, Glen, etc. Undoubtedly they all have their attractions and stories, this land being what it is. Bainsford, for instance, used to be Brainsford, and allegedly commemorated an English knight, Sir Brian le Jay who was slain at the Battle of Falkirk when his horse got bogged down in the burnside mud here. And near Carronshore stands the gaunt remains of an early 17th century tower-house called Skaithmuir, belonging to the Elphinstone family, direly ravaged and shorn of its features for industrial purposes, but still bearing an inscribed window-lintel dated 1607. Flanking this are the initials of Alexander, 4th Lord Elphinstone and his wife. These scorned initials relate to a man who rose to be Lord High Treasurer of Scotland and was appointed by the Scottish Parliament to treat for an early, and abortive, union with England in 1604. Scratch the surface of Scotland almost anywhere, and the drama lies revealed.

Fallin, Throsk and South Alloa. Some places, by their siting or natural and other resources, retain an importance right down the centuries; others rise and fall. The group here dealt with, Fallin, Throsk and South Alloa, set in the carselands of the winding Forth south-east of Stirling, offer an example of the latter fate. Fallin and Throsk were not considered to be worth separate mention in gazetteers of the late 19th century; while South Alloa features with something of a flourish. Today, the last has sunk almost without trace, while the former are sizeable communities.

Fallin lies on the A.905, in the flat lands 3 miles from Stirling and about five miles north-west of Airth. It owes its rise to coal-mining; and though this industry has faded, as is now so frequently the case, Fallin nevertheless continues to spread, with a great expansion of local-authority housing. For, with road transport what it now is, this area is not inconveniently distant from booming Falkirk and Grangemouth, as well as Stirling. It is not a beautiful place, but has greatly improved in appearance for all that, since the days of grim miners' rows and unsightly pitheads. From the road, the windings of Forth are not obvious; yet the great river flows close by —indeed, there was a small harbour here once. This is on the southern edge of the area where the Battle of Bannockburn was fought in 1314, when the vast English army was penned into these then marshlands and suffered terrible slaughter.

About a mile to the north lies the interesting but insufficiently appreciated fortified laird's house of Steuarthall, formerly called Wester Polmaise. Its position would be very strong, before the land was drained. It consists of a tall square and whitewashed tower with a semicircular stair-turret, dating probably from the early 17th century, and a more commodious and lower wing to the east. There is a heraldic panel with the motto *GANG FORWARD*, and the initials A.S. and A.H., referring to Sir Alexander Stirling and his Hamilton wife. He was of the Garden family, a 17th century judge. Here is thought to have been detained the unfortunate Lady Grange, by her husband—another judge—before her enforced captivity and death in the Hebrides, in 1732.

Throsk, a mile east of Fallin, with its modern housing and guarded gates, has grown up because of the siting of a services ordnance depot here. It also possessed a little harbour on the Forth, and a railway-bridge spanned the river. Nearly another mile to the east, at the road junction, is the interesting farmhouse of Kersie Mains, formerly a laird's house of the 17th century, with possibly an earlier nucleus. It appears as a mansion with park in Pont's map of 1654. It is an L-shaped building with a square stair-tower, its formal south-facing front in marked contrast to its more ancient-seeming rear. It is thought to have been built by the Monteith family, who also once owned the lands of Kerse, at Grangemouth.

Here is the little dead-end road to South Alloa, or Alloa Ferry, just across the Forth from that thriving Clackmannanshire town. This was a place which seemed destined for vigorous life and development, and has instead almost faded away. It was important enough to give its name to a branch railway—the South Alloa branch of the Scottish Central, of which it was the terminus. From here a steam ferry plied to Alloa. An ambitious project was authorised here, by special Act of Parliament in 1873, for a £300,000 development, in £10 shares, to construct a dock, with entrance lock 136 yards long, a large harbour with quays, jetties, warehouses and so on. Alas, all collapsed before erection. As did the proposal to bridge the river here, another Act authorising the spending of £60,000 on the project. The railway bridge eventually built, in 1883, is at Throsk 1½ miles up.

Just opposite South Alloa is a great river island, known as Alloa Inch, on which is even a farm of 80 acres.

Fintry. There are four Fintrys in Scotland—although the village in Aberdeenshire spells its name Fintray. The area of Fintry just north of Dundee takes its name from this Stirlingshire district, because it was another property of the same Graham family—whence came Graham of Claverhouse, Bonnie Dundee. The fourth Fintry is the one which the name seems to suit, *fionn traigh*, a small bay of white sand on Big Cumbrae island in the Clyde.

We are concerned here with the highly attractive valley, and hills, in West Stirlingshire, with its village and parish. The hills are a green, grassy sub-range of the Lennox Hills, lying to the north of the Campsie Fells and reaching their highest point at Stronend (1677 feet.) Their summit area is rounded and very much a plateau; but there is a notable rocky escarpment ringing much of this, at around the 1300-foot contour. The Water of Endrick circles the range to east and south, and it is its valley which gives Fintry parish its distinctively picturesque character.

The river, once called the Anderwick, makes a sharp bend westwards about three miles from its source, within a hundred or two yards of the great Carron Valley Reservoir; and soon thereafter plunges over a steep lip, to form the magnificent 94-foot-high waterfall known as the Loup of Fintry. This, being in a deep ravine, is not visible from the road—although its roar can be heard, for it is only 200 yards distant. It is well worth visiting. The views from here, down the valley, are fine. Also hidden from the same B.818 road, on the north side, is Loch Walton, a pleasantly secluded troutful water, with islets.

The road descends the valley much more steeply than on the Carron side, passing the site of an ancient Graham castle near Spittalhill, half-way down—which name indicates some former hospice or shelter, also. The sharply-climbing Crow Road, B.822, turns off southwards at Gonachan, near here, at first in the Gonachan Glen, to cross the watershed of the Campsie Fells, rising to 1154 feet near the source of the Carron, before descending steeply to Campsie village. Splendid vistas of the Clyde basin are to be had from this road.

Half a mile farther down the Endrick, the road reaches the Clachan of Fintry, the older part of the village. High on the north, crowning a rocky knoll, is the dun of Craigton; and to the south of the village, and much higher, soars Dunmore, with another fort on top. Fintry, it seems, was well protected in prehistoric times. At the Clachan, the inn of that name is ancient, but now a modern hotel. The church is an unambitious structure built in 1823, but on the site of an older building; for the parish church is recorded here as early as 1207, dedicated to St. Modan; and there are pre-Reformation gravestones in the kirkyard, one of which bears the outline of a knightly sword. The bell, still in the tower, is dated 1626, and was made by a Glasgow hammerman named W. Maine. In a detached house to the east lived the famous Tom Johnston, Labour leader and probably Scotland's finest Secretary of State. Not far from the Clachan Inn is a Youth Hostel.

The other part of the village, Newton of Fintry, lies almost half a mile to the west, and has its own interest, having been founded by a forward-looking cotton-manufacturer named Peter Spiers of Culcreuch in 1794 as a sort of model village for the workers. Certain of their cottages remain. The mill did not prove successful, however, and was eventually abandoned, although its mill-lade is still discernible. To the north almost a mile, stands in a large estate Culcreuch mansion itself, a fine fortalice of the late 15th century, oblong, thick-walled and parapeted, to which has been added a tall gabled wing of the 18th century. Culcreuch was a property of the Galbraith family, descended from the Celtic Earls of Lennox. It was taken and held by the Commonwealth forces during the Civil War. In 1632 it was sold to the second son of the famous John Napier of Merchiston, inventor of logarithms. In the late 18th century Culcreuch was acquired by the aforementioned Peter Spiers, of the Elderslie family.

The Endrick's valley widens out noticeably, west of Fintry, until it is a mile across. The road forks at Newton, the B.822 swinging north to rise below the shoulder of Stronend and over the Kippen Muir, to the Carse of Forth and Flanders Moss area; the B.818 to continue westwards to join the A.875 near Killearn, passing on the way modern Ballikinrain Castle, now a Church of Scotland Residential School. Old Ballikinrain, across the road and near the river, is an 18th century mansion of two periods, with a good and typical façade. An old draw-bar, with slot in the walling, still features at the entrance, relic of the fortified era. This was another Napier property, from the 15th century, until sold in 1862.

Flanders Moss. Geography sometimes combines with history, and even with national character, to make a place significant on a major scale. Names like Stirling Bridge, the Tor Wood, Ettrick Forest and the Pass of Killiecrankie spring to mind. Such a place is the Flanders Moss. It is a strange area still, although now only a fraction of the size once it was; and, because of what it has meant to Scotland, should be a lot better known than it is.

It is difficult to delimit the Flanders Moss, in the Carse of Forth. Today it is normally taken to be the extreme western end of the latter; but even so it is in two portions, one south-east of the Lake of Menteith, the other south-west, with a 2-mile-wide island of firmer ground, at Cardross, dividing them. And even this is not very clear, because the northern portion of the western part has a separate identity as the Gartrenich Moss; also the eastern section has sundry sub-sections, such as the Poldar Moss, the Carse of Boquhapple and the Blairdrummond, Ochtertyre and Drip Mosses. It would, therefore, be very hard to state where one begins and another ends. For convenience, then, and because it is historically sensible, we may consider the entire vast tract of the flood-plain of the upper Forth, from where it issues out of its hills at Aberfoyle almost to Stirling itself, as the Flanders Moss; the damp green heart of the Carse of Forth, 3 to 4 miles wide by about fourteen miles long—say, 50 square miles of level marshland through which the Forth and its tributaries, great and small, coil and meander under the sternly watchful regard of the great brown mountains of the Highland Line—that prospect which the late Sir D. Y. Cameron loved so much to paint, and so magnificently captured.

A large part of all this has been drained and reclaimed, of course. Much of it is now rich arable, especially the eastern portions, where the activities of the Moss Lairds, as they were called, in skimming off the top peat and floating it down the Forth to the sea, in the early 19th century, did so much to bring worth and wealth out of wilderness. But much remains wild, empty, remote, a place of vast vistas, seeping, spilling, spreading waters, rustling reeds, the sigh of winds and the cries of birds—perhaps twenty squares miles of it.

Two long straight roads flank this great green barrier—for that is what it is—to north and south, the A.84 and A.811 respectively, from Stirling, fine level highways for motorists to speed along with but little appreciation of what stretches on their low-lying sides. Four small side-roads even venture to cross parts of the Moss—but these are by no means straight. Strangely enough, it is not from these crossing roads that any true aspect of the Flanders Moss is to be gained; they lie too low amongst it all. But up on the higher ground on either side, or from the A.81, Glasgow–Aberfoyle road, which joins the other two at the western end—here it is worth while to pause and look and consider.

For, apart from the wide and stirring prospects themselves, you see something that has strongly moulded history. Here, in the very narrow, waist of Scotland, is a natural feature of profound importance. You could call it a moat—the moat of half of Scotland. Even modern drainage can do little with much of it; and in the past it represented an almost impassable barrier—save for the utterly desperate, the notably light-of-foot and the MacGregors, who knew the secrets of its hidden tracks, reaches and islands, and made good use of that knowledge, part of the reason for Rob Roy's phenomenal success. For this 4-mile-wide barrier stretched all the way across the land from the roadless mountains of the Ben Lomond group right to Stirling—where the river itself became too wide to bridge. Hence the vital significance of Stirling Bridge—and why most of the great battles of Scotland were fought thereabouts. The Flanders Moss and the Firth of Forth between them cut Scotland in two.

From earliest times this had its great impact. The Romans came here, and were held up. There are two conflicting stories. One, that they were in fact responsible for the flooding desolation of it, by Severus's army cutting down the great forest here and so playing havoc with the natural drainage; and the other, that they found the Moss already there, and sought to build a causeway across it, unsuccessfully, parts of which Rob Roy used to make use of, though under a foot or so of mud and water, for driving his purloined herds of Lowland cattle across to the security of his Highland fastnesses. Be that as it may, the Moss continued to represent a hopeless obstacle, not only for travellers and drovers but for military commanders; and so was partly responsible for the prolonged maintenance of the clan system in the North, and the very delayed opening up of the Central Highlands. As late as 1715, before the Battle of Sheriffmuir, Rob Roy offered to lead part of the Jacobite army across the mosses, by secret ways known to him, in the Frew area, and so to outflank the Duke of Argyll, commander-in-chief of the government forces based on Stirling—a move which could have altered the course of history, for Argyll was in two minds as to his allegiance, and was being abused and ill-supported by London. However, 'Bobbing John', Earl of Mar, in typically vacillating fashion, failed to make use of the MacGregor's specialised knowledge, and Sheriffmuir was fought and lost—and with it the Stewart cause.

Frew. This is not a name which bulks large on the Scots scene—though, strangely enough, it is not so very uncommon as a surname, there being, for instance, no fewer than twenty-six such entries in the Edinburgh telephone directory. Undoubtedly many even knowledgeable Scots have never heard of it as a place-name. Yet it has meant much down the centuries, and could, at least once, have been a turning-point in Scots history. Frew is an area, not a single place, lying athwart the River Forth about eight miles west of Stirling, and 2½ miles south of Thornhill. In other words, it is in the watery middle of what was formerly the eastern, Blairdrummond, section of the great Flanders Moss. It is quite a large area, for East Frew and West Frew, both farms, are 2 miles apart; but it is no centre of population, even now. The important feature, of old, lay between these two—the Fords of Frew. A bridge now carries the B.822 over the Forth near by; but this is a modern development, possible only because the Moss here has been drained. Until this was done, the only feasible, and far from easy, crossing of the river west of Stirling was by the hollow road over the marshes and through the Fords of Frew.

The river is wide and powerful, and looks even today when disciplined and controlled, impossible to ford. But just west of Fordhead Farm, east of the present bridge, an old track leads down a fairly steep bank, to enter the water. Its exit to the north appears to have been about eighty yards downstream; and it would be a brave man, mounted or otherwise, who ventured to cross here now. Indeed, always this crossing must have been risky, and very frequently, when the river was running high, quite impossible.

Yet it was known by some, and used to significant advantage by those prepared to take the risk. The great Montrose used it in 1645, unexpectedly to bring his army south, to win the Battle of Kilsyth. Rob Roy knew it better than any, and used it frequently to bring his cattle herds back to Inversnaid and Glen Gyle from the fat lowlands. Indeed, he is alleged to have fought a small battle here with dragoons from Cardross, as he drove his purloined beasts north from the Her'ship of Kippen in 1691—and won triumphantly. And it was here that he made his brilliant escape from the soldiers—commanded, oddly enough, by Montrose's descendant, now a Duke—celebrated in Scott's novel *Rob Roy*. Most famed of all, here he proposed to the Earl of Mar, in the Rising of 1715, that he should lead part of the Jacobite army across, to get behind and outflank the Duke of Argyll and the Government forces holding Stirling Bridge—a manoeuvre which could have altered the whole course of history, for Argyll was very weakly supported and is thought to have been ready to switch sides. But 'Bobbing John', as Mar was nicknamed, hesitated as he was ever apt to do, and did not support Rob—which was why the MacGregors were late for the Battle of Sheriffmuir next day, and the subsequent disaster.

In the later Rising of 1745, Prince Charles, having Gregor MacGregor of Glengyle, Rob's nephew, amongst his officers, did use the Ford of Frew on his march south, when Stirling Bridge had been breached against him by the Government troops.

The Forth hereabouts is at its most contorted, winding about amongst the levels in fantastic coils; indeed, just a little east of the ford, it swings away north-westwards for half a mile. The floodplain is further cut up here by the inflowing of the quite large Goodie Water, issuing from the Lake of Menteith. In former times this created its own marshy lake, called Goodie Loch, in the midst of the already waterlogged Moss. Small wonder that the Carse of Forth was a nightmare for conventional military commanders, from Roman times onwards. Today, drained, the rich farmlands spread. But still the water is there, if tamed, underlying all, and the wildfowl haunt the network of ditches, while the wild geese skeins flight at dusk and dawn.

Gargunnock. This is probably the most attractive of the string of villages which dot the northern foothills of the Touch, Gargunnock and Fintry range, along the south flanks of the Flanders Moss area. Like Kippen, it lies on the line of the old drove road, back from the fast A.811, Stirling–Dumbarton, highway, about half a mile to the south, and 6 miles west of Stirling itself. The village climbs up a spine of high ground above the carse; and being so comparatively near to the town, it is becoming a favoured residential area. Nevertheless it has not lost its traditional character and charm. Although it seems to crouch under the hills to the south—indeed, the highest point in the Touch–Gargunnock Hills, Carleatheran (1593 feet) is not much more than two miles behind—its outlook to the north, across the wide Carse of Forth to the Highland hills, gives space and a splendid prospect.

The village preserves a fair number of late 18th century houses, most of them climbing steeply up the street. The modern housing is not obtrusive. The church is very interesting and attractive, standing rather apart from the rest, on rising ground east of the main village, above the Gargunnock Burn. It was built in 1774, on the site of an older edifice, and is a sturdy place, with three crow-stepped gables and a gabled belfry and weather-vane. It has three outside stone stairways, which lead up to three separate galleries, or lofts—very individual access, presumably for lairds who had little desire for association. The old bell is preserved in the manse garden, and was made by John Meikle, of Edinburgh, in 1702. The manse itself dates from 1750, but has been added to and remodelled.

Gargunnock House lies, in its estate, half a mile to the east. It is a 'two-faced' mansion, showing quite a handsome classical south front, of 1794, pedimented, with a balustraded parapet, and whitewashed. But buried within the building, though open to the east, is an L-shaped tower-house of the late 16th century, typical with angle-turret, crowstepped gables and vaulted basements. In the 17th century another wing was added to the south-west, and this now forms part of the south façade, though it is not obvious. There was much further enlargement in the 18th century. This was early a posses-sion of the Setons of nearby Touch, later passing through many hands until Charles Stirling bought it in 1835. It remains with his descendants.

To the west of Gargunnock lies the ancient estate of Leckie, its large mansion of 1836 now an eventide home called Watson House. The estate itself is still private, belonging to Viscount Younger. But the original fortalice of Old Leckie still stands within the grounds, at present unused. It is a very fine T-shaped tower-house of the late 16th century, forming an interesting, unusual and picturesque composition. Restored, it would still make a delightful residence of character. Leckies of that Ilk held these lands from the mid-14th century. But they lost them for a while, taking the wrong side in the struggle between James I and Albany. However, John Leckie, a descendant, managed to buy back the property in 1535, and it remained with the family until David Moir, a Stirling bailie acquired it in 1659, his descendants retaining possession until recent times. The Leckies seem to have been a turbulent lot, and there is a tradition of a fierce battle between them and the Grahams fought at the western end of the parish. Three hundred yards south of Old Leckie, two bridges cross the Leckie Burn, which comes down from little Loch Logan. These formerly carried the ancient drove-road, which kept to the higher ground before drainage allowed the present roadway. The farthest away is the oldest, single-arched and less than seven feet wide, with an incised panel declaring in Latin that it was built in 1673 out of benevolence and for the sake of safety. Its successor is wider, and dates from the 18th century.

The chronicler Blind Harry made Gargunnock famous by de-scribing how William Wallace assailed and captured Gargunnock Peel, held by the English. It was situated about half a mile north-east of the village, and described as containing "within a dyk, bathe closs, chawmer and hall". No trace of this remains, unfortunately. After dealing with Gargunnock, the patriot hero proceeded, presumably by the Fords of Frew, northwards to Blackford in

Strathallan, where he met a party of English whom he slew and threw into the Allan.

Grangemouth. That Grangemouth has become Scotland's fastest-growing boom-town—as distinct from the planned new towns such as East Kilbride, Cumbernauld and so on—is not really surprising. A knowledgeable glance at any medium-scale map will reveal why. The central waist of Scotland, where the great firths of Forth and Clyde strike inland to within 30 miles of each other, coincides with the area of greatest industrial concentration and potential. And Grangemouth, where the River Carron enters the Forth, is at the highest point on the east of Scotland where ocean-going ships may reach, 50 miles inland from the North Sea. On the opposite, west, side, the mountains come down close to the Clyde, allowing no room for great and spreading development, farther to the Glasgow area. So here, on the wide carselands and levels of the Forth, but as far west as is Lanark, was not only the obvious entry and exit port for Central Scotland but the vicinity for extensive development for any industries which demanded space, sheer acreage and good transport facilities. When oil, and all its by-products, became quite suddenly vital in the modern economy, after the Second World War, Grangemouth as suddenly began to blossom phenomenally. Today it is an extraordinary sight, by day and by night, an almost nightmarish, yet stirring, conglomeration of docks, oil installations, storage-tanks, refineries, pumping-installations, cracking-plants, factories, laboratories and the like, linked together by untold miles of contorted piping, out of which, rear the vast steaming cooling-towers, the flaming gas-chimneys, the soaring cranes, derricks and masts, in their scores and hundreds. It spreads over an ever-greater area of the plain of Forth—yet all set against the splendid green-and-blue background of the shadow-slashed Ochil Hills, the towering flourish of Stirling Castle's rock, and the distant magnificence of the Highland Line—not to mention the seaward vistas of the Forth estuary itself. Surely, few vast industrial complexes can have so fair and resounding a setting—for here is the very heartland of Scotland's story, with Stirling itself only a dozen miles away. It is strange that out of the district which has produced so much of the drama of this land, now comes the proliferating, unpronounceable and polysyllabic progeny of modern science married to petroleum—polyvinylchloride, polystrene, polypropylene and all the other plastics, synthetic fibres, detergents, solvents and the like, on which our age relies—complementary to the flood of household metal products, the steel sinks, cookers, refrigerators, washing-machines and similar items spilling from the nearby Carron Ironworks and the innumerable light-castings establishments of the Falkirk area.

It was, of course, the same Carron Works, and their imitators and competitors, which gave birth to Grangemouth in the first place. For though this is not a 'new town' within the meaning of the Act,

Stirling Castle, from the south-west. The grass-grown banks are the
remains of King's Knot, famed royal garden

Stirling. A corner of the restored Old Town

as it were, it is new enough as towns go in Scotland, most of whose communities date from time immemorial. Indeed, it was not erected into a police burgh until 1872. Grangemouth is a monument to private enterprise—very private. Some would suggest wickedly so, perhaps. For it was all founded by one man, Sir Lawrence Dundas, in 1777. He was the local landowner—but only newly so—and he gave his name to the nearby village of Laurieston. Shrewdly he bought the great carseland estate of Kerse—the name is the same—in 1762, from the Hopes of Hopetoun—who must since. have scarcely ceased to bewail the day. He gained a baronetcy, his son a peerage and his descendants, still in possession, warsled their way up to being Marquises of Zetland no less. Sir Lawrence was a man of vision, obviously, and of energy—as well as being most conveniently connected with the ruler of Scotland of the period, the notorious Henry Dundas, Viscount Melville—and he was enabled to ornament that most lucrative of professions, Contractor to the Army and Commissary-General. The Carron Iron Company had been set up a few years before, near by; and the great Forth and Clyde Canal was begun in 1767, Sir Lawrence one of its main instigators—hence its Port Dundas, near Glasgow. He indeed cut the first sod of the canal. But he did more than that. It so happened that the eastern terminal of the canal was arranged to be where the Grange Burn joined the Carron and the Carron joined the Forth— Grangemouth. Just five years after Sir Lawrence bought the land. He seized his self-made opportunity with both capable hands, and the port of Grangemouth was born. Here came the iron-ore to feed Carron and the other Falkirk works, and from here was exported their products, east and west, by sea and canal. Here the coal of the adjoining Stirlingshire coal-field was shipped, and the pit-props brought in from Scandinavia—leading to a huge development of the timber trade, of which Grangemouth became the centre. From first being a 'creek', the quaint name for a sub-port, under Bo'ness down the Firth, in 1810 Grangemouth became a head port. Then came its own dockyard for shipbuilding, in 1843. At this stage, the population was only 1500. By 1881 it was 4460; by 1961 it had risen to 18,860. Today—who knows? But greatly more, and ever-growing. For here is the largest and most dynamic oil-refining and allied concentration in Scotland, with deep-sea tankers arriving in a stream from across the world—and not only this, but the oil flowing in from the West Coast deep-water terminal at Finnart on Loch Long, pumped by pipe-line across the land, further to feed Grangemouth's insatiable maw. Sir Lawrence would chuckle—as no doubt do his present-day descendants, who still own the superiority over all.

Old Grangemouth—if any of it can be called old—has been likened to a Dutch town, so flat is the area and so invaded by water. For not only does the river, the burn, the great canal and its basins dominate, but the many docks probe and extend, and there are wide water-basins for the storing and seasoning of timber, linked by channels, so that the whole affect is of pervading water. The great modern extensions, of course, have spread south and east from this watery nucleus; while the docks and oil terminals thrust out on reclaimed land into the tidal mud-flats of Forth.

Needless to say, there is little of architectural or antiquarian merit to dilate upon. The former mansion house of Kerse itself was probably the burgh's most interesting as well as ancient edifice, a large and eventually sham-Elizabethan palace, evolved from an early nucleus, standing in grounds to the west of the town. These have now been encroached upon by great factories, and the mansion is no more; but the estate-office remains there, keeping, as it were, the lairdly finger on the pulse of Grangemouth. The rule from here used to be close and autocratic—so much so that for long, for instance, no public houses were permitted in the burgh, the Earl of Zetland disapproving. Challenged, in 1881, he pointed out that his feu-charters specifically forbade the establishment of any such. The issue was taken up by the presumably thirsty burgh fathers, and went to the Court of Sessions—which held that such prohibition was contrary to public policy. However, my lord appealed to the House of Lords, who duly supported their colleague, declaring that the only question to be tried was whether the superior's undoubted rights in the matter had lapsed by disuse—which obviously they had not. Happily, this situation no longer applies, and Grangemouth's drouth may now be quenched by more than its pervading water.

To the south-east of the burgh, near the bank of the Grange Burn, is the site of Abbot's Grange, presumably one of the many farms of the Abbey of Cambuskenneth. Grangemouth's first actual church was built by the first Earl of Zetland in 1837, as a chapel-of-ease—a place of worship more convenient for the inhabitants than the faraway parish churchs at Bothkennar, Polmont or Falkirk—for Grangemouth was not a parish of itself until 1880. The present church, with its 60-foot steeple, was erected in 1866. For long its two schools were named—can you guess?—Dundas and Zetland; but today it has fine modern educational establishments emancipated from feudalism—even though, presumably, the premises still pay feu-duty to Sir Lawrence's descendants. One wonders whether modern development tycoons will make such a lasting impression as did these old Scots lairds?

Today, of course, Grangemouth has a fine new commercial and civic centre and shopping precinct, traffic-free and noise-proofed with rubber tiling. Called York Square, it has sheltered under-cover arcading, bridged by a restaurant, and complete with an ornamental pool provided with no fewer than twenty-three fountain-jets of varying heights capable of being lit up by night—so the watery motif is not overlooked. There is landscaping, with trees and shrubs, and even the public conveniences have underfloor electric heating. Grangemouth started late, but it runs well ahead in the 20th century race.

Inversnaid. To lie only some twenty-five miles, as the crow flies, from both Glasgow and Stirling, and yet to be so remote as Inversnaid, is scarcely credible. That a busy main road, A.82, Glasgow-to-the-North, runs less than a mile away, only emphasises the remoteness, since it is on the other side of Loch Lomond, and only reachable by boat—or a 55-mile detour. This is because there is no road up the east side of Loch Lomond, beyond Rowardennan, and no approach to Inversnaid, by wheeled vehicle, save by the 15-mile dead-end road from Aberfoyle, to the east. All of which undoubtedly creates its difficulties and frustrations for the folk of this little community—even though there may be blessings too, in this hectic age. It certainly makes this hamlet of Buchanan parish, Stirlingshire, an interesting place to visit.

It is attractive in its own right, however, steeped in character and history. There are two distinct localities, separated by less than a mile, but also by about 350 feet of altitude—for Inversnaid proper is at the lochside, only a few feet above sea-level; and the Garrison, fort, farm and little community at the mouth of the Snaid Glen, is near the 400-feet contour, with a steep, winding and picturesque road between.

Unless approached from the Loch Lomond steamer, or by boat from the other side, the visitor inevitably arrives at the Garrison first, a half-mile below the Arklet dam. This is now a farm, but takes its name from a small fort erected here, by the government, in the early 18th century, to seek to control the Jacobite MacGregors— Rob Roy MacGregor, captain of his clan, it will be remembered, was Laird of Inversnaid and Craigrostan. The remains of the fort-barracks stand on a knoll 250 yards above the Snaid's junction with Arklet Water, with the farm adjoining. It was placed here to control two fords which cross the said waters, on former tracks to Rowardennan, Stronachlacher and Inversnaid harbour. It consists of a square, of tower, barrack-blocks, guard-house, well and so on, enclosed within a high, loop-holed wall. Only a section of this remains, but the plans are given in the Inventory of Ancient Monuments for Stirlingshire. The building had a short but dramatic existence, being demolished more than once before it was ever completed—by the MacGregors, of course—and again later. In the subsequent Rising of 1745 it was again taken, by a son of Rob Roy, and partly demolished. Rebuilt again, it was maintained until the end of that century; but by 1823 it was ruinous and part used as an ale-house. Below, behind the schoolhouse, is a small graveyard, where a 19th century tombstone commemorates many men of various regiments who died on duty here. That not only men died, is revealed by one moss-grown headstone which says: *JANE YE WIFE OF JOHN (H)YETT OF YE BUFFS DIED MARCH YE 4 1750 AGED 37.* The famous General Wolfe served here, as a subaltern.

Rob Roy's house was across the Snaid and higher up the glen, now gone. Here took place the dastardly attack on his wife, by Graham of Killearn, factor to the Duke of Montrose, in Rob's absence; which had a profound effect on that fiery character, and therefore on history itself. The glen has no houses now, other than the farm; but once it would be scattered with the crofts of the MacGregors. From its head, the head of Glen Gyle is only a mile or so—Rob's chief's domain.

Down the steep wooded escarpment, the road twists, to the large hotel and pier. The rushing river near by forms a 30-foot waterfall, and here in 1907 was installed an early turbine, to provide direct electricity for the hotel. This large establishment, strange to come upon in so remote a place, is pleasantly sited on a terrace above the little harbour. It has always gained much of its custom from the loch steamers, and from bus-parties ferried across from Inveruglas; but now, with the much-fought-for restoration of the road from Stronachlacher, visitors may also come by car. Naturally, the harbour was always highly important, strategically as well as otherwise, and the MacGregors made full use of it to impose their turbulent will on the great loch's environs. At Inversnaid, Wordsworth celebrated in song the ferryman's daughter, in *The Highland Girl*; and his sister Dorothy expiates on the area in her Journal. Inversnaid is, too, the setting of Gerard Manley Hopkins's poem, 'This darksome burn, horseback brown'. Far from the parish church at Buchanan, a mission church was established here in 1895, with occasional services.

To the south stretches the now empty wilderness of the former Craigrostan property, in which rears Ben Lomond itself (3192 feet) and lesser peaks. A very rough and difficult path traverses this, after a fashion, now at the lochside, now high on the wooded escarpment. Over this awkward terrain Rob Roy's nephew and chieftain, Gregor MacGregor of Glengyle, on a famous occasion, drove a herd of purloined cattle from Gallangad, down near Gartocharn, a large bull making most of the running. It is about ten exceedingly hard miles to Rowardennan and the road, with the isolated houses of Cailness, Rowchoish and Ptarmigan Lodge en route, accessible, practically, only by boat. To the north of Inversnaid stretches similar untouched wilderness, all the way to Glen Falloch, beyond the head of the loch. Above the lochside, a mile or so up, is a cave, sometimes called Rob Roy's Cave, sometimes Bruce's, where both heroes are said to have taken refuge, when fugitives.

Killearn and Gartness. Killearn is deservedly one of the most favoured places in a favoured district, an attractively sited and picturesque village at the northern mouth of Strathblane, near the junction of the Blane and Endrick Waters, 17 miles north of Glasgow. Placed on the north-western skirts of the Campsie Fells and looking out to the Highland hills and Loch Lomond, it has splendid prospects. The village is in two parts, the older section strung along a ridge of higher ground on the north, the residential area in the valley. On that ridge, strangely, are three parish

churches, successors one of another. The oldest is the least prominent, a roofless building of 1734, on the site of a still older kirk,
surrounded by its large graveyard, with many ancient tombs. The
church has two tiers of round-headed windows, the upper ones
having keystones in the form of human faces. The interior now
contains the burial-places of sundry lairdly families.

The next church was built some hundreds of yards to the north,
in 1826, not particularly interesting in appearance, and now used as
a hall. It did not serve for long, for the third and present ambitious
edifice, in cruciform Early English style, built between the other
two, superseded it in 1881, partly as a memorial to a daughter of
the Orr-Ewings of Ballikinrain. It has a spire 100 feet high, and
seating for 600, designed by Bryce, the well-known Edinburgh
architect. Between this, again, and the first church, is the manse,
and in front towers the huge obelisk memorial, 103 feet high, to
George Buchanan (1506–82) born at Moss near by. It was erected
in 1788, and vies with the two church towers for domination of the
skyline. Only in Scotland, probably, would such a carping divine
and pedant be given so tremendous a monument by public subscrip-
tion. Near by, opposite the Drymen road-end, is a mid-19th
century toll-house, once with rising toll-bar, still retaining its much-
defaced stone of engraved toll-charges.

There are some pleasing late 18th and early 19th century cottages
at The Square, between the Black Bull Hotel and the old kirk,
restored by the Killearn Trust. Down the hill is an attractive
village green, now a public park, with a circular built-up well.
Considerable modern housing extends to the south, much of it
hidden by folds in the land.

Killearn House, a classical mansion built in 1816 by the first of
the Blackburn family, lies 1½ miles to the south-west. The Black-
burns replaced the old Grahams of Killearn, the most notorious of
whom, factor to the Duke of Montrose, in 1712 shamefully abused
and evicted Rob Roy's wife at Inversnaid, while her husband was
away on Jacobite business—later suffering for it at Chapellaroch
and Loch Katrine. The great modern Killearn Hospital spreads itself near by. To the south, the House policies are bounded by the
Dualt Burn, a rushing stream foaming down from Stockiemiur.
A quarter-mile below the A.809 road across Stockiemuir, the burn
makes a picturesque hidden waterfall of some sixty feet. Stockiemuir itself is a wild area of broken heather, peat and outcropping
rock, below the Whangie or Aucheneden Hill, close to the county
boundary. The Whangie is a high-set, narrow chasm, 346 feet long,
cleaving the hillside.

Between Stockiemuir and Killearn village is the Croy area,
where the A.81 and the B.834 cross, near an old bridge over the
Endrick. Croy Cunningham the maps call it now; but there was
also Croy Leckie. Rob Roy's sister Margaret married Leckie of
Croy Leckie, a small lairdship. A mile to the north, but to the west
off the main road, is Gartness, with its castle-site, hamlet, mill,

235

former railway station and famous Pot of Gartness waterfall. The castle stood on the Endrick 400 yards south-south-east of Gartness Bridge, its stones being used in the construction of the mill, now itself ruinous. It was a house of John Napier of Merchiston (1550–1617) the inventor of logarithms, the Napier family having been strong in this area. The mill has one of the castle stones, dated 1574, built in. The waterfall, the Pot, is formed by the Endrick cutting through a cleft over a series of rock ledges and creating a dramatic cauldron.

The Finnich area lies south and west, flanking the A.809 road. Hidden in woodland half a mile west of Finnich Toll is the site of the Cashel of Knockinhaglish, an early Celtic Church establishment consisting of an oval embanked enclosure, quite large, within which would be rude buildings. It is thought this was the church and settlement of St. Kessog. Many years ago excavations unearthed human bones and the foundations of buildings. Not far away, the Carnock Burn coming down off Stockiemuir like the Dualt, carves a deep winding ravine in the red sandstone rock, called Finnich Glen, to form another waterfall in a 70-foot-deep chasm known as the Ashdow, overhung with trees. Almost two miles farther to the north is the village of Croftamie, just in Dunbartonshire, with the old House of Dalnair near by, in Stirlingshire, an interesting late 17th century laird's house erected as a new manse by the evidently prosperous but determined minister of Killearn, Master James Craig, in 1684. He was a man of strong convictions, charged before the Privy Council for not praying for King William —whom he declared he "wished were drowned in the mickle pot of Great Nesse". A larger mansion was later built near by. Here is now a Youth Hostel. Dalnair was the site of a temporary Roman camp, not yet fully explored.

On the other north side of Killearn, a quarter-mile along the road to Balfron, is the hamlet of Blairessan, where a great battle is said to have been fought between Romans and Caledonians. Carbeth House lies beyond, a former Buchanan property, from which Rob Roy's great-grandmother Janet Buchanan came. And in the northeast corner of this interesting parish once stood the castle of Balglass, a strong house which is reputed to have sheltered Wallace. It was the seat of the Bontine family, a name now very little heard, one of whom murdered the minister of Campsie.

Kilsyth. The burgh of Kilsyth, situated at the head of the Kelvin valley, beneath its own Kilsyth Hills, 12 miles west of Falkirk and 12 miles north-east of Glasgow, is a go-ahead town of 10,000 people; but a place of strangely various, indeed conflicting, character. It is scarcely lovely of aspect, like most of the other Central Scotland industrial towns; yet its site is a fine one. The old town and commercial quarters, including the modern industrial estate, occupy the level ground of the haughlands of Kelvin, and are somewhat dreary of aspect; while the modern housing development

burgeons in dramatic terracing, rank upon rank, up the steeply
sloping hillsides to the north. The view gained from the A.803
through-road, Kirkintilloch–Stirling, therefore, gives a wrong impression altogether, both of the shopping centre and old main
street, which strikes off southwards, and of the very 20th century
developments above. The visitor gets no impression of age—and
indeed Kilsyth only became a burgh in 1826; yet it is a historic
place of much interest. And even its name is contradictory, for the
former village and parish was called Monaeburgh, until 1649;
Kilsyth itself being merely a divided barony belonging to the
Livingstone family, linked to the Earls of Linlithgow, one of whose
lairds, Sir James, was created Viscount of Kilsyth and Baron
Campsie, in 1661, by Charles II. It was a short-lived line thereafter, however, for the 3rd Viscount, the first's second son, took part
in the Jacobite Rising of 1715, and was duly attainted. More of him
anon.

Just why the new burgh took the name of Kilsyth rather than
Monaeburgh is not clear. It developed by cotton manufacture and
coal-mining, but suffered decline like so many others. Now, however, it thrives, with diversified industry such as the well-known
Donbros knitwear, with hosiery, chalkboard, paint, wallpaper and
other manufactures. There is a modern Town House, a large
Academy, a golf-course, the Duncansfield stadium of Kilsyth
Rangers—which on several occasions have won the Scottish Junior
Cup—and the fine public park of Colzium-Lennox—the old estate
of Colzium to the east, its 50 acres of policies, parkland and little
glens gifted to the town and utilised for sports and recreational
facilities, its mansion-house used as a museum, gallery, community
centre, aviary and so on, its gardens notable especially for the
unique annual floral display commemorating in original fashion
some outstanding theme of the year. The mansion, attractively
placed on a terraced site, was formerly a seat of the Edmonstone
of Duntreath family. The site of the older castle crowns an eminence
to the east. A track within the estate leads to the picturesque and
quite large Banton Loch and Townhead Reservoir.

Another ruined castle's site, that of the Livingstone's Kilsyth
Castle, lies on the high ground half a mile to the north. It was a
15th century place, and was held against Cromwell in 1650. The
Kilsyth lairds were still exercising feudal power in 1639, when one
hanged a servant in the barony of Bencloich.

Kilsyth's main claim to historical fame, of course, was the great
battle fought here in 1645 between Montrose and the Covenanters
under General Baillie, the winning of which gave Montrose almost
complete control of Scotland for a time. The royalist force consisted of 4400 foot, Highland and Irish, and 500 horse; but by good
tactics, and divided counsels leadership amongst the Covenanters,
the great Marquis utterly defeated 6000 foot and 1000 horse, with
subsequent tremendous slaughter, not only of the soldiery but also
of the unfortunate local inhabitants—for the loss, astounding as it

may seem, of only seven or eight men. The site of the battle was the hollow of ground to the south-east of the town, now threaded by the Forth and Clyde Canal; and in the *Old Statistical Account*, the writer describes how, to that day, not only could the situation of each army be traced, but various aspects of the battle could be followed in the names given to landmarks, such as the Bullet Knowe, the Baggage Knowe, the Drum Burn and the Slaughter Howe. In the Dullatur Bog to the south great numbers of bones, skeletons, arms and relics have been dug up, including a mounted trooper fully armed. He adds: "The place where the bodies lie in any number may be easily known; as the grass is always of more luxuriant growth in summer and of a yellowish tinge in spring and harvest." A macabre story tells that when these remains were being brought to light, millions of toads issued from the site and hopped away, covering the fields, with a score or more to every yard, for miles northwards.

Kilsyth has another link with the religious and dynastic wars. In the old burial-ground, in a corner of the present cemetery, stood the old kirk, now gone. But amongst the many recumbent tombstones is an ogee-roofed mort-house on the site. Built into the wall is a stone declaring that beneath lie the bodies of the widow of James Graham of Claverhouse, Viscount Dundee, and her infant son. She was Jean Cochrane, granddaughter of the 1st Earl of Dundonald, and, after Bonnie Dundee's death at Killiecrankie, married William Livingstone, who became 3rd Viscount of Kilsyth. In Holland, with her son and nurse, she was killed when the turf roof of a house fell on them, her husband being extricated alive. Embalmed, they were brought home to Kilsyth Kirk. The family vault was accidentally opened by Glasgow students, in 1795, and the bodies found in excellent state of preservation, and reburied.

A mile west of the town, a narrow road strikes uphill. Near the farm of Balcastle is an excellent motte, the large artificial mound of an early palisade-type castle of timber, 200 yards west of a sharp road-bend. Still farther west is the mainly modern village of Queenzieburn, pleasantly set in an open position, a half-mile to the north of which used to be the Old Place of Kilsyth, another seat of the Livingstones, now gone. A cairn with burial urn was found near Queenzieburn.

Two miles on the other side of Kilsyth is Banton, its loch already mentioned. There were two villages in this foothill area, Low and High, east of the loch. Coal and ironstone were worked here, and there is still industry; but the district has a rural atmosphere. We read that the schoolmaster here in 1842, had a salary of £12 6s. 3d. with £31 of school-fees and a house.

The Kilsyth Hills to the north are part of that rather strange barrier of high ground which covers central Stirlingshire, and which, although only about sixteen miles long and ten wide, is unusual in having no true overall name but rejoices in a multiplicity of sectional names—the Dundaff, Touch, Gargunnock, Kilsyth, Fintry, Killearn and Strathblane Hills, and the Campsie

Fells. Sometimes, overall, they are termed the Lennox Hills—which see. But this is not strictly accurate. The ancient earldom and district of Lennox, or the Levenach, was based on the valley of the Leven, flowing out of Loch Lomond, and never stretched nearly to Stirling. Be that as it may, the Kilsyth Hills form an attractive background to the industrialised Kelvin valley, reaching north-wards about three miles to the Carron valley which divides the massif. The highest summits are Garrel Hill (1503 feet) and Tomtain (1484 feet). There is much modern afforestation here. A steeply-climbing but quite good road crosses from Kilsyth to Carron Bridge, rising from 190 to 1050 feet in the process, through the empty hills.

Kippen and Boquhan. Kippen, in modern times, has had two especial claims to fame—that it was the home of the famous Scottish landscape artist, Sir D. Y. Cameron, who so frequently and de-lightfully painted the magnificent prospects of the Highland Line to be seen from his very door; and that here grew the greatest vine in existence, which first planted in 1891, brought hosts of visitors—but alas, it has now been cut down to make room for houses.

But there were two earlier claims to renown, in differing spheres. Here took place, in 1691, the celebrated 'Her'ship of Kippen', when, after ambushing a herd of 200 cattle on the way to tryst, at Buchlyvie, Rob Roy and his MacGregors, driving them to cross Forth by the Fords of Frew, came near to Kippen; and could not resist the temptation to add to their winnings by a thorough harry-ing of the unfortunate village, when, it was alleged, they drove off everything with four legs. Dragoons from Cardross caught up with them just as they crossed the ford, and in the battle which followed, the troops were routed, a Gaelic song being composed to celebrate the victory. The other claim had its own significance. An old Scots Act of Parliament permitted—because it could not do otherwise—the distilling of whisky free of duty within the Highland Line. Kippen, by some ingenious feat of the imagination, claimed to be within that line, and for long was the seat of extensive distilling, until a new and spoil-sport Act was passed at Westminster in 1793, when the distillery died a death.

Kippen is the largest of the villages flanking the south side of the Flanders Moss, set on a rising spine of ground quite high above the level carselands, and slightly by-passed, blessedly, by the fast A.811, Stirling–Dumbarton, road. The village itself climbs quite steeply, its top and western end reaching the 'suburb' of Cauldhame, formerly a separate hamlet. The view from many of the north-facing houses is superb. To the south, the area is sheltered by the long escarpment of the Gargunnock and Fintry Hills, with Kippen Muir and some attractive foothills country between—this traversed by the dramatic glen of the Boquhan Burn, a picturesque valley of such natural beauty that it has, perhaps fancifully, been likened to the Trossachs in miniature. The burn issues from the heights by the fine waterfall of Spout of Ballochleam, about three miles due south of the village.

There are some good old cottages at Kippen, including that known as Taylor's Building, of mid-18th century date; as well as some attractive modern housing. Only the crowstepped gable and belfry of the original parish church survives, in the old graveyard behind the modernised and large 18th century manse. This church was built in 1691, the same year as the Her'ship; but the bell, which still hangs above, dates from 1618, so there must have been a still older building. There is a tradition that the earlier chapel stood near Dasher, a farm about a mile to the south-east. The present and modern parish church is a large and handsome edifice, built in 1825, but reconstructed this century, a work with which the artist Cameron was associated. Outside it is erected the shaft of an old market-type cross. A celebrated Covenanters' conventicle was held about a mile west of the village, in 1676; and over 200 men of the parish are said to have marshalled here and marched to the disastrous Battle of Bothwell Brig, three years later.

There are a number of interesting places round about. Boquhan Glen has been mentioned. The estate of that name lies on the low ground about a mile to the east. The fine Georgian mansion, which succeeded an older fortalice demolished about 1760, is itself demolished; but the ambitious stable-range remains in use, for the Home Farm, dating from the early 19th century, with clock-tower and cupola all very evident from the main road. Boquhan was originally Buchanan property, although Harry Cunningham seems to have been the laird at the time of his duel with Rob Roy at Arnprior.

Dasher was also mentioned, and here, near the defile of the Boquhan Burn, is an oval earthwork defended by a double rampart, possibly Pictish. Another, similar, is to be discovered at Keir Hill of Dasher (Keir, or *caer*, meaning fort); and it is here also that the pre-Reformation church of St. Mauvais is thought to have stood. Farther west, on the high ground between the village and Kippen Muir, are Arnmore and Wrightpark, the former a ruined laird's house of the Leckie family, dating from the end of the 17th century, with a lintel inscribed A.L. 1722 I.S.; the latter a large and ambitious, if somewhat bleak-seeming, Georgian mansion, with much internal fine woodwork and plaster, and, strangely enough, a vaulted basement. The house dates from 1750.

The Lennox Hills. Once, the name of Lennox meant great things in Scotland. It was a more important entity than either the Stirlingshire or the Dunbartonshire that it straddled. Lennox was one of the major divisions of the land, one of the original great mormaorships, which developed into the ancient earldoms, into which the realm was split. Lennox ranked with Moray, Mar, Strathearn, Fife and so on; and its Celtic earls were powerful indeed.

The name was originally Levanach, the plain of the River Leven, which flows out of Loch Lomond, basically the Vale of Leven, still so called. But this is all, of course, in Dunbartonshire. However, much of the surrounding country, and the many baronies of the earls, became in time included in the term The Levenachs, or The Lennox; and part of this is what is sometimes called the Lennox Hills, with contiguous parts of West Stirlingshire.

This range of hills extends from near Dumbarton itself almost to Stirling town. The name is not very descriptive or accurate, for Lennox never extended quite so far east as this. But at least it is a convenient overall name for a range, not in itself so very large, yet burdened with a great multiplicity of sectional names. Surely nowhere else in Scotland is a comparatively modestly-sized area so nominally profuse; for here are the Kilpatrick, Strathblane, Killearn, Fintry, Kilsyth, Gargunnock, Touch and Dundaff Hills, as well as the Campsie Fells; the total range only some twenty-three miles long and varying from four to ten miles in width. Why it has collected all these separate entities, I have been unable to discover.

It all makes, however, an attractive northern rampart and lung for the busy Central Scotland industrial area, giving a most pleasing background landscape and relief to much that is less picturesque of aspect. The south-western end is, of course, much in demand as a desirable residential hillfoots area for North Glasgow, with the Strathblane, Campsie, Lennoxtown, Killearn and Balfron districts greatly favoured, all within easy commuting distance of the city. The hills reach their highest point at Earl's Seat (1894 feet), with an average altitude of 1400 to 1500 feet. They are in the main grassy and without outstanding features, with much modern forestry. There is, however, a notable rocky escarpment running for miles along the northern face, overlooking the Forth valley and Flanders Moss, at about the 1250-foot contour, variously called Standmilane Craigs, Black Craig etc. The range is divided by two main interruptions—the deep valley of Strathblane, to the west, running roughly north and south, which separates the Kilpatrick Hills from the rest; and the long, high and picturesque central valleys of Carron and Endrick, running east and west, which almost meet and so dissect the entire massif. The two rivers' headwaters used to approach each other within a mile; but now the Carron Valley Reservoir has flooded still farther westwards, so that its end laps almost into the Endrick's course. Thus waters flowing into the Forth and Clyde run within almost yards of each other. The great reservoir, nearly four miles long, much of it surrounded by forestry plantations, is a scenic attraction.

Altogether, these hills, considering their closeness to great centres of population, are remarkably lonely and little traversed. Perhaps this is no bad thing.

Logie and Blairlogie. These, a parish and a village, do not seem as though they should belong to Stirlingshire at all, but to

Clackmannan. They are the first of the Hillfoots communities, leading to Menstrie, Alva, Tillicoultry and the rest. Yet, in fact, though across the Forth, they are very near to Stirling, only about two miles north-east of Stirling Bridge, behind the wooded Abbey Craig. Logie is a large parish, yet with its church and manse isolated remotely in a cleft of the Ochils; and Blairlogie, the little community, is nearly a mile away to the east. The parish is one of vehement contrast, most of it being high empty hills, while its low-lying portion could hardly be lower nor flatter, the 2-mile stretch of level carseland to the Forth, with farms, mansions and the Manor-Powis colliery.

There are three churches, one at Blairlogie and two at Logie itself, though one of these is a ruin. These two are most picturesquely-placed, tucked under a rocky wooded bluff, with a waterfall plunging near by and the dramatic peak of Dumyat soaring behind. The ruined church is the higher placed, only the west gable and part of the south front remaining; but it makes an attractive fragment in its green and leafy setting. It is not so old as it seems, dating only from 1684, although a stone of an earlier building, dated 1598, is built in. There is a belfry, some rather good windows and a sundial; also a Douglas heraldic panel, for the minister who helped to pay for the reconstruction in the 17th century. The first church is recorded as early as 1178, and belonged to the Priory of North Berwick. There are many interesting tombstones in the sloping graveyard, almost a hundred of them dating from before the 18th century. The most notable is an unusual hog-backed one, now weather-worn.

The manse is charmingly sited on a little terrace behind the old church, the sound of the waterfall always there; and at the other side are the gardens houses of the Airthrey estate, now the University of Stirling, the ancient wall of which rims the former road from Bridge of Allan, winding its way by. An old copper-mine was dug into the hillside some two hundred yards to the north. The later parish church, about an equal distance to the south, was built in 1805, and is also attractively placed and a good building.

Blairlogie village is one of the most delightful in the land. It stands on rising ground back from the A.997 road, approximately half-way between the parish church and Menstrie and consists of a huddle of picturesque old houses amidst orchards and gardens, clustered round its little whitewashed church, and under benign dominance of its own small castle. With its winding tiny streets, really only lanes, and the magnificent backcloth of the steeply-rising Ochils, it has managed to retain its old-world charm. But that it is no sleepy hollow is vouched for by the fact that the village hall is the venue for much and famed lively activity, public lectures, displays, classes and so on, of a high order, to which people flock from far and near. The castle, now called The Blair, is set on a shelf above the village, on a strong site created by the steep ravine of a burn, and is a fine little fortalice of the mid-16th century, enlarged in 1582 and in more modern times, but still only modest in proportions. The original three-storey tower is simple, with vaulted basement, crowstepped gables, pedimented dormers and a corbelled-out stair-turret and angle-turret, which last have lost their conical roofs. Indeed it is almost certain that the roof level as a whole has been somewhat lowered. There is some good woodwork within. The castle was built by Alexander Spittal, of the Stirling family, originally from Fife, in 1543. It is still occupied, and in appreciative hands.

The little United Free church, down near the main road, is plain but pleasing, a long, low white building, with a belfry and good windows. It dates from 1761, and owes its foundation to a Secessionist breakaway from the main Logie congregation. Another coppermine, of the 17th century, used to be worked at Ewe Lairs, a few hundred yards north of the village.

Down in the carselands, there is only the grass-grown site of the Castle of Manor, near the colliery, although the building was entire only a century ago. It was the 16th century seat of the family of Callander of Manor. Not far away is a reputed Roman causeway across the Forth; and to the west stands the substantial Georgian mansion of Powis House, with some good Adam features within. This was built by a family called Mayne, in mid-18th century.

Above all this area towers the shapely peak of Dumyat (pronounced Dum-*eye*-at) which, though not very high (1375 feet) is one of the most eye-catching of the Ochil summits. On its southwestern shoulder, at about the 1000-foot contour, is an early Iron Age fort, an oval enclosure with many outworks, designed to use the natural features of the site for defensive purposes. Possibly there has been a later dun built within. The name is said to mean the Dun of Maeatae. The view from Dumyat is spectacular.

Manuel. Manuel, today, means great brickworks and fireclay manufacture. But once it was a very different scene, in this green Avon-side area, the very south-easternmost corner of Stirlingshire. It was much esteemed territory, much fought over, within sight of Linlithgow Palace's towers. The lords spiritual and temporal clashed here, and traces of their ambitions still remain.

The great castle of the Livingstones, Earls of Linlithgow and of Callendar, still stands—now, unfortunately, amongst the industrial rubbish-dump of the brickworks company, who surely could do better than this for one of Scotland's major monuments of the past. It was built by the Crawfords, in the 15th century, and was called then Haining Castle; in 1540 it passed to the Livingstones. It is interesting that they then changed its name to Almond Castle, though set beside the River Avon. This clearly reveals the affinity of these two corruptions of the Gaelic word *abhainn*, meaning river, and used variously as the names of innumerable streams throughout the country—Avon, Almond, A'an, Devon, Deveron and so on. Why the Livingstones preferred Almond to Avon would be interesting to know—especially as there is another Almond not far away, in Lothian, the river which reaches the Forth at Cramond, or *Caer-almond*. The lofty square keep, of massive proportions, is still more or less entire to the wallhead, with some excellent workmanship, and deserving of a better fate.

Little over a mile away, to the south-east, is a relic of the Church's interest, the Priory of Manuel, or Emmanuel, which gives the area its modern name. Only a single tall buttress of masonry remains, on the very edge of the Avon, not far from Manuel House, and readily visible from the side-road B.825. Indeed it was so close to the river that most of the priory, a nunnery, has fallen therein, and only this fragment remains, with a pointed arched window, two string-courses and two corbels. It was founded for Cistercian nuns by Malcolm IV, in 1156. Edward, Hammer of the Scots, was here in 1301, when he wintered at Linlithgow. The chapel was fairly entire until in 1788 a spate swept most of it away.

The ruin faces down the grassy haugh of the Avon, and here in 1526 was fought the Battle of Linlithgow Bridge, between the armies of the Earls of Lennox and Arran, to try to extricate the young King James V, at his express desire, out of the clutches of the Douglases. Arran and the Douglases won, and one of that party, Sir James Hamilton of Finnart, Arran's illegitimate son, shamefully slew Lennox after he had surrendered his sword, wounded. The same character afterwards attempted the assassination of the King himself—yet he was one of the most cultured men in the kingdom, and a notable architect.

Mugdock, Craigmaddie and Craigend. This interesting and untypical south-west corner of Stirlingshire has a character all its own. Suddenly the great urban sprawl of Glasgow and its outliers ends, and open country begins. Unusual country. A glance at a large-scale map will reveal, firstly, an inordinate scatter of blue patches—small lochs. Including Bardowie and Dougalston, there are no fewer than sixteen of them, as well as many smaller ponds. Some are enlarged by dams to make reservoirs. The map also shows an area of suddenly increased altitude, of rolling foothills, high moors and large estates. All within seven or eight miles of Glasgow centre.

Mugdock is a famous name in Scots history, because of its association with the great Montrose. Lying just a mile north of Milngavie, it comprises an ancient 14th century castle—which has recently been the location for the popular TV series, *The Borderers*—a hamlet, a loch in a large wooded estate and a reservoir which acts as a storing-place for Glasgow's water supply from Loch Katrine. The castle was once a very large and important establishment, set picturesquely above its loch, and today giving little impression of its former grandeur. The tall square 14th century tower which remains was only a flanking gatehouse-tower, one of a number round a great walled courtyard, with a large central keep, now gone. The 17th century building to the west was not part of the original;

and the ruinous present centre-piece dated only from 1875. The original castle was long—320 feet long—and fairly narrow, a shape dictated by the site, which was a ridge practically surrounded by water—for the loch used to be much larger. The portcullis gateway beside its tower is still there; and there was a pre-Reformation chapel to the north.

The Grahams acquired Mugdock from Maldwin, Earl of Lennox, in the 13th century, in due course becoming Earls of Montrose. In the time of the 5th Earl and 1st Marquis, the great Montrose, the castle suffered much, owing to the hatred of his enemies. When, in 1641, he was imprisoned for five months without trial in Edinburgh Castle, Argyll and the Covenant leaders sent Lord Sinclair to demolish his "staitly house of Mugdock". However, this seems to have been only a superficial spoliation, for Montrose was living here again after his victorious campaign of 1644. Then it was again savaged by the Laird of Buchanan, on the orders of Argyll. On Montrose's execution Argyll himself grabbed Mugdock—but his own execution changed that, and it was restored to Montrose's son at the Restoration. Then it is said to have been the scene of bacchanalian orgies, when used by the notorious Earl of Middleton in his anti-Covenanter oppressions. Later the Montrose family removed to Buchanan Castle at Drymen, former seat of one of their despoilers.

A mile to the east, on the skirts of Craigmaddie Muir, is the pleasant wooded estate of Craigmaddie, its mansion and ancient ruined castle visible from the A.81. The castle crowns a rocky tree-girt bluff impressively, actually within the ring of a prehistoric hill-fort; but only the two lower storeys and vaulted basement remain. Although these represent only a simple 16th century tower, undoubtedly there was a predecessor. The Galbraiths of Baldernock—in which parish Craigmaddie stands—were a powerful family, who possibly descended from the ancient royal house of Strathclyde, and were related to the Celtic Earls of Lennox, from whom they received these lands. Sir William married a sister of the Comyn who was one of the Competitors for the Crown after the death of Alexander III, and became co-Regent of Scotland in 1255. His son married a sister of Bruce's friend, the Good Sir James Douglas. From these stem the Galbraiths of Culcreuch and other lairdships. They had a stronghold on an island in Loch Lomond still called Inchgalbraith. The later mansion of Craigmaddie, below the castle, is a handsome early 19th century edifice, attractively sited. A loch of 10 acres lies to the north.

On Craigmaddie Muir, to the east, is the celebrated Auld Wife's Lift, the strange stone formation; and near by were two chambered cairns, opened in 1792, and found to contain cinerary urns and bones. A group of others lie to the south, at Blochairn, and are thought to mark the site of a great battle between the Picts and the Danes.

Craigend Muir lies to the north of both Craigmaddie and Mugdock, and covers a great deal of high ground before the drop into the valley of Strathblane. The views are superb, to the Campsie Fells, and the Highland giants behind Loch Lomond. It is on this broken moorland that the majority of the lochs occur. The large Craigend Castle, within its estate, was built only in 1812, a Buchanan property. There is a hamlet of Craigend, but this is 3 miles to the north-east, beyond the northern slopes of the moor. Based on the castle, a great £9,000,000 holiday development project is planned for Strathblane.

Craigallion Loch lies a mile west of Craigend Castle, and is one of the largest and most picturesque of these many waters, with finely wooded shores.

Plean. There is a wide area of country lying north of Larbert, south of Bannockburn, east of Airth and west of the A.80, Glasgow–Stirling road, covering perhaps ten square miles, its western part once within the great Tor Wood. It contains no important town or village; but, by its situation in the heart of Central Scotland, has been involved in important matters. It contains a section of the Roman Road. The Battles of Bannockburn, Sauchieburn and Falkirk were fought near by, and spilled over into Plean. Here Prince Charles Edward's army camped before the 1746 Battle of Falkirk. This, then, was the cockpit of Scotland.

Unfortunately for its appearance and amenity, coal was found to underlie a great part of eastern and northern sections—with the usual results. It was quite an attractive area, scenically, once; and its western portions, rising towards the skirts of the Dundaff Hills, are still pleasant and unspoiled.

Plean itself is an undistinguished mining village on the A.9 highway, 6 miles north of Falkirk, with a vast, ugly bing rising to the west. This is really East Plean, Plean proper lying half a mile to the south, on the same road; but the larger has to all intents swallowed up the older. Here is the church, only constituted a *quad sacra* parish in 1878; and the school. Near by is the Simpson Home for old men, founded in 1831.

Plean Tower, or Castle, lies on a side-road about a mile to the east, standing on a rocky mound amongst former marshland. It is a small square fortalice of possibly 15th century construction with later alterations, which has stood within a courtyard. The tower has had a chequered history. It was a ruin, but earlier this century it was restored, after a fashion, and occupied again. Unfortunately, the parapet at the wallhead was then heightened in unsightly fashion, and its crenellations turned into windows, throwing the building out-of-scale. Although it is now a ruin again, this sorry top-hamper remains. Strangely enough, although the courtyard buildings have been vaulted, the basement of the keep itself is not. It has a fine Hall fireplace, heraldically decorated. The castle could be restored once more, to provide a house of character and modest size. Plane, as it was once named, was a Somerville stronghold for two centuries before passing to the Nicolsons of nearby Carnock.

Stirling Castle. Architectural detail on early 16th century Palace, one of the
finest Renaissance buildings in Scotland

Stirling. 15th century Church of the Holy Rude

A mile to the east, on remote rising ground, are the much more ruinous remains of a larger fortalice. It is called Bruce's Castle; but despite popular notions it has nothing to do with the hero-king. It was originally called Carnock Tower. A large castle of the early 15th century, oblong on plan, only the vaulted basements and a tall fang of masonry remains. It belonged in the 15th century to Sir William de Airth of Plean, passing to the Bruces of Auchenbowie about 1512. They retained it for about a century, when Alexander Drummond of nearby Carnock House acquired it. But he retained his own Carnock as principal manor-place of his barony, and changed the name of Carnock Tower to Bruce's Castle.

Carnock *House* lay half a mile to east, in a large wooded estate, and was another handsome castle, this time of the 16th century. The present author visited it in 1934, when, although abandoned, it was still entire. Bought by a coal-mining company, neglect and mining subsidence ensured its demolition. It was a most notable double tower of massive proportions, with parapet and wall-walk, and contained handsome heraldic plaster ceilings. Built by Sir Robert Drummond and his wife Margaret Elphinstone in 1548, it later passed to the Nicolson family, baronets of Carnock since 1637.

West Plean is now only a large farm and mansion with a small school, a mile west of East Plean, at the end of a straight stretch of the Roman Road. On the crest of Common Hill, just to the north-west, is what is described as a homestead, of native early Iron Age construction, comprising foundations of a circular farmhouse and a rectangular barn, with cobbled yard, excavated in the 1950s. Relics uncovered then indicate that it was pre-Roman in origin, dating from about Christ's time.

Cowie is a large mining village lying less than two miles to the north-east of Plean, on the side-road, B.9124. A wholly modern place, it remains little known because of its isolated position—rather extraordinary in tight-packed industrialised Central Scotland. But there is antiquarian interest here too; for just to the west of the village, on the summit of what are called the Berry Hills, is the site of an early Iron Age fort, with triple scarped defences, much damaged by the plough. Also, still farther west, aerial photography only recently discovered what the archaeologists call an enclosure, no doubt connected with the fort. Although coal-mining recedes, a tile-works has been established here; and a scheme of land reclamation is tidying up the pit detritus.

Polmont and Brightons. By its very position, where the higher ground elbows close to salt-water, and the Avon joins the Forth at a bend of the narrowing estuary, the Polmont area has always been important strategically, and for the traveller moving north or south in East Scotland. The busy A.9 highway has long threaded the village itself, with, just beyond it, the parting of the roads, west to Falkirk and north for the modern Kincardine Bridge over the Forth. Now the new motorway swings north here; and Polmont and

Brightons have become something of desirable dormitory areas for the employees of the vast Grangemouth petro-chemical plants and refineries just a mile or so to the north. Jet planes fly over constantly on their runs-in to Edinburgh Airport at Turnhouse.

So, likewise, here the Romans marched and camped, and found need to build their farthest-north wall of all Britain, Antonine's Wall, sometimes called Grim's or Grime's Dyke—but locally known as Graeme's or Graham's Dyke, for good Scots reasons. A tiny portion of it is still to be distinguished at Polmonthill, climbing up-and-down-hill, grass-grown but detectable, where the escarpment plunges down to the coastal plain, neglected but enduring. The new sewage-works near by make typical modern comment.

Called after the Emperor Antonius Pius, it was built in A.D. 142 by engineers of the 2nd Legion under Lollius Urbicus, Governor of Britain. The Wall stretches 39,726 Roman paces, or 36½ miles, from Carriden, on Forth, to Old Kilpatrick, on Clyde. On stone foundations, it is built of earth and turf, and was 24 feet thick and 20 feet high, with three forts at each end and fifteen intermediate forts at 2-mile intervals. It was defended on its north side by a fosse or ditch 40 feet wide and 20 deep, and along its south went a paved military road. The forts were erected against the Wall itself; and one, Inveravon Fort, can be traced, half a mile east of Polmont amongst the grassy hummocks, the new motorway flanking it.

Close by was the little loch which gave Polmont its name—*poll monaidh*, the poll of the hill.

As indicated, the Polmont district is developing fast. To the south of the village, the land continues to rise; and here, in what were formerly the lands of Polmont House, the rows of modern villas proliferate. The House itself, a dignified, whitewashed, Georgian mansion, still stands, rather bare now on its ridge, eyebrows raised at all this bustle and development. Beyond it the main railway-line between Edinburgh and Glasgow passes through Polmont Station; and just behind runs the Union Canal all contributing to Polmont's reputation as a traffic centre and place to be got through. On this high ground, with the delectable views northwards across the Forth and its carselands, are the former mining villages of Brightons, Redding Muirhead, Crossgatehead, Wallacestone and Shieldhill, one tending to run into another; and, as is the way with mining communities unfortunately, none very characterful or beautiful. But the vistas compensate for much.

St. Ninians. Time has not been very kind to St. Ninians. It may now be little more than a southern suburb of Stirling, but it has its own resounding identity. Because it lies where the Edinburgh–Stirling and Glasgow–Stirling roads join, on the crest of a small escarpment above the level carselands, not only is it swallowed up by the ever-encroaching town, but it has become that unfortunate entity, in modern conditions, a traffic-hub. Not that this is anything new, for the Roman Road ran through here.

Nevertheless, traces of the old St. Ninians—or St. Ringans, as was the old Scots way of pronouncing it—still exist. The early dipping main street was so narrow that, long before by-passes became normal, the high roads found it advisable to make a semi-circle round it. So, although most of its buildings have now been demolished, some of the old town's nucleus remains, a few tradi-tional houses, and the isolated clock-tower of the old parish church, which still strikes the hours. The church itself was used as a powder-magazine by Prince Charlie's army after the Battle of Falkirk in 1746, and was blown up, accidentally or otherwise, as the troops retired northwards, leaving only the tower standing, its basement being made into a burial-place for the Bruces of Auchenbowie. The replacement was built a little to the east, in 1750, a large and massive edifice, to seat 1500—for this was the seat of one of the largest parishes in Lowland Scotland, amounting to no less than 38,012 acres, and extending as far south as Dunipace and as far west as Fintry, 12 miles by 7—although, admittedly, much of it empty hills. It is not clear whether the blown-up building was on the site of the original early church, which had been established here from a remote period, dedicated to the royal 4th century Celtic saint from Whithorn on the Solway. A holy well was sited near by, also in his name. Soon after the founding of Cambuskenneth Abbey in 1147, it was granted "the church of Egglis St. Ninians with its chapels of Dunipace and Lithbert" (Larbert).

St. Ninians' greatest hour, of course, was during the two days of the Battle of Bannockburn. Bruce set up his standard at the Bore-stone, a mile to the south; and the main encounter took place in the levels a mile to the east. Here, at St. Ninians Kirk, on the first day, June 23rd, 1314, was stationed Bruce's nephew, Thomas Randolph, Earl of Moray, who by mischance chose to ride to confer with his uncle at the Borestone just as Sir Robert Clifford and an English cavalry force made a probing thrust east-about through the marshes, unexpectedly—which Moray should have ridden to cut off. Angrily the monarch reproved the unfortunate young man. "A rose has fallen from your chaplet today!" But, racing back, Moray retrieved the situation and, against odds, won an infantry engagement against heavy cavalry, a heartening preliminary victory. On the second day, it was the lot of Sir Robert Keith, Knight Marischal of Scotland, to be stationed at St. Ninians on the lip of the escarpment, where there was an excellent view over the carse, and at Bruce's signal to make a swift dash down to capture a strategic point of firmer ground from which English archers could have enfiladed the Scots host.

The hamlets of Newhouse and Bellfield lay between St. Ninians and Stirling, but these are now absorbed.

Sauchieburn and Auchenbowie. Here is a wide stretch of rural foothill country lying south and west of Stirling and north of Denny, flanked by the Plean area to the east and the Touch Hills to the west. Much of it is well-wooded—indeed it would all once be within the great Tor Wood tract—but most is now undulating farmland rising to the sheep-strewn moors. Two large and ancient estates dominate it, Sauchieburn and Auchenbowie; but, though the area could be said to cover a dozen square miles, there are no villages, or even hamlets; only a great number of scattered farms, estate cottages and the like. There are two large sheets of water, Loch Coulter to the south-west; and an islanded reservoir, contrived by damming the Bannock Burn, about a mile west of Sauchieburn House. The Bannock Burn rises some two miles farther west, in the high morasses of Touchadam Muir, at about thirteen hundred feet. Loch Coulter, a mile long and half that in width, is interesting in that, during the great earthquake at Lisbon in 1735, the water was seen to be much agitated and sank in level, temporarily, by about a dozen feet.

Sauchieburn is famed for the great battle fought there in 1488, when insurgent nobles, with the young Prince James, aged 15, defeated his father King James III—who had long infuriated them by weakly government and the raising up of favourites. The King, seeing his forces in defeat, fled the field; but was thrown from his horse near Beaton's Mill at Bannockburn; and dazed, was taken into the mill premises, where his pursuers, led it is thought by the Lord Gray, stabbed the monarch to death. In contrition and self-blame, the young King James IV ever thereafter wore an iron chain about the loins. The battle was fought at the east side of the Sauchie Burn about one and a half miles from the Borestone of Bannockburn.

The large mansion house of Sauchieburn is modern. But the original fortalice of Old Sauchie still stands, a roofless ruin but preserved, less than a mile to the south, with the estate-office housed in a later wing. It is quite a handsome, medium-sized tower-house of the early 17th century, with later additions, some of the same century, tall, L-planned, with corbelled angle-turrets and many gunloops and shot-holes, all strongly sited on the lip of a steep ravine. The 18th century extension, which houses the offices, contains some good panelling of that period. The lands were granted in 1528 to James, son of the 4th Lord Erskine, and this family presumably built the castle. In the mid-17th century the property changed hands more than once, finally being sold in 1786 to Ramsay of Barnton, with descendants of whom it still remains.

The other estate, Auchenbowie, lies 2 miles to the south-east, near the A.80 highway. The mansion is a fine, commodious place of the 17th century, somewhat altered and added to but retaining much of its original aspect. It also is L-planned, with an octagonal stair-tower, crowstepped gables and steep roofs. It was long a seat of a branch of the Bruce family, the first of whom seems to have been Provost of Stirling in 1555. A successor, William Bruce, killed a relative in a duel at the end of the 17th century. Soon thereafter, in 1708, an heiress carried the property to the Monro family, who still retain possession.

Three miles to the south-west, on high ground beyond Loch Coulter, is the remote little church of Buckieburn, off the Kilsyth–Stirling road. It seems an extraordinary place to put a church. It was built by the heritors of the upland part of St. Ninians parish in 1750. A plain edifice, with no adjoining graveyard, it is interesting in having two mural paintings by the well-known modern Glasgow artist William Crosbie, R.S.A.

Skinflats, Bothkennar and Carronshore. Skinflats is hardly a beauty-spot, yet it is surely much traduced by its name, as off-putting an appellation as one is likely to meet with in a day's journey. Strangely enough this is, in fact, merely a Scots corruption of the Dutch for beautiful meadows. It is claimed that a colony of Low Countrymen, Dutchmen or Walloons, were settled here, in the level carselands of the Forth, a couple of miles north of Grangemouth, as in so many other parts of the land, in the days when there was major trading and coming-and-going between the Scots east-coast ports and the Continent. These industrious colonists gave this part of Bothkennar parish its name—and though perhaps such utterly flat expanses are scarcely beautiful in our eyes —however nostalgically pleasing to the Dutch—the views of the Ochils, Stirling Rock and the basin of Forth, are very fine; moreover, the quality of the land itself is excellent enough for any, alluvial loam quite free from stones, mile after mile of it, only 17 feet above sea-level.

The village is not large, and now wholly modern as to housing; and not particularly attractive. It was shamefully decayed, at one time not so long ago, but now improved. Indications of a more pleasant, non-industrial occupation can still be traced—possibly the Dutchmen's legacy—in abandoned cottages, small farmeries and even orchards. Unfortunately, from a scenic point of view—if less so for the landowners, in especial the Dundas family, of Zetland —coal was discovered to underlie the good earth; so that mining development came, to create its usual blight upon the locality, however much wealth it created for more distant pockets. This changed the character of the community, and left unsightly bings rearing out of the rich carseland.

The parish, a small one, is called Bothkennar; but there is no actual community of that name—only an isolated church and manse, standing in the fields midway between the villages of Skinflats and Carronshore, the church a plain edifice, dating from 1789 and enlarged 1887, though containing traces of an earlier work. One of its ministers, the Reverend William Nimmo, wrote *The History of Stirlingshire* in 1770. In the graveyard are some tombstones with fine representations of sailing-ships, reminder of the time when Carronshore was a port.

Carronshore is a larger village, but with little of evident character, sited a mile to the west, and formerly an appendage of the great Carron Iron Company, for which it was an early port for the land-

ing of ironstone and lime, with its own little canal to the Works—
this in the days before Grangemouth grew up. Here the barges
brought ironstone from, for instance, Jovey's Neuk at Aberlady
Bay, and other sources, prior to the development of iron-ore im-
ports. Here also, much earlier, the Roman vessels used to come.
Indeed as late as 1723, the 'Coalshore of Carron' as it was called,
was described as a good harbour for ships up to 60 tons—scarcely
believable as this seems today. The Romans were said to have sailed
as far as 4½ miles up-river from the Forth at Grangemouth. The
Carron in those days represented Buchanan's *Epithalamium*, the
boundary of Rome's actual conquest of Britain.

Near by is the gaunt and gutted shell of the early 17th century
Skaithmuir Tower, a former fortalice built by the 4th Lord Elphinstone, shamefully converted into a pit pumping-station.

Slamannan. The large and scattered parishes of Slamannan and
Muiravonside, south of the plain of Forth, are little typical of
Stirlingshire, and probably often not even recognised as part of the
county. They comprise a very uneven, low hill-and-valley system,
with a fairly lofty moorland plateau area behind, of somewhat bleak
mosses and thin pastures. But there is much woodland amongst the
northern slopes and hollows, though not of a rich character. It is
not a rich countryside, indeed, dotted with small croftlike farms.
But it *was* rich in coal, and though this is played out now, inevitably
it has left its scars in bings, wasteland and less than lovely villages.

Yet there is much that is attractive here too, many quiet pastoral
valleys and unspoiled prospects, with splendid views from the high
ground across the Forth carselands to the Ochil Hills. It is populous
too, with communities large enough to be called towns at Slamannan itself, and Maddiston, and many villages, places whose history
would appear to go back only to the Industrial Revolution. Nevertheless, no little history was made hereabouts in early days, because
of the southern approaches to strategic Stirling, the vicinity of the
royal town of Linlithgow and of the great and significant headquarters of the Knights of St. John, at Torphichen, both in West
Lothian. Indeed, in this area was marshalled William Wallace's
army before the fatal Battle of Falkirk in 1298, as witness names like
Wallacestone and Wallace's Cave.

There are more domestic links with the past, however, if you look
for them. For instance, the author came across a small farmhouse
on a side-road about a mile east of Slamannan, called Pirnie Lodge.
Here was the traditional steep roofing, crowstepped gables, decorative skews and tiny windows. The door was notably ambitious,
with a roll moulding, and stone panel over the lintel bearing the
letters M.R., W.H. and I.S., and the date *1735*. Three sets of
initials are unusual; normally such only refer to a husband and wife.
Enquiries at the house, however, revealed more of interest than
merely the explanation. A young woman informed me that the
M.R. in fact stood for Master—meaning, of course, a Master of

Arts. The house had been built by her own ancestor, the Reverend William Hastie, and his wife Isabella Shaw, 235 years before. This was the first occasion in which I had seen the old Scots term of Master, referring to a university degree and used by ministers long before 'Reverend' came into fashion, incorporated in a doorway panel. Moreover, the young woman still possessed a manuscript book by the good cleric, detailing the history of the Hastie family, old even then. This, for a small, two-storeyed farmhouse of four or five rooms, spoke eloquently. Scotland has seldom been able to provide much proof of a yeoman stock of enduring vitality, however tenaciously her lairds managed to cling to their acres and fortified houses. Here, unexpectedly in unknown Slamannan parish, was a little revelation. The bonnet-lairds are not all gone.

Stirling. By any standards, Stirling is one of the major names in Scotland, one of the truly important places. It is not a city; indeed as Scots towns go, with 28,000 people, it is only nineteenth in population. Even within its own county it is smaller than Falkirk, and will probably soon be smaller than Grangemouth also. But size is not the only criterion. Its history, of course, is pre-eminent; its setting is superb; its character unique. If any place deserves to be called the heart of Scotland, geographical as well as historical, it is not Edinburgh, the capital, or Glasgow the industrial metropolis, but the Royal Burgh of Stirling. That Edinburgh did, in fact, become the capital instead, is perhaps something of an accident. Had the Forth estuary run straight, at about Bo'ness; or better still, bent southwards, Stirling almost certainly would have been established as the capital. But the Forth swings north-westwards, and the Lennox Hills come thrusting north-eastwards, to bar off from the south-west this first point where the great river might be crossed before modern steel bridges were thought of. That it was too far up-river for a deep-water port also contributed. Nevertheless, Stirling is the natural place for the capital of Scotland, and the place where the most significant events have shaped the country's history. Moreover, it links the Highlands and the Lowlands, as Edinburgh does not. Perhaps had it indeed been the permanent seat of government, the history of Scotland might have been happier.

Be all that as it may, Stirling is a place that no one who seeks to know Scotland should fail to visit, to explore, to try to understand. It lies almost equidistant from Edinburgh, Glasgow and Perth, and though not really in the geographical centre of the land—a point which would lie somewhere about Pitlochry or Aberfeldy—it is highly central for all practical purposes. It is probably further west than many realise, being only some twenty-five miles north-east of salt water at Dumbarton, but 35 north-west of Edinburgh. It lies west, for instance, of Blair Atholl, Crieff, Lanark, Dumfries, of most of Wales or of any part of England until we reach Devon. The Highland hills come within 8 miles, the nearest 2000-footer, Uamh Beag, being about a dozen miles north-west, and Ben Ledi about sixteen. Although the county town, it is not centrally placed in Stirlingshire, occupying the north-east extremity, within a mile or so of both the Perthshire and Clackmannanshire boundaries. In fact, it is as it were the hinge of Scotland where, as well as these two shires, those of Dumbarton, Lanark, the Lothians, Kinross and Fife all come close.

Needless to say, it was the great impressive towering rock, dominating all the flat lands of the Carse of Forth, and at the lowest point at which the river might be crossed, by ford or bridge, which established Stirling, from earliest days, as a place of major significance. Just when the first fortress was set up thereon, and a community grew under its shelter, is hard to ascertain. Presumably there was a fort here in pre-Roman times, a stronghold of that British people they called the Damnonii, whose chief town was not far away at Alauna, near where the Allan Water joins Forth, according to Ptolemy. The Romans themselves must have had a fort to guard *their* crossing of Forth near Drip but no traces remain; though there is an inscribed stone on the shoulder of the castle hill near Ballengeich, which is alleged to declare in Latin that this was a point for the daily and nightly watch of the Second Legion. Some say the inscription is falsified. The Roman Road itself passed slightly to the west of the Rock. Of the dark ages which followed the Roman withdrawal, little or no recorded history has come down to us about Stirling. The accounts and traditions of the Celtic missionaries have not much to say about Stirling, which was not the sort of place they would be concerned with, a fortress-city geared to war and strategic matters. We read that it was called *Mons Dolorum*, meaning the mount of grief or strife, then, as after, no doubt a place of constant battle, owing to its situation. Some scholars have asserted that the early name of Striveling comes from an anglicising of this theme—but this seems far-fetched, very few of our ancient place-names having any such conveniently English derivation. It seems more likely to have come from some suffix to the Gaelic word *srath*, or strath, for a wide valley. In the 10th century the place was apparently called Struthlinn. Other forms were Strivelyn and Strewelin. Confusingly, the area also seems to have rejoiced in the name Snawdoun, which Chalmers derives from *snau-dun*, the fortified hill on the river. There is still a Snowdon Place in Stirling.

Although the all-conquering Kenneth MacAlpine, King of the Dalriadic Scots, was evidently concerned with Stirling, and gave his name to Cambuskenneth, a mile to the east, it is not until the 12th century that its story comes clearly into view; when Alexander I had a castle here, and in fact died here in 1124. One of the first acts of his brother, David I, was to give a royal burgh charter to Stirling in 1125; but this was probably a renewal rather than a new status. A port was in operation here by 1150; and in 1226 Alexander II granted the right to hold a weekly market. And so on. Thereafter its development is chronicled, step by step—and is also, practically, the history of Scotland.

Some ask, was Stirling ever actually the capital? This cannot be answered simply yea or nay; for in medieval times it was not a term in use, nor a conception with any validity—not in Scotland, at least. The seat of government was where the king was—and the king moved around, necessarily. Parliaments met as and where required. Monarchs tended to have basic headquarters and favourite seats; but these frequently differed between reigns, and even during reigns. If Bruce, for instance, had a capital, Ayr could have been said to be it, during the early part of his reign; Dunfermline later. Nevertheless, Stirling was for most reigns the basic, most frequent and favoured seat of government, its castle not only the strongest and most impregnable fortress in the land but the most central. Edinburgh Castle, so similar in appearance, was not in fact a royal residence in the same category—and Edinburgh was too near the English border at Berwick, for comfort. James IV, married to Henry VIII's sister, Margaret Tudor, was the first monarch to actually build a palace at Edinburgh—Holyroodhouse, beside the Abbey of the Holy Rood; but even so his home was at Stirling. Here his son was born—and James V still looked on Stirling as home. Did he not call himself the Gudeman o' Ballengeich—this being a croft of land under the north-east flank of the Castle Rock, which that roving monarch used as a nickname during his incognito and amorous adventures amongst his people. Mary Queen of Scots, his daughter, though born at Linlithgow, was brought here as a child; and on her return from France became the first monarch who seemed to prefer Edinburgh as her main seat. Her son, James VI, followed suit; and it was during his reign that Edinburgh became accepted as the capital—even though Falkland in Fife was *his* favourite palace. That is, until he exchanged it for Whitehall! But even he insisted that his first and favourite son, Henry, should be born and christened at Stirling, in 1594, as 'the most convenient place for the residence of this most noble and mightie prince . . .'. It is often assumed that Edinburgh, and the Palace of Holyroodhouse, is the true and principal seat of the Scots monarchy. This is a mistake.

Certainly the first glimpse of Stirling, castle and town, seen from almost any angle of approach, is such as to leave a lasting impression on the visitor. Rising abruptly out of the level plain, the great fortress-crowned rock with the grey town climbing its steep slopes, all against a background of striking beauty and colour in almost every direction, is not one to be forgotten. Closer approach, unfortunately and inevitably, does not quite live up to first impact; since no modern industrial town could possibly retain the aspect of unspoiled medieval character. The low-lying streets of the modern town, choked with traffic as they tend to be, are less than picturesque, unworthy of the rest, and unfortunately all that most motorists see of the place. Although the approach from St. Ninians and the south, with the ring-road carrying the through-traffic by the attractive residential areas of Snowdon, Drummond and Victoria

Places, and the Queen's Road which flanks the great King's Park, successor of the royal deer-park, and now a golf-course, is pleasing, with good views. Even the large Raploch housing scheme, to the west of the Castle Rock—passing the interesting and apt-to-be-missed King's Knot on the way—though itself uninspired enough, is finely situated.

The glory of Stirling is, of course, up the hill—the ancient town of climbing streets and narrow wynds, and the great fortress above. The Castle itself deserves an entire book—for this is no mere building or group of buildings, but a splendid and complex citadel, much less spoiled than is Edinburgh Castle. This comparison with Edinburgh is inevitable. The two are so similar in type and situation. They make a pair unrivalled in northern Europe. But Edinburgh, being the capital and a large city, draws so many more visitors. Yet Stirling has much that Edinburgh lacks, or has despoiled. The Castle here has suffered vastly less modernisation and disfigurement. A list of the individual items of building will suffice to give some idea of the wealth of architectural splendour. There is the Mint, the Great Hall, the Palace, the Chapel-Royal, the King's Old Building, the Magazine, the Elphinstone Tower, the Gatehouse, the Prince's Tower, the Grand, French Spur, Over-Port and Queen Anne Batteries, not to mention the Lower and Upper Squares, the Nether Bailey, the Counter Guard, the Bowling Green and Nether Green, and the Lady's Hole. All these, crowning the soaring outcrop of sheer rock hundreds of feet above the plain. Some of these buildings are amongst the finest in Scotland.

The Great Hall and the Palace are probably the most renowned. Indeed, the former was once the most magnificent secular edifice in Scotland. Traditionally it was built by James III's low-born favourite, Thomas Cochrane, who was an artist and architect of no mean order, but who offended the nobility, when made Earl of Mar, by his arrogance, and whom they hanged like a dog over Lauder Bridge. Like his royal master, he was before his time. But he was widely travelled and brilliant, and erected here reputedly the first building in all these islands to fully display the influence of the Renaissance. Most of the work, undoubtedly, was completed in the following reign, soon after 1500, by James IV. Unfortunately the roof-line is modern, and the building has lost its parapet and walk, much changing the external appearance. Above an undercroft of vaulting, the Hall itself measures 126 by 37 feet, the ceiling 54 feet high. At the celebration for Prince Henry's christening in 1594, a ship 40 feet in height was contrived within. Not a few of the great dramas of Scotland took place within these walls.

The Palace is equally famous, its series of carved figures intriguing and unique, one of the most dramatic Renaissance buildings. It is very large, with many state apartments and presence chambers. The larger part dates from 1540, James V's period—and the Gude-man o' Ballengeich was one of the big spenders. The King's Presence Chamber ceiling originally displayed the famed 'Stirling

Heads', a series of carved wooden medallions of most notable crafts-manship, some historical, some mythological, now scattered in museums and elsewhere. Daniel Defoe, the 17th–18th century political writer, author of *Robinson Crusoe*, who was also a most able English political spy, wrote eloquently of this building, saying that it was the noblest in all Europe, and that no apartment at Windsor or Hampton Court could come near it. In the centre of this Palace block is the courtyard of the Lion's Den, where the beasts roamed and were baited for the royal amusement. Here are some very long hooked poles, the first fire appliances—the hooks for dragging burning thatch from roofs, the long shiny shafts early greasy-poles, for sliding down, to escape.

The Chapel Royal, built by James VI, the Wisest Fool in Christendom, in 1594 for the baptism of the son over whose birth he was so inordinately proud, is likewise a fine building, although less ambitious, with some notable tempera mural painting within. It was a renewal of an older building.

But even the briefest description of all the wealth here is im-possible, in the space available. It must suffice to say that Stirling Castle is a most worthy monument to the most ancient royal line in Europe. A not very good statue of Bruce, the hero-king, adorns the esplanade approach, from the east. And down to the south-west of the Rock lie what were the King's Gardens, with, stretching beyond, the great King's Park plateau, enclosed by William the Lion as early as the 12th century, extended with a New Park to the south, by Alexander II, around 1264—this New Park being used by Bruce in his strategy for Bannockburn. Immediately beneath the Rock, all that is left of the extensive gardens is the curious, geometrically-stepped mound known as the King's Knot. This was a very large parterre, measuring in all over four hundred feet square, terraced in extraordinary fashion, octagons within squares rising to a central mound, and indicative of the scale of these gardens. Though visible from the road, it can best be discerned from above. The famous Sir David Lindsay of the Mount, James V's tutor, has some-thing to say about this, in his *Farewell of the Papingoe*, written in 1539, also referring to other features hereabouts:

> Adew fair Snawdoun, with thy towris hie,
> > Thy Chapill Royall, Park, and Tabill Round.
> May, June and July wald I dwell in thee,
> > War I ane man, to heir the birdis sound
> Quhilk doth agane thy Royall Rocke resound.

Clearly, then, the Chapel Royal of 1594 was only a renewal. The Round Table refers to the King's Knot, sometimes so called; it had a legendary connection with King Arthur's Round Table and order of chivalry—as indeed had the castle itself.

At the other side of the Rock is an area of broken grassy hillocks, one called the Gowan or Gowling Hill, where a Jacobite battery was sited during the siege of 1746. Near by is the Mote or Heading Hill, where James I executed his cousin, Murdoch, Duke of Albany, and his sons and father-in-law, Lennox, in 1425, for their part in having him kept prisoner in England and usurping his kingdom in the meantime—a fierce reaction from an otherwise generous and poetic man. Here also died Sir Robert Graham and others who aided him in the murder of the same king, twelve years later, at Perth. This hill has also the strange local name of Hurly-Haaky, or Hackit, from a game which used to be played here, consisting of tobogganing down the slope, on a cow's skull, an amusement of James V. Lindsay refers to this also:

Some harlit hym to the Hurlie-Hackit.

The castle was long used as an infantry depot. Its hereditary keeper is the Earl of Mar and Kellie, who lives within sight, at Alloa. It is open daily.

The old town of Stirling is not any museum piece. It has many ancient buildings, and keeps to the old streets and wynds. But there is modern housing up amongst the old, and on the whole very skilfully fitted in and appropriately designed. Inevitably there has been much falling into ruin and demolition, over the years; but a great deal of the character of the place has been preserved, without sacrificing its lived-in atmosphere. It is the reverse of Falkirk, which though ancient and rich in history, has practically no ancient building remaining.

Only a very few of the most notable can be mentioned here. The Church of the Holy Rude. Argyll's Lodging. Mar's Work. Cowane's Hospital. Bruce of Auchenbowie's House. Norrie's House. Darnley House. Glengarry House. The Broad Street complex. The Town House. The Athenaeum. The Mercat Cross. Sections of the Town Wall. These are mainly clustered in or about the high-placed streets of St. John Street, Broad Street, Castle Wynd and St. Mary's Wynd, within the old wall which protected the medieval town to the south-east, where it was vulnerable to attack.

The Church of the Holy Rude, at the head of St. John Street, well up the hill, is a very handsome building of curiously composite character, on the site of a still earlier edifice. It was erected in two stages, the nave and tower about 1455, the choir and transepts some fifty years later. It was, in fact, divided into two distinct parish churches, West and East, in the 17th century. In 1936–40 the two parts were reunited into the very splendid parish church, a cathedral in miniature, 208 feet long. The pillared nave of five bays has a magnificent open timber roof, and a clerestory on one side only, with good ribbed vaulting in the aisles. The choir has clerestorys on both sides, clustered pillars and vaulted aisles. The fine apse, which has a floor of Italian marble, was used as a model for that Lorimer built into the Scottish National War Memorial Shrine at Edinburgh

Castle. There are many magnificent stained-glass windows, one by Burne Jones. The pulpit has 17th century panels and pilasters, though reconstructed. There are four bells in the tower, dating from the 15th, 17th and 18th centuries. There are many interesting memorials, one inscribed *HEIR LYIS ANE HONORABIL MANE CALIT ALEXANDER FOSTER LAERD OF GARDEN QVHA DEIT THE 13 IANVARE 1598*—Sir Alexander Forester, Provost of Stirling. The kirkyard contains numerous ancient gravestones, an interesting though not ancient one commemorating the Wilson sisters who were martyred by drowning at Wigtown, in Covenanting times. The Church of the Holy Rude was the scene of the coronation of the infant James VI, in 1567. Its exterior still displays signs of General Monk's bombardment during the Civil Wars period.

The great mansion known as Argyll's Lodging, in Castle Wynd, is the finest town house of its kind in Scotland—a 17th century palace. It was built, not by any of the Campbell of Argyll family but by the noted Sir William Alexander, formerly MacAlister, whose family had come from the west with the first Earl of Argyll and anglicised their name. Sir William was created Earl of Stirling in 1633 by a grateful Charles I, whose pockets he had filled. This extraordinary character, celebrated as a poet and courtier, largely promoted the idea of baronetcies, to be sold, and linked them with his schemes for colonising Nova Scotia. Viscount Canada was his subsidiary title. He it was who built up a small existing house into this great courtyard mansion, harled and formerly whitewashed, with its stair-towers, stringcourses, crowstepped gables, decorative dormers and carved heraldry which we see today, a palatial place eloquent of the kind of life that was lived in Stirling even after the kings had departed for the south. It came into the hands of the 9th Earl of Argyll in 1666, and he added the south wing, now disappeared, and sundry details. The interior has been greatly altered and subdivided for later purposes, but some good features such as handsome stairways, fireplaces, and plasterwork remain. Charles II resided here in 1650, and his brother, the Duke of York in 1681. It was the Duke of Argyll's headquarters, as Commander-in-Chief, before Sheriffmuir in 1715, and it was occupied by the notorious Duke of Cumberland in 1746, on his way north to Culloden. It was converted into a military hospital in 1799.

Mar's Work, standing between the last two, is a very different place, a century older, and now in fact only a ruined façade. But highly dramatic, the remains indicating that it has been an impressive and splendid palace also, likewise quadrangular, with much heraldic decoration and architectural flourish, though only a part of the east wing survives. It was built in 1571-72 by John Erskine, 18th Earl of Mar, who was Regent of Scotland for only two years, for the young James VI. It is doubtful, if this great palace was ever finished. This was very soon after the Reformation, and the Earl was accused of using stones from the spoiled Cambuskenneth

Abbey (the Abbey lands having been given to him) with a charge of
sacrilege. Perhaps the Regent was a little uneasy in his own mind
on the matter, for he inscribed on the lintels of the doorways to
the twin gatehouse-towers the following lines:

> *I PRAY AL LVIKARIS ON THIS LVGING*
> *VITH GENTIL E TO GIF THAIR JVGING.*

and,

> *THE MOIR I STAND ON OPPIN HITHT*
> *MY FAVLTIS MOIR SVBJECT AR TO SITHT.*

And at the rear of the gatehouse pend he adds, a little defiantly:

> *ESSPY SPEIK FVRTH AND SPAIR NOTHT*
> *CONSIDDIR VEIL I CAIR NOTHT.*

At any rate, Mar was a vast improvement on his successor as
Regent, the crudely fierce Douglas, Earl of Morton, who, in 1579,
amongst other savageries had two poor rhymesters hanged at
Stirling Mercat Cross for penning a satire upon his ways. The
young King James himself was terrified of the man, and was not
sorry to see him eventually executed on his own Maiden, the
guillotine he had invented, two years later. His palace occupied a
site at the south corner of Broad Street. Near by the Earl of Bothwell, Mary Queen of Scots's third husband, also had a palace, now
gone.

Cowane's Hospital lies just to the east of the church, an attractive
17th century building, erected in 1637 as an almshouse with 40,000
marks left by John Cowane, merchant and Dean of Guild, for "the
entertainement of decayed gild breither". E-planned, harled, with
an ogee-roofed square tower, it was built by John Mylne, the King's
Mason. Here also Cambuskenneth Abbey stones were utilised. A
statue of the founder, clad like a cavalier, surmounts the tower doorway. The principal apartment was the great Guild Hall, with
gallery and high open timber roof. Within are many items of
interest. There is an ancient terraced bowling-green to the east.
This Hospital must not be confused with Cowane's House, in St.
Mary's Wynd, which was the 16th–17th century residence of the
Cowane family. It is sometimes called Queen Mary's Palace, but
though the Queen may have lodged here on some occasion, it was
never her house. The building is in a sad state, having been used
as a carpet factory at one time, and its upper storey removed. But
remains of a stair-tower and angle-turrets reveal that it was a fine
house once. It could be rebuilt.

Bruce of Auchenbowie's House, in St. John Street near the
bowling-green, has fared better, having been restored; but it has
suffered much alteration nevertheless. It is another 16th century
town house, with vaulted basement and projecting stair-tower

which has lost its conical roof. Glengarry Lodge, sometimes called the Darrow Lodging, is another restored 16th century building, looking attractive now, with its truncated dormer windows, crow-stepped gables and stair-tower. It is in Spittal Street. Norrie's House, in Broad Street, is rather different, having been built in 1671 as part of the street frontage, not as a free-standing house; and though much of the back is a reconstruction, the narrow façade has been retained and makes a very dignified composition. James Norrie was Town Clerk at this period. Next door is another 17th century house, with double-gabled frontage, which has also been rebuilt behind, retaining the façade. Elsewhere in this handsome Broad Street are similar restorations, having an admirable effect.

In Broad Street also are the Town House or Old Tolbooth, and the Mercat Cross. The former was designed by Sir William Bruce, the King's Architect, about 1703, and is a fine steepled tolbooth, built in the classical style, with a later court-house and jail. The square clock-tower is surmounted by an ogee-roofed belfry, with bells dated 1656 and 1669. Inside there is much panelling and good fireplaces. The Mercat Cross, restored and standing in its original position outside, in the centre of Broad Street, was long removed elsewhere and broken. Only the handsome unicorn finial is original, but this is remarkably fine, with the animal bearing the Royal Arms of Scotland on a shield round its neck, with the badge of St. Andrew hanging therefrom.

The Athenaeum, much lower down the town, in a prominent position at the junction of Spittal Street and King Street, is an interesting comparison to the old Town House in Broad Street—for this was its successor. It has a very superficial resemblance thereto. Why it should be called the Athenaeum is not clear. Possibly it was just an ironic nickname, since the 1814 Guildry records advocate the substitution for the old Meal Mercat, which stood here, of "a genteel building of three storeys in the place where the said Mercate stands, containing two elegant shops, with suitable apartments above for assembly-rooms, library and reading-room, with a steeple in the centre". This genteel and elegant edifice was in due course erected, steeple and all—though a later writer disposes of the result with "the style is poor Italian, and there is a spire". Despite the typical early 19th century preoccupation with taste, gentility and sensibility, the result is a distinct come-down from the authentic and traditional buildings up the hill. It has a curved front, rusticated ground-floor façade, and a tall square clock-tower topped by a circular drum and then an octagonal spire. A statue of William Wallace, oddly enough in apparently a Roman toga, stands incongruously on top of an over-massive porch, obviously an afterthought.

Just across Spittal Street, is the Corn Exchange, where stands the still later and quite imposing Municipal Building. To these has recently been attached a large and highly modern addition, with a quite ambitious entrance. Stirling certainly keeps on trying. The figure 4 motif, used in old and new, refers to the fact that Stirling was one of the original four royal burghs of Scotland.

Tribute must be paid to the very fine modern housing in the traditional style with which the Stirling authorities have replaced ancient derelict building, and preserved the character of the old upper town—even though some of the lower-placed efforts are less successful, in the outer suburbs. No expense appears to have been spared in this direction, and it reflects great credit on the municipality. A particularly attractive close, or enclave, strikes off St. John Street just below the Erskine Marykirk, a cul-de-sac of delightful housing. A pity that the adjoining church's neglected forecourt should be such an eyesore. The climbing gardens contrived on the site of demolished property between Spittal Street and Baker Street are also pleasing. Stirling High School is near by.

The Carnegie-founded Burgh Library, containing Reference, Magazine and Children's Rooms, as well as the Lending Departments, occupies an impressive building just opposite the Burgh Chambers, and is all thoroughly modernised. But round the side, to the south, is the Back Walk, and a portion of the ancient Town Wall, strengthened in 1547, at the time of the English invasion and Battle of Pinkie, with one of its bastions more or less intact. There is more of it behind the Municipal Buildings, and elsewhere.

It is impossible to mention here the many other public buildings; but reference should be made to the Smith Institute, an Italianate museum and art gallery in Albert Place under the Castle Rock, near the Public Halls. Spittal's Hospital, also, the oldest of the town's charitable endowments, is an interesting 17th century house—although the foundation was in 1530, as a panel with that date declares, founded for the support of the poor by Robert Spittal, tailor to James IV—the same benefactor who built the bridge at Bannockburn.

Stirling, because of its situation, is limited in the directions in which it can expand. So most of the modern development has had to take place to the south-east or the north-west, in the level carse-lands. Here there is much of industry, dealing particularly with agricultural requirements—machinery, fertilisers, seeds, bacon-curing and so on. Notable is the great new auction marts complex, about a mile out on the Drip Road to the north-west, a little town in itself, with many sale-rings, vast assembly pens, covered hall and precinct, offices, banks, shops, a restaurant, loud-speaker address system and so on, all most spacious, clean, convenient—and with glorious views as an unusual bonus. Cattle sales, amongst the largest in Scotland, are held here on Wednesdays and Thursdays each week, stirring occasions. Near by is the very modern St. Marks parish church.

Apart from these agriculture-linked industries, there are many others including pre-cast concrete, engineering, carpet-making, confectionery, tobacco and rock-wool. The hotel and catering trades, not unnaturally, are well to the fore.

Although sited at Causewayhead and Bridge of Allan, the new University of Stirling falls to be mentioned here. Its establishment was only attained after a long and vehement struggle, in competition with the claims of other areas—such as Inverness. Its setting, in the pleasant hillfoots estate of Airthrey Castle, is scenically quite the finest of any university in the land, amongst parkland, woods, green knowes and beside a serpentine loch, with the Ochils rising abruptly behind, and all the spread of the carse and windings of the Forth lying below. Airthrey Castle itself, an Adam house, enlarged later, was once the seat of that Robert Haldane, the eccentric founder of Congregationalism in Scotland, mentioned under Glen Eagles. It is retained as offices of the university. It is intended to have two-thirds of its students in residence—and in delightful residential conditions, between woods and loch. The many modern-style scholastic buildings are scattered about the property in attractive fashion, crowning a knoll here, tucked into a hollow there, with imaginative use of the environment, and retention of the trees. At the time of writing, the establishment had reached only about one-third of its planned size and complement. It is the closest to an American type university in the country with no faculties, and two semesters in the year; and has ambitions to blaze a trail in academic standards combined with the demands of technical times. An exciting new project here is the building of a theatre and arts complex, to be called the MacRobert Centre.

Another venture in the direction of cultural matters was the inaugurating by the Town Council, in 1958, of the Stirling Annual Festival Fortnight, for music, drama and the arts generally, an ambitious project which takes place in May each year, with concerts, recitals, exhibitions and other displays. While not intended to rival Edinburgh's great International Festival, it is a fine gesture on the part of a town of only 28,000 people. Set up five years later, was the Scottish Tartans Information Centre, opened by the Lord Lyon of Arms, in the Old Tolbooth, Broad Street, housing a fine collection, popular with overseas visitors especially.

No account of Stirling would be complete without reference to the famous Stirling Bridge—even though the present structure is not that which featured in Wallace's resounding victory. It is a picturesque, humpbacked and narrow edifice of four arches, probably of the 15th century, spanning the river to the north of the town, just to the west of the A.9 crossing, and now only open to foot traffic. Previous bridges had been of timber, and are marked on old maps as early as the mid-13th century. The strategic importance of this crossing has been emphasised. One of the arches of the present bridge was severed by General Blakeney in 1745, in an attempt to prevent the Jacobite army from entering the town. It is sad that the approaches to this significant and handsome structure should be so seedy. But it is still much-photographed—and, choosing your angle, a highly attractive picture can still be obtained.

But, though Cornton, Causewayhead and Bridge of Allan stretch ahead, on the way to the North, this is quite the wrong note on which to leave Stirling, a town of tremendous character, vigour and vision, which has played, and surely always will play, a major part in Scotland's affairs.

Strathblane and Blanefield. The name of Strathblane can cause some confusion, since it applies to a village and parish, but also to a fairly long and famous valley—in which is another village, that of Blanefield. The Blane Water, in its early reaches called the Ballogan Burn, rises high on the west shoulder of Earl's Seat (1897 feet) the highest of the Campsie Fells, and flows south, dropping to the low ground, at the former Ballogan House, in a three-stage waterfall known as Spout of Ballogan, which can be seen from the main A.81 highway. A series of cultivation terraces lie to the east, also visible from the road. The river then swings westwards along the wider valley, and a mile on is Strathblane village, at the junction of A.81 and A.891.

This is an attractively-sited place, growing rapidly with modern housing, a popular residential area for Glasgow commuters and others—Glasgow being only 11 miles away. There is a very distinct valley, with the Campsies rising steeply to the north, and high moors to the south. There is a fine new school, a large roadhouse-type inn and everywhere burgeoning rows of 'executive' houses. The parish church, dating from 1802 and replacing an earlier building castigated as 'mean', stands on a hillside site to the east of the village, with a quite modern manse opposite. There is a very pleasant garden in front, planted to the memory of Sir Archibald Edmonstone 8th baronet of Duntreath. A great number of old tombstones surround the church, and, strangely, amongst them a single standing-stone of much greater antiquity. Beneath the floor of the church are other tombs, one reputed to be the grave of the Princess Mary, sister of James I, and her husband Sir William Edmonstone; another, one of the Montrose family, possibly the 3rd Marquis who died 1684. Strathblane was once notable for a religious hospital; today, to the south of the village, is a Children's Home Hospital. Passing nearby is a twisting, climbing 'back-road', parallel with the main A.81 to Glasgow, very attractive amongst the cluster of small lochs on the moorland, with splendid views.

Blanefield village, of more modern origin, and where a calico-works developed, lies a mile to the west, at another road junction, in a sylvan wooded setting. The main road here swings north-westwards through a narrow gap which divides the Strathblane Hills part of the Campsies from the Kilpatrick Hills of Dunbartonshire. It is quite a pass, richly wooded. Less than a mile along is the characterful early 18th century laird's house of Middle Ballewan, a house of the Craig family, with a mineral spring near by. A similar distance farther, on the left, and within a great estate under the dramatic wooded hill of Dumgoyach, is the notable castle of Duntreath, since the mid-15th century the seat of the Edmonstone

family. This was once a very important courtyard-type castle. Now
only the large 15th century keep remains, restored and still occupied
by the present Edmonstone baronet. It is a massive oblong tower,
with crenellated parapet and wall-walk, and an unusual porch-like
arrangement for the original door, carried up as a sort of buttress
containing a winding stair. Once there was much subsidiary building within curtain-walling, including a gatehouse-tower known as
the Dumb Laird's Tower. Duntreath was originally a property
of the Celtic Earls of Lennox, but came to Sir William Edmonstone
of Culloden, about 1434, who had married the Princess Mary,
daughter of Robert III. One of the 17th century lairds was born
dumb, but otherwise seems to have been quite effective. Thereafter,
the family removed to Ireland for a century, and Duntreath sank
into ruin. During this period, we read, its chapel, still used,
"underwent a crash during divine service"—an alarming experience
for the worshippers. The Edmonstones returned in 1783, but to
Colzium near Kilsyth; and it was not until 1863 that Duntreath
was restored. On the estate, on the ridge near Dumgoyach farmhouse, are a group of five standing-stones, only one still upright.

Beyond Duntreath, the soaring peak of Dumgoyne (1402 feet)
though only an outlier of Earl's Seat, begins to dominate the view,
at the other side of the widening strath from Dumgoyach. By the
roadside, is the distillery of Glengoyne. Half a mile farther, the road
forks, and about a mile along the left and main fork, a side-road leads
down to the Blane, where there is an old, narrow bridge of 1732.
Near by was the former Mosshouse Tower, where in 1506 was born
the famous scholar and historian George Buchanan, James VI's
cordially-loathed tutor. The great modern Killearn Hospital lies
spread ahead, within the northern mouth of Strathblane. A
£9,000,000 holiday centre development is planned, based on
Craigend Castle, with hotel, golf course, swimming pools, artificial
ski-slope and chairlift.

Torwood. The map, and the gazetteers, will indicate that Torwood is just a small village in Dunipace parish, 2 miles north of
Larbert, a picturesque glimpse of which presents itself from the
main A.9 highway on the way to Stirling. To some extent today, this
is true. There is the village, mainly of low-browed cottages amongst
trees, stretching along a side-road which rises at an angle to the left,
to link eventually with the Glasgow–Stirling, A.80, road, near
Snabhead behind Bannockburn, after passing West Plean.

But the name means so much more than this. Tor Wood was one
of the important topographical factors of Scotland's history, for
centuries. For this was one of the great forests of the land, to rank
with Ettrick, covering a vast area of the foothill country between
Falkirk and Stirling; and because it lay in the very waist of Scotland,
the most strategic area, it was inevitably not only the haunt of
fugitives innumerable but played a large part in the tactics of
armies. Tor Wood could be reached, by secret ways across the

Flanders Moss, from the Highland fastnesses; it had all the empty tracts of the Kilsyth, Dundaff, Touch, Gargunnock, Fintry and Campsie Hills behind it: and so was an almost impenetrable sanctuary which could not be surrounded nor sealed off. Here have lurked almost every one of Scotland's heroes, at one time or another —as well as a great many rogues, traitors and rebels. Here, in security, armies could assemble, to descend upon the rich plains of Forth and Lothian. Here broken remnants have fled, to fight another day.

William Wallace is probably the name which springs to mind most prominently in connection with the Tor Wood. Here he escaped, after the disaster of the Battle of Falkirk, and here he frequently found refuge thereafter. Wallace's Oak has undoubtedly long disappeared, although a shoot of it was said to be thriving until 1835. Here, at Torwood Castle, Bruce frequently met Comyn, while they were uneasy Joint-Guardians of enemy-occupied Scotland, to transact state business in an atmosphere of mutual antipathy. Here much of Bruce's force assembled before Bannockburn; and he used the Wood in his battle strategy. Here Donald Cargill, fiery Presbyterian preacher, in 1680, after long banishment, before a large outdoor congregation, formally excommunicated Charles II and others, including Bloody Mackenzie of Rosehaugh and General Tam Dalziel of the Binns. The thorn tree which served as pulpit is still said to grow. He was hanged a year later at Edinburgh, aged 71. Prince Charlie's Jacobite army made use of the Tor Wood also for its descent upon Hawley's dragoons at the second Battle of Falkirk, in 1746. And so on. Scotland would not have been the same without the Tor Wood.

Today little of the forest remains, although the area is still patched with woodland. The Roman Road crosses it, on high ground west of the village. Between the two, half a mile from the A.9 road, is the Tappoch broch, excavated in 1864 and 1948, one of the circular, dry-stone, beehived-shaped castles of our early Iron Age ancestors, a long way south of most of its fellows. Its walls still rise to about five feet. Probably it dates from just after the Roman exodus. Torwood Castle itself still stands, though somewhat dilapidated, the main features surviving, half a mile south-west of the village. But this is a much later building to that which Bruce used, belonging to the mid-16th century, with 17th century courtyard extensions. It is a handsome and commodious fortalice on the L-plan, plain at the outer sides, decorative at the inner, well supplied with shot-holes. It should be better maintained. The family of Forester of Garden took their name from the office of Keepers of the Royal Forest here, from the mid-15th century until 1635, when the first Lord Forrester of Corstorphine acquired the property. The courtyard was rimmed by three ranges of building, most now gone.

Touch. This is another of those names—pronounced 'toosh', by the way—which has declined in importance and recognition, partly because there is no village of the name, and the district lies away from a main road. But the Touch area and barony was a significant one, once—inevitably, considering its situation so close to Stirling and the strategic heart of Scotland. Indeed, amongst the Touch foothills is the Gillies Hill, where the Scots clerics and baggage-train were stationed at Bannockburn. Touch, therefore, occupies the north-east corner of the Lennox Hills, so vital in the military history of the land—and in consequence was much coveted. One of Bruce's staunchest supporters—and later his brother-in-law—Sir Alexander Fraser, Chamberlain of Scotland, was laird of Touch; and indeed the property was then called Touch-Fraser. Although there is no village, the name is still maintained in Touch House, the Touch Hills, Touchadam Muir (the source of the Bannock Burn), Touch Mollar and so on.

The estate lies 2 miles or so south-west of Stirling, beyond Cambusbarron village, stretching up into the hills. The house is a most notable one, having three distinct aspects. The nucleus, a tall, slender keep of the late 15th or early 16th century, rises five storeys, with a parapet and wall-walk. Then a long typical 17th century range stretches to the north-east, incorporating more ancient work at the west. Lastly, to the south, was erected a most handsome Adam front, probably the finest piece of Georgian architecture in the county, its triangular pediment decorated with scroll-work and Seton heraldry. Internally there are many excellent features, such as panelling, plaster ceilings, fireplaces and graceful stairways. The whole makes a splendid and impressive composition. Sir Alexander Seton, only son of the 1st Earl of Huntly—before he, a Seton, married the heiress of the Gordons and took over the chiefship of that clan—acquired Touch in the 15th century. He became Hereditary Armour-Bearer and Squire of the Royal Body. The line retained possession until earlier this century.

There is another interesting house on the Touch estate—Seton Lodge, probably built as a dower-house, at the turn of the 18th and 19th centuries, a smaller but attractive building of the period, with Adam characteristics. An 18th century dovecot stands near by. There are a number of prehistoric sites on the property, and a Bronze Age food vessel was discovered here. Up on Touch Muir is the site of a dun, and also an enclosure, probably a farmstead connected therewith.

Wallacestone, Westquarter and Laurieston. Lying on the high ground to the south-east of Falkirk, Wallacestone is one of those somewhat stark little communities which dot these north-facing uplands of South Stirlingshire, unlovely in themselves but with a tremendous prospect over the level plain of Forth. Indeed it is because of this viewpoint quality that it got its name; for here, at the eastern end of the Callendar ridge was where Sir William Wallace traditionally viewed the battlefield of Falkirk in 1298.

Local legend asserts that this is where Wallace took up position before the battle. But this cannot be true, for it was in this Maddiston area that the English army made its approach, and it is known that it was down in the boggy area of the plain, in the Mungal district, that the main battle was fought, the Scots facing *eastwards*. Much more likely is that the hero gained this height as he was being led, exhausted and reluctant from the stricken field, after the cavalry of the less than co-operative Scots nobles had ridden off, and from here looked back in pain and anguish. It is known that he was led off to the side of the field, cutting through English cavalry. This seems the right area. A monument now stands on the ridge, amidst modern housing, inscribed on one side HIC STETIT 11 DIE AUGUST A.D. 1228. And on the other *Erected to the Memory of that Celebrated Scottish Hero, Sir William Wallace, 3rd August 1810*.

It is an old story, but still important to the Scots. Long may it remain so.

Downhill from Wallacestone is a very different community. Westquarter was an ancient estate, set about the deep, steep banks of an attractive wooded ravine of the Westquarter Burn. Long the seat of a branch of the powerful local family of Livingstone, the original fortalice was erected by Sir George Livingstone of Ogilface, popular at the Court of James VI, the King's Justiciary for the trials of witches, and created a baronet of Ulster in 1625. The Livingstones retained possession until comparatively recent times, but only the 17th century dovecote and the walled garden now remain of their establishment. Stirlingshire County Council took over the property some years ago, and rehoused here the entire population of the former mining village of Standrigg, in a very attractive modern housing scheme, seeking to retain as much of the sylvan character of the place as was possible. The result is notably successful, with old trees, green banks and multi-level housing, and the winding ravine with its two linns and steep woodland paths threading all, a model for other local authorities. This steep Westquarter Glen was reputed to have given the English cavalry a lot of trouble in 1298, and it might well have been up here that Wallace found his way from the field.

Westquarter lies on the eastern outskirts of Laurieston, a village with an unusual history and much changing of name. Of great importance here was the Roman fort of Mumrills, which lies just north of the A.9 highway, by Sandy Loan. It was one of the *praesidia* established by Agricola in A.D. 80. The first occupation lasted only for a single winter. But in A.D. 142, in an attempt to regain lost ground, Mumrills was selected as the largest *castella* on the Antonine Wall, and was probably the headquarters of the general commanding the frontier. It had ramparts of clay, and within were stone buildings, a headquarters, commandant's house, barracks, granaries, baths, etc. The place was thoroughly excavated, from 1923 onwards, and fullest descriptions may be read in the *Proceedings of the Society of Antiquaries of Scotland* for 1928–29. There is not a great deal to see now, the ground having been returned to agricultural use; but a vast amount of relics were recovered— pottery and decorative ware, coins, metal weapons, implements and adornments, bone and horn tools—even footprints of a wild-cat on Roman brick. It makes a fascinating study.

The adjoining village sank into insignificance after all this grandeur, becoming known as Langtoun. In 1756 Francis, 6th Lord Napier, descendant of the famous inventor of logarithms, Napier of Merchiston, feu it out as a planned urban development, and the name was changed to New Merchiston. Nail-making and weaving were the industries fostered. The church was built in 1788, seemingly first as a meeting-house for the Macmillanites. Later the village became the property of Sir Laurence Dundas of Kerse, progenitor of the Marquis of Zetland's family, and the name was again changed to Laurieston, in his honour. A brewery and distillery were set up, but owing to the quantity of iron in the local water, the products did not keep well. Today, owing to the proximity of both Falkirk and Grangemouth, Laurieston burgeons anew as a housing area. A most attractive winding country road runs behind the Callendar ridge from here to Glen and the upper areas of Falkirk, quite different from the general character of the area.

APPENDIX

Places of special interest, some open to the public, others where access or view is usually possible, or can be arranged.

(*Indicates property in care of Ministry of Public Building and Works; †indicates property of National Trust for Scotland)

CLACKMANNANSHIRE

Clackmannan: *Tower
Dollar: †Castle Campbell
Fishcross: Sauchie Tower
Menstrie: †Castle and Baronetcy Room

PERTHSHIRE

Aberfeldy:
 Castle Menzies
 Croftmoraig Stone Circle
 Dull Sanctuary Stones
 Grandtully Castle
 Grandtully, *St. Mary's pre-Reformation Church
 Weem pre-Reformation Chapel and Menzies memorials
Abernethy: Celtic Church Round Tower
Auchterarder:
 St. Kattans pre-Reformation Church
 *Tullibardine pre-Reformation Church
Balquhidder: Ancient Parish Church, Rob Roy's Grave and Stones
Blair Atholl:
 Blair Castle
 Clan Donnachaidh Museum
Blairgowrie: Loch of Lowes Nature Reserve
Callander: Kilmahog Mill
Coupar Angus:
 Abbey
 Bendochy Parish Church and Stones
Doune:
 Blairdrummond Safari Park
 Car Museum, Doune Lodge
 Castle
Dunblane:
 Cathedral
 Scottish Churches House
Dunkeld:
 *Cathedral
 †Hermitage and Nature Trail
 †Little Houses
 Rumbling Bridge, Strathbraan

Dunning: St. Serf's Church and Stone
Forgandenny: Ancient Parish Church
Forteviot:
   *Dupplin Cross
   Parish Church—Celtic Stones and Bell
Fortingall: Parish Church and Ancient Yew
Fowlis-Wester: Ancient Parish Church and Stones
Innerpeffray:
   Old Library
   Pre-Reformation Church
Killiecrankie: †Pass and Information Centre
Ben Lawers: †Information Centre
Meigle: *Celtic Stones Museum
Meikleour: Beech Hedge
Muthill:
   *Ancient Church
   Drummond Castle Museum
Perth:
   Balhousie Castle—Black Watch Regimental Museum
   Bell's Sports Rotunda
   †Branklyn Garden, Barnhill
   *Huntingtower Castle
   New Scone—Greystanes Housing and Stone Circle
   Pittheavlis Castle
   St. John's Kirk
   Scone Palace
Pitlochry:
   *Dunfallandy Stone
   North of Scotland Hydro Board Exhibition Hall and Fish Pass,
      Loch Faskally
   †Lynn of Tummel Nature Trail
Port of Menteith: *Inchmahome Priory
Strathyre: Forestry Centre and Museum

STIRLINGSHIRE

Bannockburn: †Bruce Statue and Rotunda
Bonnybridge: *Rough Castle Roman Camp
Fintry: Loup of Fintry Waterfall
Stirling:
   *Cambuskenneth Abbey
   *Castle
   Church of the Holy Rude
   Cowane's Hospital
   Scottish Tartans Information Centre
   Wallace Monument, Abbey Craig
Strathblane:
   Bardowie Castle and Loch
   Mugdock Castle and Loch

INDEX

Main cities are indicated in bold figures.

T

Dullator Bog, 238
Dumgoyach, 264, 265
Dumgoyne, 265
Dumyat, 13, 189, 242, 243
Dunalastair Reservoir, 165
DUNBARNEY, 79, 80
DUNBLANE, 71, 72, 73
Dunblane Cathedral, 71
Duncan I, 70, 74, 82, 144
Duncan, Rev. Richard, 64, 105
Duncansfield Stadium, 237
Dunchroisk, 110
Duncrevie, 93
Duncrub, 77
Dundaff Hills, 199, 210, 211, 216, 241, 246
Dundas family, 57, 58, 95, 212, 230, 231, 232, 251, 269
Dundas Port, 231
Dundee, Viscount, 32, 55, 108, 224, 238
Dundonald, Earl of, 238
Dundurn, 58, 125
Dunfallandy, 129
Dunfallandy Stone, 129, 161
Dunfermline Abbey, 3, 8, 150, 152
Dunfermline, Lord, 16
Dun Gael, 83
Dunidea, 120
DUNIPACE, 212, 200, 213, 248, 265
Dunira, 58, 95
DUNKELD, 74, 69
Dunkeld Cathedral, 40, 147
Dunkeld, Little, 147
Dun Monadh, 141
Dun Mor, 172
Dunmore, 192, 195
Dunmore, Earls of, 192
Dunmore Hill, 58, 181
DUNNING, 76, 14, 28, 149
DUNSINANE, 167, 9, 56, 134
Dunsinnan, 57, 168
Dunsinnan, Lord, 57
Dunruchen, 49
Duntreath Castle, 264, 265
DUPPLIN, 81
Dupplin, Battle of, 81
Dupplin Cross, 19, 81
Dupplin, Viscounts, 82
Duthieston, 71

E
Each, Ben, 53
Eagles, Glen, 14, 92, 263

Earl's Seat, 241, 264
Earlstoun, or Easterton, 14
EARN, BRIDGE OF, 50
Earn, River, 50, 57, 63, 79, 94, 103, 104, 105
Earthquake House, Comrie, 58
Eas Gobhain, 180, 181
Eastbow Hill, 92
Easter Rhynd, 141
Ecclesbreck, 216
Ecclesiamagirdle, 80
Edendon River, 31, 94, 95
Edgar, King, 138
Edinample Castle, 126
EDINBELLIE, 195, 196
Edinburgh, 254, 255
Edinchip, 36, 111, 126
Edmonstone family, 68, 110, 237, 264, 265
Edradour, 162
Edward I, 30, 33, 190, 206, 212, 244
Edward II, 200
Edward III, 152
Edward VII, 153
Eilean Dubh, 184
Eilean nan Bannoamh, 105
ELCHO, 141, 142
Elcho, Lord, 141
Elizabeth, Princess (Winter Queen), 52
Ellen's Isle, 184
Elphinstone family, 192, 221, 222, 247
Elphinstone, Lords, 132, 252
Elphinstone, Tower, 192
Emmanuel Priory, 244
Endrick Water and Valley, 195, 207, 209, 211, 213, 214, 224, 225, 235, 236, 241
Enochdhu, 120
Eonam, Milton of, 96
Ericht, Loch, 31, 95
Ericht River, 45, 46, 47, 49, 56
Errochty River, Glen, 31, 94, 178, 179
ERROL, 78, 79
Erroll, Earls, Countesses of, 52, 78, 97, 115, 131, 163
Erskine family, 5, 6, 138, 139
Erskine, Lords, 250
Esher, Viscount, 53
Evelick Castle, 112

F
Fair Maid's House, Perth, 153
Falcon Stone, 28